PEARSON BUSINESS REFERENCE AND WRITER'S HANDBOOK

PEARSON BUSINESS REFERENCE AND WRITER'S HANDBOOK

Roberta Moore
Patricia Seraydarian
Rosemary Fruehling

Prentice Hall

Boston Columbus Indianapolis New York San Francisco Upper Saddle River
Amsterdam Cape Town Dubai London Madrid Milan Munich Paris Montreal Toronto Delhi
Mexico City Sao Paulo Sydney Hong Kong Seoul Singapore Taipei Tokyo

Editor in Chief: Vernon Anthony
Senior Acquisitions Editor: Gary Bauer
Editorial Assistant: Megan Heintz
Development Editor: Linda Cupp
Director of Marketing: David Gesell
Marketing Manager: Leigh Ann Sims
Marketing Assistant: Les Roberts
Project Manager: Christina Taylor
Senior Operations Supervisor: Pat Tonneman
Senior Art Director: Diane L. Ernsberger
Cover and Interior Designer: Candace Rowley
Full-Service Project Management: Nesbitt Graphics, Inc.
Composition: Nesbitt Graphics, Inc.
Printer/Binder: C.J. Krehbiel
Cover Printer: Lehigh-Phoenix Color Corp./Hagerstown
Text Font: New Century Schoolbook

Library of Congress Cataloging-in-Publication Data

Moore, Roberta
Pearson business reference and writer's handbook / Roberta Moore, Patricia E. Seraydarian, Rosemary T. Fruehling.
p. cm.
Includes bibliographical references and index.
ISBN 978-0-13-514053-6 (alk. paper)
1. English language--Business English--Handbooks, manuals, etc.
2. English language--Grammar--Handbooks, manuals, etc. 3. Business writing--Handbooks, manuals, etc. I. Seraydarian, Patricia E., II. Fruehling, Rosemary T., III. Title.
PE1115.M66 2009
808'.042--dc22

2009004933

Prentice Hall
is an imprint of

www.pearsonhighered.com

10 9 8 7 6 5 4 3 2 1
ISBN-10: 0-13-514053-6
ISBN-13: 978-0-13-514053-6

CONTENTS

PREFACE

Welcome to the *Pearson Business Reference and Writer's Handbook.* This book has been designed and organized for the sole purpose of aiding students and professionals in achieving the production of high-quality written communications. Writers who produce well-written and error-free documents are able to do so not because they have memorized all of the rules and principles of good writing and language usage, but because they use all of the tools and resources available. This is critical to the writing process. With this in mind, the authors' approach is to provide within one publication two integrated streams of information:

1. A *Business Reference Manual* that can be used to quickly access answers to questions pertaining to grammar, usage, sentence construction, abbreviations, word usage, spelling, and all the necessary basics to ensure correct and error-free writing.
2. A *Writer's Handbook* with detailed guidelines and examples of good writing that can be applied to developing content, designing, and formatting the various kinds of communications that writers encounter on the job.

This two-books-in-one approach gives you all the information you need—in one place—and it can also be conveniently downloaded on your desktop. You will not only be able to solve writing problems quickly at the point of context, but also be able to use the guidelines and models to improve the style and content of your communications and improve your overall writing skills.

Use **Part One: Grammar, Mechanics, and Usage** to subsidize your electronic editing devices and your own memory of English grammar rules and usage principles. **Part Two: Writing Process and Style** will help you become a more skillful writer; good business writing is not a goal in itself, but a skill needed to meet business and career goals. Following the principles and guidelines outlined in this part is key to synthesizing the rules of grammar with the techniques of effective writing style. **Part Three: Document Content, Format, and Design** focuses on the specific writing challenges that are most relevant to the business setting. The suggested solutions are current, realistic, and practical. Because technology has affected writing style and the writing process itself, this handbook incorporates the use of electronic writing, editing, and proofreading tools and is expressly written for users who produce documents from start to finish. **Part Four: User Reference Tools** provides a glossary and indexes to help you quickly find the solutions you need.

With this distinctive approach as its guide, the *Pearson Business Reference and Writer's Handbook* combines three valuable qualities: it is comprehensive, up-to-date, and easy to use.

INSTRUCTOR RESOURCES

Supplements are available to download from the Instructor's Resource Center. To access supplementary materials online, instructors need to request an instructor access code. Go to **www.pearsonhighered.com/irc**, where you can register for an instructor access code. Within 48 hours of registering you will receive a confirming e-mail including an instructor access code. Once you have received your code, locate your text in the online catalog and click on the Instructor Resources button on the left side of the catalog product page. Select a supplement and a login page will appear. Once you have logged in, you can access instructor material for all Prentice Hall textbooks.

- Online Instructor's Manual
- Online PowerPoint Presentations

ONLINE STUDY GUIDE AND WORKSHEETS

No need to buy a student workbook! Download the *Online Study Guide* and *Worksheets* from the book website **www.pearsonhighered.com/robertamoore.** The online study guide provides writing applications, allowing students to analyze writing and apply the handbook's principles along with materials to assist with memorizing of concepts and rules and mastering how to use the handbook in workplace writing.

DOWNLOADABLE EBOOK

An access code for the downloadable ebook version of the *Pearson Business Reference and Writer's Handbook* is automatically packaged with a new copy of the printed handbook. The ebook contains the complete handbook in a fully searchable format. Download it to your computer to use whenever you write. Instructions for downloading the handbook are printed on the access code package.

ACKNOWLEDGMENTS

Sharon Carson, Palo Alto College

BJ Hathaway, Northeast Wisconsin Technical College

Deborah Kitchin, City College of San Francisco

Jane McDowell, Columbus State Community College

Shirley Reid, Indian Hill Community College, Ottumwa, IA

Margaret Taylor, Coastline Community College

HOW TO USE THIS HANDBOOK

This book employs a *functional approach,* with features that enable you to quickly access principles of Standard English and guidelines for effective writing and design of business documents. It provides answers to questions that writers encounter and examples of how to handle specific writing challenges and produce modern business communications. The principles, guidelines, and examples are basic, clearly worded, and to the point. The following pages will assist you in understanding how this functional approach works.

COLOR CODING

Four main **Parts** are color coded to help you locate the 12 **Sections** quickly.

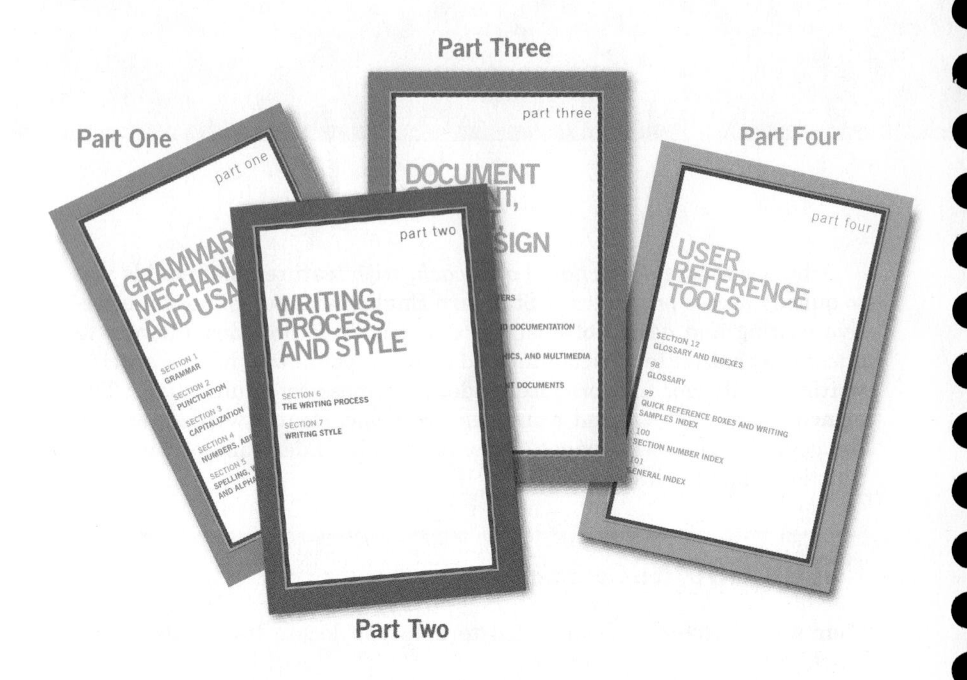

SECTION CONTENTS

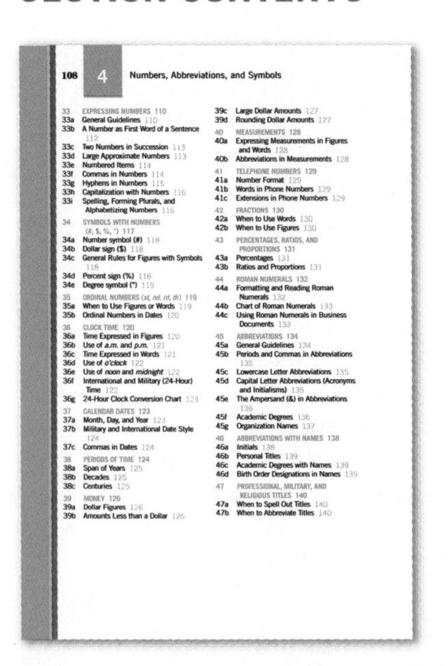

108 4 Numbers, Abbreviations, and Symbols

The detailed **Section Contents** listing on the back of the opening page provides an overview and quick reference to **Topics** and **Sub-topics** by page number.

EASY-REFERENCE FEATURES

Topic Numbers and Titles

Topics are clearly worded and numbered consecutively from 1 to 101.

Sub-topics are lettered a to z within each **Topic.**

Running heads show the Topic (left) and the last Sub-topic (right).

Sub-headings guide you to details within each Sub-topic.

Cross-references help you find additional information.

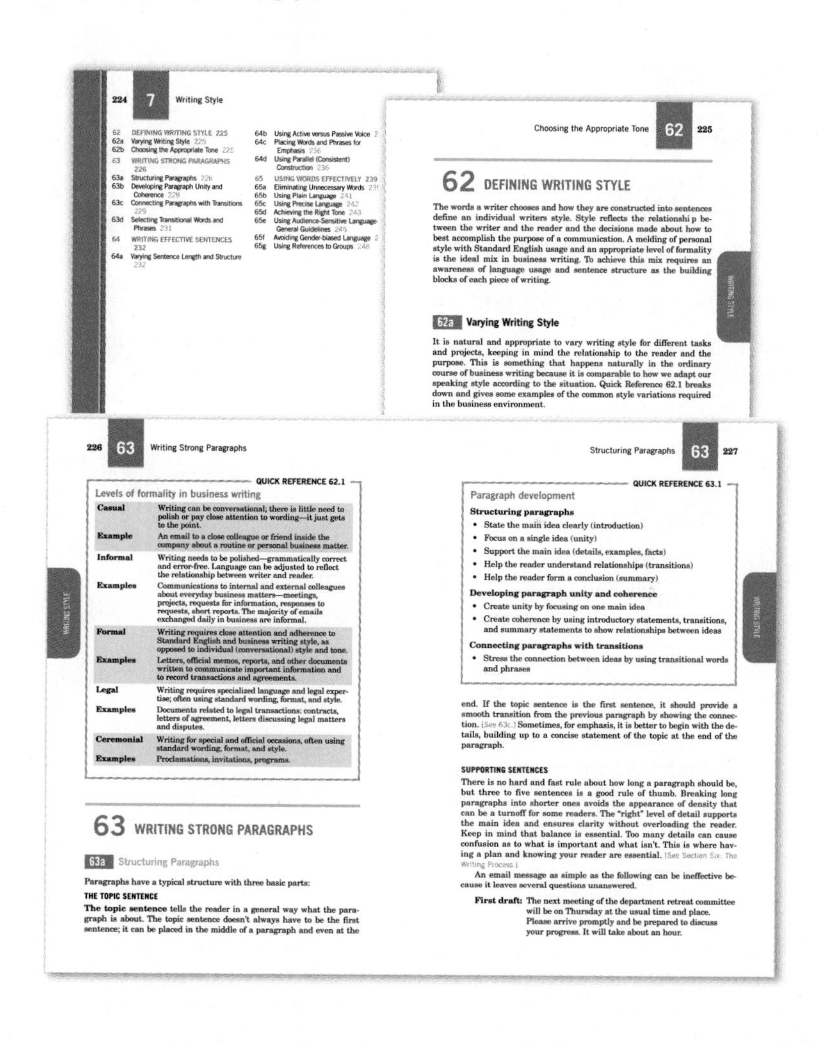

224 **7** Writing Style

Choosing the Appropriate Tone **62** 225

62 DEFINING WRITING STYLE

The words a writer chooses and how they are constructed into sentences define an individual writers style. Style reflects the relationshi p between the writer and the reader and the decisions made about how to best accomplish the purpose of a communication. A melding of personal style with Standard English usage and an appropriate level of formality is the ideal mix in business writing. To achieve this mix requires an awareness of language usage and sentence structure as the building blocks of each piece of writing.

WRITING STYLE

62a Varying Writing Style

It is natural and appropriate to vary writing style for different tasks and projects, keeping in mind the relationship to the reader and the purpose. This is something that happens naturally in the ordinary course of business writing because it is comparable to how we adapt our speaking style according to the situation. Quick Reference 62.1 breaks down and gives some examples of the common style variations required in the business environment.

226 **63** Writing Strong Paragraphs

QUICK REFERENCE 62.1

Levels of formality in business writing

Casual	Writing can be conversational; there is little need to polish or pay close attention to wording—it just gets to the point.
Example	An email to a close colleague or friend inside the company about a routine or personal business matter.
Informal	Writing needs to be polished—grammatically correct and error-free. Language can be adjusted to reflect the relationship between writer and reader.
Examples	Communications to internal and external colleagues about everyday business matters—meetings, projects, requests for information, responses to requests, short reports. The majority of emails exchanged daily in business are informal.
Formal	Writing requires close attention and adherence to Standard English and business writing style, as opposed to individual (conversational) style and tone.
Examples	Letters, official memos, reports, and other documents written to communicate important information and to record transactions and agreements.
Legal	Writing requires specialized language and legal expertise; often using standard wording, format, and style.
Examples	Documents related to legal transactions: contracts, letters of agreement, letters discussing legal matters and disputes.
Ceremonial	Writing for special and official occasions, often using standard wording, format, and style.
Examples	Proclamations, invitations, programs.

WRITING STYLE

63 WRITING STRONG PARAGRAPHS

63a Structuring Paragraphs

Paragraphs have a typical structure with three basic parts:

THE TOPIC SENTENCE

The topic sentence tells the reader in a general way what the paragraph is about. The topic sentence doesn't always have to be the first sentence; it can be placed in the middle of a paragraph and even at the

Structuring Paragraphs **63** 227

QUICK REFERENCE 63.1

Paragraph development

Structuring paragraphs
- State the main idea clearly (introduction)
- Focus on a single idea (unity)
- Support the main idea (details, examples, facts)
- Help the reader understand relationships (transitions)
- Help the reader form a conclusion (summary)

Developing paragraph unity and coherence
- Create unity by focusing on one main idea
- Create coherence by using introductory statements, transitions, and summary statements to show relationships between ideas

Connecting paragraphs with transitions
- Stress the connection between ideas by using transitional words and phrases

WRITING STYLE

end. If the topic sentence is the first sentence, it should provide a smooth transition from the previous paragraph by showing the connection. [See 63c.] Sometimes, for emphasis, it is better to begin with the details, building up to a concise statement of the topic at the end of the paragraph.

SUPPORTING SENTENCES

There is no hard and fast rule about how long a paragraph should be, but three to five sentences is a good rule of thumb. Breaking long paragraphs into shorter ones avoids the appearance of density that can be a turnoff for some readers. The "right" level of detail supports the main idea and ensures clarity without overloading the reader. Keep in mind that balance is essential. Too many details can cause confusion as to what is important and what isn't. This is where having a plan and knowing your reader are essential. [See Section Six: The Writing Process.]

An email message as simple as the following can be ineffective because it leaves several questions unanswered.

First draft: The next meeting of the department retreat committee will be on Thursday at the usual time and place. Please arrive promptly and be prepared to discuss your progress. It will take about an hour.

Quick Reference Boxes

Quick Reference Boxes summarize important information and guidelines. The boxes are numbered according to the **Topic** in which they appear. You can use these numbers to find what you need quickly.

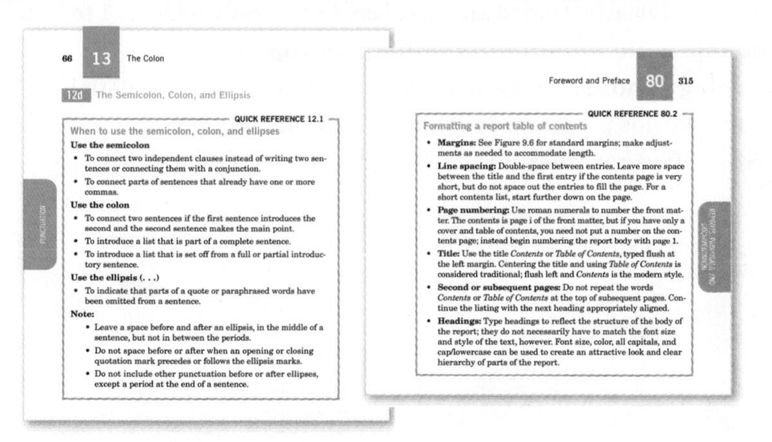

66 13 The Colon

12d The Semicolon, Colon, and Ellipsis

QUICK REFERENCE 12.1

When to use the semicolon, colon, and ellipses

Use the semicolon

- To connect two independent clauses instead of writing two sentences or connecting them with a conjunction.
- To connect parts of sentences that already have one or more commas.

Use the colon

- To connect two sentences if the first sentence introduces the second and the second sentence makes the main point.
- To introduce a list that is part of a complete sentence.
- To introduce a list that is set off from a full or partial introductory sentence.

Use the ellipsis (. . .)

- To indicate that parts of a quote or paraphrased words have been omitted from a sentence.

Note:

- Leave a space before and after an ellipsis, in the middle of a sentence, but not in between the periods.
- Do not space before or after when an opening or closing quotation mark precedes or follows the ellipsis marks.
- Do not include other punctuation before or after ellipses, except a period at the end of a sentence.

Foreword and Preface 80 315

QUICK REFERENCE 80.2

Formatting a report table of contents

- **Margins:** See Figure 9.6 for standard margins; make adjustments as needed to accommodate length.
- **Line spacing:** Double-space between entries. Leave more space between the title and the first entry if the contents page is very short, but do not space out the entries to fill the page. For a short contents list, start further down on the page.
- **Page numbering:** Use roman numerals to number the front matter. The contents is page i of the front matter, but if you have only a cover and table of contents, you need not put a number on the contents page; instead begin numbering the report body with page 1.
- **Title:** Use the title *Contents* or *Table of Contents*, typed flush at the left margin. Centering the title and using *Table of Contents* is considered traditional; flush left and *Contents* is the modern style.
- **Second or subsequent pages:** Do not repeat the words *Contents* or *Table of Contents* at the top of subsequent pages. Continue the listing with the next heading appropriately aligned.
- **Headings:** Type headings to reflect the structure of the body of the report; they do not necessarily have to match the font size and style of the text, however. Font size, color, all capitals, and cap/lowercase can be used to create an attractive look and clear hierarchy of parts of the report.

Writing and Design Guidelines and Samples

Dozens of figures show sample documents that provide models for content, format, and design of all kinds of business documents.

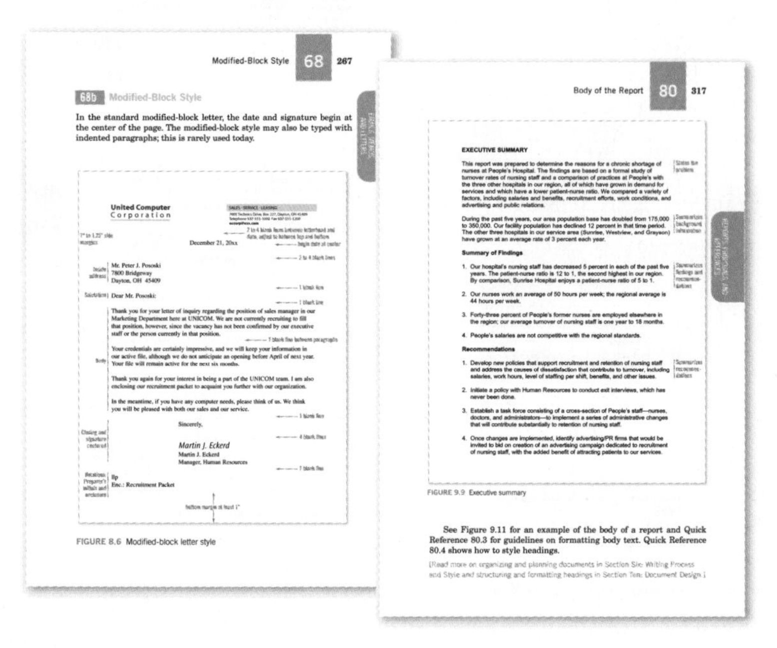

Modified-Block Style 68 267

68b Modified-Block Style

In the standard modified-block letter, the date and signature begin at the center of the page. The modified-block style may also be typed with indented paragraphs; this is rarely used today.

United Computer Corporation

SALES · SERVICE · LEASING

December 21, 20xx

Mr. Peter J. Pososki
7800 Bridgeway
Dayton, OH 45409

Dear Mr. Pososki:

Thank you for your letter of inquiry regarding the position of sales manager in our Marketing Department here at UNICOM. We are not currently recruiting to fill that position, however, since the vacancy has not been confirmed by our executive staff or the person currently in that position.

Your credentials are certainly impressive, and we will keep your information in our active file, although we do not anticipate an opening before April of next year. Your file will remain active for the next six months.

Thank you again for your interest in being a part of the UNICOM team. I am also enclosing our recruitment packet to acquaint you further with our organization.

In the meantime, if you have any computer needs, please think of us. We think you will be pleased with both our sales and our service.

Sincerely,

Martin J. Eckerd
Martin J. Eckerd
Manager, Human Resources

llp
Enc.: Recruitment Packet

FIGURE 8.6 Modified-block letter style

Body of the Report 80 317

EXECUTIVE SUMMARY

This report was prepared to determine the reasons for a chronic shortage of nurses at People's Hospital. The findings are based on a formal study of turnover rates of nursing staff and a comparison of practices at People's with the three other hospitals in our region, all of which have grown in demand for services and which have a lower patient-nurse ratio. We compared a variety of factors, including salaries and benefits, recruitment efforts, work conditions, and advertising and public relations.

During the past five years, our area population base has doubled from 175,000 to 350,000. Our facility population has declined 12 percent in that time period. The other three hospitals in our service area (Sunrise, Westview, and Grayson) have grown at an average rate of 3 percent each year.

Summary of Findings

1. Our hospital's nursing staff has decreased 5 percent in each of the past five years. The patient-nurse ratio is 12 to 1, the second highest in our region. By comparison, Sunrise Hospital enjoys a patient-nurse ratio of 5 to 1.
2. Our nurses work an average of 50 hours per week; the regional average is 44 hours per week.
3. Forty-three percent of People's former nurses are employed elsewhere in the region; our average turnover of nursing staff is one year to 18 months.
4. People's salaries are not competitive with the regional standards.

Recommendations

1. Develop new policies that support recruitment and retention of nursing staff and address the causes of dissatisfaction that contribute to turnover, including salaries, work hours, level of staffing per shift, benefits, and other issues.
2. Initiate a policy with Human Resources to conduct exit interviews, which has never been done.
3. Establish a task force consisting of a cross-section of People's staff—nurses, doctors, and administrators—to implement a series of administrative changes that will contribute substantially to retention of nursing staff.
4. Once changes are implemented, identify advertising/PR firms that would be invited to bid on creation of an advertising campaign dedicated to recruitment of nursing staff, with the added benefit of attracting patients to our services.

FIGURE 9.9 Executive summary

See Figure 9.11 for an example of the body of a report and Quick Reference 80.3 for guidelines on formatting body text. Quick Reference 80.4 shows how to style headings.

Quick Reference Tools

Topic 99: Quick Reference Boxes and Writing Samples Index on page 434.

This index lists alphabetically by keyword the titles of boxes that summarize information and the figures that depict sample documents. The box numbers correspond to Topic numbers; the sample numbers correspond to the Section (1–11) in which the figure is located.

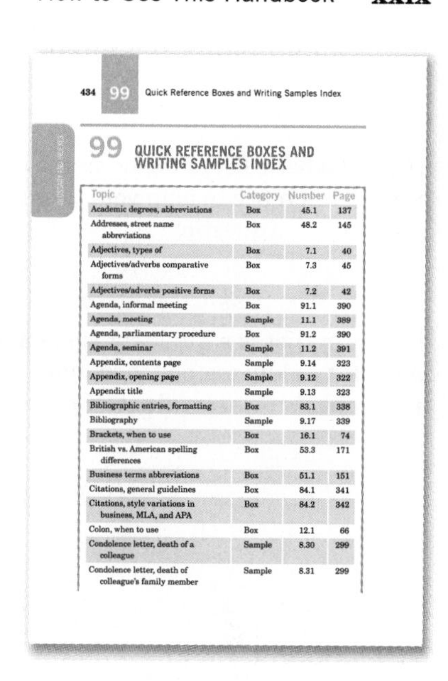

434 99 Quick Reference Boxes and Writing Samples Index

99 QUICK REFERENCE BOXES AND WRITING SAMPLES INDEX

Topic	Category	Number	Page
Academic degrees, abbreviations	Box	45.1	137
Addresses, street name abbreviations	Box	48.2	145
Adjectives, types of	Box	7.1	40
Adjectives/adverbs comparative forms	Box	7.3	45
Adjectives/adverbs positive forms	Box	7.2	42
Agenda, informal meeting	Box	91.1	390
Agenda, meeting	Sample	11.1	389
Agenda, parliamentary procedure	Box	91.2	390
Agenda, seminar	Sample	11.2	391
Appendix, contents page	Sample	9.14	323
Appendix, opening page	Sample	9.12	322
Appendix title	Sample	9.13	323
Bibliographic entries, formatting	Box	83.1	338
Bibliography	Sample	9.17	339
Brackets, when to use	Box	16.1	74
British vs. American spelling differences	Box	53.3	171
Business terms abbreviations	Box	51.1	151
Citations, general guidelines	Box	84.1	341
Citations, style variations in business, MLA, and APA	Box	84.2	342
Colon, when to use	Box	12.1	66
Condolence letter, death of a colleague	Sample	8.30	299
Condolence letter, death of colleague's family member	Sample	8.31	299

Topic 100: Topic Index on page 441.

This index lists Topic titles alphabetically *by keyword*. Use it to quickly locate a Topic or Sub-topic by *its number or by the page number.*

Topic Index 100 441

100 TOPIC INDEX

Topic/Sub-topic Title	Number	Page
Abbreviations	**45**	**134**
academic degrees	45f	136
acronyms and initialisms	45d	135
ampersand (&) in abbreviations	45e	136
general guidelines	45a	134
lowercase letter abbreviations	45c	135
organization names	45g	137
periods and commas in abbreviations	45b	135
Academic courses and degrees, capitalization	**32**	**106**
Adjectives and adverbs	**7**	**40**
adjective and adverb forms	7e	42
adjectives	7a, 7b	40
adverbs	7c	41
comparative forms	7h	44
comparisons using *less/more, less/fewer, more/most*	7j	46
differentiating adjectives and adverbs	7d	41
good/well and *bad/badly*, usage	7g	43
irregular comparative forms	7i	46
linking verbs with adjectives	7f	43
Apostrophes and asterisks	**19**	**83**
the asterisk	19c	84
contractions, apostrophe	19a	83
possession, apostrophe	19b	83
Business messages, composing	**71**	**279**
Business terms, abbreviations	**51**	**150**
common business abbreviations	51a	150
foreign words and phrases	51b	156
Calendar dates	**37**	**123**
commas in dates	37c	124
military and international style	37b	124
month, day, and year	37a	123

Topic 101: General Index on page 456.

This traditional detailed index provides complete coverage and includes cross references to help you find information by page number.

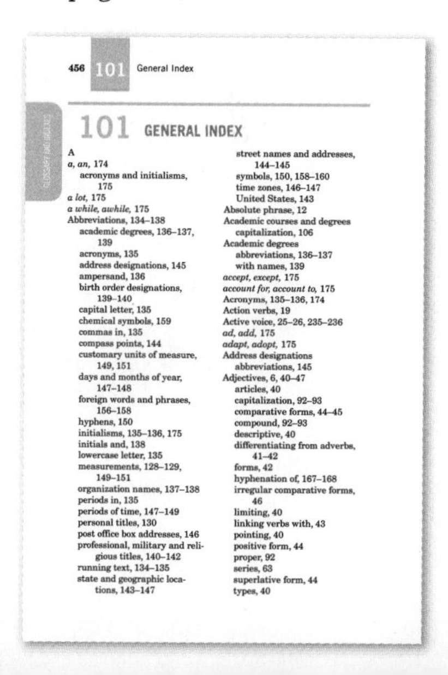

456 101 General Index

101 GENERAL INDEX

A
a, an, 174
acronyms and initialisms, 175
a lot, 175
a while, awhile, 175
Abbreviations, 134–138
academic degrees, 136–137, 139
acronyms, 135
address designations, 145
ampersand, 136
birth order designations, 139–140
capital letter, 135
chemical symbols, 159
commas in, 135
compass points, 144
customary units of measure, 149, 151
days and months of year, 147–148
foreign words and phrases, 156–158
hyphens, 150
initialisms, 135–136, 175
initials and, 138
lowercase letter, 135
measurements, 128–129, 149–151
organization names, 137–138
periods in, 135
periods of time, 147–149
personal titles, 130
post office box addresses, 146
professional, military and religious titles, 140–142
running text, 134–135
state and geographic locations, 143–147
street names and addresses, 144–145
symbols, 150, 158–160
time zones, 146–147
United States, 143
Absolute phrase, 12
Academic courses and degrees
capitalization, 106
Academic degrees
abbreviations, 136–137
with names, 139
accept, except, 175
account for, account to, 175
Acronyms, 135–136, 174
Action verbs, 19
Active voice, 25–26, 235–236
ad, add, 175
adapt, adopt, 175
Address designations
abbreviations, 145
Adjectives, 6, 40–47
articles, 40
capitalization, 92–93
comparative forms, 44–45
compound, 92–93
descriptive, 40
differentiating from adverbs, 41–42
forms, 42
hyphenation of, 167–168
irregular comparative forms, 46
limiting, 40
linking verbs with, 43
pointing, 40
positive form, 44
proper, 92
series, 63
superlative form, 44
types, 40

Find it Fast

The alphabetic list of topics on the outside of the back cover flap provides a quick reference to help you access answers to common writing problems and reference questions.

Writing Process Checklist and Assessment Tool

This checklist is a guide for remembering and practicing the necessary steps for producing polished business writing. Use the accompanying assessment tool to evaluate your own or others' written work.

ABOUT THE AUTHORS

ROBERTA MOORE is a writer, editor, and author residing in New York City. She has held editorial and executive positions with some of the nation's leading publishing houses, specializing in business education, office technology, and business English and communications. In addition to developing hundreds of educational programs, she has traveled throughout the country conducting training workshops for teachers and publishing professionals and speaking at educational conferences and on college campuses. Ms. Moore also does consulting in the field of corporate communications, specializing in employee diversity training and issues of special interest to the small business community, as well as writing speeches for top executives, newsletters, and a variety of corporate literature.

Ms. Moore is coauthor of *English for Careers: Business, Professional, and Technical,* Tenth Edition, published by Prentice Hall, as well as seven other textbooks in the fields of English, communications, college success, and career development.

DR. PATRICIA SERAYDARIAN is a business educator and author of 16 publications—the majority on business communications and word processing—and corporate trainer residing in Las Vegas, Nevada. She has taught business education at the high school and postsecondary levels, and was a State Supervisor of Vocational Business and Distributive Post-Secondary Business Education in Michigan.

In addition to authoring textbooks, Dr. Seraydarian has done extensive consulting work, specializing in grammar review and proofreading seminars for secretaries. Among her clients were General Motors Corporation, Michigan Consolidated Gas Company, and Livonia (MI) Public Schools. She has also published several books in the field of religion.

DR. ROSEMARY T. FRUEHLING is an internationally known educator and lecturer in the field of business education. She has taught at both the high school and postsecondary levels. She has also conducted business education teacher-training seminars for the United States Department of Defense and served as a consultant to such business firms as Honeywell, General Mills, International Milling, Crocker Banks, and Warner-Lambert Pharmaceutical Company. In addition, Dr. Fruehling served as director of the Office of Software Technology Development for the State of Minnesota. Before that appointment, she was postsecondary vocational education section manager in the Division of Vocational-Technical Education of the Minnesota State Department of Education.

Dr. Fruehling is author of more than 20 business education books, including several bestselling business communications, psychology, and human relations texts.

part one

GRAMMAR, MECHANICS, AND USAGE

SECTION 1
GRAMMAR

SECTION 2
PUNCTUATION

SECTION 3
CAPITALIZATION

SECTION 4
NUMBERS, ABBREVIATIONS, AND SYMBOLS

SECTION 5
SPELLING, WORD DIVISION, WORD USAGE, AND ALPHABETIC FILING

GRAMMAR section one

1 Grammar

1 BASIC SENTENCE STRUCTURE

Understanding basic sentence structure makes it easier to detect whether a sentence has a grammatical error, thus allowing more focus on making other improvements in your writing—style, tone, and word choice. This section covers important points of grammar related to how words function as different parts of speech in sentences and how to formulate grammatically correct sentences.

1a The Parts of Speech

The parts of speech are *nouns, pronouns, verbs, adjectives, adverbs, prepositions, conjunctions,* and *interjections*. Language works in a fluid way that allows words to function as different parts of speech, depending on where and how they are used in each sentence. Grammar rules provide the framework for using words correctly as different parts of speech, offering a fundamental understanding of how to construct sentences.

QUICK REFERENCE 1.1

The parts of speech

Nouns name people, animals, places, and things; abstract concepts and qualities; activities; time and measurements. They tell *who, whom, what,* or *where* in sentences.

A common noun is a nonspecific name, and need not be capitalized unless it is part of a proper name, a title, or the first word in a sentence: *elementary school, children, street, building.*

A proper noun is a specific name and should always be capitalized: Scott Jamison, Microsoft, the Washington Monument, the Chrysler Expressway.

Collective nouns are most often common nouns that name nonspecific groups: *team, committee, senate, jury,* but they can be proper nouns as well, such as the US Senate. The most important thing to remember about collective nouns is that they are singular or plural, depending on whether the group is acting as a unit or its members are acting separately.

Pronouns, such as *he, she, it, them, who, everybody*, substitute for nouns. Pronouns prevent needless repetition of nouns.

Verbs are action words, such as *eat, love, count;* **linking** (state-of-being) **verbs,** such as *is, are, be, am,* and **auxiliary** (helping)

CONTINUED→

GRAMMAR

QUICK REFERENCE 1.1 → CONTINUED

verbs, such as *is, are, have, has, had, will, were,* which are used with other verbs.

Adjectives modify nouns—*beautiful* dress, *tall* person, *overwhelming* task; and pronouns—they are *nice,* I am *tired,* it is *wet.*

Adverbs modify verbs—walk *slowly*, write *well;* adjectives—*extremely* charming man; and other adverbs—*unusually* quick recipe.

Conjunctions, such as *and, or, but, so, because, although, either . . . or,* join words or parts of sentences. (*Words:* We will take Bill *and* Gloria in our car. *Parts of a sentence:* We wanted to go to the golf tournament, *but* bad weather made us change our plans.)

Prepositions, such as *of, in, into, with, to, between, from,* link nouns or pronouns to other parts of a sentence to show relationships. A **prepositional phrase** begins with a preposition and ends with a noun or pronoun, which is called the object of the preposition. The professor will be *in his office* this afternoon *from 2 to 4 p.m.*

Interjections are expressive words used to show emotion. They are usually followed by an exclamation mark. *Never! Wonderful! You're joking!*

1b Subjects and Verbs (Predicates)

A **sentence** is a group of words that expresses a complete thought. It must include a **subject** and a **verb** (a **predicate**). The **subject** of a sentence tells *who* or *what*. The simple subject of a sentence may be one word or a group of words; the complete subject may include modifying words or phrases.

Simple noun subject: **Debra** handled the details.

Simple pronoun subject: **She** handled the details.

Complete subject: **The futuristic new medical center** is extraordinary.

A simple subject may be understood; this is known as an **imperative sentence** or a **command** in which the subject is understood to be *you.*

Leave the report with the receptionist at the front desk. [*You* leave the report. . . .]

The verb and words that modify the verb are the predicate of a sentence. By definition, a verb expresses action (such as *write, plan, move*) or state of being (such as *is/are/am, was/were, be/been*). A verb works with the noun, pronoun, or phrase that is the subject of the sentence to make it a complete thought.

My brother Lester **hopes** to get an athletic scholarship.

Lester **enjoys** running track and playing soccer.

Lester **is running** track and **playing** soccer at school this year.

Subjects usually precede the verb but sometimes are placed after it.

The new computer will be delivered on Thursday.
subject verb

The new employees were eager to learn.
subject verb

Here are the reports you wanted.
verb subject

There could have been many good reasons for his behavior.
verb subject

1c Direct and Indirect Objects

An **object** in a sentence answers the question *whom?* or *what?* after the verb. An object may be "direct" or "indirect"; that is, it receives the action directly or indirectly.

DIRECT OBJECTS

When the object answers the question *what?* or *who/whom?* it is direct.

I gave the directions to Veronica. [*What* did I give?]
verb object

I left Veronica at the restaurant with the clients. [*Whom* did I leave?]
verb object

Mr. Beatty mailed the package. [*What* did Mr. Beatty mail?]
verb object

INDIRECT OBJECTS

When an object answers the question *to whom? for whom? to what?* or *for what?* it is indirect. Indirect objects generally appear before the direct object, but an object answers the same questions when it comes after a verb, preposition, or verbal (see 3b).

Dr. White presented her nurse with a dozen roses. [*nurse* is the indirect object; *roses* is the direct object]

The manager gave the courier the new proposal. [*courier* is the indirect object; *proposal* is the direct object]

GRAMMAR

2 SUBJECT-VERB AGREEMENT

2a Basic Rule of Agreement

One of the most important principles of grammar is **subject-verb agreement**: The subject and verb *must agree in number*—if the subject is singular, the verb must be singular; if the subject is plural, the verb must be plural.

To form the **singular present tense** of most verbs, add an *s* to the basic verb form.

The division manager decides all salary increases.
subject verb

To form the **plural present tense,** do not change the basic verb form.

Division managers decide salary increases for their departments.
subject verb

2b Subjects Joined by *and*

With more than one subject joined by *and,* use a plural verb.

The security guard and the manager meet every Monday.
subject subject verb

The desk, chair, and credenza are being moved to your new office.
subjects subject verb

The exception is when two or more words represent a single person or thing; in this case, use a singular verb.

Peanut butter and jelly is my favorite sandwich.
subject verb

The chairman and CEO is the first speaker on the agenda.
subject verb

2c Subjects Joined by Other Connectors

When subjects are joined by *neither . . . nor, either . . . or, not only . . . but also,* the verb should agree in number with the subject closest to it. That subject will determine whether the verb is singular or plural.

Either you *or* David is responsible for closing the store.
subject subject verb

Not only the president, *but also* his cabinet members are responsible for setting policy.
subject subject verb

2d Collective Nouns as Subjects

Collective nouns name a group; examples are *team, committee, herd,* and *jury*. The decision to use a singular or plural verb with a collective noun will depend on how it is used in the sentence. If the group is acting as one entity, use a singular verb; if its members are acting separately, use the plural form.

Singular: The committee votes on all new contracts. [*The committee* is a unit and is, therefore, singular.]

Plural: The faculty vote on all new contracts. [*Faculty* refers to multiple individuals, so the plural is correct. To make this sound better, use *faculty members*.]

Singular: The jury is not allowed to talk to any of the principals in the case. [The collective noun *jury* refers to one entity, so a singular verb is correct.]

2e Pronouns as Subjects

Pronouns have three classifications, called cases:

Nominative case: I, he, she, it, you, we, they, who

Objective case: me, him, her, it, you, us, them, whom

Possessive case: my, mine; his, her, hers; its; your, yours; our, ours; their, theirs; whose

Pronouns that are subjects or that refer to the subject are always in the nominative case.

NO: Us graduates are planning a farewell party.
subject verb

Graduates is the subject and the pronoun refers to it, so use the nominative case.

YES: We graduates are planning a farewell party.
subject verb

Speakers often mix nominative and objective case pronouns:

NO: Him and I are going to the convention.
subject subject verb

Him is in the objective case, and *I* is in the nominative case. The pronouns must both be in the nominative case.

YES: He and I are going to the convention.
subject subject verb

[Read more about pronoun case in 6b.]

Speakers frequently use objective case pronouns with forms of the verb *to be*. In writing, however, take care to use the nominative case of pronouns after verbs such as *is, are, am, was, were, been,* and *being.*

NO: It was **me** who called.

YES: It was **I** who called.

NO: The prize-winning customer was **him**.

YES: The prize-winning customer was **he**.

2f Pronoun Subjects That Can Be Singular or Plural (Indefinite)

Indefinite pronouns refer to a nonspecific person or thing or more than one person or thing. Some are always considered singular and take a singular verb, others are always plural and take a plural verb, and others go either way, depending on usage.

Common indefinite pronouns that are always singular are: *anybody, no one, nobody, someone, somebody, everybody, everyone.*

Anybody (subject) is (verb) welcome to attend the event.

Everyone (subject) is (verb) planning to take a long weekend.

Some indefinite pronouns are always plural: *both, few, many, most, some, several.*

Few (subject) are (verb) willing to take risks, but those who do usually succeed.

Most (subject) of their products are (verb) well made and durable.

Some indefinite pronouns may be singular or plural: *all, any, more, none, other,* and *some.* In these cases, you need to refer to the number of the **antecedent** (the word to which the pronoun refers).

None (subject) is missing (verb).

When *none* is followed by a prepositional phrase with a plural object, a plural verb can be used because the sentence will simply sound better.

None (subject) of the employees want (verb) to move to the new office.

To arrive at the correct verb in the preceding example, ask yourself: *None of whom?* The antecedent is *employees,* which is plural. Therefore, the correct verb is the plural *want.*

All the food was good and none is left.
subject verb subject verb

The pronoun *(all)*, the antecedent *(food)*, and the pronoun *(none)* are singular, thus singular verbs *(was, is)* are used. The number of the verb used is determined by the sense of the sentence.

[For a complete list of indefinite pronouns, see 6i.]

2g *You* as a Subject

The pronoun *you* always requires a plural verb even though its usage may refer to a single person.

You were the favorite for the Employee of the Year Award. [single person]

You are invited to attend the conference as guests. [more than one person]

3 PHRASES IN SENTENCES

A **phrase** is a group of words that may contain a subject or a verb but not both. Phrases play different roles in sentences; they can function as subjects, verbs, and modifiers. To ensure that sentences make sense, notice whether phrases are connected appropriately to other parts of the sentence to avoid dangling constructions or misplaced modifiers.

3a Essential and Nonessential Phrases

A group of words that serves solely to modify a part of a sentence may be an **essential phrase**—one that is necessary to the meaning of the sentence—or a **nonessential phrase**. To determine if a phrase is nonessential, the sentence must make sense without it.

Nonessential: The forecast of a severe snowstorm, **the third one of the year**, was the reason I changed my travel plans.

The nonessential phrase modifies snowstorm. It is set off with commas because it is not essential to the meaning of the sentence.

Essential: The student **who was put on suspension** is going to be given a chance to make up the work.

The phrase modifies *student* and is essential because it is needed to identify the specific student; therefore, it is not set off with commas.

[Read more about punctuating phrases in sentences in Section Two: Punctuation.]

3b Phrases Functioning as Subjects

Verbals are verb forms that function as nouns, adjectives, or adverbs in sentences. Verbals are frequently used at the beginning of sentences as part of an introductory phrase. Sometimes these phrases function as the subject of a sentence.

Gerund phrase: the *-ing* form of a verb is a **gerund**; alone or in a phrase it can function as the subject of a sentence.

Going to the meeting (subject) is (verb) impossible for me because I am too busy.

Working (subject) was (verb) the last thing I wanted to do on Saturday.

Infinitive phrase: a group of words that looks like the infinitive verb form (*to go, to get, to see*) because it begins with *to,* but functions as the subject in the sentence.

To err on the side of caution (subject) is (verb) the sign of a manager who does not take risks.

To sit quietly with a book (subject) is (verb) my form of relaxation.

3c Phrases Functioning as Modifiers

An **absolute phrase** is a group of words that contains a noun or pronoun and a participle and modifies the whole sentence. Remember that this type of phrase is a modifier and not the subject of the sentence.

Having merged the regional offices, we now have only two branches instead of four.

Considering the number of invitations sent, I expected a much better turnout.

A **prepositional phrase** starts with a preposition (such as *of, in, with, for*) and ends with a noun or pronoun object. Prepositional phrases function as modifiers.

Toward the end of last year, the quality assurance committee began its work.

At the bottom of the handout, you will find a key to the colors used in the chart.

A **participial phrase** (also called a **verbal** because it contains a verb form) is a group of words that contains a present or past participle. This type of phrase functions only as a modifier, not as a subject even though it might appear to be a subject (see *gerund phrase* in 3b).

Working late every night for a month, the staff finished the project ahead of schedule.

Walking away, he seemed to resent what I thought was constructive criticism.

Offered the chance to relocate, I became excited about moving out west.

Ignored by the audience, he talked on to the end of his boring presentation.

[Read about punctuating parts of sentences and use of commas in Section Two: Punctuation.]

DANGLING VERBALS

When an introductory verbal phrase functions as a modifier, care needs to be taken to make sure the phrase is not "dangling" in a way that distorts the meaning of the sentence. A dangling verbal phrase may result in sentences that are amusing, confusing, or distracting.

NO: **Ignored** by the audience, **the room** emptied while the speaker talked on. [meaning: the room was ignored]

YES: **Ignored** by the audience, **the speaker** talked on while the room emptied. [meaning: the speaker was ignored]

NO: **Looking perfect** for the interview, **a passing cab** splashed muddy water on Jessica. [meaning: the cab was looking perfect]

YES: **Looking perfect** for the interview, **Jessica** was splashed with muddy water from a passing cab. [meaning: Jessica looked perfect]

4 CLAUSES IN SENTENCES

A **clause** is a group of related words that contains a subject and a verb. An **independent clause**, also known as a **main clause**, can stand alone as a sentence because it expresses a complete thought. A **dependent clause**, also known as a subordinate clause, cannot stand alone because it depends on the rest of the sentence for its meaning.

GRAMMAR

4a Types of Sentences

A **simple sentence** consists of *one independent clause.* A simple sentence with only one independent clause can be long or short:

Our company offers outstanding benefits.

Our company offers outstanding benefits that include liberal vacation time and end-of-year bonuses.

A **compound sentence** consists of *at least two independent clauses.*

The company offers outstanding benefits and our employees appreciate them.

(The company offers outstanding benefits — independent clause; our employees appreciate them — independent clause)

A **complex sentence** consists of *one independent clause* and *one or more dependent clauses*.

When I get to the office, I will call him about the matter.

(When I get to the office — dependent clause; I will call him about the matter — independent clause)

Before going to the supply store, I took a look at the stock room, although I was sure we were low on everything.

(Before going to the supply store — dependent clause; I took a look at the stock room — independent clause; although I was sure we were low on everything — dependent clause)

A **compound-complex sentence** consists of at least *two independent clauses* and *one or more dependent clauses.* In the following examples, the independent clauses are underlined.

When I graduate, I plan to attend Westmont College; later I will move to Chicago.

(When I graduate — dependent clause; I plan to attend Westmont College — independent clause; later I will move to Chicago — independent clause)

4b Connecting Independent Clauses

WITH A COORDINATING CONJUNCTION

The coordinating conjunctions are *and, but, for, nor, or, so,* and *yet.* Place a comma before the conjunction that connects the second clause to the first. However, when one (or both) of the clauses is very short, and is joined by *and* or *or*, the comma can be omitted.

You will need to double your efforts, **or** I'm afraid the funding will dry up.

We need higher profits **or** we'll go broke.

The end-of-year sales were lower than expected, **and** we will need to cut staff during the first quarter.

He was late **and** we could not start without him.

Our expectations of the new model were high, **for** we had invested millions to develop it.

We expect higher profits next year, **yet** we will forge ahead whether or not our goals are met.

[Read more about connecting clauses with conjunctions in 4d]

WITH A TRANSITIONAL WORD OR EXPRESSION

Transitions are words and phrases that help readers move effortlessly from one idea to the next *closely related* idea. They may be used in the beginning or middle of sentences, as well as to join independent clauses. When a transitional word or phrase connects independent clauses, insert a semicolon—not a comma—before the transition. A comma would result in a comma splice.

The company offers outstanding benefits; **however**, they are very expensive.

Dr. Jackson is not a specialist; **therefore**, I recommend that you see someone else.

A refund has been credited to your account; **in addition**, we are enclosing a $25 gift card to compensate for the error.

[Read more on the use of transitional words and expressions in Topic 63.]

Here are some common transitional words and expressions:

also	however	therefore
thus	for example	that is
in fact	nevertheless	in addition
furthermore	otherwise	consequently

WITH PUNCTUATION

Punctuation alone—a semicolon, a colon, or a dash—may also connect independent clauses.

Two closely related independent clauses with equal emphasis may be connected with a semicolon.

Remember, the meeting starts promptly at 9 a.m.; don't be late.

Subscribe to our new online encyclopedia; it's the best investment you can make in your child's education.

When an independent clause is used to introduce a second clause that you wish emphasized, the clauses may be separated with a colon.

The presentation must achieve our key goals: it needs to provide a rationale for reorganizing and motivate the staff to cooperate.

GRAMMAR

Please observe the smoking policy: smoke only in areas designated with a "Smoking Permitted" sign.

When an independent clause is followed by a second clause that you wish to de-emphasize, they may be separated with a dash. The preceding example could be changed to emphasize the first clause as follows:

Please observe the no smoking policy—smoke only in areas designated with a "Smoking Permitted" sign.

4c Avoiding Comma Splices and Run-on Sentences

When two independent clauses are not joined by a conjunction, do not separate them with a comma. Doing so creates what is known in grammar as a comma splice or a run-on sentence.

A **comma splice** occurs when you place a comma between independent clauses without a conjunction to connect them. A **run-on sentence** occurs when you join independent clauses with no punctuation at all. Correct these errors in one of the following ways: (1) separate the independent clauses into separate sentences; (2) join the clauses with a comma and a coordinating conjunction; (3) separate the clauses with a semicolon.

COMMA SPLICE

The CEO's mandate is to expand the sales division into global markets, he is giving us a time frame of three years.

RUN-ON

The CEO's mandate is to expand the sales division into global markets he is giving us a time frame of three years.

CORRECTIONS

The CEO's mandate is to expand the sales division into global markets, and he is giving us a time frame of three years. [joined with a coordinating conjunction]

The CEO's mandate is to expand the sales division into global markets; he is giving us a time frame of three years. [joined with semicolon]

The CEO's mandate is to expand the sales division into global markets. He is giving us a time frame of three years. [separated into two sentences]

4d Connecting Dependent and Independent Clauses

WITH PUNCTUATION

When a sentence begins with an introductory dependent clause, separate it from the main clause with a comma.

When I get to the office, I will call him about the matter.
dependent clause independent clause

Unless you have a particular preference, I will appoint you to the group that needs the most help.
dependent clause / independent clause

After you finish proofreading the report, please make six color copies.
dependent clause / independent clause

In these examples, the independent clauses could be punctuated as short sentences. Remember, however, that a dependent clause cannot stand alone. A dependent clause that begins with a capital letter and ends with a period is a sentence fragment (see 4e).

When two dependent clauses introduce the main clause, place a comma only before the main clause. The following are examples of complex sentences with two dependent clauses:

After you revise the report and Janice has finished proofing it, please make six color copies. [no comma between dependent clauses]
dependent clause / dependent clause / independent clause

When I graduate, I plan to move to Ohio, if the job market is good.
dependent clause / independent clause / dependent clause

Before going to the supply store, I took a look at the stock room, although I was sure we were low on everything.
dependent clause / independent clause / dependent clause

WITH A CONJUNCTION

Dependent conjunctions, also called **subordinate conjunctions**, precede a dependent clause.

We offered him the job, **although** I had hoped for someone more experienced. [A comma is used because the clause is nonessential.]

We cannot accept your proposal **unless** you can lower the costs substantially. [The clause is essential, so no comma is used.]

The following words are often used as dependent conjunctions:

after	although	as	because
before	even though	if	since
so	that	than	unless
until	when	which	while

[Read about use of commas with clauses in Topic 11.]

Correlative conjunctions are connecting word pairs that join dependent and independent clauses. The following words are correlative conjunctions:

either . . . or

neither . . . nor

not only . . . but also

both . . . and

We **neither** agreed to the contract terms, **nor** did we approve the schedule. [two independent clauses]

The designs were **not only** poorly done, **but also** they were two weeks late. [two independent clauses]

The designs were **not only** poorly done, **but also** two weeks late. [an independent and dependent clause]

4e Correcting Sentence Fragments

A **sentence fragment** is a group of words lacking a subject or a verb, but punctuated as if it were a complete sentence. Except in very informal writing, a sentence fragment should be edited to make it a complete sentence. The sentence fragment is in boldface in the following examples.

NO: The student demonstrated her negative attitude. **Flinging verbal accusations as she left the group.**

YES: Flinging verbal accusations as she left the group, the student demonstrated her negative attitude. [corrected by connecting the two clauses with a comma and changing their order to make the fragment an introductory clause]

In the next example, there are two possibilities for correcting the fragment.

NO: One thing is important. **Taking time to proofread your work.**

YES: Taking time to proofread your work is important. [corrected by rewriting]

YES: One thing is important: taking time to proofread your work. [corrected by changing the period to a colon]

A sentence fragment may be used intentionally, especially in dialogue, advertising, and informal writing, but it is best to avoid them in business writing.

[Read more about colon use in Section Two: Punctuation.]

4f Parallel Construction of Words, Clauses, and Phrases

When joining words, phrases, or clauses, express like elements—two or more nouns, pronouns, adjectives, clauses, or phrases—in parallel form. In the following examples, note that the two phrases being joined have parallel wording.

> My two favorite tasks are **welcoming visitors** to the office and **making appointments.** [The conjunction *and* joins two present participles: *welcoming* and *making*.]

It would be poor writing to express the same thoughts in this way:

> My two favorite tasks are **to welcome** visitors to the office and **making** appointments. [In this sentence, the first element is expressed as an infinitive phrase, and the second element is a present participle.]

When editing your writing, double-check for parallel construction.

> **NO:** **To use the swimming pool** or **if you need a spa appointment,** please see the first floor receptionist.
>
> **YES:** **To use the swimming pool** or **to make a spa appointment,** please see the first floor receptionist.

[Read more on parallel construction in Section Seven: Writing Style.]

5 VERBS

5a Types of Verbs

By definition, a **verb** is a word that expresses action or state of being.

Action verbs tell what the subject of the sentence is doing.

work	worry	invite	write	dance
receive	have	own	love	read
call	run	think	relax	proofread
do	hop	work		

State-of-being verbs, also called **linking verbs**, include forms of the verb *to be* and verbs of the senses, as well as others. These verbs "link" the subject of the sentence to a word or words that tell something about the subject.

be	being	been	am	are
is	was	were	become	seem
remain	appear	feel	sound	taste
smell	look			

Helping verbs, also called **auxiliary verbs**, are used with other verbs to show time, possibility, or emphasis. A helping verb may precede the main verb—either an action or a linking verb.

Some linking verbs also function as helping verbs:

be	been	am	is
are	was	were	

A few action verbs also function as helping verbs:

do	does	did	have	has	had

The following are *always* helping verbs:

may	must	might	shall	will
could	can	should	would	

Verbs are also categorized as transitive or intransitive. A **transitive verb** is one that requires an *object* to complete the meaning of the sentence. An object is a noun or pronoun or verbal phrase that answers *who, what,* or *which* directly after the verb.

The sales rep **delivered** the new software today. [*Delivered* what? The answer is the object: *software.*]

An **intransitive verb** is one that does not need an object to complete its meaning.

Jose **left.**

Verbs can be transitive or intransitive depending on their use in the sentence. To determine the case of a verb, ask *who? what?* after the verb. If the question is answered by words in the sentence, the verb is transitive.

5b Verb Tense

Verb tense indicates the *time* that an action takes place.

SIMPLE TENSES

The four **simple tenses** are present, past, present participle, and past participle.

- **Present tense** refers to action that is being taken at this time. The *singular present tense* typically adds an *s* to the regular verb form.

  The division **manager reviews** all team member policies at our annual meeting.

The *plural present tense* usually does not change the regular verb form.

All division managers **review** team member policies at our annual meeting.

- **Past tense** refers to action that occurred at an earlier time (the past). A helping verb (*had, has, have*) is *never* used for the simple past tense.

  Julia **won** the walkathon by just 20 seconds. [not *had won*]

  We **reviewed** all team member policies at our annual meeting.

- **Present participle** (the *-ing* form) refers to action that is in the process of taking place.

  We **are reviewing** all team members at our annual meeting.

- **Past participle** (needs a helping verb) refers to action that is completed.

  We **have reviewed** all team member policies during our annual meeting.

FUTURE AND PERFECT TENSES

The **future tense** refers to action that will occur at some time in the future. The **perfect tenses** are the *present perfect,* the *past perfect,* and the *future perfect*. The past participle is used to form the perfect tenses.

- **Future tense** uses helping verbs because English (unlike other languages) has no principal verb form to express the future. The most common of these helping verbs are *will, should, can, may,* and *must.* Either *shall* or *will* is correct, but in all but the most formal communications, *will* is standard usage.

  We **will review** all team member policies at next year's annual meeting.

  The CEO **will schedule** the next meeting.

  She **should plan** the next meeting within 30 days.

  You **may go** to lunch at noon, but please don't take more than an hour.

- **Present perfect tense** refers to action that began in the past, has been completed in the present, or is continuing into the present time. It is made up of the *past participle* (the third principal part of the verb) and one of two helping verbs: *has* or *have.*

  Ergonomic factors **have become** a major concern of today's business world.

  Tom Fallon **has talked** with the applicant.

- **Past perfect tense** refers to action that was completed before another past action. The past perfect tense uses *had* as its helping verb.

  My parents found it difficult to sell the family home because they **had owned** it for more than 40 years.

  My brother **had mastered** Italian before he accepted a position in Italy.

- **Future perfect tense** refers to action that will have been completed before a specific time in the future. The future perfect tense is constructed by adding *shall have* or *will have* to the past participle.

  Sally **will have earned** her doctorate before she launches her new research study.

  Will you have completed your book before you move to London?

  She **will have solved** the problem, so you can cancel the technician order.

5c Regular and Irregular Verbs

The majority of verbs are **regular verbs**—which means they form the past tense and past participle by adding *ed* or *d: walk/walked, look/looked, die/died, propose/proposed.*

Irregular verbs form the past tense and past participle by changing form in different ways. Examples are *give/gave/given, write/wrote/written,* and *take/took/taken.* Forms of these commonly used words are easy to remember, but others are harder: *bring/brought/brought,* for example, or *lie/lay/lain* and *lay/laid/laid.*

Many dictionaries provide the spellings of words in their different grammatical forms, so it is good to have one handy when proofreading. See Quick Reference 5.1 for a summary of regular and irregular verb forms. For an extensive list of irregular verbs, see Quick Reference 5.2.

5d Forming Tenses of Verbs

[Read more about usage of verbs in Topic 1 and 2.]

QUICK REFERENCE 5.1

Verb tenses

Regular verbs

Regular verbs form the past and past participle by adding *d* or *ed*.

Present	Past	Present Participle	Past Participle
talk	talked	talking	talked
calculate	calculated	calculating	calculated
act	acted	acting	acted

Irregular verbs

Irregular verbs form the past tense by changing their spelling in other ways. Most irregular verbs are so commonly used that we know their forms without thinking.

Present	Past	Present Participle	Past Participle
go	went	going	gone
buy	bought	buying	bought
do	did	doing	done
drive	drove	driving	driven

Some verbs that do not change

Present	Past	Present Participle	Past Participle
bid (offer)	bid	bidding	bid
cut	cut	cutting	cut
hurt	hurt	hurting	hurt

GRAMMAR

5e List of Irregular Verb Forms

QUICK REFERENCE 5.2

Commonly used irregular verbs

Present Tense	Past Tense	Past Participle (always used with helping verbs)
am, is, are	was, were	been
become	became	become
begin	began	begun
break	broke	broken
bring	brought	brought
buy	bought	bought
choose	chose	chosen
come	came	come
cost	cost	cost
do	did	done
draw	drew	drawn
drink	drank	drunk
drive	drove	driven
eat	ate	eaten
fall	fell	fallen
feel	felt	felt
give	gave	given
go	went	gone
get	got	gotten
have	had	had
hide	hid	hidden
hold	held	held
hurt	hurt	hurt
is	was	been
know	knew	known
lay	laid	laid
lie	lay	lain
ring	rang	rung
rise	rose	risen
see	saw	seen
set	set	set
sit	sat	sat
shrink	shrank	shrunk
speak	spoke	spoken

CONTINUED →

QUICK REFERENCE 5.2 → CONTINUED

Present Tense	Past Tense	Past Participle (always used with helping verbs)
sing	sang	sung
sink	sank	sunk
sleep	slept	slept
strike	struck	struck
swim	swam	swum
take	took	taken
teach	taught	taught
think	thought	thought
wear	wore	worn
write	wrote	written

5f The Voice of Verbs (Active and Passive)

Verbs are *active* or *passive.* In the **active voice**, the subject performs the action. In the **passive voice**, the subject is the receiver of the action.

Active voice: Maria **wrote** the letter yesterday.

Passive voice: The letter **was written** by Maria yesterday.

The active voice places more emphasis on the doer of the action; it is clear and direct and, in general, makes writing more effective. Passive construction can make writing dull and formal. Often writers make the mistake of using the passive voice because they feel it creates a more lofty or businesslike tone. Clear, direct language is usually preferable, but not always.

Notice how the following sentences shift tone and ease of communication when changed from passive to active voice.

Passive: The new editor **was welcomed** warmly by the staff.

Active: The staff warmly **welcomed** the new editor.

Passive: A rousing speech on competitive tactics **was delivered** by David Ortega.

Active: David Ortega **delivered** a rousing speech on competitive tactics.

Passive: A retirement luncheon **was given** by the HR department for the director.

Active: The HR department **gave** the director a retirement luncheon.

Use the passive voice when you wish to invoke a more formal tone or to de-emphasize the doer of the action, as in the following:

> The design judged least effective **was submitted** by Graphic Artists, Inc.

The passive voice imparts a more tactful tone than the active voice.

> Graphic Artists, Inc. **submitted** the least effective design.

Another way to say it is:

> Graphic Artists, Inc. had the least effective design, according to the judges.

This uses the active voice, but softens it with an explanatory phrase.

These examples show the numerous ways you can use words to impart the exact tone that suits your purpose. Keep in mind that a document composed entirely of active voice sentences would become just as monotonous to read as one with sentences composed entirely in passive voice. Varying active and passive voice makes writing rhythmic and is useful in adding interest and appropriate emphasis where needed.

[Read more about how to use active and passive voice to vary sentence structure in Section Seven: Writing Style.]

5g Verb Mood (Indicative, Imperative, Subjunctive)

Indicative, imperative, and subjunctive mood of verbs convey the manner in which you want the action in a sentence to be interpreted by the reader.

Indicative mood makes a statement or asks a question:

> She **is** the corporate general counsel.
>
> **Is** he the one who should receive the report?

Imperative mood gives a command or makes a request:

> **File** that letter with the others.
>
> Please **call** me about the conference.

Subjunctive mood expresses doubt, a wish, or a condition contrary to fact:

> I wish I **were** staff director.
>
> If I **were** you, I **would have attended** the meeting.

Use the **subjunctive** mood in sentences that involve the use of hypothetical conditions (not true, but discussed as if they were true). Words such as *wish, would, like, if, though, unless,* and *whether* usually require the subjunctive mood. Helping verbs used to form the subjunctive mood include *may, might, should, would, could.*

Indicative: They **invited** me, but I **didn't go** to the reception. [statement of fact]

Subjunctive: Even **if they had invited me,** I **would not have gone** with them to the reception. [hypothetical; in truth, they did not invite me]

Indicative: She **is** now the manager, and the office **runs** more smoothly. [statement of fact]

Subjunctive: If she **were** the manager, the office **might run** more smoothly. [hypothetical; she is not the manager]

Imperative: **Attend** the meeting. [a command]

Subjunctive: If I **were** you, I **would attend** the meeting. [contrary to fact; I am not you]

Imperative: You **go** to the meeting in my place. [command]

Subjunctive: I wish you **would go** to the meeting in my place. [a wish]

Note that when *to be* is the verb, the third person singular form *were* is also used for first and second person in the subjunctive mood.

First person indicative: I **am** going to the meeting.

First person subjunctive: If I **were** going to the meeting, I would take you with me.

Second person indicative: You **are** going to the meeting.

Second person subjunctive: If you **were** going to the meeting, I would go too.

Third person indicative: He **is** going to the meeting.

Third person subjunctive: If he **were** going to the meeting, I would go too.

Note that not all sentences beginning with *If* or with other phrases that sound hypothetical are in the subjunctive mood. It always depends on the exact message you want to convey to the reader.

Not subjunctive: If he **was** sick yesterday, he should not have come to work. [The meaning is "He probably was sick."]

5h Split Infinitive in Verb Phrases

An **infinitive** is the word *to* plus a verb: *to go, to begin, to finish, to visit.* The grammar rule that applies to infinitive use was once an absolute: *never* *split an infinitive*. But, as with so many strict rules of grammar, popular usage in speech migrated into writing, and the rule became more relaxed.

Now the rule has been modified to suggest: Do not use a *lengthy modifier* between the parts of an infinitive verb phrase. Edit a sentence like the following to avoid having a split infinitive verb phrase.

Lengthy modifier: She was determined **to**, *within set time limits,* **plan** the reception for the sales meeting.

Revised: She was determined **to plan** the reception for the sales meeting *within set time limits*.

Sometimes short modifiers read more smoothly and make the sentence more understandable when the infinitive is split.

Awkward: He made a suggestion **to train** *more thoroughly* the new receptionists.

Revised: He made a suggestion **to** *more thoroughly* **train** the new receptionists.

Awkward: Make sure **to arrange** *carefully* the seating chart for the head table.

Revised: Make sure **to** *carefully* **arrange** the seating chart for the head table.

6 PRONOUNS

6a Definitions of Types of Pronouns

The simple definition of pronouns is that they are words that take the place of nouns. This topic covers the types of pronouns and provides guidelines that prevent common mistakes made when using pronouns in writing.

QUICK REFERENCE 6.1

Types of pronouns

- **Demonstrative pronouns** point to and identify a noun or pronoun: *this, these, that, those. This* and *these* refer to things or people nearer in distance or time. *That* and *those* designate things or people farther away in distance or time.
- **Indefinite pronouns** refer to unspecified people and things: *all, many, everything, anything, several, many, nobody, few, somebody, everything.*

CONTINUED→

GRAMMAR

QUICK REFERENCE 6.1 ➞ CONTINUED

- **Interrogative pronouns** are used to ask a question: *who, whom, what, which,* and *whose.*
- **Personal pronouns refer to people and things:** *I, me, you, he, she, her, him, they, them, we, us, it, one.*
- **Possessive pronouns show possession:** *my, mine, his, hers, yours, ours.*
- **Reflexive pronouns** refer back to the subject or a clause in a sentence: *myself, themselves, yourself,* and other words with the suffix *self* or *selves;* also *each other, one another.*
- **Relative pronouns** refer to nouns expressed elsewhere in the sentence: *that, which, who, whomever.*

6b Pronoun Case

Pronoun case refers to the three forms of *personal pronouns* that perform different functions in sentences: **nominative case** pronouns are used as subjects; **objective case** pronouns are used as objects; **possessive case** pronouns show possession. Quick Reference 6.2 lists these pronouns and the pronoun case for each type.

QUICK REFERENCE 6.2

Pronoun case

Type of pronoun	Nominative case	Objective case	Possessive case
Personal pronouns	I	me	my, mine
	he, she	him, her	his, her, hers
	it	it	its
	you	you	you, yours
	we	us	our, ours
	they	them	their, theirs
	who	whom	whose
Relative pronouns	who	whom	whose
	which	which	of which
	that	that	
Interrogative	who	whom	whose
	which	which	
	what	what	

6c Pronoun-Antecedent Agreement

Personal pronouns replace specific nouns used elsewhere in a sentence. For clarity, the **pronoun reference** must agree in number (singular/plural) and gender (masculine/feminine) with its noun or pronoun **antecedent**. A pronoun and its antecedent must both be singular, or they must both be plural.

The **company** installed **its** new computer network yesterday.
singular reference singular pronoun

When our **assistants** come in, **they** will find a surprise.
plural reference plural pronoun

The **students** bring **their** own laptops to class.
plural reference plural pronoun

6d Personal Pronouns: First, Second, and Third Person

QUICK REFERENCE 6.3

Personal pronouns

Personal pronouns refer to people—*I, me, he, she, him, her, you, we, us, they, them*—or things: *it*. They have three categories: first person, second person, and third person. Each *person* has a singular and a plural form.

First-person pronouns: the person or people speaking or writing:

Singular: I me my mine myself
Plural: we us our ours ourselves

Second-person pronouns: the person or persons spoken or written to:

Singular or plural: you your yours
Singular only: yourself
Plural only: yourselves

Third-person pronouns: the person(s) or thing(s) spoken or written about:

Singular masculine: he him his himself
Singular feminine: she her hers herself
Singular neutral: it its itself
Plural neutral: they them their theirs themselves

6e Agreement with More Than One Antecedent Joined by *and*

When a pronoun's antecedent is more than one noun or pronoun joined by the word *and,* the antecedent is plural and the pronoun should be plural:

Ms. Templeton and I would like you to see **our** point of view this time.

Jackie and I would like to meet with you this week, and **we** are free every afternoon.

Ms. Smith and her assistant met yesterday. **They** said the meeting was very productive.

Bob and Enrique will be happy with **their** promotions.

6f Agreement with More Than One Antecedent Joined by *or*

When a pronoun's antecedent is more than one noun or pronoun joined by *or* or *nor,* the pronoun reference should agree with the nearer antecedent in number (singular or plural):

Either Kai or John must present **his** ideas first.

Neither Mary nor her assistants may take **their** break right now.

6g Agreement with Gender

A pronoun reference and its antecedent must both be male, female, or neutral:

Both male: Mr. Williams leaves **his** office each day at six o'clock.

Both female: Ms. Fontana opens **her** doors at eight every morning.

Both neutral: The company must balance **its** books.

Many nouns—for example, *manager, employee, mechanic, secretary, assistant, supervisor*—can refer to males, females, or both. Some pronouns are similarly indefinite: *one, each, every, everybody, either, neither, somebody*.

When you use a gender-neutral noun or pronoun antecedent, compose the sentence so that the reference is also gender-neutral. Sometimes, to avoid being gender-specific, it is necessary to rewrite the whole sentence. Here are some options:

1. Use pronouns that represent both genders, such as *he or she, she or he, him or her, her or his,* and so on. (But you don't want to repeat this kind of phrasing in sentence after sentence.)
2. Make the noun plural and use *they* or *their.*
3. Rewrite the sentence to avoid the problem.

NO: When we find a new doctor, **he** will no doubt be well qualified.

YES: When we find a new doctor, **he or she** will no doubt be well qualified.

OR

BETTER: Any new doctor we find will no doubt be well qualified.

NO: Any nurse who works in corporate health knows **she** is making good money.

YES: Nurses who work in corporate health know **they** are making good money.

NO: Everybody in the engineering department wants **his** workstation to be comfortable.

YES: Everybody in the engineering department wants **his or her** workstation to be comfortable.

OR

BETTER: Everybody in the engineering department wants a comfortable workstation.

6h Agreement with Indefinite Pronouns

Indefinite pronouns refer to a nonspecific person or thing or more than one person or thing; they may be singular or plural: *all, many, everything, anything, several, many, nobody, few, somebody, everything.*

Several of my friends attended the financial management seminar.

Nobody admitted to using the defective printer.

Please don't remove **anything** from the files while the legal case is pending.

Some indefinite pronouns are always singular, some are always plural, and some may be either, depending on the meaning intended.

The following examples show agreement with indefinite pronouns.

NO: **Each group member** must bring **their** notes to the meeting.
singular antecedent — plural pronoun

YES: **Each group member** must bring **his or her** notes to the meeting.
singular antecedent — singular pronoun

OR

Make antecedents and pronouns plural to avoid "his or her" phrasing.

BETTER: **All group members** must bring **their** notes to the meeting.
plural antecedent — plural pronoun

NO: Everyone must clear **their** own desk at the end of each day.
singular antecedent plural pronoun

YES: Everyone must clear **his or her** desk at the end of each day.
singular antecedent singular pronoun

OR

Reword the sentence to avoid "his or her" phrasing.

BETTER: All employees must clear **their** desks at the end of each day.
plural antecedent plural pronoun

6i List of Indefinite Pronouns

QUICK REFERENCE 6.4

Indefinite pronouns

Always singular	Always plural	Singular or plural, depending on their use in the sentence
another	both	all
anybody	few	any
anything	many	more
each	others	most
every	several	none
everybody		some
everyone		
everything		
much		
neither		
nobody		
nothing		
no one		
one		
somebody		
someone		
something		

GRAMMAR

6j Relative Pronouns (*who/whom, who/that, which/that*)

Relative pronouns refer to nouns expressed elsewhere in the sentence:

This computer is the one **that** needs repair.

Those computers, **which** were purchased five years ago, are being replaced.

My assistant, **who** is out sick today, will help you get settled tomorrow.

This topic covers pairs of relative pronouns that are commonly confused.

WHO AND *WHOM*

One quick way to test the use of *who* and *whom* is to remember that *who* is the nominative pronoun case (use as the subject of a sentence) and *whom* is the objective pronoun case (use as an object in a sentence).

Subject: The manager is the one **who** makes those decisions. [*Who* refers to *the manager,* the subject of the sentence.]

Object: Those decisions are made by **whom**? [*Decisions* is the subject and *whom* is the object of the preposition *by.*]

When in doubt about *who/whom,* extract the phrase from the sentence and turn it around to see whether the nominative or objective case applies.

NO: Please let us know **who** we should speak to about this issue. [We should speak to who? *Who* is the object of *speak to* and is therefore incorrect.]

YES: Please let us know **whom** we should speak to about this issue. [We should speak to whom? *Whom* is correct because it is the object.]

Note the difference in these two correct sentences:

Objective: He was the one to **whom** we looked for leadership. [We looked to whom? *Whom* is the object.]

Nominative: He was the one **who** provided leadership. [*Who* refers to the subject *he.*]

Objective: Is Lois the person **whom** we selected for that position? [We selected *whom*? *Whom* is the object of the verb *selected.*]

(**Note:** *Whoever* and *whomever* follow the same rules as *who* and *whom. Whom* is always correct after a preposition: *about whom, to whom, by whom, for whom,* and so on. This is one very simple way to test your usage.)

[Read more about prepositions in Topic 8.]

WHO AND *THAT*

The following simple rules will help you remember how to use these pronouns:

1. Use *who* to refer to a specific person.
2. Use *that* to refer to groups of people.
3. Use *that* to refer to general or specific things.

Specific person: Mr. Santiago, **who** was our top performer last year, is leaving the company.

Miranda is the person **who** won the sales contest.

Group of people: Phoenix is the location of the sales team **that** won the vacation to Hawaii.

We will be interviewing the four people **that** are most qualified.

Group of things: Our company has three departments **that** deal with different aspects of technology.

Specific thing: The new team-building seminar is one **that** you should not miss.

WHICH AND *THAT*

Use *which* and *that* to refer to nouns other than persons. Use *that* to introduce an **essential phrase.** If the sentence cannot be understood without the phrase, it is essential.

Begin **nonessential phrases** with *which*. Set off a nonessential phrase with commas if it falls in the middle of the sentence. Do not set off clauses beginning with *that*.

Nonessential: The new software is state-of-the-art, **which** gives us an advantage. [The sentence can stand on its own without the phrase introduced by *which*.]

The new equipment, **which** is state-of-the-art, gives us an advantage. [The two parts of the sentence surrounding the phrase that begins with *which* can stand alone.]

When the information is essential to the meaning of the sentence, introduce the phrase with *that,* with no punctuation.

Essential: Installing new software **that** is state-of-the art will give us an advantage. [The phrase beginning with *that* is essential to the meaning of the sentence.]

He asked me to mail him a copy of the book **that** was recommended by the employment counselor. [The phrase beginning with *that* is essential to clarify the specific book.]

6k Interrogative Pronouns *(who/whom, what/which)*

Interrogative pronouns ask a question. The interrogative pronouns are *who, whom, what, which,* and *whose.*

WHO AND *WHOM*

Writers often confuse the use of *who/whom,* although the distinction has become less important as common usage has made *who* in place of *whom* more acceptable, particularly in spoken English. It helps if you recall that *who* is the nominative case and *whom* is the objective case, which means that you would use *who* as a subject and *whom* as an object in a sentence (see 6b).

Subject: Who would be the best person to represent our group?

Object: Whom should we ask to join our group?

Subject: Who did the last presentation?

Object: To whom did you just speak?

Check this usage by changing the sentence structure: You [*subject*] just spoke to whom [*object*]?

WHAT AND *WHICH*

Confusing the use of these pronouns can be blamed on habits of speech, which allow their use interchangeably most of the time. However, in writing, the misuse of one for the other is more likely to strike the reader as an error.

Here is an easy rule to keep in mind: *What* is correct when referring to one; *which* is correct when referring to more than one.

NO: What one of these packages did you open by mistake? [more than one]

YES: Which one of these packages did you open by mistake?

BETTER: What package did you open by mistake?

YES: What beverage is most appropriate to serve after lunch? [one]

YES: Which beverages are most appropriate after lunch? [more than one]

6l Demonstrative Pronouns *(this/these, that/those)*

Demonstrative pronouns point to and identify a noun or pronoun: *this, these, that, those. This* and *these* refer to things or people that are close in distance or time.

This computer needs repair.

These are the books that are past due at the library.

That and *those* are used to point to things or people at a farther distance or time.

That vacation policy is fairly new.

Those staff members are the ones we will be training.

Don't insert unnecessary words when using demonstrative pronouns. For example:

NO: This <u>here</u> computer needs repair.

NO: That computer **<u>there</u>** in the library is fairly new.

(**Note:** *This* and *that* are singular; *these* and *those* are plural.)

6m Indefinite Pronouns

Indefinite pronouns are used when the person or thing being referred to is identifiable but not specified. Indefinite pronouns include *all, many, everything, anything, several, many, nobody, few, somebody, everything*. Indefinite pronouns may be singular or plural.

Singular: Everything is dependent on the outcome of the survey.
Nobody admits to using the defective printer.

Plural: Many members **are** upset with the vote.
Few are willing to commit to long work hours on the project.

[For a list of indefinite pronouns see 6i; for subject-verb agreement with indefinite pronouns see 2f; for pronoun-antecedent agreement with indefinite pronouns, see 6h.]

6n Reflexive Pronouns

Reflexive pronouns refer back to the subject or a clause in a sentence: *myself, themselves, yourself,* and other words with the suffix *self* or *selves;* also *each other, one another.*

Use reflexive pronouns in two situations only:

1. To emphasize the noun (or pronoun) to which the reflexive pronoun refers:

   The **employees themselves** ran the office while the management team was away.

   Never mind, **I** will do it **myself**.

   The executive editor and the news director promised to plan the writing conference **themselves**.

   They help **each other** all the time, which explains why they are so successful.

GRAMMAR

2. To direct the action back to the subject of the sentence:

   I cannot give **myself** credit for that work.

   You should all congratulate **yourselves** on a job well done.

   She asked **herself** a million times why she ever wanted this project.

The most common error both writers and speakers make with reflexive pronouns is to use them in place of objective case pronouns (see 6b):

NO: Return the signed copy to Mike or **myself** by Friday.

YES: Return the signed copy to Mike or **me** by Friday.

NO: Georgia, the attached form must be signed by Monique or **yourself.**

YES: Georgia, the attached form must be signed by Monique or **you**.

6o Possessive Pronouns

Possessive forms of pronouns show ownership or possession.

Pronoun	Possessive
I	my, mine
you	your, yours
she	her, hers
he	his
it	its
one	one's
we	our, ours
they	their, theirs
who	whose

POSSESSIVE PRONOUNS WITH GERUNDS

Writers sometimes have trouble using the correct possessive pronouns before **gerunds** (words ending in *ing*). When a pronoun modifies a gerund (a present participle used as a noun, see 3b), use the possessive form:

NO: **Me** calling you is not inconvenient.

YES: **My** calling you is not inconvenient.

Maria's quitting made the rest of the staff unhappy.

Her quitting made the rest of the staff unhappy.

Jim's working overtime brought in several new orders.

His working overtime brought in several new orders.

POSSESSIVE PRONOUN *WHOSE*

Writers sometimes confuse the possessive form of *who—whose*—with the contraction of *who is—who's*.

NO: **Whose** going to be first on the program? [Use of the possessive makes no sense here.]

YES: **Who's** going to be first on the program? [Who is going to be first would be equally correct. The contraction makes the sentence more informal in tone.]

Another construction of the same sentence might be:

YES: We need to decide **whose** turn it is to go first on the program.

6p Pronouns in Comparisons with *than* and *as*

When making comparisons, be sure the sentence actually compares the items intended. Using the incorrect form of a pronoun can lead to faulty comparisons:

NO: Sandy can sell better than **him**. [Compares unlike things—Sandy's ability to sell—with him.]

YES: Sandy can sell better than **he**.

The correct pronoun in the preceding sentence (*he*) is in the nominative case because the full phrases are being compared: *Sandy can sell* is being compared to *he can sell*. By adding the missing words, it is easy to see which pronoun is correct.

Compared items are not always in the same case. More examples:

I like **her** better than **him**. [*Her* and *him* are being compared. Both are in the objective case.]

I like **her** better than **he** does. [How *I like her* is being compared to how *he likes her*. *Does* merely substitutes for *likes*. *Her* is the object of *like*; *he* is the subject of *likes*.]

Writers and speakers often leave one or more of the last words out of the sentence when the comparison involves two phrases. Cutting the last phrase short is all right as long as the comparison remains clear. For example:

He can run as fast as they [can run].

My boss is as tall as I [am tall].

If your desk chair is higher than mine [is high], we can trade.

GRAMMAR

7 ADJECTIVES AND ADVERBS

7a Adjectives

Adjectives modify nouns: *beautiful* dress, *tall* person, *overwhelming* task—and pronouns: they are *nice,* I am *tired*, it is *wet.*

Nouns: The **good** news is that we are under budget.
[The adjective *good* describes the noun *news.*]

Pronouns: She is **qualified** for the position.
[The adjective *qualified* describes the pronoun *she.*]

Adjectives perform a variety of functions, as outlined in Quick Reference 7.1.

7b Definitions of Types of Adjectives

QUICK REFERENCE 7.1

Types of adjectives

- **Descriptive adjectives** tell "what kind." To tell what kind of *suit,* you might choose *tailored, dressy, casual, red, pinstripe,* and so on.
- **Limiting adjectives** "limit" nouns in the sense of quantity; they tell "how many." Limiting adjectives are words such as *more, any, many, enough, most, several, few.*
- **Articles** are the words *a, an,* and *the*. They are used in front of nouns, adjectives, and adverbs to tell *which one*. *The* is a "definite" article; *a* and *an* are "indefinite articles."
- **Pointing adjectives** are similar to articles; they signal a noun, and they also tell *which one*. Pointing adjectives are easy to memorize because there are only four: *this, that, these*, and *those. This, that, these*, and *those* are also pronouns. They are adjectives when they precede a noun.

this pencil these ideas that decision those programs

7c Adverbs

Adverbs modify (or describe) verbs, adjectives, or other adverbs. Adverbs typically answer *How? When? Where? Why?* and *To what extent?*

The speaker **artfully** explained a **complex** subject. [*Artfully*, an adverb, describes the verb *explained*; *complex*, an adjective, describes the noun *subject.*]

Verbs: We need to move **swiftly** to capture a bigger market share. [The adverb *swiftly* modifies the verb *move.*]

Other adverbs: We are moving **very** swiftly to capture a bigger market share. [The adverb *very* modifies the adverb *swiftly,* which modifies the verb *are moving.*]

Adjectives: Our marketing plan is **exceptionally** thorough. [The adverb *exceptionally* modifies the adjective *thorough,* which modifies the compound noun *marketing plan.*]

Parts of sentences: **Clearly,** our new marketing plan is our best hope for success. [*Clearly* is an adverb that modifies an independent clause.]

7d Differentiating Adjectives and Adverbs

Because both are modifiers, adjectives and adverbs are sometimes confused. Many adverbs end in *ly*. Many adverbs ending in *ly* are adjectives that become adverbs when the *ly* is added. However, do not assume that all words ending in *ly* are adverbs. Such words as *motherly, fatherly, lively, lovely*, *clearly,* and *lonely* are adjectives.

The following comparisons show the difference in usage of adjectives and adverbs:

Adjective: It was a **sudden** snowfall and driving was hazardous. [The adjective *sudden* modifies the noun *snowfall.*]

Adverb: The snow fell **suddenly** and driving was hazardous. [The adverb *suddenly* modifies the verb *fell.*]

Adjective: The keynote speaker wore a **beautiful** dress. [The adjective *beautiful* modifies the noun *dress.*]

Adverb: The keynote speaker wore a **strikingly** beautiful dress. [The adverb *strikingly* modifies the adjective *beautiful.*]

When forms of adverbs and adjectives are close in spelling, the word you are modifying will tell you which form to use. See Quick Reference 7.2

for some of the forms that can be confusing. Your dictionary will also help with identifying problematic adjective and adverb forms.

7e List of Adjective and Adverb Forms

QUICK REFERENCE 7.2

Adjective and adverb forms

Adjective	Adverb
bad	badly
busy	busily
cheap	cheap/cheaply
close	close/closely
daily	daily
early	early
fair	fair/fairly
fast	fast
former	formerly
good	well
hard	hardly
hourly	hourly
important	importantly
last	last
late	late/lately
loud	loud/loudly
monthly	monthly
only	only
past	past
quick	quick/quickly
real	really
right	right/rightly
short	short/shortly
similar	similarly
slow	slow/slowly
strong	strongly
usual	usually
weekly	weekly
whole	wholly
wrong	wrong/wrongly
yearly	yearly

7f Linking Verbs with Adjectives

Sometimes commonly used adjectives and adverbs seem to defy the rules of usage. This can occur because verbs known as **linking verbs** require the use of an adjective instead of an adverb. There are relatively few linking verbs; they include the following:

- Forms of the verb *to be* (*is, are, been, was, were,* and so on)
- Words that describe demeanor, such as *become*, *seem*, *remain,* and *appear*
- Verbs related to the senses, such as *taste, look, smell, feel,* and *sound*

For example:

> She **was happy** about the change in her duties. [The adjective *happy* modifies the subject pronoun *she,* not the verb *was.*]
>
> Dr. Robinson **seemed concerned** about the results of my tests. [The adjective *concerned* modifies the noun *Dr. Robinson*, not the verb *seemed.*]

Because these forms are used frequently in everyday speech, writing them correctly is usually not difficult.

7g Correctly Using *good/well* and *bad/badly*

A couple of forms give many writers trouble because they are often used incorrectly in conversation: *good/well* and *bad/badly*.

GOOD AND *WELL*

Good is always an adjective; *well* is an adverb except when it refers to a person's health—in which case it is an adjective.

> **Adjective:** You look good. [*Good* is referring to appearance.]
>
> **Adjective:** You look well. [*Well* is referring to health.]
>
> **Adverb:** You speak well. [*Well* is describing the action verb *speak.*]

BAD AND *BADLY*

Bad is always an adjective and *badly* is always an adverb; you decide which to use based on the type of word you want to modify. If you are modifying a linking verb, use the adjective *bad*. If you are modifying an action verb, use the adverb *badly.*

- The social worker **felt bad** about the family's situation. [*Felt* is a linking verb, so the adjective form *bad* is used.]
- The social worker **handled** the situation **badly**. [*Badly* modifies the action verb *handled*, so the adverb form is used.]

7h Comparative Forms of Adjectives and Adverbs

Adjectives and adverbs show comparison through one of three forms: *positive, comparative,* and *superlative*. In grammar terms, these are called *degrees*—meaning degree of comparison.

The **positive form (first degree)** describes the base word without comparison:

David is a **busy** person.

This draft does not provide a **complete** assessment of the flood damage.

The **comparative form (second degree)** compares two things:

David is **busier** than Malcolm.

Please draft a **more complete** assessment of the flood damage than the one we have.

The **superlative form (third degree)** compares three or more things:

David is the **busiest** employee in the department.

This draft provides the **most complete** assessment of the flood damage of any to date.

CHOOSING THE RIGHT COMPARATIVE FORMS

The number of syllables in the adjective or adverb usually determines the correct way to form the comparison. One-syllable words typically form the comparative by adding *er*, and the superlative by adding *est* to the root word. Words of two or more syllables typically form the comparative by adding *more* or *less* in front of the word, and the superlative by adding *most* or *least*.

Positive	**Comparative**	**Superlative**
great	greater	greatest
large	larger	largest
pretty	prettier	prettiest
boring	more boring	most boring
difficult	less difficult	least difficult
dangerous	more dangerous	most dangerous

These rules are summarized in Quick Reference 7.3.

QUICK REFERENCE 7.3

Comparative forms of adjectives and adverbs

Comparing two things

Use the **comparative form** of adjectives and adverbs to compare *two things.* For most comparative forms, add *er*; for words with two or more syllables use *more* or *less.*

NO: This is the **greatest** of the two numbers.

YES: This is the **greater** of the two numbers.

NO: Which of the two has the **highest** salary?

YES: Which of the two has the **higher** salary?

NO: Of the two letters, which is **most** legible?

YES: Of the two letters, which is **more** legible?

Comparing three or more things

Use the **superlative form** of adjectives and adverbs to compare *three or more things.* For one- and two-syllable words, the superlative is most often formed by adding *est.* For words of more than two syllables, form the superlative by adding *most* or *least* to the positive form.

Of the all the options we have, taking the train is the **easiest** way to get there.

Last year, we had our **highest** sales in the third quarter.

Walking to work is the **slowest** method, but I need the exercise.

Month-end balances are the **most difficult** to compute.

Tatum is the **most responsible** employee in the shipping department.

He felt **least qualified** to take on the new project.

For clarity when comparing a thing or person within a group, use the superlative form and add *other* to exclude the compared item from the group.

NO: Their security system is **safer** than *any* in the neighborhood. [The word *any* includes the system mentioned in the sentence.)

YES: Their security system is **safer** than *any other* in the neighborhood. [Now the security system being cited is excluded.)

7i Irregular Adjective and Adverb Comparative Forms

A few words are irregular in how they form comparisons; the easiest way to write them correctly is to remember them. These words change completely to show comparison, as opposed to adding the *er/est* ending or adding the words *more/less, most/least.*

Modifier	Comparative	Superlative
good/well	better	best
bad	worse	worst
fewer	fewer	fewest
little (degree)	less/lesser	least
many/much	more	most

ADJECTIVES WITH NO DEGREES OF COMPARISON

Some adjectives do not permit comparison: *round*, *unique*, and *perfect.*

- A **round** ball cannot be rounder or roundest.
- **Unique** means one of a kind, thus there can be no degrees of uniqueness.
- **Perfect** means without flaw, thus an object cannot be more or less perfect.

(**Note:** Adding *most* or *very* in front of *unique* has become common in everyday usage, but it is absolutely incorrect.)

7j Comparisons Using *less/more, less/fewer, more/most*

Modern grammar usage allows liberties that weren't acceptable in the past. Even though these rules are being eroded by popular usage of incorrect forms, in many situations a person's level of education and/or intelligence is still negatively judged when these forms are misused.

The first is never use *more* with an *er* ending or *most* with an *est* ending. The following examples are common misuses of these forms:

NO: The new policy for excessive absence is **more stricter** than before.

YES: The new policy for excessive absence is **stricter** than before.

NO: The second choice is **more better**.

YES: The second choice is **better**.

NO: That is the **most cheapest** copy paper I have seen.

YES: That is the **cheapest** copy paper I have seen.

Do not confuse the use of *fewer* and *less* when comparing amounts. *Less* is both an adjective and an adverb; it is used *only* to describe things that are *conceptual* or *abstract* and *cannot be counted*. *Fewer* is an adjective only and is used to describe things that *can be specified* or *counted.*

NO: We are getting **less orders** than usual for the time of year. [Orders can be counted, so *less* is incorrect.]

YES: We are getting **fewer orders** than usual for the time of year.

NO: The new styles have **less problems** than the old ones. [Problems can be specified; it is not an abstraction.]

YES: The new styles have **fewer problems** than the old ones.

YES: She seems **less ambitious** than she used to be.

YES: He is **less successful** than his younger brother. [Ambition and success are abstractions.]

8 PREPOSITIONS

8a Function of Prepositions

Prepositions are words that connect a noun or pronoun to another word in the sentence to show relationships. A **prepositional phrase** begins with a preposition and ends with a noun or pronoun, which is the *object* of the preposition.

Please leave the file **on my desk**. [*On* is the preposition; *on my desk* is the prepositional phrase; *desk* is the object of the preposition.]

In the supply closet you will find what you need.

8b Commonly Used Prepositions

The distinction between prepositions and adverbs is sometimes unclear. Remember that prepositions can never function alone in a sentence. On the other hand, adverbs can serve alone as modifiers. Quick Reference 8.1 lists common prepositions.

QUICK REFERENCE 8.1

Prepositions

The following words are often used as prepositions:

about	at	except	of	toward
above	behind	for	off	under
across	below	from	on	until
after	beneath	in	over	up
against	beside	inside	since	upon
along	between	into	through	with
among	by	like	to	within
around	during	near		

8c Unnecessary Prepositions

Writers and speakers frequently make the mistake of adding unnecessary prepositions. If you can remove a preposition without changing the meaning or making a sentence less clear, remove it.

Where did you buy that [at]?

Where are you going [to]?

Where will we eat [at] today?

I wish this project were over [with].

All [of] my coworkers worked overtime.

What was I thinking [of]?

8d Prepositions at the End of Sentences

If possible, avoid ending a sentence with a preposition, unless doing so will create an awkward sentence as in the following examples:

Acceptable: I wish I knew what you were thinking **about**.

Awkward: I wish I knew **about** what you were thinking.

The first sentence is concise and to the point; the second is grammatically correct, but it is awkward.

Sentences ending in prepositions are more frequent in conversation than in writing. Be aware of this tendency and compose sentences to convey your meaning without awkwardness and to achieve the right degree of formality. Both of the following are correct, depending on whether you are writing a formal or an informal communication:

Formal: To whom did he give his report?

Informal: Who did he give his report to?

8e Using the Correct Preposition

Some verbs require the use of specific prepositions in certain constructions. For example: agree *with* a person but agree *to* a plan; differ *with* when you disagree but differ *from* when you compare. Also, some writers fail to observe the proper distinction between closely related prepositions: *in* or *into, between* and *within*. Quick Reference 8.1 clarifies these distinctions.

8f Frequently Used Verb-Preposition Combinations

QUICK REFERENCE 8.2

Verb-preposition combinations

agree on (something)
agree to (something)
agree with (someone)
apologize for (something)
apologize to (someone)
argue with (someone)
argue about (something)
blame (someone) for (something)
blame (something) on (something)
borrow from
center on
conform to
decide between
decide on
depend on
dream about, of
excuse (someone) for
feel like
have confidence in
have influence over
hear of
insist on
independent of
object to
participate in
provide for
provide (someone) with
relate to
rely on
separate from
show up at
speak about
succeed in
take advantage of
take care of
think about
think of
throw away
wait for
warn about
worry about

PUNCTUATION section two

9 BASIC RULES OF SENTENCE PUNCTUATION

9a Statements and Polite Requests

Use a period at the end of **declarative sentences** (statements) and **imperative sentences** (polite requests).

Declarative: Our new administrative assistants attended the seminar.

Imperative: Please sign the document and return the original to me.

A **polite request** may be worded like a question, but the writer is not asking for an answer. The writer is looking for some kind of action in response.

May I please have a response within 30 days.

Would you go to the accounting office to verify your Social Security number.

Your word processor's grammar/spell checker may indicate the period as an error, so avoid the mistake of automatically accepting the change.

9b Exclamations and Interjections

Use an exclamation point at the end of an **exclamatory sentence** to indicate emotion or emphasis. Used sparingly, exclamations can express strong feelings such as eagerness, joy, disbelief, urgency, or anger. When overused, they lose their impact.

I can't wait to see it!

Congratulations on a super job!

You have been chosen to represent our membership!

An exclamation point may also be used in place of a question mark when strong emphasis requires it.

How could you honestly think that's what I meant!

Interjections are expressive words used alone or in a short phrase to show emotion. They are usually followed by an exclamation mark.

Whew! What a day!

Congratulations!

Well done!

9c Direct and Indirect Questions

Use a question mark at the end of a **direct question.**

Did you know that Margaret was promoted to regional manager?

Who will read the applications, interview the candidates, and make the final decisions?

Use a period at the end of an indirect question. An **indirect question** states what the speaker is asking instead of asking directly.

The manager asked if our reports could be finished by the end of the week.

My question is whether retirement insurance benefits are applicable to a surviving spouse.

Here is the second sentence asked as a direct question. Note the use of quotation marks.

I asked, "Are retirement insurance benefits applicable to a surviving spouse?"

9d Other Forms of Questions

Sometimes a question falls within a statement. Use a question mark at the end of a declarative sentence that contains a question.

The budget for the project will be increased, won't it?

Let's plan a trip to Mexico, shall we?

Use a question mark enclosed in parentheses to express doubt or uncertainty of a word or phrase in a statement.

We are having a birthday celebration for our CEO, who will be 58 (?) on December 15.

An **elliptical question** is a shortened form of a question and should end with a question mark. Capitalize the first word of each question.

When will the project be finished? Two weeks? One month? Ninety days?

My manager tells me you are enrolling in the MBA program at Wharton. When? [*When* represents the shortened form of the question *When are you enrolling*?]

9e Spacing and Ending Punctuation

Leave one space after the ending punctuation of a sentence. Some writers still follow the rule used with typewriters of leaving two spaces. This is acceptable in word processing documents as long as the spacing is consistent throughout. However, in material that is to be professionally printed one space after periods is the standard. See Topic 20 for general rules of spacing and function.

10 PUNCTUATION IN LISTS AND OUTLINES

10a Listed Items Within Text

Although there are various options for punctuating a list of items, it is important to treat punctuation and capitalization consistently throughout a document.

When text contains listed items (numbered, lettered, or bulleted), use a period (or a question mark) at the end of each item when the items are complete sentences.

Here is the order of the October 23 workshop on global warming:

1. The moderator will present an overview and introduce the panelists.
2. Each panelist will give a 6-minute presentation.
3. The moderator will conduct a 30-minute panel discussion.
4. The audience will ask questions of the panel members.

When listed items are not complete sentences, punctuation is optional. When no period is used, do not place a period at the end of the last item.

Our goals for the coming quarter are:

- Increased profits
- Decreased breakage and theft
- Decreased employee absence

Sometimes a list of items is part of a lead-in sentence. In this case, each item may begin with a lowercase letter.

If you have received new equipment, you need to:

- select modems 35X and 39X
- use USB 12-ft. cables
- purchase surge protectors (8 and 12 stations)

10b Standard Numbering in Outlines

QUICK REFERENCE 10.1

Formal outline format

Number outlines in this order to show hierarchy of topics: roman numerals, capital letters, arabic numerals, lowercase letters. If a topic or subtopic doesn't have more than one division, do not divide it; thus, in order to have an A you need a B, to have a 1 you need a 2, and so on.

Outline for presentation

I. Introduction
II. History of Project
  A. Pre-merger Status
    1. Had undefined goals
    2. Used poor planning
    3. Adopted unmanageable procedures
  B. Post-merger Process
    1. Returned to planning stage
    2. Simplified process
    3. Set focused goals
      a. Cost containment
      b. Target dates
      c. Measurable outcomes

10c Periods and Spacing in Lists and Outlines

Use a period after a number or letter in a list and align the entries. You needn't align the periods, unless your word processor does so automatically.

I. Project overview
II. Development process

III. Timeline
IV. Resources needed
V. Launch

Leave at least two spaces after the number and align turnover lines at the indent.

Our goals for the coming quarter are:

1. Increased profits
2. Decreased breakage and theft
3. Decreased employee absence
4. Increased employee morale

11 COMMA USE IN SENTENCES

The comma is the most frequently used punctuation mark and the one most often used incorrectly. A comma indicates a pause in a sentence or a shift of emphasis. Commas give long sentences a rhythmic quality, guiding the reader through a string of related clauses and phrases.

Using commas correctly is of prime importance in writing clear, easy-to-understand sentences. Misusing a comma can result in changing the meaning of a sentence or making a train of thought impossible to follow. This can happen whether the problem is missing commas or commas where they don't belong.

To use commas correctly, think of them as having three basic uses in a sentence:

1. To set off elements (words, phrases, and clauses) of a sentence
2. To separate elements listed in a series
3. To separate elements (numbers or words) that could be confusing if run together

11a To Set Off Clauses

Use a comma before a coordinating conjunction that separates two independent clauses. An **independent clause** has a subject and a verb and could stand alone. The coordinating conjunctions are *and, but, for, or, nor, so,* and *yet.*

John was with the company for two years, but I did not get to know him well.

We need a down payment of $1,000, and the check should be made out to me.

If either or both of the independent clauses are very short, the comma can be omitted when joined by *and* or *or*.

He asked and I accepted.

Eric will fax the letter before noon tomorrow or Romena will drop it off.

[Read more on compound sentences in 4a and conjunctions in 4b.]

In a sentence with one independent clause and one or more **dependent clauses** (a dependent clause has a subject and a verb but cannot stand alone as a complete sentence), separate the clauses with a comma.

While I am taking management classes, (dependent clause) please excuse me from attending Thursday afternoon meetings. (independent clause)

If you cannot attend the meeting, (dependent clause) please send someone to take notes. (independent clause)

When you go to the trade show, (dependent clause) pick up some catalogs for the staff. (independent clause)

You can recognize a dependent clause by its first word—a dependent conjunction. Common dependent conjunctions are:

after	even though	until	while
although	if	when	
as	since	whether	
before	so that	which	

When the dependent clause falls at the end of the sentence, you do not need to separate it with a comma if it is clear to the reader that the phrase is modifying the main clause of the sentence.

Please excuse me from Thursday afternoon meetings while I am taking management classes.

Please send someone to take notes if you cannot be at the meeting.

11b To Set Off Words and Phrases

INTRODUCTORY WORDS AND PHRASES

Use a comma after an **introductory word** or **phrase** that introduces the main message of a sentence.

Yes, I am available for lunch next Tuesday.

In case of an emergency, please contact the security desk.

When you have the time, please call me.

You may omit the comma after a short "place" or "time" introductory phrase—unless the comma is needed for clarity or to follow some other punctuation rule.

Very often I take the long way home for the scenery.

In 2009 I received my master's degree from Hampton University.

In 1999, the year I graduated from college, I moved to California. [Commas set off a nonessential phrase.]

NONESSENTIAL AND ESSENTIAL MODIFIERS

Nonessential modifiers are not essential to the meaning of the sentence. They are usually set off from the rest of the sentence by commas. **Essential modifiers** define or distinguish the elements they modify; therefore, they are essential to the meaning of the sentence. Essential modifiers are not set off by commas.

Single words can function as essential or nonessential modifiers. In the following sentence the writer wants to place the emphasis on *brother;* the name is given as additional information but it is the relationship that is important.

Nonessential: My brother, Pat, started this business.

In the next sentence the writer wants to emphasize which brother.

Essential: My brother Pat started this business.

A **phrase** does not have both a subject and a verb and thus cannot stand alone. To test whether a modifying phrase is essential or nonessential, remove it from the sentence. If the basic sentence retains its meaning, set it off with a comma. If the phrase or clause is needed to fully understand the sentence, do *not* set it off with a comma.

Nonessential: The old house, **built in 1920,** is being used to store our archives. [The phrase *built in 1920* gives added information about the old house but is not essential to the information that it houses our archives.]

Essential: The old house **being used to store our archives** was built in 1920. [The phrase *being used to store our archives* is essential to explaining which house was built in 1920.]

Nonessential: The Bates file, **which I could not find,** is the file I need for our meeting. [The clause adds information about the file but is not essential to the understanding of what specific file is needed for the meeting.]

Essential: The file **that Robert borrowed** is the one I need for our meeting. [This sentence implies that there is more than one file. Without the clause *that Robert borrowed* the reader would not know which file the writer meant. Thus the *that* clause is essential.]

(**Note:** *Which* typically introduces a nonessential phrase and *that* usually introduces essential phrases.)

Most prepositional phrases are "essential" and shouldn't be enclosed in commas. In addition, do not use a comma to separate a subject from its verb.

We will attend the conference in St. Louis next month.

Explain in a few words your reasons for refusing the promotion.

[Read more about prepositions in Section One: Grammar.]

11c With Transitional Words

Transitional words form a bridge to connect two elements of a sentence. Frequently used transitional words are *therefore, furthermore, also, too, however, thus*. Quick Reference 11.1 lists common transitional words.

Use two commas when you want to set off transitional words that interrupt the main flow of the sentence.

It could be**, also,** that he was not feeling well.

I would still**, however,** like to delay that question.

We must agree**, therefore,** not to discuss this issue.

A transitional word is often placed at the beginning of a sentence when it provides a transition from the previous sentence. Use a comma to separate it from the rest of the sentence.

Her request came at the last minute. **Therefore,** I refused to accept her share of the work.

Our business priorities are in the United States. **Furthermore,** we cannot afford to travel outside the country.

Our profit goals have not been met. **Thus,** we must approach the new year cautiously.

(**Note:** To join the two independent clauses in these sentences, use a semicolon in place of the period and retain the comma after the transitional word [see 12c].)

Sentences with transitional words sometimes flow more smoothly when the interrupting element is placed first in the sentence, as shown in the following pairs of examples.

Acceptable: I would, **however,** still like to delay that decision.

Better: **However,** I would still like to delay that decision.

Acceptable: We must, **therefore,** agree not to discuss this issue.

Better: **Therefore,** we must agree not to discuss this issue.

You may omit the comma if you want to de-emphasize the transitional word.

Perhaps he proceeded to check the printer after reading the installation instructions.

I must say that **unfortunately** I did not enjoy the seminar.

When the transitional word functions differently, not as a transition or an aside, do not separate it from the rest of the sentence.

However difficult it is, she is determined to succeed.

(**Note:** Do not use a comma to separate an introductory adverb that serves as a transition at the beginning of a sentence.)

Tomorrow I will get to work early. [*Tomorrow* is an adverb that answers *When?*]

[Read more about transitional words and expressions in Topic 63 and Quick Reference 63.2.]

QUICK REFERENCE 11.1

Common transitional words

also	for example	incidentally
actually	frankly	moreover
apparently	furthermore	perhaps
consequently	generally	therefore
conversely	however	unfortunately
finally	ideally	too

PUNCTUATION

At times, a single-word transition or insertion of the writer's opinion appears at the end of a sentence. These are nonessential elements that should be separated from the rest of the sentence with a comma.

Let's wait until next week to discuss that, **however.**

Our earnings have declined, **unfortunately.**

I don't want to stay an extra hour, **frankly.**

DIRECT PERSONAL ADDRESS

When directly addressing a person, set off the name with commas.

I know, **Mark,** you will understand that it is impossible for me to get away from the office this week.

Barbara, I am so grateful for your assistance during my recent trip to California.

CONTRASTING EXPRESSIONS

Use commas to set off phrases that contrast two ideas. The word *not* often appears in these phrases.

She was in favor of, **never in opposition to,** the proposal.

The administrators, **not the supervisors,** made most of the decisions.

We're going to Chicago, **not Detroit.**

11d With Items in a Series

WORDS, PHRASES, AND CLAUSES

The series comma is used to separate three or more items in a series (phrases or words) with a connecting word (*and* or *or*) before the last item. The use of the series comma varies among different businesses and professions. Most businesses use a comma before the conjunction, while many journalistic enterprises do not. Therefore, it is not considered incorrect to omit the series comma, but always be consistent within each document.

Word series

We have offices in New York, London, and Beijing.

Please donate new toys, books, clothes, and crafts to the children's charity event.

Phrase series

Each employee was advised to create a new password, memorize it, and change it frequently.

Clause series

Marketing employees focus on promotions, the sales staff works on the front line, and our research team monitors purchasing trends.

SERIES OF ADJECTIVES

Two or more adjectives are often used together to describe a noun. Separate the adjectives with a comma when they both modify the noun.

This time let's hire an **efficient, knowledgeable** assistant. [Both *efficient* and *knowledgeable* modify *assistant*, so use a comma.]

When the first adjective modifies the second adjective, do not use a comma.

We want a **light blue** color for the walls. [The adjective *light* modifies *blue*, so no comma is needed.]

A simple test can be used to determine whether or not to use a comma. Say the sentence with the word *and* in place of the comma. If the sentence makes sense with *and* added, use a comma.

YES: We've had a **good fiscal** year.

In this case *good* and *fiscal* are two separate adjectives, both modifying *year*. With *and* inserted the sentence does not make sense:

NO: We've had a **good and fiscal** year.

In this case omit the comma. On the other hand, a sentence such as the following does need a comma.

We've had a **long, challenging** year. [*long* and *challenging* modify *year*]

11e In Place of Omitted Words

When words or phrases are repeated in similarly structured phrases and clauses, you can sometimes avoid being repetitive by omitting words. Indicate the omission with a comma.

Those driving to our new office should take Highway 95, and those going to our old branch, Maryland Parkway. [The comma between *branch* and *Maryland Parkway* replaces the phrase *should take*.]

Some standard "sayings" omit words because they are clearly understood without them. In this case a comma stands in for the omitted words.

First come, first served. [Those who come first will be served first.]

Been there, done that. [I've been there and I have done that.]

11f Commas in Numbers

NUMBERS USED AS FIGURES

In figures with four or more digits, place a comma after each set of three digits, starting from the right. The comma is optional in four-digit numbers, but useful for clarity and consistency with larger numbers.

> 1,250 or 1250
> 22,375
> 100,000
> 1,225,337
> 110,000,000

In a list of figures, such as a table, align the commas in the figures.

Do not use commas in numbers that "identify," such as addresses, serial numbers, page numbers, and so on.

> The information can be found on page 1268 of the encyclopedia.
>
> He lives at 18626 Anglin, about two miles south of the freeway exit.

12 THE SEMICOLON

12a To Connect Ideas in Sentences

The semicolon is a convenient punctuation mark when you want to strongly connect ideas in independent clauses without using a conjunction. The semicolon indicates equal emphasis on the two ideas.

> Her ability to smooth ruffled feathers was unbelievable; she solved many an office controversy. [If you connect the two ideas with *and,* the emphasis shifts to the second idea.]
>
> Auditing their finances is never easy; we have three people working on it full time. [If you connect the two ideas with *but,* the emphasis shifts to the second idea.]
>
> Mary Beth planned the project; David implemented the process; Kim evaluated them both. [Here you could just as easily use a comma with *and* before the last element. The semicolons make the statement a little less formal.]

12b To Connect Parts of Sentences That Have Commas

Use a semicolon rather than a comma to connect parts of sentences that already have one or more commas. This is done solely to improve readability.

> The building borders on a park, a highway, and a busy street; but it still has beautiful views from every aspect.

In the following sentence the semicolon separates two closely related independent clauses:

> On the other hand, I do understand her rationale; it is just a bad time to make the suggested change. [The conjunction *but* could have been used in place of the semicolon, but the sentence reads more concisely without it.]

In the next example, semicolons are used to separate items in a series that have commas. Readability is improved.

> The three people to invite are Richard Georgio, vice president, Human Resources; Paul Chang, CFO; and Dianne Sebastian, vice president, Labor Relations.

12c To Connect Clauses with Transitional Words or Phrases

When a transitional word or phrase connects two independent clauses, use a semicolon to separate the clauses. Use a comma following the transitional word. Transitional words and phrases include:

accordingly	nevertheless
consequently	otherwise
for example	that is
furthermore	therefore
however	thus
in fact	moreover

> He awoke late; therefore, he was late for the meeting.
>
> There is no truth to the rumor that we ran out of sweet rolls at the meeting; in fact, we had a surplus.
>
> I did not attend the meeting because of a medical emergency in my family; otherwise, I would have been there.

[See 11c for commas with transitional words and phrases. Read more about using transitional words and phrases to connect ideas in sentences and paragraphs in Section Seven: Writing Style.]

PUNCTUATION

12d The Semicolon, Colon, and Ellipsis

QUICK REFERENCE 12.1

When to use the semicolon, colon, and ellipses

Use the semicolon

- To connect two independent clauses instead of writing two sentences or connecting them with a conjunction.
- To connect parts of sentences that already have one or more commas.

Use the colon

- To connect two sentences if the first sentence introduces the second and the second sentence makes the main point.
- To introduce a list that is part of a complete sentence.
- To introduce a list that is set off from a full or partial introductory sentence.

Use the ellipsis (. . .)

- To indicate that parts of a quote or paraphrased words have been omitted from a sentence.

Note:

- Leave a space before and after an ellipsis, in the middle of a sentence, but not between the periods.
- Do not space before or after when an opening or closing quotation mark precedes or follows the ellipsis marks.
- Do not include other punctuation before or after ellipses, except a period at the end of a sentence.

13 THE COLON

13a To Introduce Sentence Elements

Colons are interesting marks of punctuation. They announce: Something else is coming! Following are the instances when a colon should be used to introduce part of a sentence.

A FULL SENTENCE

Use a colon to connect two sentences when the first sentence introduces the second and the second makes the main point.

> She asked me an important question: Will the new budget be ready by the end of this month?

Capitalize the first word of the second sentence for special emphasis only; otherwise, do not use a capital letter.

> The cost will be $500: that is the minimum charge for one day.
> [Equal emphasis on both clauses]

A LIST WITHIN A SENTENCE

Use a colon to introduce a list that is written as part of a complete sentence:

> I promised my employees three things: fairness, integrity, and loyalty.
>
> Here are the names of the new committee members: Richard Dupont, Annalee Yang, and Charles Baxter.

A LIST SET OFF FROM TEXT

Use a colon to introduce a list that is set off from a full or partial introductory sentence.

> Our committee has three goals:
>
> 1. To determine the issues in question
> 2. To keep the team well informed of the actions of the committee
> 3. To reach an equitable solution to the problem.

13b In Business Letters

Use a colon after the salutation in a business letter.

> Dear Mr. Powell:
>
> Dear Customer Service Department:

Use a colon with a subject line in a letter.

> Re: Account #23456

[Read more about punctuating parts of business letters in Section Eight: Email, Memos, and Letters.]

13c In Expressions of Time and Ratios

Use a colon to separate hours and minutes and parts of ratios.

4:55 p.m.

ratio of 2:1

13d In Titles of Publications

Use a colon to separate a publication's title and its subtitle.

Talking Smart: A Guide to Powerful Oral Presentations

[Read more about styling titles of publications in Section Three: Capitalization.]

14 THE ELLIPSIS (. . .)

14a To Replace Omitted Words

An ellipsis (. . .) is three periods used to indicate a place where words have been omitted. Use a space before and after an ellipsis in the middle of a sentence. At the end of a sentence, use a fourth period.

IN A QUOTE

In direct quotations, use an ellipsis to indicate that parts of the quote have not been included. For spacing with quotation marks, see 14b.

Molly said, "I was pleased with the banquet and . . . we'll do it again next year, for sure."

WHEN PARAPHRASING

You might also paraphrase a quote (put it in your own words) and still want to indicate that you have left out part of what was said.

The memo said the rules are effective immediately . . . plans for training will be announced next week.

FOR TRANSITION OR EMPHASIS

In informal communications, writers often use the ellipsis as a way to transition between phrases to indicate a pause that is slightly more significant than a comma. An ellipsis used in this way is a device to indicate that more could be said or to intentionally leave a thought hanging.

The meeting didn't go well . . . much worse than I expected, in fact.

The meeting went great . . . will fill you in later.

I'm not happy with the outcome of the meeting. We'll discuss later . . .

You can borrow my laptop computer for the meeting . . . I do hope you will remember to lock it up this time. [This sentence uses an ellipsis to indicate missing words that indicate feelings of mistrust. The reader "can fill in the blank."]

14b Spacing

Leave a space before and after an ellipsis, in the middle of a sentence, but not in between the periods. Do not space before or after the ellipsis when an opening or closing quotation mark precedes or follows it. The most important thing to remember about spacing, as always, is to be consistent. Check your document to make sure you've spaced on both sides of the ellipsis mark.

14c With Other Punctuation

Omit other punctuation along with the omitted words. For example, do not include a comma before or after an ellipsis.

NO: He said, "The best solution is not always the easiest, . . ." and then proposed a possible way to solve the conflict.

YES: He said, "The best solution is not always the easiest . . ." and then proposed a possible way to solve the conflict.

When an ellipsis comes at the end of a sentence, leave the period and add the ellipsis. Space before the next sentence.

The policy states that "vacation can be carried over to the following year. . . . The exact number of days depends on the employee's length of service."

15 THE DASH

A dash can be used to replace other punctuation marks—most often, commas or parentheses—to set apart nonessential parts of sentences.

QUICK REFERENCE 15.1

When to use the dash

- To signal that words set off from the rest of the sentence are nonessential, but still important.
- To emphasize part of a sentence.
- To insert important information as an aside without disrupting the flow of the main message.

15a To Emphasize Part of a Sentence

Whereas other punctuation could always be used, dashes can add interest and impact to a statement and help convey the writer's intended emphasis. Use dashes sparingly, especially in formal writing; otherwise the emphatic effect will be lost.

TO SUMMARIZE

We will be visiting several Midwestern cities to promote the book—Milwaukee, Chicago, and Minneapolis.

New York, Los Angeles, and Chicago—these are the most competitive markets for our products.

TO EXPLAIN OR CLARIFY

The course bulletins—undergrad and grad—give details of our classes.

The workshop will cover diversity management—specifically, hiring, retaining, and promoting an inclusive workforce.

TO ADD A CONTRASTING POINT

This year's conference was sparsely attended—unlike last year's, which was fully booked.

FOR EFFECT OR EMPHASIS

I'm not sure that the schedule allows adequate time—but we'll push ahead anyway.

We're holding a golf tournament in May—an ideal reward for the top salespeople.

15b In Place of Commas or Parentheses

Dashes may be used in place of commas or parentheses to set off or separate sentence elements. A dash is a clearer signal to the reader that the set-off information is important.

Compare the following sentences and note how the emphasis shifts when you use dashes in place of commas or parentheses:

Commas: Please mark off the meeting dates, March 15 and 16 and April 10 and 11, on your calendar.

Parentheses: Please mark off the meeting dates (March 15 and 16 and April 10 and 11) on your calendar.

Dashes: Please mark off the meeting dates—March 15 and 16 and April 10 and 11—on your calendar. OR Please mark off the meeting dates on your calendar—March 15 and 16, and April 10 and 11.

The last sentence uses one dash to interject the most important information at the end of the sentence, where it has the most impact.

15c To Interject an Aside

Dashes also let you insert an **aside**—information that is useful but not essential to meaning—without disrupting the flow of the main message.

> The items we need to get started—markers, pads, and pens—are located in the supply cabinet on the second floor.

Place a dash before the final phrase when you want to "tack on" information without starting a new sentence.

> I'll need some supplies to get started—black and blue markers, yellow legal pads, and pens. [You could also use a colon to introduce the list.]

15d Spacing

Do not space between a dash and the words that come before and after it, unless this is the house style of your organization. Spacing requires careful proofreading to make sure all the dashes are consistent.

15e With Other Punctuation and Capitalization

Punctuation

Use *both* an opening and a closing dash, as opposed to other punctuation marks, to enclose a nonessential phrase or clause.

> **NO:** We asked for two-day shipping—the same as usual, and the package still has not arrived.
>
> **YES:** We asked for two-day shipping—the same as usual—and the package still has not arrived.

Use other punctuation as appropriate if it belongs with the set-off phrase and ends the sentence.

> The package arrived—just in time, I might add. [In this sentence, the phrase *I might add* after the comma modifies *just in time,* so the comma instead of a dash is correct.]

Capitalization

Do not begin the first word of a phrase set off by a dash with a capital letter unless it is a proper noun.

Gregory Smith—his number is in my Rolodex—should also be invited.

Please invite the two new members of our staff—Gregory Smith and Jon Yu.

15f Size of Dashes

In most word processing programs a dash is formed by typing two hyphens. After you type the next word and hit the space bar, the hyphens turn into a dash. This is known as an *em dash* (—) because it is the size of an "m" on the keyboard.

An *en dash* (–)—which is longer than a hyphen and shorter than a dash (and the size of an "n" on the keyboard)—forms when you type a single hyphen with spaces before and after.

Within written text, use the *em* dash; the *en* dash is most often used in dates, for example 1964–1968 or 1964–68.

16 PARENTHESES AND BRACKETS

16a When to Use Parentheses

The purpose of using parentheses is to avoid disrupting the flow of a sentence while providing additional or explanatory information that is not essential or is an aside to the main message. *Placing words within parentheses de-emphasizes them.*

The committee recommended three possible sites for our next annual meeting: Miami, Charleston, or Atlanta. (The majority of our commissioners come from the Southeastern United States.) [The words in parentheses are nonessential.]

Please review the proposed agenda (see attachment) and be prepared to discuss these items at our next meeting, September 15. [The words in parentheses are an aside.]

16b Punctuation and Spacing

COMPLETE SENTENCE

If the material within parentheses is a complete sentence, use the appropriate end punctuation and place it inside the closing parenthesis.

When you are ready to discuss the report, please call my assistant to schedule an appointment. (We need to do this ASAP!) [The words in parentheses are a separate, complete, exclamatory sentence.]

I was very impressed with John Hughes. (He was well qualified for the position—and charming.) [The words in parentheses are an aside that is a complete sentence.]

CLAUSES AND PHRASES

Punctuate clauses and phrases within parentheses as you would any clause or phrase, but place commas and periods used to punctuate the complete sentence on the outside of the closing parenthesis. Never place a mark of punctuation in front of an opening parenthesis.

When you are ready to discuss the report (ASAP, I hope), please call my assistant.

If you need to eat dinner in the hotel, I recommend Joe's Place, which is located on the mezzanine (they have superb steak).

SPACING WITH PARENTHESES

Do not insert space after an opening parenthesis or before a closing parenthesis.

16c For Reference and Clarification

TO ENCLOSE NUMBERS OR LETTERS OF LISTED ITEMS

Use this style with numbers in running text. If you choose to list the items on separate lines, use a period after the number.

The main topics for the report are: (1) sales to date, (2) breakdown by territory, (3) new product introduction, and (4) special promotions.

TO ENCLOSE THE ABBREVIATION OF A NAME

The American Medical Association (AMA) is holding a huge conference downtown, so please plan to get an early start when you leave for the airport.

Always spell out a name the first time it is used in a document; then give the abbreviation in parentheses if you intend to use the abbreviation in the rest of the document.

The American Association of Retired Persons (AARP) lobbies for the interests of senior citizens before Congress. AARP is very zealous in presenting those concerns.

TO ENCLOSE THE NUMERIC VERSION OF A SPELLED-OUT NUMBER

Use parentheses to clarify numbers in legal writing or other important documents where you want to prevent misunderstanding.

> The contract will terminate automatically in five (5) years, unless both parties agree to renewal prior to the expiration date.

TO SET OFF DATES AND REFERENCES

> World War II (1939–1945) was a turning point in history.
>
> Your question is answered in Chapter 7 (see pages 125–129).

QUICK REFERENCE 16.1

When to use parentheses and brackets—summary

Use parentheses to avoid disrupting the flow of a sentence.

- When you want to provide additional or explanatory information
- When information is nonessential or an aside to the main message

Use parentheses for reference and clarification.

- To enclose numbers or letters of listed items
- To enclose the abbreviation of a name
- To enclose the numeric version of a spelled-out number
- To set off dates and references

Use brackets within quotations.

- To enclose words that you insert in the middle of a quotation for clarity or to add information
- When a quotation contains an error, indicate that the error is not yours by inserting the word [*sic*] in brackets.
- When you need to insert a parenthetical phrase within a parenthetical phrase, place the second phrase in brackets.

Punctuation with parentheses and brackets

- If the material within parentheses or brackets is a complete sentence, use the appropriate end punctuation and place it inside the closing parenthesis or bracket.
- Place commas and periods used to punctuate the complete sentence on the outside of the closing parenthesis or bracket.
- Never place a mark of punctuation in front of an opening parenthesis or bracket.
- Do not put a space after an opening or before a closing parenthesis or bracket.

16d When to Use Brackets

Use brackets to enclose letters or words that you have inserted into the middle of a quotation for clarity or to add information.

Mr. Langford's request clearly stated, "Upon your return to the office [from vacation], begin work on the quarterly report."

When a quotation contains an error, indicate that the error is not yours by inserting the word *sic* (which means "It is thus in the original") in brackets. In the following sentence, the word *expenses* should be *expense*.

The contract spelled out your obligation as follows: "The contractor must submit all expenses [*sic*] reports within 30 days of the time they are incurred." [Note that the word *sic* is in italics.]

When you need to insert a parenthetical phrase within a parenthetical phrase, place the second phrase in brackets.

We are going to begin the retreat at the Burlingame Hotel and Spa on Friday. All staff members are required to be there by 6 p.m. (I realize you need to arrive the next day [May 3] and have passed this information along to Mr. Ellis.)

17 QUOTATION MARKS

17a Direct Quotations

Use double quotation marks with a **direct quotation**, which means the words are the exact spoken or written words of someone other than the writer. When you use quotation marks, it is extremely important to make sure the quote is exact.

The applicant said, "I am really looking forward to working with all of you."

AT THE BEGINNING AND END OF A PARAGRAPH

When a quotation continues to a new paragraph, *do not* use a closing quotation mark at the end of the first paragraph, but *do* use an opening quotation mark to start the new one, and place the closing quotation mark wherever the quotation ends.

Ms. Winslow, our consultant, discussed the fact that workers in the mail room spend little time each day interacting with workers from other departments. "In addition," she said, "the lack of natural lighting in the basement will, over time, lead to lower levels of physical energy.

"Solutions to these problems have been tested by some of my other clients and I have their permission to share these ideas with you." Her first suggestion is to introduce mail workers to staff members in the departments they service. Second, we need to "make it clear that mail workers are an important part of the organization's communications system."

Several more suggestions were given. Ms. Winslow promised to send us a copy of her complete presentation.

OMITTING WORDS FROM DIRECT QUOTATIONS

If you partially quote a statement or paragraph from spoken words or a written source, use an ellipsis mark to indicate where words have been omitted, but place the quotation marks at the beginning and end of the quoted statement.

> An audience member asked, "What is the source of the scientific information . . . and where can I find it?" [Use a space before and after an ellipsis mark.]

[Read more on use of ellipses in Topic 14.]

17b Indirect Quotations

Do not use quotation marks with **indirect quotations** when you are **paraphrasing**—summarizing or using your own words instead of the speaker's exact words.

Direct quotation: Pamela said, "I quit!" [These are the speaker's exact words.]

Indirect quotation: Pamela said she is quitting. [The writer reports *what* the speaker said but paraphrases.]

Robert and Jackie said they would not attend the wedding.

17c Quotations Within Quotations

When quoted material contains other quoted material or a title enclosed in quotes, use single quotation marks within double quotation marks.

> Sean said, "If you sing 'Danny Boy' one more time, I will never come to another St. Patrick's Day party of yours."
>
> According to Diane, "Maureen said, 'I will not work on a holiday!' and then slammed the door."
>
> Gavin said, "All three of us have finished reading the article 'Creating an Effective Business Environment.'"

17d Spacing with Quotation Marks

Always place periods and commas inside quotation marks. Never space between other punctuation and a quotation mark. Also, do not space between single and double quotation marks.

> The speaker introduced her presentation, "All You Can Eat," by saying, "This diet will change your life."
>
> The judge said, "'Take the Last Train Home,' the award winning poem, was one of the best ever submitted to our contest."

17e Commas with Quotation Marks

SETTING OFF DIRECT QUOTES

When a quotation comes in the middle of a sentence, set it off with a comma *in front of* the opening quotation mark and a comma *inside* the closing one.

> Her opening words, "Women have more opportunities in technology than at any time in our history," were met with loud applause.

When you interrupt a quotation within a sentence, use two sets of quotation marks; set off each part of the quotation with commas.

"I must say," he added, "that you all have done a great job despite the many interruptions."

Do not use a comma before a partial direct quotation integrated into the words of the sentence.

We were instructed to tell callers to "please hold while I ring his office," when transferring a call. [The phrase at the end of the sentence is set off with a comma for clarification, but the first part of the sentence is clearer without using a comma before the quote.]

No commas are needed to set off the quotes in the following two sentences because they are integral to the sentence:

He said that we should "feel free to walk out the door" if we were in danger of missing our scheduled flights.

I couldn't help thinking "why should I care" as I listened to the impassioned speaker.

COMMAS WITH OTHER WORDS IN QUOTES

Punctuate titles and other words enclosed in quotes as you would if they were not part of a quotation.

Enclose in commas: Each of us has to memorize Abraham Lincoln's most famous speech, "The Gettysburg Address," as our final assignment for the course.

No commas needed: Each of has to memorize "The Gettysburg Address" as our final assignment for the course.

17f Punctuation Within and Outside Quotation Marks

PERIODS AND COMMAS WITH CLOSING QUOTATION MARKS

Always place periods and commas inside closing quotation marks. Do not space between the comma or the period and the quotation mark.

Richard said, "Let's create our own manual 'database.'"

"You must locate and use the recyclable disposal bin," admonished the teacher.

QUESTION MARKS AND EXCLAMATION POINTS WITH CLOSING QUOTATION MARKS

When the quoted words are a question or exclamation, place the ending punctuation mark inside the quotation mark.

QUICK REFERENCE 17.1

Summary of quotation mark use

Direct quotations

- Use double quotation marks around a *direct quotation* (when the words are the exact spoken or written words of someone other than the writer).

Indirect quotations

- Do not use quotation marks with indirect quotations (when you are paraphrasing—putting in your own words—the speaker's words).

Quotations within quotations

- When quoted material contains other quoted material or a title enclosed in quotes, use single quotation marks within double quotation marks.

Spacing with quotation marks

- Never space between other punctuation and a quotation mark.
- Do not space between single and double quotation marks.

Punctuation with quotation marks

- When a quotation comes in the middle of a sentence, set it off with a comma *in front of* the opening quotation mark and a comma *inside* the closing quotation mark.
- Always place periods and commas inside closing quotation marks; place semicolons and colons outside.
- When the quote is a question or exclamation, place the ending punctuation mark inside the quotation mark.
- When the entire sentence is the question or the exclamation, place the punctuation outside the quotation mark.
- Place colons and semicolons outside quotation marks. Do not space between the ending quotation mark and the colon or semicolon.

Quotation marks with words and phrases

- Enclose in quotation marks informal language, slang expressions, clichés, or language that is purposely used incorrectly; words referred to as words; and definitions.

With titles

- Place quotation marks around titles of short literary works, such as poems or articles, and parts of longer works, such as the chapters of a book or sections of a report.

The visitor asked, "Where is Human Resources?" [The words enclosed in quotation marks are the direct question, so the question mark is placed before the closing quotation mark.]

When the director opened the conference room door, we all yelled, "Surprise!"

When the entire sentence is the question or the exclamation, place the punctuation outside the quotation mark. Compare the following sentences to the preceding ones:

Did the visitor ask, "Where is Human Resources"? [Both the sentence and the quotation are questions, so place the question mark after the closing quotation mark.]

The sign clearly read "Do NOT drink the water"! [The sentence as a whole is an exclamation, so place the mark outside.]

(**Note:** Do not leave a space between the quotation mark and the question mark or exclamation point.)

COLONS AND SEMICOLONS WITH QUOTATION MARKS

Place colons and semicolons outside of quotation marks. Do not space between the ending quotation mark and the colon or semicolon.

The consultant is not just "one of the team"; he is our only hope of writing a successful grant by the deadline.

Place a hold on all the articles marked "CO": Custom Order.

To introduce a quotation with a full sentence, use a colon rather than a comma after the introductory sentence.

The committee's report was brief: "We have considered all solutions to this problem and find none acceptable."

These were her exact words: "Never make a promise that you don't intend to keep."

17g Quotation Marks with Words and Phrases

INFORMAL LANGUAGE

Quotation marks are sometimes used to draw attention to words and phrases. For example, a writer may use slang, clichés, or language that is purposely incorrect or informal.

His was a real "fly-by-night" business. [*"Fly-by-night"* is a cliché that is also informal.]

The candidate's wife was a real "loose cannon." [*Loose cannon* is a slang term used to describe someone whose words and actions are unpredictable.]

WORDS REFERRED TO AS WORDS

To clarify a reference to a word in a sentence, place the reference in quotes:

In the second paragraph of the instructions, I advise you to replace "dangerous" with "hazardous."

An equally acceptable option is to use italics in place of quotes.

In the second paragraph of the instructions, I advise you to replace the word *dangerous* with *hazardous*.

DEFINITIONS

Use quotation marks to enclose a definition. Enclose in quotes or italicize the word being defined.

Television comes from Greek and Latin roots meaning "to see far."

17h Quotation Marks with Titles

Place quotation marks around titles of short literary works (such as poems and articles); use italics for titles of complete works.

Believe it or not, I base my philosophy on a poem by Robert Frost, "The Road Not Taken."

Today I read an interesting article, "America's Best Places to Live," in the August issue of *Money* magazine.

Also use quotation marks to indicate titles of parts of longer works, such as the chapters of a book or the sections of a report.

"Managerial Fitness" is the title of the second chapter in Professor Din's book.

(Read more on style of titles in 18a and in Section Three: Capitalization.)

17i Quotation Marks as Symbols in Measurements

Single and double quotation marks are used to symbolize feet and inches.

Patti is 5'6" tall.

Word processing programs allow you to insert straight quotation marks (10') instead of using the "curly" quotation marks on the keyboard.

18 ITALICS

18a To Indicate Titles

Italicize the titles of complete works: books, magazines, newspapers, plays, films, exhibitions, and television and radio shows.

Consumer Reports is a magazine widely read by today's savvy consumers.

Did you see *Les Miserables* when it was on Broadway?

You are invited to attend the opening reception for the exhibition *Frida Kahlo: A Study in Self-Portraiture* on June 28 at 7 p.m.

18b To Indicate Words Used as Words

Use italics or quotation marks to indicate words referred to as words.

The word *fragile* should be stamped in red on all of the boxes that are being shipped.

18c To Show Emphasis

Use italics to emphasize words.

As we have discussed in your performance reviews, you have *too many absences* to be considered for a promotion.

Writers sometimes use all caps for emphasis. Keep in mind that all caps is widely considered the equivalent of shouting in writing. In some written copy—for example, safety instructions—this might be appropriate.

This medication should NOT be taken if you are going to operate a motor vehicle.

DO NOT connect this machinery to an electrical outlet before reading the complete instruction manual.

In most other circumstances, italics is preferred:

This document is confidential. Please do *not* show it to anyone outside the department.

18d To Indicate Foreign Words and Phrases

Italicize foreign words or phrases.

The expression *s'il vous plait* is familiar to most Americans.

The Hebrew term for Holocaust Remembrance Day is *Yom Hoshoah*.

Many foreign words and expressions are established as part of the English language and should not be italicized. Consult a dictionary if you are unsure. If you do not find it listed, then the word or phrase should definitely be italicized.

19 THE APOSTROPHE AND THE ASTERISK

19a To Form Contractions

A **contraction** is a shortened form of two words written as one with an apostrophe in place of the missing letters. The more contractions you use, the more informal your writing becomes. As a general rule, confine use of contractions to informal communications. Avoid them completely in very formal or legal communications.

cannot	can't
he is	he's
should not	shouldn't
it is, it has	it's
you are	you're

Certain contractions can be confusing to the reader. For example, *it's* can mean either mean *it is* or *it has*. To avoid this confusion, write out the words.

Do not confuse *it's* for the possessive form *its,* which should never be written with an apostrophe.

19b To Show Possession

SINGULAR AND PLURAL WORDS

Use an apostrophe to show possession or ownership. Before inserting the apostrophe, determine whether the word (usually a noun or sometimes a pronoun) is singular or plural. Singular nouns become possessive by adding the apostrophe and *s*.

Singular: The baby's toys were scattered all over the floor of the child care center.

Plural nouns already ending in *s* become possessive by adding the apostrophe after the *s*.

Plural: The babies' toys were scattered all over the floor of the child care center.

If a plural possessive noun does not end in *s*, add *'s* to make it possessive.

Women's shoes are on sale until September 5.

NOUNS ENDING IN *S*

Some singular nouns ending in *s* are difficult to pronounce when you add another *s* to form the possessive. In this case, add only an apostrophe to the final *s* of the base word.

Awkward: The princess's title dated back to the 15th century.

Better: The princess' title dated back to the 15th century.

JOINT POSSESSION

To indicate that one item is jointly owned by two persons, add *'s* to the second name only.

Karen and Tom's car is in the garage.

SEPARATE POSSESSION

To indicate that each person possesses an item, add *'s* to both names.

Chuck's and Laura's offices are on the fourth floor.

19c The Asterisk

An asterisk may be used to refer to a footnote at the bottom of a page or table. Use two or three asterisks for subsequent notes on the same page. If you have more than three footnotes on a page, or if they are spread throughout a document, use numbers for references instead.

---

*Data is for the fiscal year beginning June 20xx.
** Projections based on historical data.
***Projections subject to revision in next report.

[Read more on formatting footnotes in 83b.]

20 SPACING AFTER PUNCTUATION

QUICK REFERENCE 20.1

Spacing after punctuation—summary

After end of sentence punctuation (Topic 9)

Leave only one space after ending punctuation. When proofing your document, check to make sure you have spaced consistently. This is especially important if you are preparing an important word processing document, such as a formal letter or report, or a document for layout. Consistent spacing is critical to a well-designed publication.

After punctuation in a list (Topic 10)

Leave one or two spaces after the number and before the first letter of the listed item; be consistent. When a listed item carries over to another line, align text under the first letter of the item, not the number.

With an ellipsis (Topic 14)

Leave one space before and after an ellipsis except when directly following or preceding a quotation mark.

With dashes (Topic 15)

Do not space before and after a dash, unless this is the preferred style in your organization. If you use this style, proofread carefully to make sure you have consistently added spaces around dashes throughout a document.

With parentheses (Topic 16)

Do not space after an opening or closing parenthesis.

With quotation marks (Topic 17)

Always place periods and commas inside quotation marks. Never space between other punctuation and a quotation mark. Also do not space between single and double quotation marks.

CAPITALIZATION

section three

3 Capitalization

21 BASIC SENTENCE CAPITALIZATION

The first word of a sentence is always capitalized, but rules for capitalizing words *within* sentences vary.

21a After a Colon

Do not capitalize the first word after a colon when the colon connects two independent clauses, unless the second clause is a direct quotation.

> He gave me a sound piece of advice: not to sell my business until I had consulted a financial advisor.
>
> He gave me a sound piece of advice: "Do not sell your business until you have consulted a financial advisor."

[Read more on punctuation of quotations in Topic 17.]

Some writers choose to capitalize a clause introduced by a colon to show emphasis. This is acceptable, *provided the clause could stand alone as a complete sentence*. The two sentences following are similar and both are correct.

> These are the admission criteria: You must have a bachelor's degree in a science subject, and your grade point average must be above 3.0.
>
> Here are two reasons for not taking the position: the commute is more than two hours a day, and the company has a poor reputation.

Never capitalize the first word after a colon when the clause following it is not a complete sentence and could not stand alone.

> The proposal needs work in the following areas: data analysis, evaluation criteria, and recommendations.

If the word following the colon is a proper noun or adjective, capitalize that word.

> The professor speaks three languages: English, Spanish, and Mandarin.

Do capitalize when you have a one-word introduction after the colon.

> Source: U.S. Census Bureau
>
> Note: For further information see Appendix B.

21b Questions Within a Sentence

Capitalize the first word of a complete question within a sentence.

The question is, When may I see my personnel file?

Capitalize elliptical questions within a sentence.

Was Jenny's promotion approved? When? By whom?

21c Sentence in Parentheses

Do not capitalize the first word of a sentence within a sentence when it is enclosed in parentheses.

We now have a membership of 725 (can you believe that?).

Do capitalize the first word of a sentence in parentheses when it is not part of another sentence.

We are developing an online newsletter for members. (This is the most cost-effective way to distribute information.) Would you be willing to contribute a monthly article?

[Read more about use of parentheses in Topic 16.]

22 LISTED ITEMS

22a Items Listed in Paragraph Copy

When items are listed vertically, capitalize the first word of each item, whether or not it is a complete sentence. If the listed items are complete sentences, end with a period; if not, use no end punctuation.

When you come to the meeting, please bring the following:

1. A printout of the current budget for the Centennial Anniversary program
2. The file on the 75th anniversary celebration
3. The sample programs you have collected for our review

Do not capitalize the first word of listed items when they are part of a paragraph:

We need the following information for the report: (1) data supporting the conclusions; (2) a list of sources for the data; (3) information you want placed in the appendix.

The items listed here are expressed in parallel form: that is, they are all written in the same style to aid quick reading and understanding. Make this a practice in your writing. In this case, the subjects are all nouns: *data, list,* and *information*.

22b Items Listed in Outlines

Capitalize the first word of each item in an outline.

I. Need for budget increase
  A. Business growth
    1. Expand sales staff
    2. Increase market share
  B. Staff oversight
    1. Develop consistent processes and procedures
    2. Implement new training programs
II. Itemization of expenses

This example also shows how to construct headings using parallel wording, as follows.

I. Noun—Need
II. Noun—Itemization
  A. Noun/verb—Business growth
    A-1. Verb—Expand
    A-2. Verb—Increase
  B. Noun/verb—Staff oversight
    B-1. Verb—Develop
    B-2. Verb—Implement

[Read more about parallel heading structure in 85e.]

23 NOUNS AND ADJECTIVES (GENERAL RULES)

23a Proper Nouns and Adjectives

Proper nouns refer to specific people, places, or things; they always begin with a capital letter.

Common nouns name classes or groups of people, places, and things and begin with a lowercase letter.

Proper nouns	**Common nouns**
Mayor Goodman	mayor
Sears Tower	building
United States Congress	legislators
Mount Whitney	mountain
Dr. Gonzalez	doctor
President of the United States	president

Also capitalize fictitious names that are in common usage:

the Big Three (refers to the three major U.S. auto companies—Chrysler, Ford, and GM)

the Big Board (refers to the New York Stock Exchange)

the Big Apple (refers to New York City)

Proper adjectives are words derived from proper nouns; they should be capitalized.

Adjective	**Noun**
American ideals	America
Machiavellian plot	Machiavelli
Constitutional amendment	Constitution

23b Capitalizing *the*

Do not capitalize *the* before a proper noun unless it is part of the official name or publication title. *The* in front of a name is usually a simple article.

The Atlanta Journal-Constitution

the Empire State Building

the Eiffel Tower

The Red Badge of Courage

23c Compound (Hyphenated) Proper Nouns and Adjectives

Do not capitalize prefixes and suffixes used to form compound proper nouns or adjectives unless the prefix is the first word in a sentence or part of a proper noun or title.

Many of today's journalistic practices are attributed to the post-Watergate era in politics.

The Ming Dynasty-style vase was actually a cheap imitation.

The longest article, "The Post-Depression Era," was the most interesting reading.

[Read more about forming compound nouns and adjectives in Topic 53.]

24 PERSONAL NAMES AND TITLES

24a Names of People

Capitalize names as written by the person. Most names begin with all-capital letters, but some spellings do not. Others are unusual, have more than one possible spelling, use hyphenation, and so on, as shown in the following examples. Always check the correct spelling of names to avoid embarrassment.

James R. Brauer

Patricia Gould-Bensen

Albert van den Berg

Edward de Souza

When including a nickname with a person's name, capitalize and enclose it in quotation marks.

Once again, Dennis "Ace" Pérez got the biggest sales bonus of the year.

Elliot "Lee" Murphy is the most effective legislator in the senate.

24b Professional Titles with Names

PRECEDING THE NAME

Capitalize an official title when it is part of the name.

Judge Judy is one of the most popular personalities on television.

Chairperson Elroy McKenzie presides over the monthly board meeting.

Captain Marian C. Rogers commands the 13th District of our police.

Use lowercase for an official title when it is not being used as part of the name.

My cousin, who is a **judge,** might be willing to advise us on the legalities.

As **chairperson,** Elroy McKenzie presides over the monthly board meeting.

Dr. Jonathan Douglas, a favorite **dean** on campus, is leaving to work for another university.

Capitalize such titles as *governor, mayor,* and *senator* when referring to a specific person. Do not capitalize them otherwise, unless it is the style of a specific publication or organization.

Governor Woods has not yet decided to run for a second term.

The **governor** is undecided about running for a second term.

Senator Jefferson's office has not responded to our request for an interview.

We contacted the **senator's** office for an interview, but have not received a response.

Betty Adams, mayor of Harrisonville, is considering a run for Congress.

(**Note:** Some organizations and publications have their own in-house capitalization rules. For example, a city government may capitalize *Mayor* or a company may capitalize *Chairman* or *President* when referring to the office or the person holding it.)

ARTICLES WITH TITLES

Do not capitalize articles and prepositions (such as *the, a, an, of*) preceding a personal title unless they begin a sentence.

The Honorable Judge Thomas Beckett will be the guest of honor.

This year's award winner is **the** Honorable Judge Thomas Beckett.

FOLLOWING THE NAME

In general, capitalize a professional title when it follows a name.

Holly Ramsey, Director, Applications Development, has been running the department for five years.

Please contact **Dr. Lois Carlson, Professor of Psychology,** for a copy of the latest study.

Do not capitalize occupational titles used without a person's name.

All of the **marketing managers** are away at a sales meeting.

Note: Some organizations' style is to not capitalize a person's professional or job title when it directly follows the name; this is also acceptable so long as it is applied consistently.

24c Relationship Titles

Capitalize relationship titles when they are used as part of a person's name.

Capital: My **Aunt Meredith** lives in Oklahoma.

Lowercase: My **aunt** lives in Oklahoma.

Do not capitalize *mother* and *father* except when they are part of a name or an official title:

Capital: **Mother Teresa** was known throughout the world for her work on behalf of the poor.

Lowercase: My **mother** will be out of the country when I go home for the holiday.

25 ORGANIZATION AND PRODUCT NAMES

25a Companies

Capitalize the names of companies exactly as they are written by the company. Keep in mind that company names often have unique spellings, capitalization, and spacing.

Wal-Mart

PricewaterhouseCoopers

MetLife

UnitedHealth Group

25b Commercial Products

Capitalize names of products as written by the manufacturer. Be aware of the use of the superscript symbols ™ for trademark and ® for registered, which companies use to indicate their exclusive use of a name or slogan. These symbols can be omitted in everyday business writing, but in information that will be distributed publicly, the general practice is to use the symbol at first mention.

Apple iPhone

BlackBerry®

Do not capitalize a descriptive term that follows a brand name unless is it a part of the brand (legal) name.

Campbell Soup
Alka-Seltzer Plus
Bayer Aspirin
Dell computers
Sony electronics

25c Government Entities and Agencies

Capitalize the names of government agencies and their shortened forms.

The **US Congress** passed new tax legislation that favors small businesses. [Note that periods are not required in the abbreviation for *United States,* but using them is also correct.]

The Daily News reported that **Congress** passed a new tax bill.

The **United States Supreme Court** has made the first Monday in October famous. That is the day the **Court** reconvenes after the summer recess.

Always capitalize *United States* and spell it out when used alone or with the full name *United States of America.*

Representatives of the **United States** attended the World Conference on Poverty in Geneva.

Capitalize the names of government entities when they refer to specific names or places. Do not capitalize government terms when they refer to government entities in general.

Five boroughs make up the **City of New York.**

The **State of California** has the largest Hispanic population in the United States.

The **Department of Homeland Security** is a **federal** agency.

Banks and **state agencies** will be closed on **federal** holidays.

The governor of the **Commonwealth of Massachusetts** has worked in **state government** for many years.

25d Departments and Entities Within Organizations

Capitalize department names and other organizational entities when referring to a specific unit within a firm; do not capitalize general references to them.

Specific: The **Human Resources Department** will be closed on Friday for staff training.

General: We are updating the computer systems in the **human resource departments** in all our office locations.

Mike works in **Marketing,** but he travels the majority of the time. [refers to a specific department]

General: The budget calls for a big increase in **research and development** next year. [general reference]

Specific: The **Department of Rail Operations** created a **Policies and Procedures Task Force** to write a new employee manual.

General: The director of the **rail department** appointed a **task force** to develop a new employee manual.

25e Athletic Organizations and Events

Capitalize the names of specific athletic organizations and sporting events.

New York Racing Association	the Belmont Stakes
National Football League	the Super Bowl
International Olympic Committee	the Olympic Games

26 LOCATIONS AND DIRECTIONS

26a Geographical Place Names

Capitalize names of specific locations, but lowercase names of general locations:

Minneapolis	city
New Mexico	state
Canada	country

Capitalize the word *city* when it is part of the city's official name or when referring to a government unit.

The population of **New York City** is now over nine million.

If you drive due south, you will see signs for the **city** of Nashville.

The **City of Nashville** paid for the advertising campaign promoting tourism.

26b Regional Names

Capitalize regional names when they refer to specific geographical regions. Do not capitalize such terms when they are used to indicate general locations.

CAPITALIZE

Debra and Suzanne were raised in the **South.**

Fishing is a major commercial and tourist industry in the **Northwest.**

The company is planning to open a second office in the **Far East.**

LOWERCASE

The drive will take you through the **western** part of the state.

We are taking our vacation up **north** this summer.

The Finger Lakes are located in the **western** part of New York State.

Capitalize regional terms referring to groups of people.

The owners of the new restaurant are true **Southerners.**

Many people now living on the East Coast are native **Midwesterners.**

26c Directions

Do not capitalize directional names when they refer to general directions.

Drive **south** on I-75 from Detroit to get to Ohio.

We hope to rent a time-share unit just **east** of Fort Myers.

27 PERIODS OF TIME AND HOLIDAYS

27a Time Periods

Capitalize days of the week and the names of months.

Wednesday	Saturday
February	November
American Indian Heritage Month	African American History Month

Do not capitalize the names of the seasons or the word *season* when used with a proper noun.

The **fall** is usually our busiest selling season.

The **summer** catalog must be mailed no later than March.

We are planning a special promotion for the Christmas **season.**

Capitalize the names of historical periods.

Middle Ages

Bronze Age

the Roaring Twenties

the Industrial Revolution

It is customary to dispense with capitalizing the names of comparable contemporary periods, but either form is considered correct.

the information age

the digital age

the civil rights movement OR the Civil Rights Movement

Do not capitalize the names of decades or centuries in general references.

Protesters were everywhere in the **seventies.**

The **twenty-first century** has only just begun.

The many broadcasts of **millennium** celebrations from around the world were awesome.

27b Holidays and Special Observances

Capitalize names of holidays.

Memorial Day

Fourth of July

Flag Day

New Year's Day

Do not capitalize the words *new year* when used as a general reference.

After the **new year,** our stores will no longer be open after 6 p.m.

Capitalize the names of religious observances.

Good Friday

Passover

Ramadan

Capitalize the names of cultural observances.

African American History Month
Italian American Heritage Month
Holocaust Remembrance Day
Hispanic Heritage Month

27c Historical Events and Documents

Capitalize the names of current and historical documents and legal acts.

the US Constitution OR the Constitution
the Civil Rights Act of 1964
the Magna Carta
the Kyoto Treaty

(**Note:** US may be written with or without periods.)

CAPITALIZATION

28 GROUPS OF PEOPLE AND LANGUAGES

28a Races, Nationalities, and Ethnic Groups

Capitalize the names of races, nationalities, and ethnic groups:

African American
American Indian
Arabic
Asian
Caucasian
English
Filipino
Haitian
Hispanic or Latino (or Latina)
Russian

28b *Black* and *White* When Referring to Race

Do not capitalize the words *black* and *white* when referring to the African American or Caucasian racial groups.

28c Hyphenation of Names of Racial and Ethnic Groups

The trend is to drop the hyphen from names of racial and ethnic groups when coupled with the word *American,* when used as either a noun or an adjective.

African American
Asian American
Hispanic or Latino American
European American

28d Languages

Capitalize the names of languages.

English
Spanish
French
Arabic
Russian

29 RELIGIOUS TERMS

In general, capitalize all religious terms that are proper nouns. When in doubt, consult a dictionary. The following guidelines cover broad categories of religious terms.

29a Religions

Capitalize the names of religions and members of religious groups.

the Baptist religion
the Mormon church
the Catholic church
Protestants
Buddhists
Muslims

29b Supreme Beings and Holy Texts

Capitalize names that refer to a supreme being.

God
the Messiah
the Almighty
the Holy Spirit
Allah
Buddha

Capitalize the names of religious writings, books, and their parts.

the Bible
the Old Testament
the Gospel of St. Matthew
the Qur'an (or the Koran)
the Torah
the Ten Commandments

When using the term *bible* as a figure of speech, do not capitalize it.

For the first two months, the procedures manual was my bible for learning the job.

Use lowercase letters for general references to religious terms.

a god
a scripture
a church
a holy book
biblical references

29c Religious Events and Observances

Capitalize names of important religious events and holidays.

the Crucifixion
Holy Communion
the Exodus
Ramadan
the Resurrection
Passover

Do not capitalize general references to most religious observances, but check your dictionary to be sure.

> You are invited to attend the **christening** of my son.
>
> Some religions do not believe in **baptism.**
>
> I am requesting permission to leave early to attend a **Passover seder.** [Capitalizing *seder* is optional.]

30 TITLES OF PUBLICATIONS AND ARTISTIC WORKS

30a General Rules

Capitalize the main words in titles of published and artistic works. Do not capitalize prepositions (such as *in, on, of*) and articles (*a, an, the*) except when they are the first word of a title or subtitle. Lowercase conjunctions (*and, but, or*) unless they appear as the first word of a title or subtitle.

Technology has created a relaxation of these traditional rules, and it is common to see capitalized prepositions and conjunctions in titles and headlines, particularly in newspapers, in spite of the rules. Businesses also have in-house styles, and many, especially in advertising, bend the rules when it comes to writing commercial names, tag lines, and headlines.

To indicate a title in typed text copy, use italics for complete works (books, magazines, newspapers, exhibitions, films, plays, and radio and television programs) and quotation marks for short works and parts of complete works. (In handwriting, indicate italics by underlining.)

> Enclosed is a copy of our annual publication, *Progress Report for Investors.*
>
> The classic *The Catcher in the Rye* by J. D. Salinger is still required reading in most schools.
>
> Here is a copy of *A Guide to Good Health: The Nutrition Plan for Women Over 40.*

In cases where a publisher or creator of a work does not follow the traditional rules, write the title as it was originally intended; however, err on the side of following general standards.

> *AARP The Magazine* is published by the American Association of Retired Persons. [the publisher's spelling]

(**Note:** Many publications no longer follow the convention of italicizing titles. In business, however, this convention should be followed as long as it doesn't violate the style used in your organization.)

30b Short Works and Parts of Publications

Capitalize short works and parts of works according to the same rules as complete works. Short works include poems, songs, games, and sections or parts of publications—chapters, articles in newspapers, and magazines—whether in print or online. In typed or handwritten text, indicate titles by enclosing them in quotation marks instead of italicizing them. The same is true for titles of artistic works such as paintings and dance.

> Read the second chapter, "Capturing Your Audience's Attention," in the book *Mastering Presentation Skills*.
>
> Members of the New York City Ballet company will give a benefit performance of "Sleeping Beauty" at the charity event.
>
> We must request the publisher's permission to reprint the poem "Stopping by Woods on a Snowy Evening" by Robert Frost.

30c Compound Words in Titles

Do not capitalize the second element in compound words in titles unless the word is a proper noun.

> The title of my article is "Five Ways to Boost Your Self-esteem."
>
> *Welcome to the Twenty-first Century* was number three on the best-seller list.
>
> The newspaper article you need is "Reliving the Post-Vietnam War Era" by Ira Jordan.

30d Short Words

Always capitalize the verbs *is* and *be* in titles. Do not capitalize *to* when it is used as part of an infinitive.

> My poem, "The Best Is Yet to Be," is being published in the *Everyday Poetry* journal.

PREPOSITIONS AND ADVERBS

Capitalize short words in titles when they function as adverbs instead of prepositions.

> Your article, "Moving Up in the Organization," is scheduled for publication in the next issue of the newsletter. [*Up* is an adverb in this sentence.]

HEADLINES

Word processing programs do not make distinctions between short and long words when you use the automated "change case" feature. This has led to many publications, including major ones like *The New York Times,* dispensing with the rules of capitalization regarding prepositions, conjunctions, and short words. In fact, capital and lowercase letters for prepositions and conjunctions are often inconsistently written within a single headline. Nevertheless, when you have the option of following the standard rules, it is recommended that you do so.

31 REFERENCES TO ONLINE TECHNOLOGY

31a Online Terminology

Capitalize *Internet* but not *intranet*, which refers to a company's internal Web site. Capitalize *World Wide Web* when referring to it in writing; follow the style of your organization or publication in capitalizing the term *Web.* Acceptable spellings:

Web site   web site   website

Web site addresses should be written exactly as used by the owner. Some systems are case-sensitive; others are not. If you capitalize words in a Web site name that was created in lowercase, your message might not transmit.

The **Web site** of the NAACP is www.naacp.org.

When referring to Web sites by title, capitalize them according to standard rules for titles of complete works and parts of works, as described in Topic 30.

The terms *email* and *online* are not capitalized except when they are the first word in a sentence.

31b Programming Languages

Capitalize the names of programming languages.

Java

C++

Fortran

ASCII [When used within a sentence, may be in lowercase.]

At one time, programming words included an imbedded space **[foo_bar].** The trend is now to eliminate that, and capitalization is used **[FooBar].**

32 ACADEMIC COURSES AND DEGREES

Capitalize the major words in the titles of specific academic courses. Do not capitalize general areas of study.

I enrolled in Philosophy 101.

Her minor is in economics.

All freshmen must take history, English, and math. [*English* is capitalized as the name of a language.]

Capitalize abbreviations of academic degrees, but do not capitalize them when they are spelled out.

Diane received her bachelor's degree from Southern Florida University.

Kevin is pursuing an MBA at Harvard.

Margarita Kennedy, PhD, will be the commencement speaker.

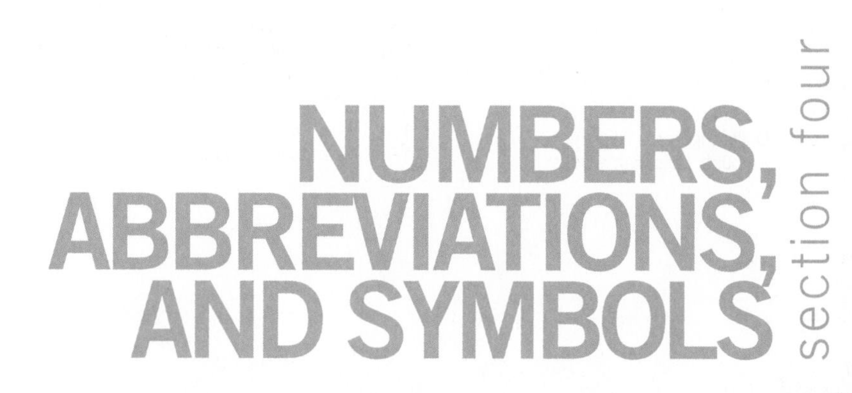
NUMBERS,
ABBREVIATIONS,
AND SYMBOLS
section four

4 Numbers, Abbreviations, and Symbols

33 EXPRESSING NUMBERS

33a General Guidelines

Almost all business documents contain some type of numerical data—even if only the date on a letter or the time of a meeting in an email. Using established conventions for writing numbers in words and figures ensures clarity—readers expect to see numbers expressed in a standard way, and doing so avoids confusion. The guidelines in this section make it easy to look up the rules that govern number usage in running text and in text heavy with numerical data.

When expressing numbers in writing, the key elements are accuracy and consistency. Always check numbers to make sure they are correct, and, to the extent possible, treat numerical information consistently in each document.

General Rule for Using Words or Figures in Text

In running text—paragraph copy excluding headings, tables, graphics, and other special parts of documents where numbers are almost always written as figures—write the numbers zero through ten in words and write numbers above ten in figures.

> We now have 25 employees who are eligible for three weeks of vacation.
>
> Please pick up the seven volunteers; use the company van that holds eight passengers.
>
> When the number of workshop registrants reaches 150, we will close the online registration site.

This rule is subject to many exceptions that arise in the effort to achieve clarity. Following are some typical situations where you might need to apply different criteria to ensure that numbers are expressed clearly and consistently.

ADDITIONAL RULES FOR CLARITY AND CONSISTENCY

In both formal documents and documents where you want to de-emphasize numbers, you may opt to write all numbers in words because figures stand out more.

> Over the past **fourteen years**, the company has been sued **twenty-three times.** [Words de-emphasize the number 23.]

QUICK REFERENCE 33.1

General rules for expressing numbers

Expressing numbers in running text (33a and 33b)

- Write numbers zero through ten in words and numbers above ten in figures.
- Always spell out a number that begins a sentence.

Punctuation in numbers (33f and 33g)

- Figures above the thousands must have commas: 10,000, 100,000
- It is optional, but recommended, to use a comma in figures of four digits: 1,000.
- When four-digit numbers appear with figures above the thousands, use a comma for consistency: 5,250, 10,300, and 400,250.
- The words for numbers between 21 and 99 are compound words and require hyphenation: twenty-one, thirty-five.
- The words for numbers above 99 are not compound words, so do not need hyphenation: one hundred, three thousand.
- Hyphenate numbers expressed as fractions: one-third, three-quarters.

Capitalization with numbers (33h)

- Do not capitalize numbers expressed in words except to begin a sentence or to follow some other rule for capitalization.
- Do not capitalize *dollars* or *cents* or the words *million, billion,* and *trillion* when writing amounts of money in words or figures: five dollars; 20 cents; $1 billion; a million dollars.

Spelling, forming plurals, and alphabetizing numbers (33i)

- When numbers are used in proper names, spell them exactly the way they are written by the person, organization, or other entity.
- To form the plural of a number expressed in words, add *s* (tens) or *ies* (forties).
- When alphabetizing numbers, written figures come before letters of the alphabet.

When several numbers in a sentence or paragraph designate similar things, it is clearer to express them in the same form—all figures or all words.

> Juan ordered **12 dozen pencils** and **5 pencil sharpeners** for test day; however, he forgot to order the **6 timers** we need. [A number under 10 can be expressed in figures if needed for emphasis and consistency.]

In copy with many numbers, or where you want to emphasize numbers, use figures for zero through ten.

> Once we have **25 people enrolled,** we can decide whether we want to admit **1 to 5 additional students,** but we must keep the number **under 30.** [All numbers refer to students.]

When numbers refer to dissimilar things, they need not be expressed in similar form.

> Once we have **25 people enrolled**, we can schedule the workshop in **three to five days.** [The figures and words refer to different things.]

In legal documents, numerical amounts are often spelled out and repeated in figures in parentheses.

> Your mortgage balance is **twenty-one thousand and forty-seven dollars ($21,047).**
>
> We will execute the agreement upon receipt of your payment of **six hundred and fifty dollars ($650).**

In formal documents, such as invitations, dates and times may be written out.

You are cordially invited to attend a reception in honor of
City Councilwoman Jennifer Yung Su
July twenty-seventh, 20xx
at eight o'clock in the evening
at the Country Gardens Clubhouse
2807 Seaside

33b A Number as First Word of a Sentence

Always spell out a number that begins a sentence, even in text with heavy numerical data.

> **Twenty years** ago the founders of the company saw a need in the marketplace.

To avoid spelling out a number, revise the sentence.

> **One hundred people were contacted:** 46 refused the interview, 22 accepted, and 32 asked for more information before making a decision.
>
> **OR**
>
> **Our office contacted 100 people:** 46 refused the interview, 22 accepted, and 32 asked for more information before making a decision.

When a number is too long to spell out (more than two words, with a hyphenated word counting as one), revise the sentence.

> **NO:** **55,273** parts were shipped last month, but 75 percent of them were returned.
>
> **YES:** **The number of parts shipped last month was 55,273,** but 75 percent of them were returned.

33c Two Numbers in Succession

When a number modifies another number, spell out one of the two to avoid confusion.

> **NO:** Our company has **12 15-story buildings** in Boston.
>
> **YES:** Our company has **twelve 15-story** buildings in Boston.
>
> **OR**
>
> Our company has **12 fifteen-story** buildings in Boston.

When two numbers appear next to each other, use a comma to separate them or revise the sentence to avoid placing them together.

> In **2007, 125** employees were relocated.
>
> **OR**
>
> **One hundred twenty-five** employees were relocated in 2007. [Always spell out a number that is the first word of a sentence.]

33d Large Approximate Numbers

Express large indefinite or approximate numbers in figures or words; with figures above the ten thousands, use the words *million, billion,* or *trillion*.

> The world has more than **six billion** people.
>
> The company's net worth is **several hundred million** dollars.

The population of the United States is more than **300 million.**

In New York City, more than **8 million** people use public transportation daily.

In written text, express large figures as a decimal (2.4 million) or a whole number (2,404,900), depending on the need to be exact. Treat such numbers consistently within each document.

Opening an office overseas enabled us to reach an additional **1.2 million** customers.

After opening the overseas office, we sold an additional **1,253,50** units. [Note that this number is also rounded off to the nearest 100s.]

33e Numbered Items

Use figures to number and label items in text and captions.

Figure 9 illustrates the sales history of **Model JT109** for the past five years.

Your report on sales in **Region 3** is due no later than this Friday by 2 p.m.

We have run out of item **No. 203A** in blue and white, but it is still available in red.

33f Commas in Numbers

Using a comma in figures of four digits is optional.

The downtown outlet purchased **1500** copies of the book and put **1000** more on reserve.

OR

We received **1,044** requests for the book in one hour!

With a mix of numbers in the thousands and higher and with copy that includes dates, using the comma is recommended.

In the first half of the decade, our staff increased from fewer than **2,000** to more than **3,500** employees. After the merger in 2005, the number jumped to more than **10,000** worldwide.

Align commas in lists of figures, for example, in a table. The right-justified alignment setting will automatically achieve this.

Thousands	Hundred Thousands	Millions	Billions
1,000	100,000	1,000,000	1,000,000,000
2,000	200,000	2,000,000	2,000,000,000
12,000	120,000	12,000,000	12,000,000,000

[See 37a for comma use in dates.]

33g Hyphens in Numbers

Avoid spelling out numbers with more than two words (a hyphenated word counts as one word). Words that express numbers between 21 and 99 are compound words and require a hyphen:

twenty-one
thirty-five
eighty-eight

Words that express numbers higher than 99 are not compound words and do not need a hyphen:

one hundred
three thousand
two hundred fifteen

Fractions need a hyphen:

one-third
three-quarters (or three-fourths)
one-half
two-thirds

Numbers expressed as words or figures need a hyphen when used to form a noun or adjective.

The school accepts **three-year-olds,** but they must pass an admissions test. [*Three-year-olds* is a noun.]

The new **45-story** office building was fully rented before construction began. [The number/word modifying building, *45-story*, is a compound adjective.]

When two modifiers that modify the same noun are separated, use a hyphen after each modifier instead of repeating the noun. Use a space after the first hyphen.

> We will only accept tenants who are willing to sign a **two- to four-year** lease.
>
> The community theater's new production is a **three- or four-part** comedy.

33h Capitalization with Numbers

Do not capitalize numbers expressed in words unless they are the first word of a sentence, part of a title, or follow some other rule for capitalization.

> **One hundred** people called in for the video conference.
>
> **OR**
>
> At least 100 people called in for the video conference.

Do not capitalize *dollars* or *cents.*

> We offer **one dollar** off on the first purchase and **fifty cents** off on the second.

Do not capitalize *million, billion,* and *trillion* when they refer to general amounts of money expressed in words or figures.

> If the contract is under **a million,** the home office doesn't need to sign off.
>
> We expect the contract to be at least **$1.5 million,** so it will need approval.

Do capitalize labels that refer to numbers, for example, *No., Section, Region*.

> Remodeling of schools will begin in **Region 3.**
>
> I correctly answered item **No. 17** on the exam.

33i Spelling, Forming Plurals, and Alphabetizing Numbers

Spell numbers in proper names exactly as written by the person, organization, or other entity.

> We bought our house through **Century 21 Real Estate.**
>
> I need a copy of the film ***101 Dalmatians*** for a special screening.

U2 has been one of the most popular bands in the world since the mid-1980s.

Our new vice president is **Jason Farnsworth III.**

To form the plural of a number written in words, add *s* or *ies*. Do not use *'s*.

As baby boomers started to reach their **sixties,** companies began facing large losses of talent due to retirement.

Tens of thousands of dollars were expended to test the new prototype.

Do not use an *s* to form the plural of a figure unless the figure expresses historical time; otherwise, express plurals in words.

The new employees are all in their **twenties.** [NOT 20s]

Many World War II veterans were born in the **1920s.** [OR '20s]

When alphabetizing a list, place items beginning with arabic numbers above items with letters of the alphabet; roman numerals come after arabic numerals and before letters.

3-2-1 Software Solutions

307th Armory

IV Guys Menswear Shop

Aaron's Department Store

[Read more about filing rules in Topic 55.]

34 SYMBOLS WITH NUMBERS (#, $, %, °)

Use symbols only with numbers expressed in figures. When more than one figure is used in succession, repeat the symbol with each number.

Please confirm my order for Items **#20A, #34C, and #12E.**

Let me know if you want the meal that costs **$25, $35, or $50** per person.

During the last three quarters, sales were up **2%, 2.5%, and 2.7%** respectively.

When the symbol is expressed in words, the opposite is true—place the word for the symbol only at the end of the list.

Sales are expected to rise **5 to 10 percent** during the holiday season.

34a Number symbol (#)

Use the number symbol in lists of item numbers or in tables; it is interchangeable with the abbreviation *No.* Otherwise, use the word *number.* Be consistent in your choice.

#23 **OR** No. 23

34b Dollar sign ($)

Use the dollar sign to express dollar amounts in figures; never add the word *dollars* when the dollar sign is used.

We can deliver the project two weeks early for an additional **$1,500.**

The hotel quoted a nightly rate of **$265.**

Our consulting rate is **$50** per hour or **$350** per day.

34c General Rules for Figures with Symbols

QUICK REFERENCE 34.1

Symbols with Figures (#, $, %, °)

- Use symbols only with numbers expressed in figures. If more than one figure is used in succession, repeat the symbol with each number, except in columns of figures in tables.
- The number symbol (#) is interchangeable with the word *number* and the abbreviation *No.*
- Use the dollar sign ($) to express dollar amounts in figures; never add the word *dollars* when using the dollar sign.
- Use percent (%) and degree (°) symbols only in heavily numerical copy or for special emphasis; otherwise use the words *percent* and *degrees.*

34d Percent sign (%)

Use the percent sign with heavily numerical information. In other, more isolated occurrences use the word *percent*.

We suggest an annual salary increase of **2.5%** after six months, **5%** at the end of a year, and **3% to 5%** in subsequent years—if performance is maintained.

Even with a corporate discount of **20 percent,** the hotel you suggested is too expensive.

The poll numbers indicate we're ahead by **10 to 15 percent.**

34e Degree symbol (°)

Use the degree symbol in text for emphasis, for example, when giving cooking directions or weather information; otherwise use the word *degrees*.

Cool season crop seeds germinate at **40° to 80°.** Warm season crop seeds germinate at **50° to 90°.**

Preheat the oven to **425°** and bake for 40 minutes.

The temperature in the office will be set at **68 degrees** at all times to save on energy costs.

35 ORDINAL NUMBERS (*st, nd, rd, th*)

Ordinal numbers indicate a ranking or place within a series. Ordinals are formed by adding *st, nd, rd,* or *th* to an arabic number.

first	1st
tenth	10th
fifty-third	53rd
thirty-second	32nd

35a When to Use Figures or Words

In general, spell out ordinal numbers in running text that are expressed in one or two words. A hyphenated word counts as one word (*thirty-first*).

The organization's **eighteenth** annual convention will be held next year.

They will celebrate their **forty-second** wedding anniversary this year.

Jason will celebrate his **sixth** birthday next month.

We are having our holiday party early for the **third** year in a row.

If the ordinal number has more than two words when written out, use numerals.

> This is the **125th** annual celebration of the founding of the California Express.

35b Ordinal Numbers in Dates

When the day follows the month, use numerals without ordinal endings.

> We will meet on **October 31.** [NOT October 31st]
>
> Please join us for lunch on Wednesday, **June 10,** at 12:30 p.m.

When the date precedes the month, use ordinal numbers in words.

> The **tenth** of October
>
> The **thirty-first** of January
>
> The **fourteenth** of February

---

36 CLOCK TIME

36a Time Expressed in Figures

When expressing time in figures, use *a.m.* and *p.m.* (always with periods and no space between the letters) to indicate morning, afternoon, and evening. Do not use *a.m.* and *p.m.* with time expressed in words (see 36c). In running text, use lowercase letters.

> The airport shuttle leaves at **7 a.m.**
>
> My return flight arrives on Tuesday at **4:56 p.m.**

When using figures for time on the hour, do not add zeroes:

> My calendar is open from **3 to 4:30 p.m.**
>
> We will expect you to arrive around **7 p.m.**

The exception is in a set of figures where fractions of time are listed along with times on the hour. For consistency, use zeroes in numbers designating hours.

> **Breakfast:** 8:15 to 9:00 a.m.
>
> **Workshop I:** 9:15 to 10:00 a.m.
>
> **Workshop II:** 10:15 to 11:00 a.m.

36b Use of *a.m.* and *p.m.*

When giving time frames, do not repeat *a.m.* and *p.m.* if both numbers refer to morning or afternoon, unless other words fall between the numbers:

> The session will run from **11:30 a.m. to 1:30 p.m.**
>
> The reception will last from **6 to 7 p.m.**
>
> The meeting time is **9:30 to 10:30 a.m.**
>
> The flight leaves at **9 a.m.** and arrives in Phoenix at **11:24 a.m.** [Times are separated in the sentence, so *a.m.* needs to be repeated.]

Three styles can be used to write *a.m.* and *p.m.*, but lowercase is preferred because it is easiest to type and looks better in text copy.

Lowercase:	a.m. and p.m. [preferred use in most running text]
Capital letters:	A.M. and P.M. [used in some types of copy, e.g., advertising]
Small caps:	A.M. and P.M. [used by some publications]

Always be consistent in usage in each document. When proofreading, make sure you have placed a period after each letter (but never two periods at the end of a sentence).

36c Time Expressed in Words

When expressing time in words, do not use *a.m.* or *p.m.* Instead indicate time of day with *morning, afternoon,* or *evening.*

> I will set my alarm for **six o'clock in the morning** and leave home by **seven.**
>
> We didn't leave the party until some time after **eight in the evening.**

Words de-emphasize numbers, so use figures when you want the time to stand out.

> The car service will pick you up at your home between **6:45 and 7 a.m.**

When no specific time is given in figures, do not use *a.m.* or *p.m.* in place of the words *morning, afternoon,* or *evening*.

NO:	We are going to get together **in the a.m.** to discuss our strategy.
YES:	We are going to get together **in the morning** to discuss our strategy.

36d Use of *o'clock*

The word *o'clock* may be used with time expressed in either words or figures, but it is used most often in formal writing and invitations. It is usually used when the time is expressed in words.

The ceremony will begin at **six o'clock in the evening.**

36e Use of *noon* and *midnight*

Use *midnight* or *noon* with or without the figure 12. This is clearer than 12 a.m. or 12 p.m., which readers might misconstrue.

The luncheon will begin at **12 noon** and end at 1:30. [Using the figure here makes it easier to see the exact time.]

In the following sentences the time is clear without the figure:

Our shipping room opens at **midnight.**

Let's meet at **noon.**

(**Note:** When referring to midnight, it can be confusing as to whether you mean the beginning or the end of the day. Using 11:59 p.m. or 12:01 a.m. and the date is the way to avoid such confusion.)

36f International and Military (24-Hour) Time

Most of the countries in the world, as well as the US military services, use the 24-hour clock, which begins at 0:00 (midnight) and ends at 23:00. Thus, 2 p.m. in the United States would be designated 14:00.

US military time does not always use the colon, so 2 p.m. would be designated 1400.

The private returned to the base at **1830** on Sunday, after a weekend at home. [1830 is 6:30 p.m.]

International time is usually written with a colon, although this may vary.

In Paris the conference call is scheduled for **14:15,** which is 2:15 p.m. in New York.

STATING TIME ON THE 24-HOUR CLOCK

The word *hours* is sometimes used to state the time on the 24-hour clock, but this usage is not universally customary. Here are some examples of how to express 24-hour clock time in spoken words. Variations, such as half-past or 20 after the hour are common, just as they are with the 12-hour clock.

0000 (or 00:00) midnight

0300 (or 03:00) oh three hundred or three hundred hours

36g 24-Hour Clock Conversion Chart

CONVERTING THE 24-HOUR CLOCK TO THE 12-HOUR CLOCK

24-hour clock	12-hour clock	24-hour clock	12-hour clock
00:00	12:00 a.m. 12 midnight (start of day)	12:00	12:00 p.m. 12 noon
01:00	1:00 a.m.	13:00	1:00 p.m.
02:00	2:00 a.m.	14:00	2:00 p.m.
03:00	3:00 a.m.	15:00	3:00 p.m.
04:00	4:00 a.m.	16:00	4:00 p.m.
05:00	5:00 a.m.	17:00	5:00 p.m.
06:00	6:00 a.m.	18:00	6:00 p.m.
07:00	7:00 a.m.	19:00	7:00 p.m.
08:00	8:00 a.m.	20:00	8:00 p.m.
09:00	9:00 a.m.	21:00	9:00 p.m.
10:00	10:00 a.m.	22:00	10:00 p.m.
11:00	11:00 a.m.	23:00	11:00 p.m.

37 CALENDAR DATES

37a Month, Day, and Year

When writing calendar dates, express the month in words and the date in figures. Do not use ordinal numbers (ending in *st, th, rd,* and *nd*). Place a comma between the day and year.

He was born **January 27, 1884.**

In very informal writing, dates can be expressed in all figures: 5/26/10.

37b Military and International Date Style

The US military and international style of writing dates is to reverse the day and month. No punctuation is needed. Use this style in military or international correspondence.

17 July 2008 [Do not use commas.]

37c Commas in Dates

When writing a date that includes the month, day, and year, place a comma after the year when it falls in the middle of a sentence, unless some other mark of punctuation follows.

On **February 1, 1999,** the Brady family founded the West End Youth Center.

We released the report on **August 8, 2007,** at the annual conference.

One week after my promotion, on **August 3, 2005**—a day I will never forget—the merger with our biggest competitor was announced.

When a date is written with only the month and year, no comma is needed after the year, unless it is being used to punctuate the sentence for another reason.

The merger of **August 2006** tripled the company's net worth.

Construction started in **May 2009,** and we were to have the building ready for occupancy no later than **February 2010.** [The comma is needed to join the two parts of a compound sentence.]

A comma is not needed in military and international date style, as shown in 37b.

[See 33f for use of commas with regular numbers.]

38 PERIODS OF TIME

Recommended styles vary, depending on whether dates are isolated or heavily cited in written material. Use a consistent style throughout each document, even if one section is heavy with dates and another is not.

38a Span of Years

To indicate a continuous span of years, use the words *from/to* in running text.

I worked at General Contracting Inc. **from 1999 to 2005.**

In text with many dates and in tables, use a hyphen (-) or an en dash (–) to indicate the span. Do not space before or after the hyphen or en dash to connect a span of years.

1991 to 1993 [preferred in running text]

1991-1993 [preferred in lists of figures, tabular material, and text heavy with similar figures]

OR

1991–1993

In the hyphenated form, use complete numbers for both years in running text where numbers are infrequent.

Sales revenue for the past three five-year periods were as follows: **1996-2000, $5 million; 2001-2005, $6.2 million; and 2006-2010, $5.9 million.**

When long lists of such numbers are used in text or in tabular material, shorten the second year: 2002-05.

38b Decades

Use figures and an *s* without an apostrophe to express decades in four digits.

By **the 2010s,** we should show a profit. [NOT 2010's]

Most of our employees finished college during **the 1990s.** [NOT 1990's]

Although '08 means 2008, avoid this style in business writing, except when referring to a year of graduation such as "the class of '08" or when referring to decades. Use either figures or words when expressing decades in two digits.

His style of dress is a throwback to the **sixties.**

Huge shoulder pads were fashionable in the **80s.**

38c Centuries

In running text, the preferred usage is to express centuries in words instead of figures, but both are correct. Do not capitalize *century* unless it is part of a title or to follow some other capitalization rule.

The personal computer was a **twentieth-century** invention. [*Twentieth-century* is a compound adjective in this sentence, so it is hyphenated.]

By the beginning of the **21st century,** personal computers were already considered a necessity for every home.

When used as a compound adjective, hyphenation is required; when used as a noun, no hyphen is needed.

Noun: nineteenth century or 19th century

Compound adjective: nineteenth-century invention or 19th-century invention

39 MONEY

39a Dollar Figures

Generally, use figures to express amounts of money in running text. Write whole numbers without decimals or zeroes unless they are part of a list of figures that requires decimals; then show decimals for all.

The total amount you owe for the lunch is **$35.**

In the second quarter our department spent just over **$2,000** for office supplies.

The amounts spent for the supplies are as follows: **paper cups, $9.37; paper plates $32.00; utensils, $14.00; coffee service, $98.02.**

39b Amounts Less than a Dollar

In running text, use figures followed by *cents* for amounts under $1 when they are used in isolation.

The board is scheduled to approve a toll increase of **50 cents** for tunnel crossings and **95 cents for bridges.**

When written with other figures above $1, express all of them with the dollar sign.

The packs of writing pads are **$8.95,** and the pens are **$.25** each.

39c Large Dollar Amounts

Always use numerals for dollar amounts up to the thousands: $1,000, $3,255.

> We have only **$12,000** in the bank, but our credit line is being increased.

For larger amounts, omit the zeroes and use the words *million, billion,* and *trillion* after each figure. Always include the dollar sign: $10 million, $10.5 million.

> The proposed extension of the commuter rail system is estimated to cost at least **$15 billion** over five years, with approximately **$900 million** budgeted for the first year of construction.

When several large numbers appear in succession, repeat the word *million, billion,* or *trillion* after each figure.

> Our sales revenue over the past three years was **$1 million, $1.2 million, and $4 million** respectively.

Words can be used instead of figures to express large numbers, depending on the desired emphasis.

> I want to alert you that the project is expected to run at least **one and a half million dollars** over budget; see the attached spreadsheet.
>
> **OR**
>
> I want to alert you that the project is expected to run at least **$1.5 million** over budget; see the attached spreadsheet.

39d Rounding Dollar Amounts

When it is not necessary to use exact figures, readers find it easier to comprehend rounded numbers, especially for large amounts. Use qualifying words such as *more than, less than, almost, approximately, about* to indicate that the figure is inexact.

> The cost of the conference registration plus travel is **about $1,000.**
>
> By the year 2020, our revenues are projected to be **more than $10 billion.**
>
> Sales declined, and we had to cut **almost $2 million** from the advertising budget.

Large numbers can also be rounded to one or two decimal points. This is recommended for tables or lists of numeric data in text where specificity is needed. For example, the figure $10,233,491 can be rounded to $10 million, $10.2 million, or $10.23 million.

40 MEASUREMENTS

40a Expressing Measurements in Figures and Words

Generally, use figures to express measurements.

The flooring needed is for an office **10 feet by 12 feet.**

The flooring needed is for an office **10′ × 12′.**

BUT

Eileen gained **more than five pounds** this week.

When two related numbers modify a noun, hyphenate them or use a slash to create one unit.

My vision is no longer **twenty-twenty.**

OR

My vision is no longer **20/20.**

Express fractions in measurements as numerals or decimals; be consistent in each document.

We need another **3½ feet** of cable. [numeral]

He measured the desk at **5.5 feet.** [decimal]

Sales were up only **0.95 percent** from last year. [Use the zero before the decimal point to prevent misunderstanding.]

Always express temperatures, sizes, and dimensions as figures.

Last night the temperature dropped to **5°.**

Jenny now wears a **size 8,** and she is **5′ 9″ tall.**

Let's purchase a **5′ × 9′** area rug for the foyer.

40b Abbreviations in Measurements

When measurements occur infrequently, use figures and the words *feet, yards, inches, pounds,* and so on, spelled out.

Every letter weighing **1 ounce** or less requires one first-class stamp.

This package weighs **2 pounds 5 ounces**. [Do not use a comma between the pounds and ounces because they are one item.]

When measurements occur frequently, and in technical material, use abbreviations.

The rugs we ordered for the executive offices are different dimensions: **Ellison, 10 × 12 ft; Darnell, 8 × 10 ft; and Cheung, 6 × 6 ft.**

(**Note:** The abbreviation appears only at the end of each set of measurements and does not require a period.)

[Read more on abbreviation of measurements in Topic 50.]

41 TELEPHONE NUMBERS

41a Number Format

Three formats are commonly used for writing telephone numbers, and all are correct. Use the style that prevails in your company or industry.

- Hyphens between sets of numbers is the most widely used style: 800-555-2900
- A period between sets of numbers is the latest style: 800.555.2900
- Enclosing the area code in parentheses and hyphenating the seven-digit number is the traditional style: (800) 555-2900

Internationally, the most widely used format is either a space or a comma between the groups of numbers.

41b Words in Phone Numbers

Some companies use words as part of their phone number for ease of memorizing. Always write them exactly as the company does. Consider whether it is a good idea to provide the all-digit translation as well, depending on the context.

800-266-COMPUTE translates to 800-266-7883.

41c Extensions in Phone Numbers

Many business phone numbers include an extension. They can be written as follows:

555-517-2825, ext. 103 or x103

In formal text, spell out the word extension:

555-363-2878, extension 4302

42 FRACTIONS

When expressing fractions, make sure they are reduced to the lowest common denominator: 2/24 should be written as 1/12. A number made up of a whole number and a fraction is known as a **mixed number.** When you create fractions with a slash (/), leave a space between the whole number and the fraction: 2 5/8 feet.

42a When to Use Words

Generally, use words to express two-word fractions in text, except in technical documents with many fractions and in measurements (express all measurements in figures in numeric-heavy text; see Topic 33).

We received a "yes" response from **two-thirds** of the people invited.

Surveys show that at least **three-quarters** of the voters would like to have the polls open for an additional two hours.

When fractions are unusual and awkward to write in words, use figures:

The next step will require an **11/32** drill bit.

Hyphenate two-word fractions:

one-fourth

one-eighth

one-sixteenth

One-half of those polled did not have a preference for either A or B.

The board must have a **two-thirds** majority vote to pass the proposal.

Do not hyphenate *a half, a fourth, a third,* etc.

The recipe calls for **a half dozen eggs.**

At least **a third of the board members** were absent the day the vote was taken.

42b When to Use Figures

Express fractions in figures in text when you want to emphasize numerical data, in copy that has a lot of numerical information, and in tables.

The race for the fund-raiser is a 5K, which is **3.1 miles.**

In text with isolated fractions that you want to express in figures, round off to a number that can be expressed as a decimal instead of a fraction: 10.5 looks better in text than 10½. Note that the keyboard automatically decreases the size of some fractions when you hit the space bar: ½, ¼, ¾.

The measurements are **1¼ ft by 2½ ft.**

Do not mix these automated keyboard-size fractions with regular-size fractions you create by typing a slash: 4/5. Use a consistent style throughout a document by turning off the automated feature of your word processing program.

The measurements are **1 1/3 ft, 2 5/8 ft, and 2 1/2 ft.**

43 PERCENTAGES, RATIOS, AND PROPORTIONS

43a Percentages

Express percentages in figures. Use the % symbol in tables and documents heavy with numerical data; otherwise, use the word *percent*. When writing a series of percentages, use the word *percent* at the end; when using the % symbol, include it after each figure.

I will ask for a **10 percent** raise next year.

Only **15 percent** of my students scored **90 percent** or better.

My scores on the unit tests were **65, 75, 80, and 91 percent.**

My scores on the unit tests were **65%, 75%, 80%, and 91%.**

43b Ratios and Proportions

A **ratio** is a numerical expression of a comparison in quantity, amount, or size; use a colon between the numbers with no space:

The ratio of professionally trained to amateur athletes in the competition is **3:1.**

The ratio can also be expressed as **3 to 1.**

Like a fraction, a ratio should be reduced to its lowest common denominator. Thus, a ratio of 24:12 should be expressed as 2:1.

Proportions express an amount compared to a whole; use words or figures.

One out of every four athletes is an amateur.

Three out of five professors at the university have doctoral degrees.

A proportion can be expressed with a hyphen to show the relationship of two numbers.

The chances for recovering the money are **50-50.**

44 ROMAN NUMERALS

44a Formatting and Reading Roman Numerals

Roman numerals are formed by the use of seven letters, as shown in the following list. A bar above a roman numeral means that it is multiplied by 1000:

Arabic Numbers	Roman Numerals
1	I
5	V
10	X
50	L
100	C
500	D
1000	M
5000	$\overline{V}$
50,000	$\overline{L}$
100,000	$\overline{C}$

All other numbers are formed by adding or subtracting from these base numerals. When smaller roman numerals precede larger ones (e.g., IV), subtract the smaller from the larger to get the result (5 minus 1 is 4). When smaller roman numerals come after larger ones (e.g., XV), add the numbers to get the result (10 plus 5 is 15). When roman numerals are the same (e.g., XX), add them (10 plus 10 is 20).

Note: The terms *arabic* and *roman* do not need to be capitalized when referring to these numeric systems.

44b Chart of Roman Numerals

QUICK REFERENCE 44.1

Roman numerals

1	I	21	XXI	500	D
2	II	22	XXII	600	DC
3	III	23	XXIII	700	DCC
4	IV	24	XXIV	800	DCCC
5	V	25	XXV	900	CM
6	VI	26	XXVI	1000	M
7	VII	27	XXVII	1500	MD
8	VIII	28	XXVIII	2000	MM
9	IX	29	XXIX	2500	MMD
10	X	30	XXX	5000	$\overline{V}$
11	XI	40	XL	10,000	$\overline{X}$
12	XII	50	L	50,000	$\overline{L}$
13	XIII	60	LX	100,000	$\overline{C}$
14	XIV	75	LXXV	500,000	$\overline{D}$
15	XV	80	LXXX	1,000,000	$\overline{M}$
16	XVI	90	XC		
17	XVII	100	C		
18	XVIII	200	CC		
19	XIX	300	CCC		
20	XX	400	CD		

44c Using Roman Numerals in Business Documents

Use roman numerals in business documents to number front matter pages of reports, to label the main sections of outlines and long documents, and to label parts of legal agreements. Other common uses of roman numerals are to number sections of legislation, to show birth order in names, to denote annual events, and to number volumes of books and magazines.

Use roman numerals in capital letters for all of the above purposes except page numbers. Always use lowercase for numbering front matter pages (Table of Contents, Preface, Introduction, etc.) of a report or manuscript.

[Read more about formatting front matter in Section Nine: Reports, Proposals, and Documentation.]

45 ABBREVIATIONS

45a General Guidelines

Abbreviations are shortened forms of words and proper names; some are punctuated with periods, some are not, and these conventions are constantly changing. This section provides guidelines regarding when to abbreviate and when not to, proper forms for abbreviation, and style guidelines for different writing situations.

As texting and instant messaging have become widespread, use of abbreviations has multiplied and become a part of everyday communication in many arenas. Nevertheless, in business correspondence, the norm is still to spell out most words and use standard abbreviations as outlined in this section. When writing any kind of business communication, if you are deciding whether or not it is appropriate to abbreviate, observe the very wise old advice: "When in doubt, spell it out."

Official abbreviations of the names of organizations, products, projects, and programs can be abbreviated in running text. When a name that has an abbreviation comes up frequently in a document, it is a good idea to use the abbreviation instead of repeating the full name again and again. When you intend to use an abbreviation frequently in a document, spell it out on first use and put the abbreviation in parentheses immediately after it. After that, you may assume that your reader will understand. (If no official abbreviation exists for a company or product name, do not invent one; it is common, however, for employees to invent in-house abbreviations for programs and projects.)

> When I worked for the **Environmental Protection Agency (EPA),** I found the caseload to be very heavy. Routinely, **EPA** caseworkers are expected to work on far more cases than can be handled effectively.

Do not confuse abbreviations with shortened forms of words that are in general usage, and, therefore, do not need explanation—for example, *TV* for *television, ad* for *advertisement,* and *PC* for *personal computer.* Such common usage is continually expanding; reading widely and consulting a dictionary are the best ways to keep abreast of changes in such usage.

Do not space between a period at the end of an abbreviation and a mark of punctuation—question mark, exclamation point, comma, colon, or semicolon.

Have you signed the contract for the work with Mentors, **Inc.?**

Please schedule a morning break, e.g., at **10:15 a.m.;** please announce it from the podium.

45b Periods and Commas in Abbreviations

Many common abbreviations, including US for United States, are written without periods today. Academic titles—MA, BS, and PhD—and measurements—ft, in, lbs—are examples of abbreviations where periods have been dropped. Others, such as *a.m.* and *p.m.,* and personal titles (*Ms,. Mrs.,* etc.) still require periods.

Never use two periods when an abbreviation that ends in a period concludes a sentence, but do use any other appropriate ending punctuation. This is something to check for in proofreading because it can easily happen accidentally.

We will be finished with the last exam no later than **8 p.m.**

Can you stay late to monitor the exam ending at **8 p.m.?**

45c Lowercase Letter Abbreviations

Most abbreviations expressed in lowercase letters have periods; no space is required between the letters.

a.m. p.m. i.e. e.g. etc. vs. ibid. op.cit.

45d Capital Letter Abbreviations (Acronyms and Initialisms)

Acronyms and **initialisms** are capital letter abbreviations of organizations, corporations, and other entities—such as the UN (United Nations). An acronym is pronounced as a word, for example, NATO (North Atlantic Treaty Organization). An initialism is pronounced letter by letter, as in CEO (Chief Executive Officer). Acronyms and initialisms are always written without periods.

EXAMPLES OF ACRONYMS

NASDAQ National Association of Security Dealers Automated Quotations

NASA	National Aeronautics and Space Administration
OSHA	Occupational Safety and Health Administration
SIDS	Sudden Infant Death Syndrome
PAC	Political Action Committee

EXAMPLES OF INITIALISMS

CFO	Chief Financial Officer
NCAA	National Collegiate Athletic Association
WWW	World Wide Web
ABC	American Broadcasting Company
RFP	Request for Proposal

Plurals of acronyms and initialisms are usually formed by adding an *s* without an apostrophe.

The company has had three **CEOs** over the last five years.

We have three **RFPs** pending.

45e The Ampersand (&) in Abbreviations

Do not use the ampersand (&) as an abbreviation for the word *and* in running text except in very informal writing or when it is part of an official name. When the ampersand is part of an official name, write it with or without spaces before and after, depending on how it is written by the organization.

AT&T

Billingsley & Co.

45f Academic Degrees

Modern style is to omit periods in abbreviations of academic degrees. In running text, either spell out the name of the degree in lowercase letters or use the capital letter abbreviation; academic degrees are widely known and do not need to be spelled out on first use.

I earned my **bachelor of arts** degree from Loyola University. [Your spell checker might indicate this as an error, but it is the style experts recommend.]

He received a **BA** in special education from Western Michigan University.

She has been writing her **PhD** dissertation for six months and hopes to finish it by the end of the year.

QUICK REFERENCE 45.1

Abbreviations of common academic degrees

AA	Associate of Arts
BA	Bachelor of Arts
BFA	Bachelor of Fine Arts
BS	Bachelor of Science
CPA	Certified Public Accountant
DD	Doctor of Divinity
DDS	Doctor of Dental Surgery
EdD	Doctor of Education
JD	Juris Doctor (Doctor of Law)
MA	Master of Arts
MBA	Master of Business Administration
MD	Doctor of Medicine
MS	Master of Science
MSN	Master of Science in Nursing
MSW	Master of Social Work
PhD	Doctor of Philosophy

[See 46c for style of names with academic degree abbreviations.]

45g Organization Names

Capital letter abbreviations of organization names are usually written without periods.

NATO FBI CIA UN FDA NAACP IRS

Most acronyms and initialisms can be written without periods and without spaces between the letters. [See 51a.]

The **AARP** provides a broad range of services to persons over fifty.

The **NAACP** is the nation's oldest civil rights organization.

CNN was the first 24-hour national news network.

If an organization uses periods in its name, follow the preferred usage.

JP Morgan Chase & Co. is listed in the Fortune 500.

Company names frequently contain abbreviations that indicate type of entity. The most common are:

Co. Company

Inc. Incorporated

Corp. Corporation

LLC Limited Liability Company

Ltd. Limited

PC Professional Corporation

In general, do not use commas to set off these abbreviations. In listings of company names, be consistent.

Georgia Interiors Inc.

H&M Construction LLC

Rockland Construction Inc.

In correspondence with a company, follow its preferred style.

We are pleased to have this opportunity to do business with Kramer & Sons Architectural Engineering, Ltd.

46 ABBREVIATIONS WITH NAMES

46a Initials

Abbreviations in names are usually initials. Write names exactly as they are written by individuals or follow general guidelines if you are not sure.

Use a period after a single initial at the beginning of a name, and add a space after.

J. Lawrence Hudson

Leave no space between two initials at the beginning of a name, but space after the second initial.

J.L. Hudson

Space before and after a middle initial.

Zelika C. Horton

Some famous names are abbreviated with all initials; no periods are needed.

FDR (Franklin Delano Roosevelt)

JFK (John Fitzgerald Kennedy)

46b Personal Titles

Personal titles include *Mr., Mrs., Ms.,* and *Dr.* (*Miss,* the title that designates a single woman, is rarely used anymore; *Ms.* is generally preferred.) Always use a period and a space after these abbreviations.

Ms. Ella Arnett
Mr. James B. Frye
Mrs. Olivia S. George
Dr. Gwendolyn C. Baker

46c Academic Degrees with Names

Omit periods in abbreviations of academic degrees with names; separate the abbreviation from the name with a comma:

Arnold T. Rosenberg, EdD
Juan Ortero, PhD
Miriam Gonzalez, CPA

When a person's academic title falls within a sentence, enclose it with commas.

We have asked Carol Brunson Day, PhD, to be our luncheon speaker.

In such cases, do not use Dr. before the name. Other titles before the name may be used if they differ from the abbreviated title.

Rev. Robert Elder, DD or Rev. Dr. Robert Elder
Mrs. Nicole Hodges Persley, PhD or Dr. Nicole Hodges Persley

46d Birth Order Designations in Names

Always abbreviate birth order designations (*Jr.* and *Sr.*) and use them with the full name only. Use no punctuation in front, but do use a period after the abbreviation.

Edward O. Bloom Jr.
Roberto Aguirre Sr.

The designations II and III (for second and third) are not abbreviations, so they do not require periods.

James B. Irving II
Watson Hines III

If a family order designation precedes a title, separate it with a comma.

Jonathan David III, MD, is closing his medical practice.

Ellison J. Bronson Sr., DDS, has opened a new office.

47 PROFESSIONAL, MILITARY, AND RELIGIOUS TITLES

47a When to Spell Out Titles

When used with names, either the full name or the last name, spell out professional, military, and religious titles and capitalize them.

President Dwight D. Eisenhower **OR** President Eisenhower

Senator Edward M. Kennedy **OR** Senator Kennedy

Professor Andrea Lewis teaches accounting and general math.

Please forward the document to **Vice President Hugo Smith.**

We have invited **Rabbi David Rubinoff** to give the invocation at the luncheon.

Spell out professional, military, political, and religious titles in running text when they are not used with a name: *general, lieutenant, president, vice president, senator, congressman, congresswoman, governor, mayor, pastor, bishop,* and so on. Do not capitalize them.

All of the candidates for **president** are well qualified.

Working for the **governor** was a great experience.

His goal is to become a **captain** in the Air Force.

47b When to Abbreviate Titles

In letters, abbreviate titles in the inside address and on envelopes, but always spell out the title in the salutation.

Inside address: Sgt. Carlton Thomas

Salutation: Dear Sargeant Thomas

Abbreviate professional, military, and political titles in listings and in informal writing, but spell them out in running text in documents, such as letters, memos, and reports. (See 47e for a list of title abbreviations.) Use these abbreviations only when the title precedes a first name and a surname.

Gov. James Blanchard **OR** Governor Blanchard
Capt. Mallory Thomas Captain Thomas

In abbreviations of professional titles made up of two words, space between the words.

Lt. Col. Jennifer E. Davis

Either place abbreviations for professional titles in front of the name or use an academic title after the name; do not use both when they denote the same thing, and be consistent in style throughout each document.

Dr. Aari Shunami **OR** Aari Shunami, MD

When a professional title is different from the academic degree, or when a personal title is needed, both may be used.

Ms. Aari Shunami, MD
Professor Diane Laing, PhD
Chairman David McKenna, DDS

47c Use of *The Honorable* and *The Reverend*

The Honorable is a title of distinction for elected government officials such as judges and members of Congress. *The Reverend* is a religious title. Both should be spelled out, and *The* should be capitalized. Use the abbreviations *Hon.* and *Rev.* only without *The*.

The Honorable Luther James Harrison has been on the bench for 25 years.

We invited **The Reverend Thomas J. Leonard** to give the benediction.

Please include a "thank-you" to **Rev. Tom Leonard** in your closing remarks. [Abbreviation used in informal writing.]

47d Use of *Esq.*

Esq. for *Esquire* is always abbreviated and placed at the end of the name. It originated as an unofficial title denoting gentry in England, but in the United States it is mainly used by lawyers. Because it is technically a personal rather than a professional title, do not use a personal title (Mr., Ms., Mrs.) in front of the name.

Margaret Snow, Esq. **NOT** Ms. Margaret Snow, Esq.

47e Abbreviations of Professional, Military, and Religious Titles

Quick Reference 47.1 lists common title abbreviations. Note that the titles of Chief Justice, Justice, Judge, Congressman and Congresswoman, and Mayor should always be spelled out; thus abbreviations are not included in this list. The title Representative, which can be abbreviated as Rep., is usually substituted for Congressman and Congresswoman when an abbreviation is desired.

QUICK REFERENCE 47.1

Selected professional, military, and religious abbreviations

Professional Titles		Military Titles		Religious Titles	
Atty.	Attorney	Adm.	Admiral	Bp.	Bishop
Chair	Chairperson	Brig. Gen.	Brigadier General	Ch.	Chaplain
CEO	Chief Executive Officer	Capt.	Captain	HE	His Eminence, His Excellency
CFO	Chief Financial Officer	Col	Colonel	Hon.	Honorable
COO	Chief Operating Officer	CO	Commanding Officer	Msgr.	Monsignor
Dir.	Director	Cpl.	Corporal	R	Rabbi
Esq.	Esquire	CPO	Chief Petty Officer	Rev.	Reverend
Gov.	Governor	ENS	Ensign		
Hon.	The Honorable	Gen.	General		
Lt. Gov.	Lieutenant Governor	Lieut. or Lt.	Lieutenant		
PM	Prime Minister	Maj.	Major		
Pres.	President	MP	Military Police		
Prin.	Principal	Pvt.	Private		
Rep.	Representative	Sgt.	Sergeant		
Sen.	Senator				
VP	Vice President				

48 STATE AND GEOGRAPHIC LOCATIONS

48a Specific Geographic Locations

Spell out the names of geographic locations—cities, counties, states, countries, and regions—within the body of correspondence, reports, and other formal business documents.

Our office is relocating to **Stamford, Connecticut,** in the spring. [NOT Conn. or CT]

Please contact my associate, Mr. Hudson, when you are in **Los Angeles.** [NOT in LA]

48b State and US Territory Abbreviations

In the inside addresses of letters, spell out the state name or use the two-letter postal abbreviation (see Quick Reference 48.1).

Oklahoma City, Oklahoma **OR** Oklahoma City, OK

On envelopes and mailing labels use only the two-letter state abbreviations. The US Postal Service recommends that two spaces separate the state and the ZIP code.

Livonia, MI 48152

(**Note:** Longer state abbreviations—for example: Ariz. for Arizona and Calif. for California—are rarely used today.)

48c United States

Spell out *United States* when using it as a noun. When using it as an adjective, it can be abbreviated.

Bill Gates is one of the wealthiest people in the **United States.**

Bill Gates ranks very high on the list of top **US philanthropists.**

Periods are no longer required in the abbreviation, but it is acceptable to do so and many publications still do.

USA **OR** U.S.A

US **OR** U.S.

QUICK REFERENCE 48.1

Two-letter postal abbreviations of US states and territories

Alabama	AL	Kentucky	KY	Oklahoma	OK
Alaska	AK	Louisiana	LA	Oregon	OR
Arizona	AZ	Maine	ME	Pennsylvania	PA
Arkansas	AR	Maryland	MD	Puerto Rico	PR
California	CA	Massachusetts	MA	Rhode Island	RI
Colorado	CO	Michigan	MI	South Carolina	SC
Connecticut	CT	Minnesota	MN	South Dakota	SD
Delaware	DE	Mississippi	MS	Tennessee	TN
District of Columbia	DC	Missouri	MO	Texas	TX
Florida	FL	Montana	MT	Utah	UT
Georgia	GA	Nebraska	NE	Vermont	VT
Guam	GU	Nevada	NV	Virgin Islands	VI
Hawaii	HI	New Hampshire	NH	Virginia	VA
Idaho	ID	New Jersey	NJ	Washington	WA
Illinois	IL	New Mexico	NM	West Virginia	WV
Indiana	IN	New York	NY	Wisconsin	WO
Iowa	IA	North Carolina	NC	Wyoming	WY
Kansas	KS	North Dakota	NC		
		Ohio	OH		

48d Compass Points and Street Names

Spell out the names of compass points in text copy.

The top sales representatives received a trip to the **West Coast.**

Brenda Hobson left the company two weeks ago and moved **east.**

Drive **southwest** on Rampart Drive to find our office.

Do not use periods in abbreviations of compass points.

North	N	Northwest	NW	Northeast	NE
South	S	Southwest	SW	Southeast	SE
East	E	West	W		

Compass points that are part of street names may be abbreviated or spelled out, depending on common usage in the location itself. (When in doubt, spell it out.)

110 E. Oak Street

116 West Truman Avenue

528 South Lake Street

Compass points that indicate an area of a city at the end of a street address are abbreviated in most locations. Separate with a comma.

4010 204th Street, NE

1600 Bedford Place, SW

For address labels for mass mailings, US Postal Service guidelines require all capital letters and no periods or other punctuation.

110 OAK ST E

116 W TRUMAN AVENUE

528 LAKE ST S

48e Street Address Designations

Spell out all the words in a street name in the inside address of letters. On envelopes and labels, standard abbreviations may be used, as shown in Quick Reference 48.2. These abbreviations require periods.

QUICK REFERENCE 48.2

Abbreviations for address designations

Avenue	Ave.	Lane	Ln.
Boulevard	Blvd.	Parkway	Pkwy.
Center	Ctr.	Place	Pl.
Circle	Cir.	Plaza	(spell out)
Court	Ct.	Road	Rd.
Drive	Dr.	Square	Sq.
Expressway	Expwy.	Street	St.
Highway	Hwy.	Terrace	Ter.
Junction	Jct., Junc.		

48f Post Office Box Addresses

For post office boxes write PO in caps, with no spacing or periods.

PO Box 290

If there is a street address, place the box number below it (PO boxes take precedence over street addresses for delivery, and post office scanners read from the bottom up).

Tropical Designs
34485 Tropical Way
PO Box 145
Kissimmee, FL 34741

48g State and US Territory Time Zones

Use all caps and no periods or spaces for time zone abbreviations (see Quick Reference 48.3).

QUICK REFERENCE 48.3

United States and territories time zones and abbreviations

Standard Time/ Daylight Saving Time	Abbreviations	Standard/Daylight	
Mainland			
Eastern standard/ daylight time	EST/EDT	Eastern time	ET
Central standard/ daylight time	CST/CDT	Central time	CT
Mountain standard/ daylight time	MST/MDT	Mountain time	MT
Pacific standard/ daylight time	PST/PDT	Pacific time	PT
Puerto Rico, US Virgin Islands			
Atlantic standard/ daylight time	AST/ADT	Atlantic time	AT
Alaska			
Alaska standard/ daylight time	AKST/AKDT	Alaska time	AKT
Hawaii			
Hawaii-Aleutian standard/daylight time	HAST/HADT	Hawaii-Aleutian time	HAT

The conference call is scheduled for 1 p.m. **PST.** [Pacific Standard Time]

Three variations denote time zones:

1. Standard time—use when daylight saving time is not in effect
2. Daylight saving time—use when daylight saving time is in effect
3. Standard and daylight—use on materials that cannot be changed when time changes from standard to daylight and back again

49 PERIODS OF TIME

49a Abbreviations for Days and Months

Do not abbreviate names of days and months in running text. In tables or graphic materials, the standard abbreviations listed in Quick Reference 49.1 may be used. These abbreviations require a period.

QUICK REFERENCE 49.1

Abbreviations for days and months of the year

Days	Standard	Months	Standard
Sunday	Sun.	January	Jan.
Monday	Mon.	February	Feb.
Tuesday	Tues.	March	Mar.
Wednesday	Wed.	April	Apr.
Thursday	Thu. or Thurs.	May	None
Friday	Fri.	June	None
Saturday	Sat.	July	None
		August	Aug.
		September	Sept.
		October	Oct.
		November	Nov.
		December	Dec.

49b Abbreviations for Units and Periods of Time

In text, spell out the names of specific units and periods of time. Abbreviations may be used in tabular material or graphics when space is limited and in informal communications. These abbreviations require a period.

QUICK REFERENCE 49.2

Abbreviations for units and periods of time

second/seconds	sec./secs.
minute/minutes	min./mins.
hour/hours	hr./hrs.
week/weeks	wk./wks.
month/months	mo./mos.
quarter/quarterly	quar.
year/years	yr./yrs.
annual/annually	ann.
decade/decades	dec.
century/centuries	cent.

ESTIMATED TIMES

ETA estimated time of arrival
ETD estimated time of departure

ERAS

Use capital letters with no spaces or periods in abbreviations for eras. CE and BCE are contemporary forms of AD and BC (without religious connotation). Choose one set or the other for consistency.

CE	Common Era	**OR**	AD	in the year of our Lord (*Anno Domini* in Latin)
BCE	before the Common Era	**OR**	BC	before Christ

Place the abbreviations after the year:

800 CE 20 BCE
10 BC 1059 AD

50 CUSTOMARY UNITS OF MEASURE

Spell out standard units of measurement in text when only a few figures are used. If measurements are extensive, use abbreviations; abbreviations may also be used in technical writing, tables, and illustrations.

Use lowercase letters without periods. All abbreviations are written as singular, so do not add *s* or *es* to form plurals.

QUICK REFERENCE 50.1

Abbreviations for customary units of measure

Measurement	Abbreviation
inch, inches	in
foot, feet	ft
yard, yards	yd
mile, miles	mi
ounce, ounces	oz
gallon, gallons	gal
pound, pounds	lb
miles per gallon	mpg
miles per hour	mph
revolutions per minute	rpm

50a Writing Sets of Measurements

Spell out units of measure unless text is technical or informal. When writing a set of measurements that are the same unit of measure, place the spelled out word or abbreviation after the last number. Use the word *by* or the symbol × with spaces before and after.

The painting in the lobby measures **3 by 4 feet.**

OR

The painting in the lobby measures **3 × 4 ft.**

If a set of measurements contains different units of measurement, indicate the unit of measure after each number.

The desk is an odd size: **5 feet, 2 inches × 3 feet, 1 inch.**
[Commas are needed.]

The corner office measures **14 ft 10 in × 16 ft 9 in.**
[No comma is needed.]

50b Use of Symbols for Measurements

When a symbol replaces a word, repeat it after each number.

The executive office needs a new rug that measures **14′ × 20′**.

The corner office measures **12′ 10″ × 20′ 6″**.

(**Note:** If your software includes fonts with straight or slanted apostrophes and quotation marks, use these instead of the curly style.)

50c Hyphens in Measurements

When measurements form compound adjectives, they require hyphenation:

a 10-oz bottle of milk

a 14-pound turkey

50d Abbreviations for Customary and Metric Measurements

Metric measurements follow the same style rules used for customary measurements: spell out the terms in nontechnical material. Quick Reference 50.2 lists abbreviations for the most commonly used customary and metric units of measure.

51 BUSINESS TERMS

51a Common Business Abbreviations

Quick Reference 51.1 provides an extensive list of abbreviations commonly used in business settings. Note that some require periods and others do not.

QUICK REFERENCE 50.2

Abbreviations for customary and metric units of measurement

Temperature		Length/Width		Weight	
C	Celsius, centigrade	cc	cubic centimeters	gr wt	gross weight
F	Fahrenheit	cm	centimeter	lb	pound, pounds
		ft	foot, feet	nt wt	net weight
		in	inch, inches	vol	volume
		yd, yds	yard, yards	wt	weight

Distance		Liquids		Other	
kg	kilogram, kilograms	g	gram, grams	doz, dz	dozen, dozens
K, km	kilometer, kilometers	gal	gallon, gallons	cal	calorie, calories
m	meter, meters	kg	kilogram, kilograms	dpi	dots per inch
mi	mile, miles	L	liter, liters	hp, HP	horsepower
mg	milligram, milligrams	oz, ozs	ounce, ounces	kw	kilowatt, kilowatts
mm	millimeter, millimeters	pt	pint, pints	MHz	megahertz
mpg	miles per gallon	qt, qts	quart, quarts	V	volt, volts
mph	miles per hour				

QUICK REFERENCE 51.1

Business abbreviations

A

AA	administrative assistant, Associate of Arts, Alcoholics Anonymous
acct.	account, accountant
ad	advertisement
admin.	administrator, administrative
aft.	affidavit
agt.	agent
ann.	annual
aka	also known as
amt.	amount
anon.	anonymous, anonymously
AP	accounts payable
approx.	approximate, approximately
APR	annual percentage rate
AR	accounts receivable

CONTINUED →

QUICK REFERENCE 51.1 → CONTINUED

ARM	adjustable-rate mortgage
ASAP	as soon as possible
ASCII	American Standard Code for Information Interchange
assn.	association
assoc.	associate
asst.	assistant, assorted
att.	attached, attention, attorney
Attn:	Attention
Atty.	Attorney
AV	audiovisual
Ave.	Avenue
avg.	average
AWOL	absent without leave

B

bal.	balance
BL, B/L	bill of lading
bldg.	building
BO	back order
bros.	brothers
BS, B/S	bill of sale

C

©	copyright
c, cc	courtesy copy/copies, carbon copy
C	Celsius, centigrade
cap	capital
CD	certificate of deposit, compact disc
CEO	chief executive officer
CFO	chief financial officer
CFP	certified financial planner
chg.	charge
CIF	cost, insurance, and freight
CIO	chief information officer
CKO	chief knowledge officer
Co.	company
c/o	care of
COB	close of business
COD	cash (or collect) on delivery
COLA	cost-of-living adjustment
cont.	continued
COO	chief operating officer
corp.	corporation
CPA	certified public accountant
CPI	consumer price index
CPM	cost per thousand
CPS	Certified Professional Secretary

D

d/b/a,	dba doing business as
depr.	depreciation
dept.	department
dir.	director
dis, disc	discount
dist.	district
distr.	distributor, distribution, distributed
div.	division, dividend
DJIA	Dow Jones Industrial Average
doz., dz	dozen, dozens
DP	data processing
dpi	dots per inch
dup.	duplicate
DVD	digital video disc, digital versatile disc

E

ea.	each
ed., eds.	editor/editors, edition
EEO	equal employment opportunity

CONTINUED →

QUICK REFERENCE 51.1 → CONTINUED

e.g.	for example
enc., encl.	enclosed, enclosure
EOE	equal opportunity employer
EOM, e.o.m.	end of month
Equip.	equipment
Esq.	Esquire
est.	estimate, estimated
ETA	estimated time of arrival
ETD	estimated time of departure
ext., ex., x	extension
F	
F	Fahrenheit
FAQs	frequently asked questions, fax, facsimile
fed	federal
FIFO	first in, first out
fin.	finance
fl.	floor
FOB	free on board
frt.	freight
fwd.	forward
FY	fiscal year
FYI	for your information
G	
GDP	gross domestic product
gen.	general
GM	general manager
Gov., gov.	Governor
gov., govt.	government [not *gov't*]
H	
HMO	health maintenance organization
hp, HP	horsepower
HQ	headquarters
HR	Human Resources
I	
ID	identification
i.e.	that is, namely
Inc.	Incorporated
incl.	including, inclusive
info.	information
ins.	insurance
inst.	institute
intl.	international
inv.	invoice
IOU	I owe you
IPO	initial public offering
IQ	intelligence quotient
IRA	individual retirement account
ISP	Internet Service Provider
J	
JIT	just in time
Jr.	Junior
K	
K	thousand
L	
l, ll	line, lines
LBO	leveraged buyout
L/C	Letter of Credit
LCL	less-than-carload lot
leg.	legal
lg.	large
LIFO	last in, first out
LLC	limited liability company
LLP	limited licensed partners
Ltd.	Limited
M	
m	meter(s), married
M&A	mergers and acquisitions
max.	maximum

CONTINUED →

QUICK REFERENCE 51.1 → CONTINUED

MBA	master of business administration
MC	master/mistress of ceremonies
mdse.	merchandise
med.	medium
memo	memorandum
mfg.	manufacturing
mfr.	manufacturer
mgr.	manager
mg	milligram, milligrams
mgt., mgmt.	management
mi.	mile, miles
min., mins.	minute, minutes
min.	minimum
MIS	management information system
misc.	miscellaneous
mkt.	market
MO	mail order, money order
mo., mos.	month, months
Ms.	Miss, Misses, Mrs.
ms., mss.	manuscript, manuscripts
msg	message
MSP	moved, seconded, and passed
mtg.	meeting, mortgage
N	
n/30	net in 30 days
NA or n/a	not applicable, not available
nd	no date
NGO	nongovernmental organization
No., no., nos.	number, numbers
NMI	no middle initial
NSF	not sufficient funds
NV or N/V	no value
O	
OAG	*Official Airline Guide*
OD	overdraft
OJT	on-the-job training
OK	okay
opt.	optional
org.	organization
orig.	original
O/S	out of stock
OTC	over the counter
P	
p., pp.	page, pages
P&L, P/L	profit and loss
PC	personal computer, Professional Corporation, politically correct
pd.	paid
PE	printer's error(s)
P/E	price/earnings (ratio)
PERT	program evaluation and review technique
PIN	personal identification number
pkg.	package(s)
PO	purchase order, post office
POA	power of attorney
POE	port of entry
pop.	population
POP	point of purchase
POS	point of sale
POV	point of view
PP	parcel post
ppd	postpaid, prepaid
PR	public relations
pr.	pair, pairs
pres.	president
prod.	product
prs.	profit sharing

CONTINUED →

QUICK REFERENCE 51.1 → CONTINUED

PS	postscript
pt., pts.	part, parts; pint, pints; point, points
ptr.	partner

Q

QA	quality assurance
Q&A	question and answer
qtr.	quarter, quarterly
qty.	quantity

R

®	registered trademark
R&D	research and development
re:, in re:	in regard to
rec'd	received
reg.	registered, regular
REIT	real estate investment trust
req	requisition
ret.	retired
retd.	returned
rev.	revised, revision, review
RFD	rural free delivery
RIF	reduction in force
Rm	room
ROA	return on assets
ROE	return on equity
ROI	return on investment
RSVP	please respond (accept or decline)

S

/S/	signed by
S&H	shipping and handling
SASE	self-addressed stamped envelope
SC, sc	small caps
sec.	second, seconds
sec., secy.	secretary
sect.	section
sm.	small
SO	shipping order
soc.	society
SOP	standard operating procedure
sq.	square
Sr.	Senior
SSN, social	Social Security Number
std.	standard
sub.	subsidiary
svc.	service

T

t/a	trading as
TBA	to be announced
TBD	to be determined
TK	to come
™	trademark
TRA	trust account
treas.	treasury, treasurer

U

univ.	university
UPC	Universal Product Code
URL	uniform resource locator

V

VAT	value-added tax
VCR	videocassette recorder
VIP	very important person
vol.	volume (measurement)
Vol.	Volume (book)
VP	vice president
v.	versus (when used as a legal term)
vs.	versus
viz.	that is; namely

CONTINUED →

QUICK REFERENCE 51.1 → CONTINUED

W		wt.	weight
w/	with	WWW	World Wide Web
WAN	wide area network	WYSIWYG	What you see is what you get.
WATS	Wide Area Telephone Service	**Y**	
whsle.	wholesale	YOB	year of birth
wk.	week	yr., yrs.	year, years
w/o	without	YTD	year to date
wpm	words per minute		

51b Foreign Words and Phrases

Many words that have their origin in foreign languages are used routinely in English. In the past the convention was to use italics for such words and phrases, but this is no longer necessary. However, foreign words, phrases, and abbreviations that are not commonly understood by English speakers should be shown in italics and translated into English where appropriate.

Quick Reference 51.2 lists some of the commonly used abbreviations that stem from foreign words and expressions; note that many require a period.These abbreviations need not be written in italics.

QUICK REFERENCE 51.2

Abbreviations of foreign words and expressions

Abbreviation	Meaning	Example/explanation
ad hoc	improvised; also, for a particular end or purpose	The CEO appointed an ad hoc committee to explore new locations.
c., ca.	approximately [Latin, *circa*]	The photograph was taken c. 1990.
CV	resume,* usually academic [Latin, *curriculum vitae*]	Please send us a copy of your CV prior to the interview.
e.g.	for example [Latin, *exempli gratia*]	You will temporarily provide assistance to the HR Department, e.g., answering phones and updating the database.

CONTINUED →

*Resume is no longer considered a foreign term, and the accent over the *e* has been dropped.

QUICK REFERENCE 51.2 → CONTINUED

Abbreviation	Meaning	Example/explanation
et al.	and others [Latin, *et alii*, with a period after *al*]	Baker, Ronald, et al., *The Art of Being Ready*, Treetop Publishing, New York, 2007.
etc.	and so forth [Latin, *et cetera*]	Please send someone to pick up equipment for the presentation—posters, flip chart, handouts, etc.
i.e.	that is [Latin, *id est*]	I believe the data is only somewhat reliable, i.e., the numbers are accurate but they are taken out of context.
ibid.	in the same place [Latin, *ibidem*]	Use in footnotes or bibliography to indicate that a reference is exactly the same as the one preceding. [1] Ibid., p. 23
loc. cit.	in the place cited [Latin, *loco citato*]	Use in footnotes or bibliography to indicate a subsequent reference to a work previously cited. [2] Anderson, loc. cit., pp. 24–26
MO	a method by which something is done [Latin, *modus operandi*]	The competition's MO is to launch new spring products right after the winter holidays.
op. cit.	in the work cited [Latin, *opere citato*]	Use in footnotes to indicate that a reference is the same as the preceding one. Must include the author's name. [3] Marbury, op. cit., p. 134
pro tem	for the time being [Latin, *pro tempore*]	Dr. Cruz was appointed president pro tem of the association.
RSVP rsvp	please reply [French, *répondez s'il vous plaît*]	Usually placed at the end of an invitation, with contact information.
vs. *and* v.	against [Legal writing uses *v.*; otherwise, use *vs.;* spell out in running text: *versus.*]	The trademark infringement case of Jackson Printing v. Jackson Ltd. was dismissed. [legal writing]

CONTINUED →

QUICK REFERENCE 51.2 → CONTINUED

Abbreviation	Meaning	Example/explanation
vis à vis	In relation to [French, face-to-face]	Let me know what you want us to do about canceling the Putnam project vis à vis the notification process.

52 SYMBOLS

Check other sections of this manual when you have questions about using symbols in text. Keep in mind that the words for many symbols, such as *dollar* and *percent,* are preferred in running text; some symbols are used most frequently in informal writing and technical material, or in graphics, tables, and schedules.

Some symbols are included on the standard keyboard; others are available on a word processing software menu. For example, in Microsoft Word, select Insert from the main tool bar and select Symbols on the drop-down menu. You will find almost any symbol you would need to use, including letters with accents.

52a Business Symbols

QUICK REFERENCE 52.1

Business symbols

Writing		Mathematical, Money, Measurement	
&	ampersand	@	at
*	asterisk	¢	cents
√	checkmark	÷	divided by
©	copyright	°	degrees
′	diacritical mark (as in *cliché*)	$	dollar sign
"	ditto	=	equals
¶	paragraph	′	feet
¶¶	paragraphs	>	greater than
®	registered	″	inch
		∧	insert

CONTINUED →

QUICK REFERENCE 52.1 → CONTINUED

Writing		Mathematical, Money, Measurement	
§	section	<	less than
/	slash (e.g., and/or)	−	minus
™	trademark	×	multiplied by
		≠	not equal to
		#	number; space; pound, pounds
		%	percent
		+	plus
		:	ratio
		π	pi
		Σ	sum of

52b Chemical Symbols

A **chemical symbol** represents the name of a chemical element. A **chemical formula** is a group of such symbols that represent a chemical compound, such as H_2O (water).

Capitalize the first letter of chemical symbols and lowercase the second letter, if there is one. Chemical symbols do not need a period.

C (carbon)

O (oxygen)

Au (gold)

Fe (iron)

52c Spacing and Punctuation with Symbols

Spacing is important with symbols because an improper space is a typographical error. Quick Reference 52.2 lists the symbols that need to have spacing rules applied.

QUICK REFERENCE 52.2

Spacing with symbols

Symbol	Rule	Example
At @	Do not space after @ in email addresses; otherwise, space before and after.	romhob@aol.com The order was for 50 embossed warm-up jackets @ $49.95 each.
And & (ampersand)	Space before and after (unless closed up in a proper name).	The building is at 432 Amsterdam Avenue, between 84th & 85th Streets. S&P (Standard and Poors)
By ×	Used in measurements; space before and after.	The room measures 20 × 13 ft.
Degree °	Do not space before; generally, spell out the word *degree* in text.	The optimum temperature for energy conservation is 68°.
Dollar $	Do not space between $ sign and the number.	$200 $3 million $1.95
Number #	Do not space after #. Spell out the word *number* in text.	My order of the executive chair (#1549) and computer desk (#1899) has not been received.
Math symbols Plus + Minus − Multiply × Divide ÷ or / Equals =	Space before and after.	2 + 2 = 4 9 × 10 = 90
Percent %	Do not space between the number and the % symbol. Spell out the word *percent* in text.	29% 100%

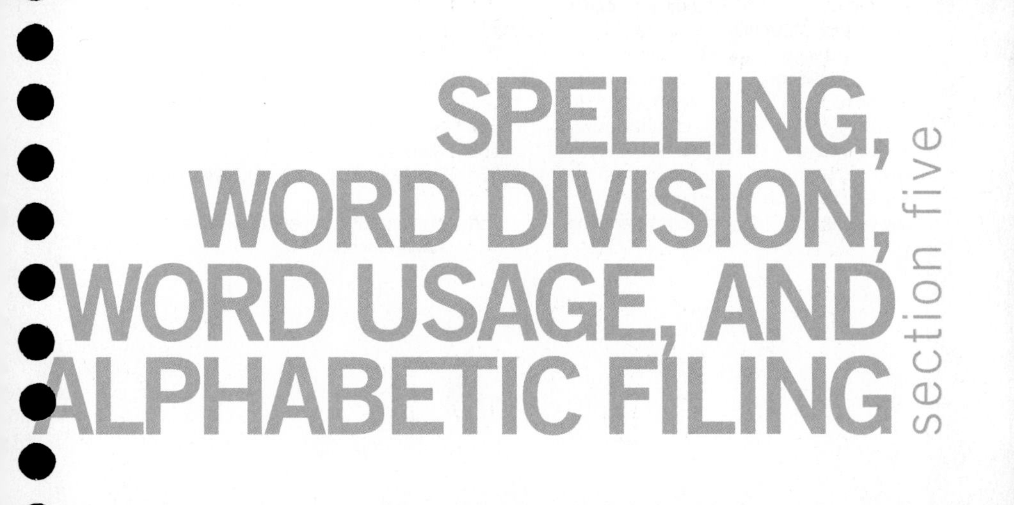

SPELLING, WORD DIVISION, WORD USAGE, AND ALPHABETIC FILING

section five

53 SPELLING AND WORD DIVISION

The English language includes many spelling rules and a great many words that do not comply with those rules. The spelling and word division topics in this section provide basic rules that help avoid most misspelling pitfalls. (In most cases, the spellings in this section follow those in *Merriam-Webster's Collegiate Dictionary, Eleventh Edition.*) The word usage section lists words and word pairs that writers frequently find confusing.

Using your dictionary and your spell checker will eliminate *most* misspellings. Spell checkers find many problems that used to plague writers, and in some cases, such as *ei* versus *ie* combinations, corrections are made as you type. To find errors that spell checkers don't pick up, always proofread to check for mistakes in word usage, verb tenses, plurals, suffixes and prefixes, and wrong and/or omitted words. Also, remember to reproof sections as you make corrections to ensure that you have not inadvertently introduced a new error.

53a Plural Forms of Nouns

Forming the plural of most nouns is a matter of remembering the spelling because you have used it and seen it so often. The guidelines in Quick Reference 53.1 will help you remember how to spell a variety of plural forms.

QUICK REFERENCE 53.1

Guidelines for spelling plurals

Common word endings	Form the plurals of most words simply by adding *s* to the singular form.	computer employee	computers employees
Words ending in *y* preceded by a consonant	Change the *y* to *i* and add *es.*	laboratory industry	laboratories industries
Words with unique spellings	Some words change to a different word to form the plural.	person child	people children

CONTINUED →

QUICK REFERENCE 53.1 → CONTINUED

Words with unique spellings (cont.)	Some words change spelling to form the plural. Some words do not change at all.	foot man goose fish deer	feet men geese fish deer
Surnames	Add *es* to surnames ending in *s, ss, x, ch, sh,* or *z*. Add an *s* to other surnames.	Bass Fox Burch Chavez Smith Rivera Radko	Basses Foxes Burches Chavezes Smiths Riveras Radkos
Words ending in *ss*	Add *es*.	address press	addresses presses
Words (originally Latin) ending in *a*, *us*, *is*, *on*, and *um*	Some have more than one plural, but generally: change *a* to *as*; *us* to *i*; *is* to *es*; *on* and *um* to *a*.	formula alumnus analysis phenomenon curriculum	formulas alumni analyses phenomena curricula
Words ending in the suffix *ful*	Add the *s* to the root word.	mouth teaspoon hands	mouthsful teaspoonsful handsful
Words ending in *f* or *fe*	Many words ending in *f* add an *s*. Some words ending in *f* change the *f* to *v* and add *es*.	proof safe shelf leaf	proofs safes shelves leaves
Words ending in *is*	Change the *is* to *es* to form the plural.	analysis basis	analyses bases
Words ending in *o*	Generally, if the *o* is preceded by a consonant, add *s*, but some add *es*; check your dictionary.	tomato veto memo zero	tomatoes vetoes memos zeros, zeroes
Hyphenated and non-hyphenated compound words	Add *s* to the first word in a compound noun to form the plural. If there is no noun in the hyphenated word, add *s* to the end of the word.	leave of absence sister-in-law show-off spin-off get-together	leaves of absence sisters-in-law show-offs spin-offs get-togethers

53b Plural Forms of Numbers

Plural forms of numbers expressed in words follow the basic pattern of adding *s* or changing *y* to *i* and adding *es:*

ten/tens million/millions twenty/twenties fifty/fifties

To form the plural of figures, add only *s*; do not use an apostrophe.

Most baby boomers were born in the **40s and 50s.**

The styles of the **1980s** are making a comeback in fashion this year.

[Read more about writing numbers in Section Four: Numbers, Abbreviations, and Symbols.]

53c Compound Words and Hyphenation

A **compound word** results when two or more words function together to form a single unit. Some compound words are hyphenated; others are not. Use of a hyphen helps readers understand that the words have a single meaning and function.

Compound words may be nouns or adjectives (see 53d). A **compound noun** may be written as one word (*airmail, database, layout*), as two words (*word processing, problem solving, decision making*), or as a hyphenated construction (*sit-in, mother-in-law, drive-in*). The question of when to use hyphens can be complex, however, because rules are not applied uniformly. Since the objective of the hyphen is to avoid confusion, after a compound word becomes widely used, the hyphen is often dropped, and some compounds eventually become one word (*bookworm, database, cyberspace, heartbreaking*).

Another variable in compound words is the coining of new usage, usually by style leaders in the media. This evolving usage makes it impossible to perfect the spelling of compound words because even dictionaries cannot keep up. The guidelines in this topic are based on the present ground rules for hyphen use. Quick Reference 53.1 outlines some general rules.

In the following sentences, the boldface words are functioning as a unit (to form a noun) and are, therefore, hyphenated as compound nouns.

We will use a **stand-in** for the close-ups.

The president had a **falling-out** with the CEO.

When such word combinations function as a different part of speech and not as a unit, do not hyphenate them.

QUICK REFERENCE 53.1

General rules for hyphenating compound words

When two words function as a unit to form a compound, use a hyphen for clarity.

We will use a **well-known** actor for the commercial.

The president had a **long-standing** relationship with the CEO.

Hyphenate a compound adjective in front of the noun it modifies; when it follows the noun, do not hyphenate it.

Please try to come up with a more **cost-effective** proposal.

I think you will find that the new proposal is more **cost effective.**

Do not hyphenate adverb-adjective combinations; the grammatical construction makes the meaning clear (the following adverbs are bold):

He is a **thoroughly** professional attorney.

The **highly** intelligent critique was biting in its wit.

Never hyphenate adverbs ending in *ly:*

The **frequently** used resource is terribly outdated.

(**Note:** If a compound word is not listed in the dictionary, it is not hyphenated.)

You might have to **stand in** line for hours to get the tickets. [*Stand* is a verb; *in* is a preposition.]

The new fashions are already **falling out** of favor with the public. [*Are falling* is a verb; *out* is a preposition.]

The two following examples are noun combinations that were originally hyphenated.

We must consider all the **trade offs.**

We thought we'd better take a **timeout.**

To decide whether to hyphenate or not, think about the function of the two words in the sentence.

The employees held a **sit-in** to protest working conditions. [*Sit-in* is functioning as a noun and needs a hyphen.]

The visitor will **sit in** the president's office until the meeting starts. [*Sit* is functioning as a verb, and *in* is a preposition, so no hyphen is needed.]

We're having a **get-together** after work tomorrow. [*Get-together* is functioning as a noun and needs a hyphen to be clear.]

Let's **get together** after work for a dinner meeting. [*Get* is functioning as a verb, and *together* is an adverb.]

[Read more about functions of words in sentences in Section One: Grammar.]

53d Compound Modifiers (Adjectives and Adverbs)

A **compound adjective** is formed when two adjectives function together as one to modify a noun or pronoun. Examples are *quick-minded* student, *high-risk* stocks, *ill-fitting* trousers.

Decide whether or not to hyphenate a compound adjective based on its position in front of or after the noun it is modifying. If the compound adjective appears before the noun, hyphenate it. (Remember to hyphenate all parts of the compound.) If the compound adjective follows the noun it is modifying, do not hyphenate it.

Follow the **easy-to-read** instructions.

The instructions are **easy to read.**

She took advantage of **on-the-job** training.

She received excellent training **on the job.**

The new office tower reflects **state-of-the-art** architecture.

The architecture of the new office tower is **state of the art.**

When using a compound adjective in a series, hyphenate after each occurrence of the first adjective and leave a space.

We are examining the possibility of doing **two-** and **five-day** versions of the course.

My manager is very **time-** and **cost-conscious,** so please notify me of any alterations to either as we proceed with this project.

Another type of **compound modifier** is created when adverbs and adjectives are combined. Though some style manuals recommend it, there is no need to hyphenate adverb-adjective combinations because the grammatical construction makes the meaning clear. The adverb modifies the adjective, and the adjective modifies the noun.

He is a **very competent** attorney. [The adverb *very* modifies the adjective *competent*.]

She supplied the **much needed** leadership. [The adverb *much* modifies the adjective *needed*.]

Never hyphenate adverbs ending in *-ly* when they combine with other modifiers.

The **frequently used** resource is terribly outdated. [The adverb *frequently* modifies the adjective *used*.]

The **newly formed** committee will handle employee complaints. [The adverb *newly* modifies the adjective formed.]

53e Compound Verbs

A **compound verb** is formed when two or more words function together as a single verb. Common compound verbs are often written as single words: *brainstorm, download, proofread, troubleshoot.* Check a dictionary for the correct spelling. If your dictionary does not list the verb as one word, use a hyphen as a connector.

Anita will **pinch-hit** for the president while he is gone.

The cooks will **deep-fry** or sauté the fish right at our table.

Do not hyphenate verb-adverb constructions:

Please **follow up** on that proposal right away.

We can't **turn down** that offer unless we have good reason.

The network decided to **black out** the game.

53f Prefixes

The generally preferred style is to *not* hyphenate most short prefixes (three or fewer letters) and many common longer ones, such as *micro-, multi-, mini-*. The following commonly used prefixes no longer require hyphenation. Note that your dictionary and spell checker might still mark some of these as errors, so decide which style you prefer and be consistent in each document.

Acceptable	**Preferred**
non-traditional	nontraditional
micro-manager	micromanager
re-emphasize	reemphasize
bi-weekly	biweekly
pre-established	preestablished

When in doubt, leave out the hyphen or consult a current dictionary. If the word is not listed, write it without a hyphen.

Some short prefixes require hyphenation for readability or meaning—for example, *anti-intellectual* and *co-op* (short for the noun *cooperative*, since *coop* is a different word).

When a word containing a prefix can also be a different word, use a hyphen between the prefix and the root to avoid confusion.

It is not worth the cost to **re-cover** the ruined sofa.

I will help you **recover** the data you lost as a result of the blackout.

Would you please **re-sort** today's mail to make sure there are no mistakes.

I hope we don't need to **resort** to double-checking the mail every day.

Prefixes preceding a word that is capitalized should be hyphenated.

We are planning our **pre-Easter** clearance sale.

53g Suffixes

Quick Reference 53.2 lists common suffixes and their usual spellings. Keep in mind that there are very few consistent rules for adding suffixes, so always consult your dictionary when in doubt.

QUICK REFERENCE 53.2

Guidelines for adding suffixes

ible* and *able	The spelling of most words is *able*, but a few end in *ible*.	agreeable payable reasonable knowledgeable permissible sensible	accountable reasonable transferable movable defensible resistible
ant/ent* and *ance/ence	The spelling is unpredictable; when in doubt, consult your dictionary.	relevant resistant assistant eminent referent persistent	relevance resistance assistance eminence reference persistence
Words ending in silent *e*	The spelling is unpredictable; when in doubt, consult your dictionary.	save eye argue mile purpose manage judge acknowledge	savings eyeing arguable mileage purposeful management judgment acknowledgement

CONTINUED →

QUICK REFERENCE 53.2 → CONTINUED

ize, ise,* and *yze	Most words ending in this sound end in *ize*.	authorize specialize economize computerize	criticize realize organize memorize
	Many common words end in *ise*.	advertise advise compromise	enterprise franchise merchandise
	A few words end in *yze*.	analyze	paralyze
cede, ceed,* and *sede	Only one word ends in *sede*.	supersede	
	Only three words end in *ceed*.	exceed, proceed, succeed	
	There are only eight words that have the "seed" sound and end in *cede*.	accede cede intercede precede	antecede concede recede secede
ment	Generally, when a root word ends in a silent *e,* do not drop the *e* before adding *ment*. (This also applies to any suffix beginning with a consonant.)	arrange state manage	arrangement statement management
Words ending in *y*	One-syllable words ending in *y* preceded by a vowel usually retain the *y* when adding a suffix.	play say bray stay	playing saying braying stayed
	Usually when a two-syllable word ends in *y* preceded by a single vowel, retain the *y* when adding a suffix.	employ employing deploy	employed employer deployed, deploying

53h American vs. British Spellings

Canada and Great Britain (and many other countries where English is spoken) use British spelling for many common words. Quick Reference 52.3 lists common variant British spellings.

QUICK REFERENCE 53.3

Differences in American and British spellings

	American	British
or, our	color	colour
	honor	honour
	favorite	favourite
	flavor	flavour
er, re	center	centre
	theater	theatre
	liter	litre
ll, l	fulfill	fulfil
	skillful	skilful
	enrollment	enrolment
og, ogue	analog	analogue
	catalog	catalogue
	dialog	dialogue
ze, se	analyze	analyse
	criticize	criticise
	memorize	memorise
	capitalize	capitalise
se, ce	offense	offence
	defense	defence
ck or k, que	check	cheque
	bank	banque
	checker	chequer
ense, ence	defense	defence
	license	licence
	offense	offence

Note: Some of these British spellings, such as catalogue and theatre are used in America and are not incorrect.

53i General Rules for Word Division

Word division is an aspect of spelling that is easy to ignore now that word processing software seems to take care of it automatically. However, a basic knowledge of word division principles is still necessary because automated hyphenation can create word breaks that interfere with comprehension of meaning. Also, copy that is justified at the right margin often creates hyphenation in several lines in succession, which can be unattractive and distracting to the reader.

The standards in this topic will help you in checking and correcting automated word processing divisions to create a polished document.

(**Note:** The rules here do not apply to professionally typeset, right-justified text over which you have no control, as in the case with the authors of this text.)

DO NOT DIVIDE

- One-syllable words
- A word if you cannot carry over at least three letters to the next line
- Words of six or fewer letters
- Abbreviations
- Contractions: *doesn't, shouldn't*
- Dollar amounts, dates, and numbers
- A proper name
- Any of the elements that compose an address: street number, street name, city, state abbreviation, or ZIP code (you may separate the street address from the city, state, or ZIP code with a turnover line)
- A URL (Web site address) or email address; the reader might mistake the hyphen for a part of the address

WHENEVER POSSIBLE AVOID DIVIDING

- Acronyms; however, if an acronym is already hyphenated, it may be divided at the hyphen: OB-GYN, KDWN- TV
- Parts of names of people; instead carry the full name over to the next line
- Groups of words that represent one unit: 39 cents; Chapter 3; 60 inches

53j Dividing Words by Syllables

Divide words only between syllables.

- Do not divide before or after a one-letter syllable.
- Avoid dividing suffixes from the root word, especially short ones.
- Leave at least two letters of the word being divided on the end of the line, and carry at least three letters to the new line.

53k Dividing Compound Words

Divide a compound word at the hyphen or between the elements of the compound word.

self-confidence	self-
salesclerk	sales-
policymaker	policy-
twenty-five	twenty-

53l Dividing Words with Prefixes and Suffixes

Generally divide at a suffix or prefix rather than within it.

Divide after a prefix: under-utilized over-sensitive inter-active

Divide before a suffix: develop-ment art-fully breath-less

When the root word ends in a double consonant, divide after the double consonant.

bill-ing
spell-ing

When adding a suffix results in a double consonant, divide between the doubled letters.

comit-ting
refer-ring

53m Dividing Words in Blocks of Type

Follow these general guidelines for dividing words in a way that maintains the readability and graphic integrity of a printed page:

- Divide words as sparingly as possible.
- Avoid hyphenating words at the end of more than two successive lines.
- Never divide the last word on the last line of a page or the last word of a paragraph.
- If a sentence contains a dash, divide after the dash:

  The monthly meeting of the Executive Committee—
  scheduled for next Friday—has been moved to the 10th floor
  conference room.

54 WORD USAGE

This topic lists words and word pairs that writers and speakers often confuse and misuse. The list is arranged alphabetically. The parts of speech are listed for each word, followed by a definition or usage notes and an example of its correct usage. Being conscientious about correct usage of words will set you apart as a skilled communicator.

a (article): Use *a* before words that begin with a **consonant** (all letters except the **vowels,** *a, e, i, o, u*) sound.

a table

a group

a band

a month

Use *a* before words that begin with a vowel but sound like a consonant when pronounced.

a once-in-a-lifetime chance (the initial sound of *once* is *w*)

a unique opportunity (the initial sound of *unique* is *y* as in *you*)

Use *a* before words derived from the word *history:*

a history

a historic event

a historical document

an (article): Use *an* before words that begin with a vowel (*a, e, i, o, u*) sound.

an identical situation

an easy route

an additional example

an unusual situation

an honor

With acronyms and initialisms (see 45d) use *a* or *an* according to the vowel or consonant sound made when the abbreviation is pronounced as a word or as individual letters.

an AARP member

an NAACP employee

a CEO of a company

a POW survivor

a lot (adjective or adverb): is always written as two words; *alot* is not a word.

The child had *a lot* of money to spend.

a while (noun): a short time period

May I use your computer for *a while*? [object of the preposition *for*]

awhile (adverb): a short time

I was finished with the task *awhile* ago. [adverb answering the question *when?*]

accept (verb): to take or receive

I *accept* your apology.

except (preposition): excluding

Everyone *except* Margaret is attending.

account for (verb-preposition): to explain, to be responsible for, to show what happened

She must *account for* the petty cash shortage.

account to (verb-preposition): to report to, to answer to

James must *account to* us for his absence.

ad (noun): a shortened form of *advertisement*

Our new *ad* will run for ten days.

add (verb): to calculate a total; to add to

Did you *add* the tax to the invoice?

adapt (verb): to adjust or conform

Employees need to learn to *adapt* to any management style.

adopt (verb): to take, acquire, or accept

We will *adopt* the new policy as you wrote it.

advice (noun): suggestion, recommendation

Do you have any *advice* for me in this matter?

advise (verb): to suggest, to recommend, to have input

Can you *advise* me in this matter?

affect (verb): to have an impact on; (noun): used in psychology to describe a person's outward demeanor—the intensity of awareness or emotion displayed.

Will my work on this project *affect* my chances for promotion? [verb]

The patient showed a heightened *affect* once the medication took effect. [noun]

effect (noun): a result; (verb) to cause

Your speech had a tremendous *effect* on your audience. [noun]

How can we *effect* a change in employee attitudes? [verb]

afterward, afterwards (adverb): at a later time; preferred usage is *afterward;* both are correct.

Dinner is at seven; *afterward*, we'll watch a movie.

aggravate (verb): to intensify or make worse (used colloquially to mean *irritate,* but avoid this usage in business writing)

Threatening to cancel the order will only *aggravate* the situation.

irritate (verb): to annoy or make impatient

It is wise not to say anything that will *irritate* your boss during a performance review.

agree on (verb-preposition): to reach an understanding with someone who is named in the sentence

George and I *agree on* the new policy for leaves of absence.

agree to (verb-preposition): to give in or compromise; to undertake an action

At least 75 percent of the committee must *agree to* our approval of the proposal.

agree with (verb-preposition): to reach an understanding with someone

I *agree with* Ivan on most issues, so we get along well.

aid (verb): to assist

With your *aid,* I can finish the project today.

aide (noun): an assistant

The nurse's *aide* attended to the patient.

all (adjective); **all of** (adjective and preposition): usually you can omit the *of*

Take *all* the copies to Suite 150.

All of the copies have been moved to the suite.

already (adverb): previously

She has *already* completed her report.

all ready (adverb-adjective): completely ready or prepared

I was *all ready* to leave when the plans were suddenly changed.

all right: completely acceptable

Your decision is *all right* with me.

(**Note:** *alright* is not a word.)

all together (adverb-adjective): completely together or in agreement

We were *all together* in one car.

We are *all together* on the importance of the petition.

altogether (adjective): entirely or thoroughly

I have *altogether* too much work to do.

He is *altogether* the laziest person I have ever met.

all ways (adjective-noun): in every way

We are in *all ways* ready for the meeting.

always (adverb): all the time

I *always* have too much work to do.

among (preposition): used to compare three or more people or things. (**Note:** Avoid *amongst*; used commonly in British but not in American English.)

Let's discuss the problem *among* the three of us.

between (preposition): used to compare two people or things

There are subtle differences *between* the twins.

and so on: additional things; other things

Please make of list of the party supplies—paper plates, cups, napkins, *and so on*.

(**Note:** In more formal writing, avoid *etc.* and use *and so on*.)

and/or: use only when three possibilities exist at the same time: (1) one of two things; (2) the other of two things; (3) both things

Your reward will be a raise *and/or* a promotion. [meaning the three options are a raise, a promotion, or both]

Agnes plans to take an extended vacation *and/or* a leave of absence. [meaning the three options are a vacation, a leave of absence, or both]

anxious (adjective): uneasy, concerned, worried

She was *anxious* about her performance review because she had not performed well in recent months.

eager (adjective): excited, enthusiastic

She was *eager* for her performance review because she had completed several successful projects in recent months.

any one (adjective-pronoun): any one person of a number of people or things or when one of a number of people or things is implied; use *anyone* in all other cases

Any one of the three assistants could do that job.

Any one of us could make a great presentation.

anyone (pronoun): any person among a number of people

Anyone planning a vacation in July should contact me immediately.

any time (adjective-noun combination): any hour; whenever; use following a preposition

Please feel free to call me at *any time.*

anytime (adverb): whenever

Anytime you are in town, give me a call.

any way (adjective-noun): any respect, method; use following a preposition

Please call me if I can help you in *any way.*

anyway (adverb): in any case or any event

Anyway, you can't leave because you have a contract.

(**Note:** *Anyways* is an outdated word; avoid using it.)

as (preposition): capacity, condition, role of; use to connect two comparative clauses

She commutes from Boston, *as* does my boss. [clause]

like (preposition): similar to; use to connect two comparative words or phrases

She is a Californian, *like* her friend Bobby. [prepositional phrase]

aren't (contraction): are not

We're going to meet today, *aren't* we?

(**Note:** In formal written text, spell out contractions.)

ain't (contraction): colloquial for *aren't;* acceptable only in very informal spoken English or when used for strong effect that would be lost if the correct form were substituted (for example, in a script)

If it ain't broke, don't fix it. OR You ain't seen nothin' yet.

assure, ensure (verb): both mean to make certain; to guarantee

Let me *assure* you the matter is closed.

I can *ensure* that our products are all fully tested.

insure (verb): to cover with insurance

Our company will be pleased to *insure* your automobile.

bad (adjective): poor, unfavorable; use to modify a noun or pronoun

He had a *bad* case of the jitters before his speech. [modifies the noun *case*]

badly (adverb): in a bad manner; to a great or intense degree; use to modify a verb or adjective

I need a vacation *badly.* [modifies the verb *need*]

because (conjunction): use to express a cause-effect relationship

I went to lunch early *because* I was hungry.

since (conjunction): use to express a time relationship; also means "in view of the fact that"

Since Bob left the company, things have not gone well in the Auditing Department.

Since three people have canceled, let's reschedule today's meeting.

being as, being that, being as how: Avoid these colloquial expressions in business writing and speaking; use *because* or *since* instead.

beside (preposition): by, near to, next to

Please put the scanner *beside* the fax machine.

besides (preposition): in addition to, also, moreover

Besides Jackie and me, three other secretaries have been selected.

bi- (prefix): two

A *bimonthly* magazine comes out every two weeks.

semi- (prefix): half; in business, *semi* means two times per year (or two times)

My *semiannual* insurance premium is due on the first of June.

borrow (verb): to take something with the intent to return it

May I *borrow* your copy of Friday's class notes?

lend (verb): to give something assuming it will be returned

I will gladly *lend* you $5.

loan (noun): something given or taken with the understanding that it will be returned

Your *loan* has been pre-approved.

bring (verb): to carry to

Please *bring* me the correspondence from Clayton Williams.

take (verb): to carry away from

Be sure to *take* these papers to the meeting.

can (verb): indicates ability

Can I play your grand piano? [Do I have the ability to play your piano?]

may (verb): indicates permission

May I play your grand piano? [Do I have permission to play your piano?]

(**Note:** This common error can be avoided by remembering the two-word clue: *ability* [can] versus *permission* [may].)

capital (noun): a sum of money; city serving as a seat of government

How much *capital* will I need to open my own business?

Lansing is the *capital* of Michigan.

capital (adjective): excellent or primary

That is a *capital* idea.

capitol (noun): a building in which the functions of government are carried out

We toured the Capitol in Washington, DC.

choose (verb): to select or make a choice

Which book will you *choose*?

chose (verb): selected, made a choice

I *chose* the nonfiction book on communications.

cite (verb): to draw reference to as an authority or proof; derived from *citation*

Be sure that you *cite* all the references used in the report.

site (noun): a particular place

The tour will include a visit to the *site* of our new headquarters.

compare (verb): to consider similarities and differences

Please *compare* the two bids and summarize their strengths and weaknesses.

contrast (verb): to consider differences

In *contrast,* Candidate A is clearly more experienced than Candidate B.

contrast (noun): a striking dissimilarity between things being compared.

There is a strong *contrast* between the first selection and the second.

complement (verb): to complete or add to

Your strengths *complement* mine; together we make a good team.

A skilled assistant is the perfect *complement* to a good manager.

compliment (noun): a comment of courtesy or praise

May I *compliment* you on your performance.

continually (adverb): repeatedly, happening frequently with brief interruptions between occurrences

Corporations are *continually* expanding through mergers with successful startups.

continuously (adverb): nonstop, taking place without interruptions

The audience talked *continuously* during the presentation.

correspond to (verb-preposition): to agree with something

Your totals do not *correspond to* mine.

correspond with (verb-preposition): to communicate with someone

Did you *correspond* with her previously?

correspondence (noun): information exchanged in writing

Keep a hard copy of all *correspondence* with our clients.

correspondents (plural noun): people who exchange information through writing

The war *correspondents* were in a very dangerous area.

could have, should have, would have (verb): use instead of *could of, should of, would of,* which are incorrect usages caused by the sound of the contractions *could've, should've,* and *would've*

I *could have* done it myself. [preferred business usage]
I *could've* done it myself. [informal usage]

criteria (plural noun); **criterion** (singular noun): standards; standard

Do you meet all the *criteria* for this position?
There is only one *criterion* for the promotion: people skills.

data (singular or plural noun): bits or pieces of information; facts or a collection of facts. *Data* is usually used in the sense of a collection or set of facts; usage of a singular verb is most often correct. Because this usage is so common, it is what looks and sounds correct to the majority of readers.

The *data* appears to be accurate.
The *data* we collected on the test scores is not correct.
The *data* shows that test scores are not an indicator of graduation rates.

desert (noun): a very arid region

On our trip out west, we drove through the *desert*.

desert (verb): to abandon

Please do not *desert* us on the last day of the seminar.

dessert (noun): the final course of a meal; a sweet food item

The guest rudely shouted, "What's for *dessert*?"
Crème brulée will be served for *dessert*.

different from (adjective-preposition): use to contrast when words or phrases are the contrasted elements

Your office is *different from* mine.

different than (adjective-preposition): use when the second element is a clause

His opinion is *different than* it was yesterday.

disinterested (adjective): impartial, objective

Our committee is so divided; let's ask the opinion of a *disinterested* party.

uninterested (adjective): having no interest, not interested, uncaring

I'm completely *uninterested* in that project.

doesn't (contraction, singular): does not

He *doesn't* care about the effect on others.

don't (contraction, plural): do not

They *don't* stock the brand we use.

eager: see **anxious**

e.g. (prepositional phrase): for example

Some of your suggestions (*e.g.,* hiring a consultant and advertising on radio) were very helpful.

i.e. (conjunction): that is, namely (used to clarify)

The expenses you incurred (*i.e.,* transportation, meals) will need to be verified with receipts.

e-mail and **email** (noun): short for *electronic mail*. This book uses the most recent spelling, *email;* however, *e-mail* is also correct. Follow the usage in your business field or organization.

ensure: see **assure**

etc.: abbreviation for *et cetera* (from the Latin) meaning *and other things* or *additional things*. In formal writing, avoid *etc.* and use *and so on*.

We are going to redecorate the office suite—new carpet, furniture, *etc.*

Please refer to rules 1-5 *and so on*.

every day (adjective, noun): each day

Our sales analyses of the previous day are delivered *every day* by noon.

everyday (adjective): commonplace, ordinary

His fits of anger, unfortunately, have become *everyday* occurrences.

every one (adjective-pronoun): one of a number of people or things

Every one of the suggestions will help boost productivity.

everyone (plural pronoun): all members of a group

Everyone must agree to the plan if we are to implement it.

farther (adverb): more distant in measurable terms

Salt Lake City is *farther* west than Omaha.

further (adverb): in addition; moreover; to a greater degree in the abstract

We will have to study the problem *further*.

fewer (adjective): use to modify nouns that can be counted

There were *fewer* people in attendance than I anticipated.

less (adjective): use to modify nouns that cannot be counted

There was *less* work on the project than I thought.

former (adjective): first of two

Of the two candidates, Craig and Lewis, I prefer the *former*. [meaning Craig]

latter (adjective): second of two

Of his two ideas, to bid higher or drop out of the competition, I prefer the *latter*. [meaning to drop out]

good (adjective): use to modify a noun or pronoun

David McKenna submitted a *good* proposal.

well (adverb): use to modify a verb or adjective

This is a *well*-written letter.

i.e.: see **e.g.**

if (conjunction): use to indicate a conditional relationship between two things

If he comes, I will leave.

whether (conjunction): use to indicate more than one alternative

She could not decide *whether* to call or write a letter.

imply (verb): to suggest something without stating it [as the writer or speaker]

Your letter *implies* that you are not happy with your job.

infer (verb): to assume something not directly stated. [as the reader or listener]

I *infer* from your letter that you are not happy with your job.

in, on (preposition): use to indicate fixed positions or places

I'll wait *in* the lobby.
We are meeting *on* the third floor.

into, onto (prepositions): use to indicate movement toward a position.

We're moving *into* a new phase.
All the toys spilled *onto* the floor.

insure: see **assure/ensure** (verbs)

irritate: see **aggravate**

it's (verb): contraction of *it is*

Unfortunately, *it's* going to rain on the day of our first softball game.

its (possessive pronoun): belonging to "it"

The committee turned in *its* report.

(**Note:** *its'* is not a word; the only correct singular and possessive form is *its.*)

last (adjective): final, concluding

Please read the *last* paragraph thoroughly.

latest (adjective): most recent, newest, current

The *latest* revision is much improved.

past (adjective): former, previous, prior

Our *past* sales records were dismal, but business is much better since the reorganization.

lay (verb): to place something down

Please *lay* the file on my credenza.

lie (verb): to recline (*lie* never takes an object); to tell an untruth

If you're feeling ill, *lie* down in the lounge and close the door.

It is highly unethical to *lie* to a client in order to get business.

lead (noun): a type of metal

We will replace all the *lead* pipes next year.

lead (verb): to take charge, to be in authority

It will help to have a senior person take the *lead* on the project.

led (verb): was in charge; was in a position of authority

As president, he *led* the company through its best and worst times.

lend, loan: see **borrow**

literally (adverb): actually, precisely, or truly

I was *literally* scared for my life during the fire.

The amount is *literally* triple what we expected to pay.

(**Note:** Do not use *literally* to introduce an exaggeration [e.g., We are *literally* drowning in paperwork.])

loose (adjective): not properly connected or attached

Now I see why the printer isn't working—the plug is *loose.*

lose (verb): to misplace; to be defeated

We cannot afford to *lose* that account!

Don't *lose* the directions or we will never find our way to the meeting.

may: see **can**

media (plural noun): plural of *medium*

Are videotaped lectures the best *media* through which to train our staff?

medium (singular noun): an intervening substance or agency through which something is transmitted

Is a lecture the best *medium* through which to train our staff?

moot (adjective): not debatable, irrelevant

That is a *moot* point, so please don't bring it up at the next meeting.

mute (adjective): unable to speak or to be heard

Although the actor was *mute,* he was able to communicate with the audience.

moral (adjective): spiritually or ethically correct

Our security guards have the highest *moral* character.

morale (noun): general feeling or attitude of confidence and pleasure

The *morale* of the staff was high after the CEO's remarks.

more important: A shortened form of "Which is *more important*. . ." is preferred over *more importantly,* especially at the beginning of a sentence

I found the missing information. *More important,* the document supports your position on next year's budget.

more importantly (adverb): in a more important manner

The reaction of the disgruntled employee was treated *more importantly* than it deserved.

no body (adjective-noun): no group or person within a larger group

No body of the government can act alone to enact a law.

nobody (pronoun): no person, no one

Nobody is allowed into the building on weekends without proper ID.

off (adverb); **off of** (adverb and preposition): usually you can omit the *of*

I can't get the smudge *off* the table. NOT Please take the glass *off of* the wood table.

oral (adjective): by mouth; spoken

We have an *oral* contract.

verbal (adjective): relating to words, either spoken or written.

The applicant's *verbal* skills were excellent.

passed (verb): sent, handed, went beyond or through

She has *passed* the stage of blind career ambition.

past (adjective): lapsed, expired, a period of time before the present

The high-volume real estate market is *past.*

past (adverb): beyond

We had to get *past* the disappointment of losing the contract.

peace (noun): condition of harmony, lacking conflict

Once he retires, we should have *peac*e in the department again.

piece (noun): portion or fragment; (verb): to put something together into a larger whole

I need one more *piece* of information to make the report complete.

You can probably *piece* your report together from these documents.

persons: the plural form of *person*; use *people* instead to refer to more than one individual

Thirty *people* attended the meeting.

percent (noun): use to express a specific number

They gave us 18 *percent* of the net proceeds.

(**Note**: *Percent* is written as a single word not two words: *per cent.*)

percentage (noun): use to express the general concept

If a large *percentage* of the people vote, our candidate will win.

personal (adjective): relating to or belonging to an individual person; private

Our Human Resources Department offers counseling on *personal* finance to interested employees.

personnel (noun): a group of employees

All our *personnel* have academic degrees.

plus (conjunction): in addition to; in writing do not use as a substitute for *and*

He requested a new printer *and* a scanner.

precede (verb): to come before or ahead of

The keynote address will *precede* the workshops.

proceed (noun): to move forward or ahead

Once you pass the Sawyer Building, *proceed* north on First Street.

Proceed with your plans; we can set a firm date later.

principal (noun): a person who has controlling authority; a school administrator

He is a *principal* in the firm.

The *principal* called a staff meeting.

principal (noun): a sum of money

The mutual fund offered a high rate of return on the *principal*.

principal (adjective): main or most important

She is the *principal* decision-maker within the group.

principle (noun): a comprehensive and fundamental law, doctrine, or assumption

Our service is based on the *principle* that the customer is always right.

raise (verb): to lift something to a higher level

Please *raise* my salary in the new fiscal year. [always takes an object]

rise (verb); to move upward or increase

If my salary continues to *rise,* I will consider myself well paid. [never takes an object]

real (adjective): true, actual

Her attitude was a *real* surprise to me.

really (adverb); actually, truly

It was *really* nice to see you.

(**Note:** The two words are not interchangeable because they are used as different parts of speech; use *real* only to modify a noun and *really* only to modify a verb: *real truth* or *really truthful*.)

reason (noun or verb): as a noun, a rationale or motive; as a verb to calculate or think

The *reason* for working late today is to try to avoid pressure tomorrow.

Please try to *reason* your way through this complex data.

(**Note:** Do not use the phrases *the reason is because* and *the reason why;* they are redundant.)

regardless: without consideration of; in spite of.

Regardless of your receipt, I cannot issue a refund on that item.

(**Note:** There is no such word as *irregardless;* it is a misuse of *regardless*.)

semi-: ***see*** **bi-**

set (verb): to place something down

Please *set* the file cabinet in the corner. [always takes an object]

She *has set* the plant on the shelf three times.

sit (verb): to be seated or remain in place

Please *sit* in the lobby until I call you. [present tense; never takes an object]

sat (verb): to be seated or remain in place

I have *sat* in the waiting room for more than an hour. [past tense of *sit;* must have helping verb]

shall, will (verb): use *will* instead of *shall* in all but the most formal writing.

We *will* finish this project next week!

simple (adjective): easy

Aaron showed me a *simple* way to organize electronic files.

simplistic (adjective): too simple, overly simplified

He has a habit of proposing solutions that are too *simplistic* to work.

since: see **because**

some time (adjective-noun): an unspecified point in time; an amount of time; use following a preposition

Please set up a meeting for *some time* next week.

Please set aside *some time* for us to meet next week.

sometime (adverb): at some indefinite or unstated time

I will call *sometime* tomorrow, if necessary.

stationary (adjective): without movement

They've added six *stationary* bikes in the gym.

stationery (noun): paper on which letters are sent

Please order more personalized *stationery* before the budget runs out.

supposed to (verb-preposition): expected; do not confuse with the present tense *suppose,* which means *believe*

We were *supposed to* check in early.

I *suppose* you are right about getting to the airport early.

take: see **bring**

then (adverb): at that time, next; in that case

Finish your work and *then* call me.

If you don't want to go, *then* stay here.

than (conjunction): when compared with

Her office is much larger *than* mine.

that (adjective): use to introduce essential modifying clauses

She needed the file *that* was on Mr. Barker's desk.

which (adjective): use to introduce nonessential modifying clauses

The new colors, *which* we saw yesterday, are unacceptable.

their (pronoun): belonging to them

Please do not notify the staff of *their* salary increases before the paperwork is processed.

there (adverb): in or at that place

You can leave the files *there*, but I don't have time to go through them.

they're (contraction): they are

They recommended the new software, so *they're* responsible for handling any problems.

themselves (reflexive pronoun): they, them

They probably find *themselves* very busy at times.

(**Note:** *theyselves* and *theirselves* are not words; the only correct usage is *themselves*.)

til, until (preposition or conjunction): up to; before; to the time that; *til* is a shortened form of *until* and should be used only informally; *until* is more broadly accepted and should be used in formal business writing.

We will be able to wait *until* July 3, but no longer. [preposition]

New employees do not receive benefits *until* they have worked for three months. [conjunction]

to (preposition): in the direction of, toward

Please give me directions *to* the hotel.

too (adverb): very, also, extremely

The report is *too* long.

toward, towards: preferred usage is *toward*; both are correct

try to, try and: the correct usage *is try* to; do not use *try and*

Try to find the Smithers file.

uninterested: see **disinterested**

unique (adjective): one of a kind; do not use to mean simply different or unusual. Do not use comparative forms (more or less) with *unique;* by definition, degrees of uniqueness are not possible.

The restored painting is truly *unique*.

He has a *unique* musical style.

I don't think the consultant's proposal is *unique* in any way.

used to (verb-preposition): accustomed to. Do not confuse with *use,* which means to make use of. Avoid *used to* when referring to the past (e.g., He used to be her secretary.) Use *was* instead.

After a while, we were *used to* it.

weather (noun): the outdoor climate

The *weather* is unpredictable.

whether (conjunction): used to indicate more than one alternative

I did not know *whether* to write her or call her.

whether: see also **if**

Web site, website (noun): A page or pages on the World Wide Web. This book uses the traditional two-word spelling, *Web site*. The one-word spelling, *website,* and the two-word spelling *web site* are also considered correct.

well: see **good**

which: see **that**

who, whoever (pronoun): nominative case pronoun; use as the subject of a sentence or clause

Who is chairing the monthly review?

Whoever wishes to attend may do so.

whom, whomever (pronoun): objective case pronoun; use as the object of a verb or phrase

Whom should I notify?

Give the invitation to *whomever* you wish.

whose (possessive pronoun): use *whose* to show possession

Try to identify the employee *whose* handwriting is best.

Whose attaché case is this?

who's (contraction): *who is* or *who has*

Please let me know *who's* going to attend the luncheon.

I'm the only one *who's* volunteered to work on Saturday.

-wise (suffix): This suffix is added to many words to form an adverb, but good writers avoid using it because there is almost always a better way of expressing it.

We have enough, *moneywise.* [acceptable]

We are doing fine financially. [preferred]

with (preposition): in the company of another

The Daugherty file is on my desk *with* the Allen file.

Janet is attending *with* David, our new chairperson.

within (preposition): inside another or encompassed by another

The solution to the problem lies *within* your proposal.

you're (contraction): you are

You're already late for the meeting.

your (possessive pronoun): belonging to you

Your work on this project must be completed by Friday.

55 RULES FOR ALPHABETIC FILING

The one basic reason for filing rules is *to make file retrieval easy*. The process of determining file order is simple: *alphabetizing*. For many, many years, ARMA, the American Records Management Association, has been the ultimate source of filing rules. The selected filing rules presented here are all consistent with ARMA rules. See the ARMA Web site for additional information.

55a General Rules

INDEXING (NAMING FILES)

In filing, **indexing** means determining the *unit* (or name) under which the file will be stored. The name most likely to be used in retrieving the record is the one to be used for indexing. Both the alphabetic order for indexing and the order of the words are determined *letter-by-letter.*

WORDS AND UNITS

The components of indexing are *words* and *units.* Each word or part of a name is a *unit*. Thus, *Gertrude Jane Hennicott* has three units. If the files are the names of persons, the units will be indexed according to the surname. The surname will be unit 1, the first name unit 2, and the middle initial or name, unit three.

Gertrude Jane Hennicott converted to indexing order would be Hennicott, Gertrude Jane.

Unit 1	**Unit 2**	**Unit 3**
Hennicott	Gertrude	Jane

A key principle of indexing is that *nothing comes before something*. When two names are very similar, establish their filing order by comparing each letter of each indexing unit until they differ. In the following example, because nothing comes after *J* it is placed before Jane.

Hennicott, Gertrude J.

Hennicott, Gertrude Jane

PUNCTUATION

Marks of punctuation are not considered when filing.

NUMBERS

Numbers expressed as figures in ascending order come *before* all alphabetical words. Arabic numbers come before Roman numerals.

55b Names of People

Unit 1 last name
Unit 2 first name
Unit 3 middle name or initial

	Unit 1	Unit 2	Unit 3
John F. Kennedy	Kennedy	John	F.
Toni Morrison	Morrison	Toni	
Sandra Day O'Connor	O'Connor	Sandra	Day
Adam Clayton Powell	Powell	Adam	Clayton

HYPHENATED NAMES

Disregard the hyphen and file the name as one word.

George Adams-Johnstone	Adams-Johnstone, George
Anita-Jo Carter	Carter, Anita-Jo
Cathy Lee-Miller	Lee-Miller, Cathy
Anne Li-Chin	Li-Chin, Anne
Mary Reese-Patterson	Reese-Patterson, Mary

NAMES WITH PREFIXES

Surnames having a prefix are filed as one unit even if the prefix is followed by a space. Examples of such prefixes are *D, De, Mc, Mac, La, St., Ste, O, Van*, and *von*. Index these names exactly as they are written.

Philip St. James	St. James, Philip	(2 units)
Betty Saint James	Saint James, Betty	(3 units)

Name	Unit 1	Unit 2	Unit 3
Brian Mackenzie	Mackenzie	Brian	
Emily MacNamara	MacNamara	Emily	
Douglas D. McKenna	McKenna	Douglas	D.
Annette St. Johns	St. Johns	Annette	
Janet Ruth von Voorheis	von Voorheis	Janet	Ruth

PERSONAL AND PROFESSIONAL TITLES

Consider a title only when it is necessary to determine the order of two names that are the same. In that case, the title is the last unit. In the alphabetized list, the title determines the order of the otherwise identical names.

	Unit 1	Unit 2	Unit 3	Unit 4
Dr. L.R. Cannaday	Cannaday	L.	R.	Dr.
Mrs. L.R. Cannaday	Cannaday	L.	R.	Mrs.
Mayor David N. Dinkins	Dinkins	David	N.	Mayor
Mrs. David N. Dinkins	Dinkins	David	N.	Mrs.
Mrs. Betty F. Forbes	Forbes	Betty	F.	Mrs.
Rev. James A. Forbes	Forbes	James	A.	Rev.
Mr. William McIntryre	McIntyre	William		Mr.
Mrs. William McIntyre	McIntyre	William		Mrs.

When files contain both numeric family order designations and professional titles, numbers are filed sequentially. The names shown illustrate the correct order of such files.

Names	Unit 1	Unit2	Unit 3	Unit 4
Gene Chavis CPA	Chavis	Gene	CPA	
Henry Ford II	Ford	Henry	II	
Henry Ford III	Ford	Henry	III	
Oscar Goodman, Mayor	Goodman	Oscar	Mayor	
Martin Luther King Jr.	King	Martin	Luther	Jr.
Martin Luther King Sr.	King	Martin	Luther	Sr.

When a title is used by many persons (Captain, Reverend, Father), file the name under the distinguishing name.

Reverend Adams	Adams, Reverend
Reverend Michael	Michael, Reverend

ROYAL AND RELIGIOUS TITLES

Names that begin with a royal or religious title and are followed by only one name are indexed as written.

Captain Kangaroo

Dr. Seuss

Pope Benedict

Princess Beatrice

Queen Elizabeth

Saint Anne

NICKNAMES

When a person uses a nickname much of the time and is known by the nickname, the nickname should be considered as unit 1. Some well-known nicknames from the sports world:

Babe Ruth for George Herman Ruth

Magic Johnson for Earvin Johnson

Nicknames are often cross-referenced by the given name.

55c Names of Businesses and Organizations

Business names are filed in the order written. As with names of people, every unit is considered to be a separate indexing unit.

	Unit 1	Unit 2	Unit 3	Unit 4
Garden Delight Florists	Garden	Delight	Florists	
Michigan Consolidated Gas Company	Michigan	Consolidated	Gas	Company
Mountain View Estates	Mountain	View	Estates	
Mountainview Presbyterian Church	Mountainview	Presbyterian	Church	
Nevada Power	Nevada	Power		
Wells Fargo Bank	Wells	Fargo	Bank	

SMALL WORDS IN BUSINESS NAMES

Every word is considered a unit except when *The* is the first unit of the name. A beginning *The* is ignored.

	Unit 1	Unit 2	Unit 3	Unit 4
A Little Night Music	A	Little	Night	Music
The Family Shoe Store	Family	Shoe	Store	The
The In Crowd Nightclub	In	Crowd	Nightclub	The

55d Names of Government Agencies and Departments

The rules for filing political and governmental names vary among sources. The most commonly applied rules are recommended here. For names that begin with United States, such as United States Department of Agriculture, consider *United States Government* or *United States Department* as the first three units when filing.

United States Department of Agriculture

United States Department of Commerce

United States Department of Labor

When an agency name has other general words in front of it, invert the name and alphabetize under the main department name, as follows:

	Unit 1	Unit 2	Unit 3	Unit 4
Office of the Justice of the Peace	Justice	of the Peace	Office of	
Bureau of Labor Statistics	Labor	Statistics	Bureau of	
Department of Small Business Administration	Small	Business	Administration	Department of

Small words such as *a, an, the,* and *of* are not considered for filing purposes. Also, ignore any punctuation used within the name.

STATE AND LOCAL AGENCIES

Many state and local entities include the name of the political division of which they are a part: department, office, bureau, and so on. Individual offices are listed under their respective state agencies.

City of Las Vegas

County of Clark

Bureau of Water and Sewage

These names are filed first under the identifying term and then by the individual name as follows:

Written name	Unit 1	Unit 3	Unit 4	Unit 5
City of Las Vegas, Bureau of Water/Sewer	Las Vegas	City of	Water/ Sewer	Bureau of
State of Ohio Motor Vehicles Division	Ohio	State of	Motor Vehicles	Division

part two

WRITING PROCESS AND STYLE

SECTION 6
THE WRITING PROCESS

SECTION 7
WRITING STYLE

THE WRITING PROCESS

section six

56 THE WRITING PROCESS

Good writing begins before words are put on paper. Each writing task or project, from the routine to the complex, has a goal that can be achieved best with planning, organizing, drafting, revising/editing (one or more times), and proofreading—these are the steps in the **writing process.** A logical writing process produces business communications that are crisp and clear and appropriate for the intended audience.

Steps in the writing process are meant to be carried out sequentially, with the editing/revising and proofreading steps being repeated as many times as necessary to achieve a polished, error-free publication. The amount of time needed on each step will vary, of course, depending on the level of complexity of the writing task.

QUICK REFERENCE 56.1

Steps in the writing process

Step 1. Plan Goal: To think through what you want your document to say and do	**Clarify your purpose** • What is the primary purpose of the document? **Identify your target audience** • Who is the primary reader? • Who are the secondary readers? **Select the type of communication needed** • Is the appropriate form an email, memo, letter, report—or some other kind of document?
Step 2. Gather and Organize Information Goal: To cover your topic logically and provide accurate and adequate information	**Decide what to include** • What is the primary topic you need to cover? • Are there secondary topics? **Gather information** • What information is needed to achieve the goal? • Is it accurate and complete? **Organize information** • What is the best way to organize the information?

CONTINUED 

QUICK REFERENCE 56.1 → CONTINUED

Step 3. Write Goal: To create a first draft that achieves its purpose	**Develop main points** • Organize content into paragraphs. • Provide supporting ideas and details. • Write concisely and clearly. **Format for function and effectiveness** • Include standard parts for the particular type of document. • Format elements for readability, visual appeal, and business standards (headings, bold face, numbering, spacing, margins, and so on). **Develop graphics if required.** • Determine the type of graphics. • Format appropriately (titles, captions, call-outs, and so on).
Step 4. Revise and Edit Goal: To improve the content, writing style, and structure of the document	**Review content and organization** • Is there unnecessary information? • Is writing clear? • Are points in logical order? **Review paragraphs and sentences** • Does each paragraph cover one main point with supporting details? • Are sentences structured correctly? • Is punctuation correct? • Are there unnecessary words? **Review word usage** • Is word choice precise? • Are there wordy expressions that can be edited? • Is word choice appropriate to the right tone and style for the audience?

CONTINUED →

QUICK REFERENCE 56.1 → CONTINUED

Step 5. Proofread	Proofread content and format
Goal: To eliminate errors in spelling, grammar, punctuation, and formatting	• Are there typographical or spelling errors? • Are there errors in grammar, punctuation, or capitalization? • Are words inadvertently omitted? • Are there word division, usage, or abbreviation errors? **Check accuracy and consistency** • Are figures, names, etc., correct and consistent? • Is information such as dates, times, etc., correct? **Check format and appearance** • Does the document have the standard parts? • Are the parts formatted correctly? • Are spacing and margins correct and consistent? • Is line spacing consistent and done according to standard guidelines? • Is page layout attractive and appropriate to the content? • Are all elements necessary to a complete document present and formatted correctly?

57 PLANNING

57a Clarifying the Purpose for Writing

It is much easier to write fluidly when you know precisely what you want the communication to accomplish. What does the situation call for? In business, the specific purpose will usually fall under one of the following broad categories:

- To pass on information
- To respond to questions and requests
- To make requests

- To instruct or direct
- To persuade

Section Eight of this book provides specific guidelines and examples for assistance in developing documents that fall into these general categories. This section focuses on principles that can be applied to all of these purposes and most others that you might encounter.

Think in terms of both the general and the specific to define your writing purpose. A general purpose would be to inform; a specific purpose would to be report on the status of a project. This thought process aids in determining the following:

- The appropriate medium (letter, email, report, and so on)
- The level of formality required (very informal to formal)
- The language and tone (friendly, official, familiar, unfamiliar)
- The content (scope and depth of information)
- The length
- The opening and closing

57b Identifying Your Reader

Although the reader for routine communications may be obvious to you, it always helps to think about the intended audience before writing. Consider the following:

YOUR RELATIONSHIP TO THE READER

This determines the appropriate medium (email, letter, and so on) and the style in which the message is delivered—the language (choice of words) and tone.

WHAT YOU WANT YOUR READER TO THINK OR DO

The purpose for writing determines this; clarifying it beforehand will lead to clarity for the recipient. If a specific action is desired, this needs to be explicitly stated.

57c Selecting the Best Form of Communication

The purpose for writing and the intended audience determine the appropriate medium. For routine business communications, the most common forms of communication are:

- Informal email message
- Formal email message in place of a printed letter
- Letter on company letterhead

- Memorandum on a printed memo form
- Report or other document in memo form or on plain paper
- Bound reports and publications

The following questions help to determine the appropriate form:

- Is this a formal or informal communication?
- Is this communication being sent internally, externally, or both?
- Do I want the receiver to share this communication with others?
- Do I need a permanent, printable record of this communication?
- Do I want the receiver to be able to have a permanent printable record of this communication?

[Read more on formal versus informal communications in Section Seven: Writing Style and format for specific types of business documents in Sections Eight through Eleven.]

58 GATHERING AND ORGANIZING INFORMATION

Simple writing tasks don't require much organizing, but it is always helpful to spend a few minutes thinking about or listing the information you intend to include in a written communication, and then sorting through and organizing the ideas. For long, complex writing projects, this step is, of course, essential.

58a Deciding What to Include

Another way to look at it is to decide what *not* to include—the two are certainly of equal importance. The following guidelines will help with this decision:

AVOID INFORMATION OVERLOAD

Avoiding extraneous information or bogging the reader down in too many details is the key to producing crisp, clear communications. Providing just the right amount of information will help ensure that yours gets the attention it deserves.

TRY TO COVER ONE TOPIC PER DOCUMENT

Businesspeople prefer reading short documents; they often skim longer ones and may stop reading before they get to the end. To keep documents at a manageable length, it is best to avoid covering unrelated topics. This is especially true with emails, where sticking to a single topic aids in creating a thread of responses that can be filed by topic or project.

When unsure about the "right" amount of information, answering the following questions will help:

- What does my reader want or need to know?
- How much background information is needed?
- What do I want my reader to do with this information?
- What information will help my reader give me the response I need?

When writing for more than one reader, consider how to balance possible differences in their level of knowledge about the topic.

58b Evaluating Information

Having all necessary materials on hand speeds the process of drafting, allowing ideas to flow undisrupted. In addition to having resources on hand, the quality of the information is a key concern. Quick Reference 58.1 provides guidelines on evaluating information gathered in preparation for writing.

After settling on the information to be used, be sure to keep clear notes regarding the use of any copyrighted material to ensure proper citation in the final document. For information on documenting sources and styling citations, see Section Nine: Reports, Proposals, and References, Topics 82-84.

QUICK REFERENCE 58.1

Evaluating the quality of information sources

- **Is the information accurate?** Does it come from a reliable source that can be verified and documented?
- **Is the information current?** Are there copyright dates or other indicators that this is the most up-to-date information on the topic?
- **Is the information relevant?** Does it directly relate to the purpose of the communication? Does the audience need the information in order to make a decision or take action?
- **Is the information sufficient and complete?** Is there enough and is anything important missing; for example, citations for quotes or original sources for images?
- **Is data accurate?** Are names, dates, prices, titles, statements, and so on correct? Did they come from reliable sources?

58c Organizing Information

Think about each communication as having a beginning, a middle, and an end—each with its own purpose. The following applies to writing a single paragraph, several paragraphs, or a long document.

BEGINNING

- Introduces a main idea or subject
- Gets the reader's attention
- Establishes a positive tone

MIDDLE

- Contains more detailed information and support for the main idea
- Leads the reader logically to the intended conclusion

END

- States the conclusion and any action you want the reader to take
- Maintains (or re-establishes) a positive tone

After deciding what information to include, consider how to organize it. Quick Reference 58.2 lists the standard ways to order information in written communications.

QUICK REFERENCE 58.2

Options for ordering information

- Most important to least important
- Least important to most important
- Causes leading to some effect
- An effect followed by its causes
- Chronological or reverse chronological (first occurrence to last/last to first)
- Problem statement followed by proposed solutions
- Response to several questions in the order in which the questions are asked
- Steps in a process (first to last)
- Proposal or request followed by rationale

58d Creating an Outline

For complex documents it is a good idea to create a complete outline with as much detail as possible to aid the drafting process. On the computer it is easy to quickly list ideas (words and phrases), and then clarify your thinking by cutting and pasting them into the most logical sequence and content areas. Quick Reference 58.3 shows a standard outline format.

QUICK REFERENCE 58.3

Standard outline format

I. First Major Heading
  A. First subheading
  B. Second subheading
    1. Supporting point
    2. Supporting point
      a. Detail
      b. Detail
  C. Third subheading
II. Second Major Heading
  A. First subheading
    1. Supporting point
    2. Supporting point
  B. Second subheading

[Read more on structuring headings in 85d and 85e.]

59 WRITING THE FIRST DRAFT

Writers have individual preferences for drafting, but a practice that works best for many is to dive in and write quickly. Let your purpose, reader, and organizational plan guide you, but don't let them stifle you. Keep going even if you occasionally lose your focus. It is more productive to add, delete, and reorganize after completing a first draft.

Stopping to think too much, to make corrections, or to revise while drafting can result in delays and blocks. A problem that seems like a problem early in the process might not be. Your feeling may change upon rereading or it might resolve itself as you go along.

59a Developing Main Points

The first draft needs to cover all the main points, whether they are in the proper order or not. If other thoughts come to mind, note them in brackets or bold letters, so the point won't be forgotten.

Include one main idea in each paragraph to systematically move the reader through the planned content, whether simple or complicated. The revision stage will be the time to step back and make sure the order of ideas is clear and logical.

Opening and closing paragraphs can be the most difficult. Draft them anyway and plan to review and revise as needed at the end of the process.

FIRST PARAGRAPH (THE OPENING)

The first paragraph should capture the reader's interest and state the purpose of the communication. Use direct language. Trying to introduce or lead up to a topic is a common writing mistake. If, when you read over what you have written, you find that your topic jumps into focus in the second or third paragraph, revise and make this your first paragraph.

Begin with what will most interest the reader. In the following example, the writer wastes the reader's time with an unnecessary introduction.

First draft: I am the vice president of the local chapter of the National Association of Retailers. We are planning our Annual Awards Luncheon, which attracts several thousand professionals each year. We are hoping that you might be able to attend as our guest speaker.

Compare the revision, which gets to the point:

Revision: I am writing on behalf of the Boston chapter of the National Association of Retailers to invite you to join us as guest speaker at our Annual Awards Luncheon on April 23, 20xx. The luncheon attracts several thousand professionals each year.

In the first example, the writer spends time with a personal introduction and an attempt to pump up the organization's event, but the reader has no idea why. In the revision, the reader's interest is aroused by a direct invitation. By cutting the explanations to the essentials, the reader is spared unnecessary verbiage, such as the writer's title—which the reader will find in the closing of the letter or email or on stationery letterhead.

LAST PARAGRAPH (THE CLOSING)

In the last paragraph, summarize your point concisely, and conclude with a statement of what you want from the reader. Ask for specific actions in clear terms. If there is a deadline, give an exact date.

The following example is a vaguely written last paragraph related to the previous example:

First draft: It is our hope that you will be able to accept our invitation. Our association is looking forward to getting your response as soon as possible. If there is any additional information you need, please don't hesitate to let me know.

Revision: We sincerely hope that you will accept our invitation. I will need to have your response no later than Friday, February 15. This will allow us to get our publicity out in time to ensure a full house. If you need any additional information, please contact me by email or phone.

The revision includes a clear deadline and an incentive—no one wants to speak to a half-empty room.

[Read more on paragraph development in Topic 63.]

59b Avoiding Writer's Block

Following the early steps in the writing process should eliminate the possibility of **writer's block**—the inability to get words on the page. After the step of adequate planning and organizing is completed, feeling blocked is likely due to stress about the task or topic, or a lack of focus. Taking a break is often an easy solution, but if writer's block doesn't dissipate quickly, here are some additional steps to take:

- **Skip the opening and move forward.** Not feeling sure about the opening might be the sticking point, so start in the middle. Once the body of the message is written, it will be easier to find the words for the introduction—or it might turn out that where you started is actually the right opening.
- **Don't expect the first draft to be the final draft.** Stick to the writing process and plan to revise. Move through the first draft quickly, and then go back to add, edit, and delete.
- **Don't stop to change words and sentences.** Save this for the revision stage. It's more important not to slow down your train of thought while drafting. Stopping to change details is distracting and can make it hard to get back on track.
- **Don't worry too much about organization.** Trying to stick too closely to an outline can be stifling. Often, order is clarified and logic becomes more apparent during the writing process itself.

- **Don't worry about formatting details.** Plan to do this in the final step to avoid wasting time carefully formatting material that you might end up moving or deleting.

59c Formatting for Function and Effectiveness

In business writing, form can be as important as content. Taking the time to include all the necessary elements and to correctly format them is a necessary step in completing the draft of any business document. It is what makes the difference between a professional communication and one that may be judged sloppy, incomplete, or even insulting to the recipient.

Format is the physical layout of type on the page. Considering the visual appeal of a communication can be as important as thinking about the content. Readers do not like documents with dense type and long paragraphs that make reading an unappealing chore. Improve readability by keeping paragraphs as short as possible and using formatting techniques such as bulleted or numbered lists, headings, and line spacing to create white space on the page. This makes it easier for readers to scan the material and places less strain the eyes.

[See Section Ten: Document Design, Graphics, and Multimedia for additional guidelines.]

59d Formatting Techniques

Quick Reference 59.1 lists formatting techniques that make written documents more readable.

QUICK REFERENCE 59.1

Formatting techniques

- **Spacing.** Standard format requires single or 1.5 line spacing for text and an extra space between paragraphs in proportion to the regular line spacing.
- **Paragraph length.** Try to open with a short paragraph to introduce your main idea; avoid overly long paragraphs throughout.
- **Headings.** In longer documents, or short ones that can be broken into topics, use headings to alert the reader to a change in topic. Headings show organization of information and make it easy for the reader to skim and find each topic.
- **Parallel structure.** Use consistent language (wording and parts of speech) for headings and listed items. This kind of consistency enhances readability by clarifying the relationship of ideas and supporting details.

CONTINUED →

QUICK REFERENCE 59.1 → CONTINUED

- **Bulleted and numbered lists.** Use numbers when the order of items is important for logic, chronology, or ranking; otherwise, bullets are an easy and attractive way to format lists.
- **Highlighting.** Boldface, italics, underlining, all caps, and variation in font style, size, and color are all effective tools for highlighting information and showing relationships. Be careful not to overuse these elements by following the guidelines in Section Ten of this manual.
- **Visual aids.** Some information, for example, facts and figures, is more easily understood in visual format. Consider whether use of tables, graphs, or charts will enhance the content of your document.

[Read more on formatting specific types of documents in the following sections: Section Eight: Email, Memos, and Letters; Section Nine: Reports, Proposals and References; and Section Eleven: Business and Employment Communications. For general guidelines on formatting and designing text and visuals, see Section Ten: Document Design, Graphics, and Multimedia.]

60 REVISING AND EDITING THE DRAFT

Start the revision by considering aspects of your writing that affect the whole piece: content, organization, and formatting. Once those aspects are sound, work from the next-largest units to the smallest—from paragraphs to sentences, to words, and finally to punctuation. This process defines the minor difference between the terms *revise* and *edit*, which are often used interchangeably. **Revising** involves reviewing the draft from the "big picture" perspective—scope of content, clarity of expression, logical flow of ideas, structure of the document as a whole. **Editing** involves more detailed analysis—sentence placement within a paragraph, sentence structure, tone, and word choices. After all, it makes no sense to struggle to find just the right word for a sentence when you might remove the entire paragraph.

Revise as many times as necessary, given the time allotment and your level of satisfaction with how well the document has achieved your purpose. Most writers can't avoid revising and editing simultaneously to some degree, and there is nothing wrong with that. However, a final edit is always a good idea.

[Read more on style at the sentence and word level in Section Seven: Writing Style.]

60a Revising Content and Organization

The best way to critically read your own writing and see it from the reader's point of view is to get some distance from the first draft. Time away from the draft strengthens objectivity. It will be easier, for example, to notice if ideas are out of order or repeated or if a sentence is unclear. The words on the page will speak more clearly for themselves with less interference from what you thought you were saying while drafting.

FOCUS ON THE DOCUMENT AS A WHOLE

In the first phase of revising, consider the document as a whole. Ask the following:

- Have I achieved my intended purpose?
- Have I included the right amount of information?
- Have I organized the information logically and clearly?
- Do I need to add or delete content?

Now is the time to adjust the contents (reorganize, add, or delete) before proceeding with further revisions. Mark up the copy and make notes, but try not to get caught up in correcting errors that can wait for the proofreading stage. Use the checklist in Quick Reference 60.1 as a guide.

QUICK REFERENCE 60.1

Checklist for revising the document as a whole

Read through the whole document to assess whether it achieves its intended purpose, contains the right amount of content, presents information in the right order, and uses the right tone for the reader.

Content

- Will the reader readily identify the purpose of the document?
- Is all necessary information covered?
- Does anything need to be cut?
- Is there content that should be added?
- Is the style and tone suitable for the situation and the reader?
- Will the reader know exactly what is wanted?

Organization

- Is the information presented in a logical order?
- Does the order of information clearly connect ideas?
- Does the order of information lead to the intended conclusion?
- Is the relative importance of ideas/details logically presented?
- Is the conclusion clear and positive?

60b Revising and Editing Paragraphs and Sentences

Begin revising at the paragraph level, by reviewing the main point statements and then reading each sentence to be sure the idea is not repeated but expanded upon. Ask yourself if each sentence serves to support the main idea. Use the checklist in Quick Reference 60.2 for this review and see the related topics in Section Seven for more on these elements of writing style.

QUICK REFERENCE 60.2

Checklist for revising and editing paragraphs and sentences (Topics 63 and 64)

Review each paragraph to look for ways to improve the details of the message.

- Does the opening paragraph capture the reader's attention?
- Does it clearly state the purpose?
- Does it focus on the reader's point of view?
- Do middle paragraphs state a main point and develop it logically?
- Do paragraphs contain sentences that form a clear organizational structure and logical flow of ideas?
- Is the last paragraph a concise conclusion?
- Does it leave the reader with an understanding of how to respond?

Review each sentence critically and look for the following:

Grammar and structure

- Are sentences grammatically complete? Are there run-on sentences, comma splices, or sentence fragments?
- Are sentences grammatically correct? Are subjects/verbs and pronouns/antecedents in agreement?
- Are phrases and clauses arranged to emphasize the most important ideas? Would some ideas come across more effectively if they were moved to the beginning or the end of the sentence?
- Are modifying words, phrases, and clauses as close as possible to the sentence elements they modify?
- Are series of elements and listed items expressed in parallel structure?

CONTINUED

QUICK REFERENCE 60.2 → CONTINUED

Sentence variety (63a)

Read sentences and pay attention to the patterns. Too much similarity in length and structure makes writing uninteresting and difficult to follow. Consider these questions:

- Is there variation in sentence length and structure?
- Are there places where sentences in succession all have the same structure?
- Are sentences too long or too short?
- Is the same rhythm repeated without variety, creating a monotonous tone?

If your answer is "yes" to any of these questions, edit those sentences to vary their structure and length.

Active versus passive voice (63b)

- Are most sentences in the active voice?
- Is the passive voice used appropriately for emphasis?

This is another way in which sentences should be varied, depending upon the emphasis you are looking for. Use the active voice most of the time, but not *all* the time.

[Read more on writing paragraphs and sentences and on writing style and tone in Section Seven: Writing Style.]

60c Revising and Editing Words

Reviewing word choice can be done throughout the revision process, and then one more time to ensure a polished document with concise and appropriate language. Use Quick Reference 60.3 as you revise words and see the related topics in Section Seven.

QUICK REFERENCE 60.3

Checklist for editing word choice (Topic 65)

Consider the individual words and ask these questions:

- Does each word contribute to clarifying the message?
- Are there "wordy" phrases that could be more concise?
- Are words in the proper order? (Sometimes word order is inadvertently changed while revising.)

CONTINUED →

QUICK REFERENCE 60.3 ➤ CONTINUED

- Is word usage precise and appropriate?
- Does the choice of words fit the intended tone and degree of formality?
- Are pronoun references clear? Do you need to remove a pronoun and repeat the reference, provide a missing reference, or revise a sentence to avoid pronoun confusion?
- Are there any "big words" that should be replaced with more common terminology for clarity?
- Are there any technical words, abbreviations, or business jargon that the reader might not understand?
- Are there any negative words that could be changed to make your message sound more positive?
- Do any words reflect bias or other lack of consideration for the reader?

[Read more on choosing the right words in your writing in Section Seven: Writing Style.]

61 PROOFREADING

When you have completed revising and polishing your writing, you are ready to proofread. Try to put some time between the task of final polishing and proofreading. It is easier to spot errors when some time elapses between readings of a document.

61a Proofreading Techniques

- **Use your spelling and grammar checker**, but keep in mind that it is not capable of finding all types of errors.
- **Generate a printout to proof and mark changes on paper.** This is the best way to spot errors, especially in long documents. (See Figure 6.1 for standard proofreading marks.) If you proofread on the computer screen, advance the copy line by line and make corrections as you go.
- **Proofread with a partner.** Read aloud from a copy while your partner checks against the final document. It is easier to catch subtle mistakes with a fresh set of eyes—and ears. Reading aloud to yourself can also uncover subtle errors.

QUICK REFERENCE 61.1

Checklist for proofreading

Spelling and word usage

Use your spelling checker to correct typographical errors and misspellings; then look for the types of errors that spelling checkers don't find.

- Omitted words
- Grammar, punctuation, and capitalization errors
- Word usage errors
- Words transposed
- Hyphenation errors
- Missing *s* and/or apostrophe in plurals and possessives

Accuracy and consistency

- Spelling of names and other proper nouns
- Inconsistencies in expression of abbreviations, numbers, or symbols
- Errors or inconsistencies in names, titles, addresses, dates, time (double-check against original sources when necessary)

Format and appearance

- Are the standard elements required for the type of document included (e.g., letter parts, report parts, and so on)?
- Are the parts formatted correctly and consistently?
- Are margins and line spacing standard for the type of document?
- Are margins and line spacing consistent?
- Is the font style and size appropriate and consistent?
- Are headings of equal weight typed in the same style?
- Is spacing above and below headings consistent?
- Is spacing between paragraphs treated consistently?
- Are there extra spaces between words or at the end of sentences?
- Does the document need headers or footers?

THE WRITING PROCESS

61b Proofreading Marks

This universal proofing language is used to mark printed copy.

Proofreading Marks	Draft Copy	Final Copy
// Align vertically	// Diane Garner Vice President	Diane Garner Vice President
≡ Capitalize	new year's eve	New Year's Eve
/ Change capital to lowercase	Holiday	holiday
][Center	] memo [	memo
⁀ Close space	stock holder	stockholder
‾^ Change word(s)	they ~~was~~ were not sure	they were not sure
∿∿ Change to boldface	The deadline is June 15.	The deadline is **June 15.**
—— Change to italics	I read Wuthering Heights.	I read *Wuthering Heights.*
Delete or omit	beginn to change, and	begin to change and
^ Insert comma	Sarasota FL	Sarasota, FL
^ Insert semicolon	exchange consequently,	exchange; consequently,
^ Insert colon	the following two pairs of shoes	the following: two pairs of shoes
^ insert period	close of business	close of business.
^ Insert hyphen	timeout or close out	time-out or close-out
^ Insert apostrophe	womens clothing	women's clothing
^ Insert quotation mark	priced as marked	"priced as marked"

FIGURE 6.1 Proofreading Marks

Mark	Marked copy	Corrected copy
# ^ Insert space	fountain#pen	fountain pen
Move left	I. Labor Relations A. Negotiations	I. Labor Relations A. Negotiations
Move right	24,000 15,250	24,000 15,250
.... stet Retain deleted characters/words	If you, Harry, and I go (stet)	If you and I go
ss Single space	This plan is under ss consideration now	This plan is under consideration now
ds Double space	ds This plan is under consideration now	This plan is under consideration now
sp or ○ Spell out	(5) days in (NYC)	five days in New York City
Start a new line	(1) Duplicate the report (2) Send it Express Mail	(1) Duplicate the report (2) Send it Express Mail
¶ Start a new paragraph	Days. ¶ We are ready.	Days. We are ready.
Transpose words or characters	Mr. Pickerign	Mr. Pickering
	the materials relevant	the relevant materials
Move as shown	soon after we will be leaving	we will be leaving soon after
Run in; no new line	Four years. We'll be	Four years. We'll be

WRITING STYLE

section seven

7 Writing Style

62 DEFINING WRITING STYLE

The words a writer chooses and how they are constructed into sentences define an individual writer's style. Style reflects the relationship between the writer and the reader and the decisions made about how to best accomplish the purpose of a communication. A melding of personal style with Standard English usage and an appropriate level of formality is the ideal mix in business writing. To achieve this mix requires an awareness of language usage and sentence structure as the building blocks of each piece of writing.

62a Varying Writing Style

It is natural and appropriate to vary writing style for different tasks and projects, keeping in mind the relationship to the reader and the purpose. This is something that happens naturally in the ordinary course of business writing because it is comparable to how we adapt our speaking style according to the situation. Quick Reference 62.1 breaks down and gives some examples of the common style variations required in the business environment.

62b Choosing the Appropriate Tone

Tone is a somewhat abstract element that is not easy to pin down and define. Simply put, it is a combination of *what* you say and *how* you say it. Tone reveals your attitude toward your audience and topic. It operates like "tone of voice," in speaking, minus the intonations and body language that contribute to a listener's interpretation of oral and person-to-person communications. In writing, choice of words and sentence construction alone create tone.

Tone is closely related to level of formality. Casual language—slang, messaging shorthand, and non-Standard English—have little place in the business environment. As a rule, business writing leans more toward formality. But don't interpret "formality" as dull and drab. Lively and friendly language is absolutely necessary to good business communication. The essential skill is the ability to adapt writing to fit the situation, as outlined in Quick Reference 62.1.

QUICK REFERENCE 62.1

Levels of formality in business writing

Casual	Writing can be conversational; there is little need to polish or pay close attention to wording—it just gets to the point.
Example	An email to a close colleague or friend inside the company about a routine or personal business matter.
Informal	Writing needs to be polished—grammatically correct and error-free. Language can be adjusted to reflect the relationship between writer and reader.
Examples	Communications to internal and external colleagues about everyday business matters—meetings, projects, requests for information, responses to requests, short reports. The majority of emails exchanged daily in business are informal.
Formal	Writing requires close attention and adherence to Standard English and business writing style, as opposed to individual (conversational) style and tone.
Examples	Letters, official memos, reports, and other documents written to communicate important information and to record transactions and agreements.
Legal	Writing requires specialized language and legal expertise; often using standard wording, format, and style.
Examples	Documents related to legal transactions: contracts, letters of agreement, letters discussing legal matters and disputes.
Ceremonial	Writing for special and official occasions, often using standard wording, format, and style.
Examples	Proclamations, invitations, programs.

63 WRITING STRONG PARAGRAPHS

63a Structuring Paragraphs

Paragraphs have a typical structure with three basic parts:

THE TOPIC SENTENCE

The topic sentence tells the reader in a general way what the paragraph is about. The topic sentence doesn't always have to be the first sentence; it can be placed in the middle of a paragraph and even at the

QUICK REFERENCE 63.1

Paragraph development

Structuring paragraphs

- State the main idea clearly (introduction)
- Focus on a single idea (unity)
- Support the main idea (details, examples, facts)
- Help the reader understand relationships (transitions)
- Help the reader form a conclusion (summary)

Developing paragraph unity and coherence

- Create unity by focusing on one main idea
- Create coherence by using introductory statements, transitions, and summary statements to show relationships between ideas

Connecting paragraphs with transitions

- Stress the connection between ideas by using transitional words and phrases

end. If the topic sentence is the first sentence, it should provide a smooth transition from the previous paragraph by showing the connection. (See 63c.) Sometimes, for emphasis, it is better to begin with the details, building up to a concise statement of the topic at the end of the paragraph.

SUPPORTING SENTENCES

There is no hard and fast rule about how long a paragraph should be, but three to five sentences is a good rule of thumb. Breaking long paragraphs into shorter ones avoids the appearance of density that can be a turnoff for some readers. The "right" level of detail supports the main idea and ensures clarity without overloading the reader. Keep in mind that balance is essential. Too many details can cause confusion as to what is important and what isn't. This is where having a plan and knowing your reader are essential. [See Section Six: The Writing Process.]

An email message as simple as the following can be ineffective because it leaves several questions unanswered.

First draft: The next meeting of the department retreat committee will be on Thursday at the usual time and place. Please arrive promptly and be prepared to discuss your progress. It will take about an hour.

Several important details are missing: the date, time, and place. It is not sufficient to assume that the recipients already know this information. Providing the details is a courtesy to the reader, as follows:

Revision: The next meeting of the department retreat committee will be on Thursday (7/19) from 2:30 to 3:30 in the 3rd floor conference room. Please be prepared to discuss progress on your assigned tasks. If you cannot attend, please let me know and send me a note on your progress so I can fill in for you. Thanks for your time.

The revision not only provides the specifics, but it also builds rapport. It eliminates the "please arrive promptly" directive, which is officious and demanding in tone. It expresses appreciation and offers an alternative if there are scheduling conflicts. This is considerate, since the date and time were set without prior discussion. In this case, the right balance of detail combines facts, alternatives, and a generous amount of courtesy.

SUMMARY SENTENCE

The **summary sentence** (usually the final sentence in the paragraph) ties together the details and points the reader forward. Not every paragraph needs a summary; a transitional word or phrase that connects ideas from one paragraph to another is often more appropriate. This is especially true when text is lengthy and needs to be broken up for readability, even though the ideas are closely related. A summary sentence at the end of a closing paragraph of a letter or a section of a longer document is more of a necessity.

63b Developing Paragraph Unity and Coherence

A good paragraph is a group of sentences that focus on a main idea. This focus is called **unity.** Good paragraphs also help the reader understand relationships between main ideas and their supporting details, and between main ideas from one paragraph to the next. This clarity of relationships is called **coherence.** It is achieved by providing introductory statements, transitions, and summary statements as described in 63a. Both unity and coherence improve when a paragraph is structured well, so that ideas build on one another and connect clearly in the reader's mind.

Contrast the following two paragraphs, which describe the same event:

First draft: Within minutes after meeting the interviewer, the applicant began to ask interesting and thoughtful questions about the company where she hoped to work. The interviewer talked about the company: its history, its achievements, and its goals for the future. He taught her much about the company's priorities and values. For example, this company was researching ways to recycle its products before most people even knew about recycling. It also won an industry award for outstanding customer service. She knew a lot about the company, and she got the job.

Revision: The applicant's job interview went well. Within minutes after meeting the interviewer, she began to ask interesting and thoughtful questions about the company where she hoped to work. Her questions prompted the interviewer to talk about the organization. By the time the interviewer began asking questions, the applicant knew quite a lot about the company's history, achievements, goals, priorities, and values. This knowledge helped her answer the questions about her potential role in the company, and she got the job.

The draft seems to be about an interview, but it lapses into a discussion of the company. It then returns briefly to the interview. The main idea is difficult to identify, and the paragraph lacks coherence. Because the paragraph has no clear main idea, it leaves questions about how the details relate to one another.

By contrast, the revision contains a main idea that is easy to identify: the woman's interview went well. Furthermore, all the details in the paragraph support this idea; the paragraph has unity. Its coherence is also better than that of the first paragraph. The stated main idea increases the coherence. In addition, the writer repeats phrases to show the reader how the ideas fit together. Notice how the following phrases help to make the paragraph coherent: *Within minutes, Her questions, By the time,* and *This knowledge*.

63c Connecting Paragraphs with Transitions

The most effective way to show the connection between ideas in paragraphs is to use transitional words and phrases. Missing opportunities to make these connections is a common flaw in writing.

Transitional words and phrases are cues that guide the reader. They make writing clear and logical. Read the draft email in Figure 7.1 on summer hours, and note how the paragraphs and sentences often begin as if nothing had come before them. Then read the revised version in Figure 7.2, after the writer added transitions.

FIGURE 7.1 First Draft Email

FROM: Human Resources
DATE: May 1, 20xx
TO: All Department Heads
SUBJECT: Summer Hours

There is a need to develop a plan for summer hours that is not disruptive to the company's operations. Last year's practice of closing early on Fridays during July and August did not work satisfactorily and will not be continued this year.

The directors feel that there should be some relief during the hot summer months. We propose each employee be permitted to take every second Friday off. Schedules must be set so that half the office staff is at work every Friday. To make up the "lost" time, each employee is required to extend his or her working hours by one hour each day.

This is only a proposal, and it will not become policy until each of you has had an opportunity to consider it. All concerns or comments will be considered, but a decision must be made no later than Tuesday May 16.

FIGURE 7.2 Revised Email

FROM: Human Resources
DATE: May 1, 20xx
TO: All Department Heads
SUBJECT: Summer Hours

A survey of managers revealed that last year's practice of closing early on Fridays during July and August did not work satisfactorily and should not be continued this year. *However*, management would like to develop a plan for summer hours that is not disruptive to the company's operations.

We propose, *therefore,* that each employee be permitted to take every second Friday off. *To minimize disruption,* supervisors will be asked to set schedules so that half the office staff is at work every Friday. *In addition,* each department head will work with staff to develop satisfactory schedules, and arrange with individual staff members to devote extra hours during the regular week to maintain normal productivity.

This proposal, *currently under review by management,* will not become policy until each of you has also had an opportunity to consider it. All concerns or comments will be considered, but a decision must be made no later than Tuesday, May 16. *Therefore,* we need to hear from you by Friday, May 12.

Note how the italicized words connect the ideas and enhance readability. See Quick Reference 63.2 for a summary of how transitions can be used.

63d Selecting Transitional Words and Phrases

QUICK REFERENCE 63.2

Common transitions and the relationships they show

Purpose	Transitions
To introduce a topic or supporting idea	to begin, in addition, besides, also, moreover, furthermore, equally important, first, then, finally, another reason (possibility, idea, etc.)
To review a point	in other words, that is, in fact, in conclusion, to summarize
To show examples	for example, namely, including, for instance, as an illustration, specifically
To compare	likewise, as, similarly, in the same way
To contrast	however, but, yet, in contrast, on the contrary, nevertheless, otherwise, nonetheless, conversely, still, at the same time, on the one hand, on the other hand
To show cause or result	consequently, because, therefore, accordingly, thus, as a result, so
To concede a point	granted, of course, to be sure, certainly
To guide a reader through time	after, before, earlier, later, meanwhile, next, now, soon, subsequently, immediately, eventually, currently
To guide a reader through space	above, below, nearby, in front of, in back of, in the foreground, in the background, at the side, adjacent to, nearby, in the distance, here, there
To conclude	finally, in conclusion, to summarize, in summary, hence, in short, in brief

64 WRITING EFFECTIVE SENTENCES

The primary function of sentences is to express ideas in understandable units of thought. In doing so, they provide the unity and coherence of your message. By paying attention to individual sentences as you revise, and using techniques to improve the order and choice of words, you can improve your writing style. This topic covers stylistic aspects of sentence construction and the next topic covers word choice.

[Read more about grammar and sentence structure in Section One: Grammar.]

64a Varying Sentence Length and Structure

There is no fixed rule of acceptable sentence length, but you should generally avoid a series of either very lengthy sentences or short choppy ones. Both are likely to lose the reader's ability to focus for very long. Sentences of varying length make reading easier and more interesting. Consider these opening sentences from a letter accompanying a designer's work sent to a potential client.

> Thank you for agreeing to take a look at my design samples. I am very excited! I understand that you are not making a commitment, but should you decide that my work fits the concept you had in mind, I assure you that I will meet your deadline.

This writer managed to convey gratitude, enthusiasm, understanding of the reader's state of mind, and reassurance—all in three sentences of varying length.

Compare the following two paragraphs:

Lacks sentence variety: Yesterday we met with the clients. We took them to lunch at Rhonda's. We talked about our new line of golf clubs. They seemed to be interested. We will call again next week. We think we can make a sale.

Sentences vary: Yesterday we took the clients to lunch at Rhonda's to talk about our new line of golf clubs. They seemed interested, so we will call again next week. There is a good chance we will make a sale. [Note that the last sentence does not repeat the word *we*, which was used three times.]

QUICK REFERENCE 64.1

Key elements of effective sentences

Varying sentence length

- Combine short sentences with conjunctions (connecting words).
- Eliminate unnecessary words in lengthy sentences.
- Break long sentences into at least two sentences.
- Read each paragraph aloud and listen for places where the rhythm and flow could be improved by varying sentence length.

Using active versus passive voice

- In the active voice, the subject of the sentence acts.
- In the passive voice, the subject of the sentence is acted upon.
- The active voice generally delivers the message with more force.

Use the passive voice

- When the doer of the action is unknown or unimportant
- When the doer of the action should not be mentioned out of tact or diplomacy
- When the action is more important than the doer (as in formal reports)

Placing words and phrases for emphasis

- Place words for impact in a way that best expresses the main point of the sentence.
- The most emphatic position is at the end of the sentence.
- The second most emphatic position is the beginning of the sentence.

Using parallel (consistent) construction

- When connecting related ideas in a sentence, be consistent in the construction of the wording.
- Avoid shifting

  From a phrase with a subject and a verb to an *-ing* phrase

  From direct to conditional

  From active to passive voice

QUICK REFERENCE 64.2

Techniques for sentence variation

- Combine short sentences with conjunctions (connecting words).
- Use transitional words and expressions to connect ideas.
- Eliminate unnecessary words in lengthy sentences.
- Break long sentences into at least two sentences.
- Change the structure of sentences by moving subjects and verbs or clauses.
- Alternate between active/passive voice for emphasis/de-emphasis.

DETECTING LACK OF VARIETY

As you read and revise document drafts, consider these questions about each paragraph:

- Do the sentences have similar structures?
- Are the sentences about the same length?
- Do the sentences sound monotonous?
- Is the same rhythm repeated throughout the paragraph or document?

CREATING VARIETY IN LENGTH AND STRUCTURE

Connect two or more short sentences:

Original: We took them to lunch at Rhonda's. We talked about our new line of golf clubs.

Rewrite: We took them to lunch at Rhonda's and talked about our new line of golf clubs.

[Read more on connecting main clauses with commas and semicolons in Section One: Grammar and Section Two: Punctuation.]

Break up long, compound sentences to form two or more shorter ones.

Original: We took them to lunch at Rhonda's to talk about our new line of golf clubs, and they seemed interested, so we will call them next week to follow up.

Rewrite: We took them to lunch at Rhonda's to talk about our new line of golf clubs. They seemed interested, so we will call them next week to follow up.

Begin with something other than the subject of the sentence; for example, a dependent clause, a prepositional phrase, or an adverb.

Original: We took them to lunch at Rhonda's and talked about our new line of golf clubs.

Rewrite: Because we wanted more time to discuss our new line of golf clubs, we took them to lunch.

64b Using Active versus Passive Voice

The choice of active or passive voice can change the tone of a sentence or paragraph. The **active voice** places the emphasis on the action of the subject. The **passive voice** places the emphasis on the object that is acted upon.

Active voice: **John rented** a **car** for the drive upstate.

Passive voice: A **car was rented** by **John** for the drive upstate.

When you write in the active voice, the message is delivered clearly and forcefully.

Active: **I received** your letter of May 8 yesterday.

Passive: Your **letter** of May 8 **was received** yesterday.

OR

Your **letter** of May 8 **arrived** yesterday.

Notice that the first sentence in the active voice places the writer squarely in the center of the action. The second option is better when writing on behalf of your department or company.

Knowing how to create active and passive sentences allows you to choose what to emphasize or de-emphasize.

ACTIVE VOICE

The active voice is usually more effective because it is more concrete. It emphasizes the "doer" of the action. Active voice sentences are generally shorter, more direct, and easier to understand. The reader can easily identify the action being expressed. For example:

Active: Mary signed the check.

Passive: The check was signed by Mary.

In the first example, the doer of the action, Mary, is clearly doing the signing. The verb is short and clear. In the second sentence, the action is dulled by the helping verb *was,* and the doer of the action is de-emphasized. In this straightforward sentence, the active voice is much better; there is no reason to use the passive.

PASSIVE VOICE

There is a definite advantage, however, to using the passive voice when you want to de-emphasize the doer of the action.

> **Passive:** The decision to cancel year-end bonuses was made by management due to slow sales in the fourth quarter.

Management wants to soften the news, so the passive voice is chosen. Here are some additional cases where the passive voice is more effective:

- When the doer of the action is unknown or irrelevant

  The building was constructed in 1984.

  The order was shipped on Thursday.
- When the doer of the action should not be mentioned out of tact or diplomacy

  An error was made in the computation of your taxes.
- When the action is more important than the doer (as in formal reports)

  Forty charge account customers were surveyed regarding their spending habits.

64c Placing Words and Phrases for Emphasis

Placing words and phrases where they can create emphasis improves the quality of writing. Follow these general guidelines and see Quick Reference 64.3 for tips on how to use words for impact.

- Place words for impact in a way that best expresses the main point of the sentence.
- The most emphatic position is at the end of the sentence.
- The second most emphatic position is at the beginning.

64d Using Parallel (Consistent) Construction

When you connect two related ideas in a sentence, be consistent in the construction of the wording. This is known as **parallel construction.** Parallel construction helps the reader see the relationship of ideas.

QUICK REFERENCE 64.3

Placing words and phrases for emphasis

Be emphatic—avoid wordiness.

Dull:	There is no product superior to Zingo in the marketplace.
Emphatic:	No product in the marketplace is superior to Zingo. **OR** Zingo is superior to all other products in the marketplace.
Dull:	I feel it fitting to submit another high-quality manuscript to your publishing group.
Emphatic:	I am submitting another high-quality manuscript to your publishing group.
Dull:	Please prepare for your participation in the meetings that will be held next month.
Emphatic:	Please prepare for next month's meetings.

Let sentences build to a natural climax; don't put the ending in the middle.

Dull:	The DVD was defective when you sent it to me.
Emphatic:	The DVD you sent me was defective.
Dull:	We are asking you to lead the session because of your excellent work.
Emphatic:	Because of your excellent work, we are asking you to lead the session.
Dull:	You will find our services effective, timely, and essential and our prices reasonable, if you compare them to others.
Emphatic:	You will find our services comparatively effective, timely, essential, and reasonably priced.

In the following example, the first sentence shifts from a negative to a positive point of view and makes the meaning fuzzy. Keeping the construction parallel makes the meaning unmistakable.

Shift: **Do not** ignore traffic signals and **stay within** the speed limit.

Parallel: **Do not** ignore traffic signals and **do not** speed.

In the next example, the first sentence shifts from a phrase with a subject and a verb to an *ing* phrase. This makes the connection between the two parts of the sentence unclear. In the second sentence, both phrases have a subject and a verb and the connection between the two ideas is clear.

Shift: The job **is scheduled** for Friday and **will be taking** only a few hours to complete.

Parallel: The job **is scheduled** for Friday and **will take** only a few hours.

In the following example, the second instruction encourages doubts by shifting from direct ("turn on") to conditional ("you should decide"):

Shift: First **turn on the computer** and **then you should decide** which program to use.

Parallel: First **turn on the computer** and **then decide** which program to use.

In the next example, the first sentence changes voice from active to passive. The sentence reads better when both phrases use the active voice.

Shift: The power failure **lasted** several hours and **was the cause** of much ruined food.

Parallel: The power failure **lasted** several hours and **caused** much food to be ruined.

OR

The power failure **lasted** several hours and **ruined** a lot of food.

Also be aware of parallel construction for a series of phrases:

Shift: At our last meeting, the project marketing team decided **to conduct** a written survey, **produce** a prototype, and **we are going to hold** focus groups.

Parallel: At our last meeting, the project marketing team decided **to conduct** a written survey, **produce** a prototype, and **hold** focus groups.

[Read more about phrases and clauses in sentences in Section One: Grammar, Topics 3 and 4.]

65 USING WORDS EFFECTIVELY

65a Eliminating Unnecessary Words

Achieving sentence clarity and conciseness is a goal of the revision step of the writing process (see 6). Here are some techniques to apply.

- Read each sentence and look for extra words that clutter the message rather than make the point.
- Take out words that add neither detail nor information.
- Check for phrases that are common in speech, but contribute to clutter in writing. These phrases often use several words when one will suffice.
- Avoid repeating a word or phrase numerous times within a sentence or paragraph. If repetition of the idea is necessary, use a thesaurus to find a synonym.

NO: There are a number of items that we need to discuss.

YES: We need to discuss a number of items.

NO: They tried a variety of different long-distance services.

YES: They tried several long-distance services.

NO: Due to the fact that he was habitually late, his supervisor put him on probation.

YES: Because he was habitually late, his supervisor put him on probation.

QUICK REFERENCE 65.1

Replacements for commonly used wordy phrases

Wordy phrase	Replacement
advance planning	planning
all throughout	throughout OR all through
along the lines of	like
am (are) in a position to	can
are in possession of	have

CONTINUED→

QUICK REFERENCE 65.1 → CONTINUED

Wordy phrase	Replacement
assemble together	assemble, gather
as to whether	whether
at about	about
at all times	always
at the present time	now
at this (that) point in time	then
attached herewith	attached
by means of	by
check into	check
complete monopoly	monopoly
continue on	continue
cooperate together	cooperate
customary practice	practice OR custom
depreciate in value	depreciate
due to the fact that	since, because, as
during the course of	during
each and every	every
for the purpose of	for, to
for the reason that	because
for your information	*Do not use* (except as FYI in informal documents)
final outcome	outcome
give consideration to	consider
in an angry manner	angrily
in due course	*Do not use* (give a specific time)
in many cases	often
information of a confidential nature	confidential information
in order to	to
in regard to	about, regarding
in spite of the fact that	although
in the event that	if, in case
in the city of Boston	in Boston
in the month of May	in May
in the near future	*Do not use* (give an approximate time frame)
is of the opinion that	believes
make an inquiry regarding	inquire about

CONTINUED→

QUICK REFERENCE 65.1 → CONTINUED

Wordy phrase	Replacement
make (made) the acquaintance of	meet (met)
new beginning	beginning
new record	record
notwithstanding the fact that	even though
past experience	experience
personal friend	friend
personal opinion	opinion
preliminary to	before
provided that	if
rarely ever	rarely
revert back	revert
service of a valuable nature	valuable service
she is a person who is often late	she is often late
he is a person you can trust	he is trustworthy
the fact that	*Do not use*
there is no doubt that	no doubt, doubtless
this is a person who	this person
with your kind permission	may
whole entire	whole OR entire (never use together)

65b Using Plain Language

Everyday words convey a message more forcefully than "big words." At all cost, avoid sounding pompous by attempting to write "to impress." Here are some additional guidelines.

- Avoid words that are unfamiliar to the average person.
- Avoid jargon except with the proper audience.
- Avoid "legalese" except in legal documents.
- Avoid vague words; aim for precise language.

Each industry and profession has its own **jargon**—words and acronyms used and understood within that field. These words can become so much a part of everyday speech that it is easy to overlook occasions when they are not appropriate for the reader. Always be aware of jargon and consider the audience when using it.

Quick Reference 65.2 lists pompous words and expressions that often creep into writing. Some of them are **legalese,** expressions appropriate in the legal field that have found their way into everyday language. Nevertheless, it is still better to use clear, plain language in business.

QUICK REFERENCE 65.2

Plain versus pompous language

Pompous words	Plain language	Pompous words	Plain language
advise	tell	initial	first
adjudicate	judge	initiate	begin, start
allege	say, claim	institute	start
am cognizant of	know	irregardless	regardless
at the present time	now, currently	it is my opinion that	I think
in receipt of	have	jeopardize	risk
ascertain	find out	perceive	see
assert	say	peruse	read
cease	stop	preplanning	planning
commence	start, begin	presume	think
converse	talk	purport	claim, mean
de facto	actual, in reality	remuneration	payment, fee
demonstrate	show	replete	full
enclosed, herewith	here is, here are	substantiate	prove
exited	left	superfluous	extra, unneeded
endeavor	try	supersedes	replaces
facilitate	help	take appropriate action	act
finalize	complete, finish, end	terminate	end
fundamental	basic	up to this time	until now
I regret to inform you	I am sorry that	utilize	use

65c Using Precise Language

Using precise language is the best technique for ensuring a clear understanding of a message. Follow these guidelines:

- Avoid starting sentences with weak phrases such as *In order to, Inasmuch as, This is to, I just want to say.* When sentences begin with *There is, There are, It is,* check to make sure these words are necessary.

- Let sentences build to a natural climax; place emphasis at the beginning or end, not in the middle.
- Use mechanical devices such as the exclamation point and dashes sparingly.
- Use **intensives**—words such as *much, very, such, too, highly, certainly, extremely, tremendously, really*—sparingly.

Imprecise words leave the reader guessing and vague words make writing dull or make the writer sound noncommittal. When it is not possible to be precise because information is not available, explain.

Vague	**Precise**
slowly	about 15 miles per hour
soon	by March 15
early afternoon	2 p.m.
Some parts remain in stock.	Twenty parts remain in stock.
I will send it shortly.	I will send it no later than next Friday.
The computer is not working.	The computer freezes when I attempt to print.
Please respond at your earliest convenience.	Please respond by November 10.
The new printer is very slow.	It takes 10 minutes to print a 100-page document on the new printer.

65d Achieving the Right Tone

Check words and phrases to ensure the appropriate tone for the audience and purpose. In general, use positive words and avoid negative ones. A positive tone can be achieved even when content is negative, usually by finding a way to turn a negative phrase around and make it positive. Here are some examples:

Negative	**Positive**
We do not hold reservations after 10 p.m.	We hold reservations until 10 p.m.
Your travel cash advance cannot be above $1,000.	Your travel cash advance can be up to $1,000.
We do not deliver on weekends.	We deliver Monday through Friday.
You will not be sorry. . .	You will be pleased. . .

Notice that the positive form is usually shorter and more direct.

AVOID THE WORD *NOT*

If a draft has a negative tone, look for sentences with the word *not* and see if they can be rewritten to make them positive. Often this requires nothing more than substituting a word or using a prefix that is less negative than *not*. The message remains negative, but the terms are actually more direct.

Negative	Positive
did not remember	forgot
did not know, not aware	unaware
not available	unavailable
not known	unknown
not on time	late
not possible	impossible
not sure	uncertain

AVOID EMOTIONALLY CHARGED WORDS

Many words tend to provoke negative feelings; avoid them by using substitutions that elicit positive emotions. Use a thesaurus if necessary.

Negative	Positive
blame	responsibility
cheap	inexpensive, less expensive
complaint	problem
defective	malfunctioning
error	mistake
fault	responsibility
overreaction	reaction
inadequate, inferior	does not meet our needs
problem	challenge, issue
reject	decline

BALANCE THE NEGATIVE BY SAYING SOMETHING POSITIVE

Sometimes negative news simply requires hitting on a positive way to balance the impact, as these examples show:

Negative: **Unfortunately,** your proposal did not meet the specifications for **the project.** [sounds cold; closes the door to future success]

Positive: **After careful review of your proposal,** we find that it does not meet the specifications for **this project.** [shows interest; leaves an opening for the future by referring to *this project*]

Negative: Because we found your request for a one-week turnaround **to be unreasonable, we are unable** to honor it. Our policy is at least 10 business days. [blames the reader for the problem; rejects the request]

Positive: Your request for a one-week turnaround **does not meet** our schedule guidelines, but **we can** have your order ready in 10 business days. [takes responsibility for the problem; offers to fulfill the request]

SENSE WHEN NEGATIVE PHRASES ARE BETTER

Every rule has exceptions, of course. Sometimes the negative construction will deliver the desired punch when you want to write an emphatic sentence:

We will always remember a client.

We never forget a client.

The second sentence, cast in a negative form, is somewhat more emphatic than the first.

HAVE EMPATHY FOR YOUR READER

Empathy is having a sense of how another person feels by imagining yourself in his or her position. One way to show empathy is to personalize messages by using personal pronouns, particularly *you* and *your* (but don't overdo it). This approach, sometimes called the "you attitude," is essential for writing that achieves harmony between sender and receiver. It uses *you* and *your,* but also employs other techniques for showing consideration for the reader's point of view. Compare the following drafts and revisions:

Draft: I would like to meet with you on Thursday afternoon to get some information. I am working on a presentation for the upcoming sales meeting and I need your help. I'm free at 3 p.m. and would like to come to your office.

The recipient has no idea why he or she should spend time in this meeting to help you with a presentation, or why you have set a date and time without consultation. This could be offensive and counterproductive.

Revision: Will you please meet with me on Thursday at 3 p.m.? I can come to your office. I'm in desperate need of your help on a presentation that's due in two weeks and I need to get started. I want to use some of your material. Thanks.

This version uses *please, you,* and *your,* but it still fails to consider the recipient's point of view. Although it conveys a sense of respect for the recipient's ability to provide assistance, unless the colleague is a very good friend, the sender still might not get the meeting. Here's a better approach.

Final Draft: I'm preparing a presentation for the sales meeting in Cincinnati two weeks from Friday. I would like to use some of the data you presented at the last staff meeting on regional buying habits and customer profiles. Your presentation was excellent and would add a lot of substance to my talk. If you don't mind sharing some of this material, I'd like to get together on Thursday so I could work on it over the weekend. How does your calendar look for the afternoon? Would 3 p.m. be okay? If not, please let me know what would work best for you.

This time the writer fully explains the purpose of the meeting and the request for material. The writer shows empathy by paying a compliment and acknowledging that the request might be refused. To avoid being vague, the writer offers a suggestion for a specific time, while also indicating deference to the recipient's schedule and time preference.

Empathizing with your reader also includes using audience-sensitive language as discussed in 65e, 65f, and 65g.

65e Using Audience-Sensitive Language—General Guidelines

Being sensitive to words that might offend the reader is a general rule that requires stopping to think about your audience and any special sensitivities its members might have. Make an effort to avoid words, examples, or images that reinforce negative stereotypes about groups or that are biased in favor of or against a specific cultural context. Also be sensitive to the needs of an audience for whom English is not the native language and take care to avoid idiomatic expressions and colloquial figures of speech. Provide international readers with context and definitions.

Here are some "dos" and "don'ts" that provide general guidance:

- Use plain language, but at the same time, be sensitive to changes in what is "politically correct" and stay abreast of current usage.
- When addressing a group, use language that would not make any person feel excluded, diminished, or devalued.
- Consider the native language of your audience; avoid idioms, jargon, and figurative language; provide context and definitions.
- Avoid using **euphemisms**—words used to camouflage unpleasant or politically incorrect words or phrases—when your "true" meaning will still be obvious and possibly offensive.
- Do, however, use euphemisms where they can be skillfully employed to avoid negative or insensitive wording. For example, in businesses *customer service* used to be known as the *complaint department* and *human resources* used to be *personnel*.

- While being sensitive to language that might offend or make others uncomfortable, also avoid going overboard with silly sounding "politically correct" terms, such as "visually challenged" for blind or "vertically challenged" for short.

65f Avoiding Gender-biased Language

Many general terms, especially job titles, have a historic male bias. These terms have more recent forms that are gender-neutral: *chair* or *chairperson* instead of *chairman, firefighter* instead of *fireman*, *police officer* instead of *policeman*. The custom of attaching *ess* or *ette* to a noun to create a feminine word for historically masculine roles has also disappeared. Instead, words like *server* for *waiter* and *waitress* and *actor* to refer to all members of the acting profession are now the norm.

[Read about use of personal pronouns to avoid gender bias in 6g.]

QUICK REFERENCE 65.3

Gender-neutral terminology

When making general references, choose a form without gender identification. These terms that include the word *man* have been replaced with gender-neutral terminology.

Outdated usage	Current usage
mankind	human beings, society, human race, humanity
manmade	synthetic, artificial, constructed, factory-made, plastic
manpower	workers, employees, crew, laborers, staff, workforce
workmen's compensation	workers' compensation
businessmen	executives, managers, businesspeople, business workers
cameraman	photographer, cinematographer, camera operator
chairman	chairperson, chair, leader, moderator, coordinator, facilitator, etc.
clergyman	member of the clergy, minister, rabbi, priest, etc.
congressmen	member of congress, congressmen and congresswomen, representatives, legislators
fireman	firefighter

CONTINUED →

QUICK REFERENCE 65.3 ➔ CONTINUED

Outdated usage	Current usage
insurance man	insurance agent
mailman	postal worker, mail carrier, letter carrier
male nurse	nurse
male secretary	secretary, assistant
policeman	police officer

WRITING STYLE

65g Using References to Groups

Be alert to changing terms for nationalities, races, religions, and other groups, such as persons with disabilities. Quick Reference 65.4 lists current terminology that is broadly accepted for such references. For example, hyphenating nationality designations is no longer appropriate when referring to minority groups of Americans: *Asian American, African*

QUICK REFERENCE 65.4

Terms used to refer to groups

Race, ethnicity, national origin

- Hispanic, Latino/Latina, Hispanic American, Mexican American, Cuban American
- American Indian, Native American, Inuit, Alaska native; use Indian for someone from India
- Asian, Asian American (or preferably Chinese, Chinese American, Vietnamese, Vietnamese American, and so on). **Do not use:** Oriental
- African American or black (keeping in mind that not all black Americans are direct descendants of Africans). **Do not use:** Afro-American.

People with disabilities

- People with disabilities or a person with a physical disability/impairment; wheelchair user, not wheelchair bound; deaf or hearing impaired; blind or visually impaired; developmentally impaired or disabled; learning disability/disabled. **Do not use:** handicapped, retarded. For guidelines on capitalizing references to groups see Topic 27.

American, Hispanic American, and so on. The term *Hispanic* itself has gone in and out of vogue—once having been relegated to government usage, and now more generally accepted, along with *Latino*.

Keep in mind, however, that it is preferable to think of people as individuals, and that citizens who are members of America's predominant minority groups are, first and foremost, Americans. Therefore, avoid identifying people by terms that signify their membership in a racial or ethnic group except when doing so is clearly relevant and appropriate.

part three

DOCUMENT CONTENT, FORMAT, AND DESIGN

EMAIL, MEMOS, AND LETTERS

section eight

66 EMAIL

Email is the primary means of communication in business and runs the gamut from very informal messages to formal communications. Another major use of email is to send documents as attachments, in place of using conventional mail or courier services. This section covers guidelines based on current business practices for writing **routine email messages** and more formal **email correspondence** used in place of printed memos and letters for communications within and outside of the organization.

66a The Email Template

THE TO WINDOW

- Include only the primary recipient(s)—those from whom a response might be expected.
- Use a semicolon or a comma to separate recipients' names/addresses.
- When names/addresses are automatically inserted from an address book, double-check to make the sure the correct one(s) are showing in the window.

THE COPY WINDOW

- Include secondary readers—they are not expected to respond.
- Separate names/addresses with a semicolon.

THE BLIND COPY WINDOW

Use blind copies sparingly. Normally, it is courteous to let the recipient know who is being copied, but blind copies are appropriate in the following instances:

- For a mass mailing outside the organization. Placing all addresses in the blind copy window protects the privacy of the recipients.
- When there is a valid reason not to let the recipient know who is being copied.
- When the primary recipient does not know the person being copied, for example, a team member or your manager.

Keep in mind that the recipient of a blind copy might reply or forward the email to the primary recipient or anyone else.

THE SUBJECT WINDOW

Limit the subject of each email to one topic, and avoid using general terms that need interpretation. There are several reasons for this:

- Limiting the topic means the email will be easier to organize and track.
- A clear specific Subject line helps the recipient prioritize your message.
- It will be easier for the recipient to decide if a response is needed and to respond quickly.

Vague	**Specific**
Meeting	May 15 Meeting
Travel Approval	Approval for Detroit Trip
Compensation	Staff Pay Increases
Vacations	Expiration of Vacation Days
Lunch	Are you free for lunch today?
Parsons Project	Costs on Parsons Project

Capitalizing the words in the Subject line is the norm in business email. Figure 8.1 is an example of a routine email message.

66b Email Messages

THE GREETING (SALUTATION)

For routine emails to coworkers and business associates, you may choose to open with a simple "Hi Chris," or "Chris," and close with your first name.

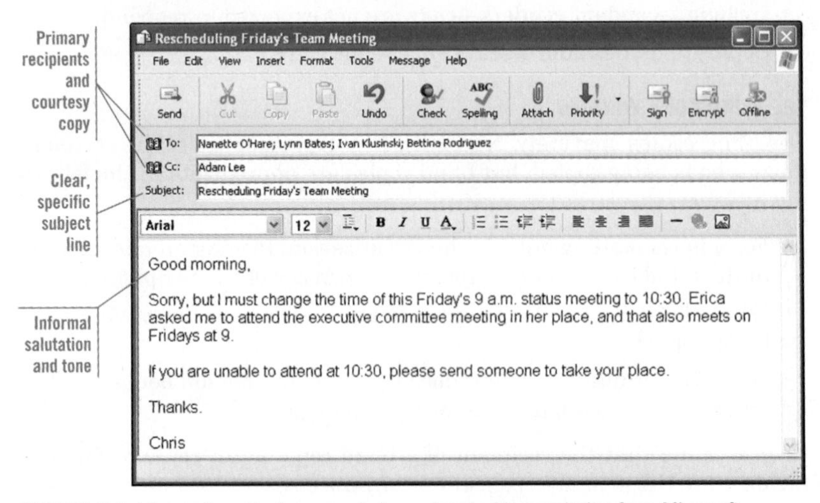

FIGURE 8.1 Microsoft product screen shots reprinted with permission from Microsoft Corporation.

It is also acceptable to use no opening or closing, which is the style used on traditional interoffice memos.

Email has opened the door to more freedom of personal expression and less formality in business writing. In the world of email etiquette, it is generally acceptable to address strangers on a first name basis. Often the traditional salutation is used with a comma to bridge the gap between formality and informality:

Dear Mary,

When writing an email that replaces a formal letter, however, it is more appropriate to use a traditional opening salutation:

Dear Ms. Lopez:

Dear Mary Lopez:

So long as the relationship with the reader dictates the choice, selecting the most suitable form should be easy. More formality is always better than less when you are not on familiar terms with your reader.

THE MESSAGE

The following are general guidelines for writing email messages for any level of formality:

- Limit each message to one topic.
- Write short, single-spaced paragraphs; do not indent paragraphs.
- Double-space between paragraphs.
- Consider your relationship to the recipient(s) and adjust your writing style and tone (level of formality, sentence structure, word choice) accordingly (see Section Six: The Writing Process and Section Seven: Writing Style).
- Observe the basic standards of good business writing, including correct grammar, punctuation, spelling, and usage.
- Remember that your email could be forwarded to others who might make judgments about your work.
- If you are sending an attachment, refer to it in the body of the message.
- If the attachment is a printed memo or letter that contains the substance of your message, do not repeat the content of the attachment in the email.
- Avoid unconventional type fonts and colors.
- Use bold, italics, and capitalization according to the same rules you would apply to printed communications on memo forms or letterhead.

- Remember that the format of the received mail may not replicate the format in which it was sent; avoid formatting problems and send an attachment instead.
- Follow the writing process—use the spelling and grammar checker, reread your draft, and correct errors, even when you are pressed for time.

THE CLOSING AND SIGNATURE

If an email has a salutation, a balancing **complimentary closing** is needed. In informal emails, the closing is a matter of personal choice. For more formal messages, choose a standard closing such as one of the following. See Figure 8.2 for an example of a formal email message.

Sincerely yours,

Sincerely,

Best regards,

Regards,

Cordially,

A **signature block** includes the sender's full name and contact information. This is especially important to include in nonroutine correspondence, but can be included in all messages.
Example of a signature block:

Barbara Westmaas
President
Wise Choices, Inc.
1275 Pine Court
Rosamond, CA 93560
Phone: 661-555-2222
Fax: 661-555-0000
bwestmaas@wci.org

66c Email Attachments

Email attachments are a quick and convenient way to send documents and other materials, such as images, Web pages, and publications. Indicate in the email what is being attached, and before hitting Send, double-check to make sure the correct file(s) is attached.

Sending large files or files created in specialized software programs might require checking with the recipient to make sure they can be opened. Converting files to PDF format makes them universally compatible. PDF files will not change format in the transmission process and the text cannot be manipulated by the recipient.

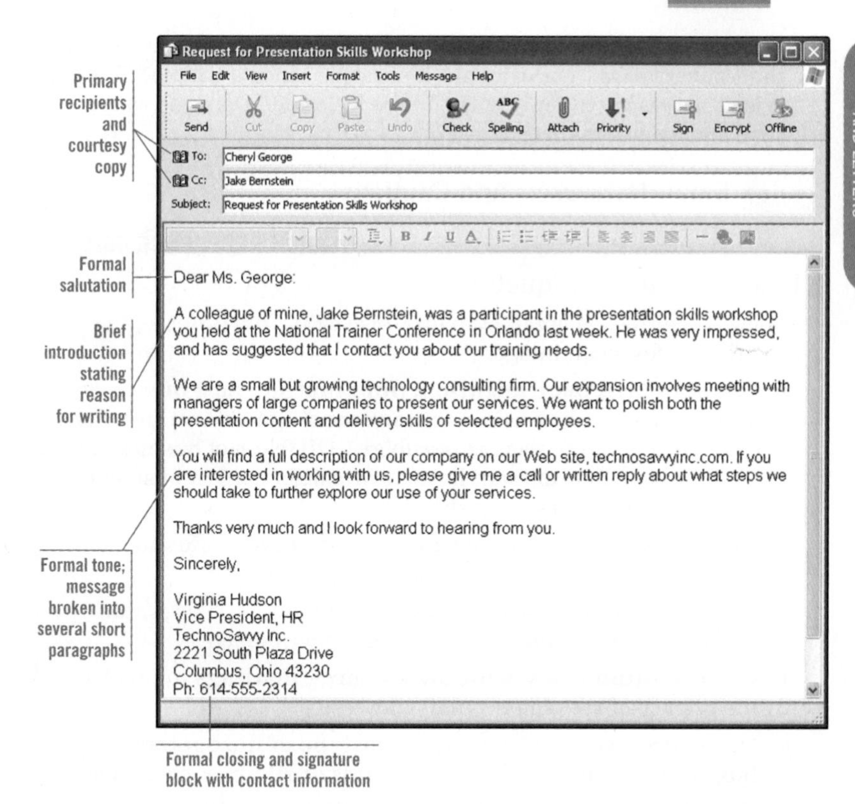

FIGURE 8.2 Microsoft product screen shots reprinted with permission from Microsoft Corporation.

66d Email Replies

When replying to email messages, keep the following in mind:

- If more than two days are needed for a response, it is courteous to send a brief message acknowledging receipt and indicating a response time. Most email systems have a function that automatically sends an "out of office" reply to be used when the recipient plans to be away from email for an extensive time.
- If the sender of an email has copied others, it is usually courteous to copy them on the reply.
- Limit the reply to the original topic to maintain one thread of communication per topic.

- When replying to an ongoing exchange of emails, know when to end the "conversation." For example, if someone sends a simple "Thanks," it isn't necessary to reply with "You're welcome." Doing so wastes time and causes mailbox clutter.

66e Email Netiquette and Cautions

QUICK REFERENCE 66.1

Business email netiquette

Follow these rules of email etiquette, also called **netiquette,** to convey a professional image.

- **Use standard capitalization, punctuation, and business abbreviations, but avoid instant message shorthand.** For example, ASAP (as soon as possible), COB (close of business), or FYI (for your information) have always been used in business. Avoid personal messaging shorthand.
- **Do not use emoticons**—faces meant to convey different emotions; reserve them for personal correspondence.
- **Do not send or forward personal messages,** jokes, chain letters, or solicitations in the business environment.
- **Use the Blind Copy window for large mailings** to protect the privacy of recipients' email addresses.
- **Never use profanity or any other type of derogatory language.** Observe business standards at all times, even in jest.
- **Never respond in anger to an email.** Wait until you are calm enough to respond in a professional manner.

Business email cautions

Know your organization's email policies. Most companies have software that monitors use of their email system. Here are a few precautions to keep in mind.

- **Personal emails.** Apply common sense to personal communications with people both inside and outside your organization. Keep in mind that companies have monitoring systems and have the right to read employees' emails.
- **Email privacy.** Emails sent on the job belong to the organization, just as paper documents do. When an email is deleted, it is most likely saved on the company's backup system or on the email provider's servers.
- **Business and legal concerns.** Do not send confidential information or make statements or commitments in emails that you

CONTINUED→

QUICK REFERENCE 66.1 → CONTINUED

would not otherwise make in written documents. Email may be forwarded to others; also, like paper documents, emails can become evidence in business and legal disputes. Employers may also use email messages as evidence of job performance.

- **Common sense use.** Avoid overuse of email. Email overload is a common problem in organizations due to overuse. Relying solely on email to communicate with coworkers can be counterproductive.
- **Security and antiviral systems.** Make sure that your computer is protected with the latest antivirus and security software; do not open attachments from unknown senders. Most companies have software that blocks spam and attachments from unknown sources; however, each employee is also responsible for ensuring that the company system does not become infected.

67 INTEROFFICE MEMOS

The **interoffice memo** (short for **memorandum**), traditionally used for all internal business communication, has largely been replaced by email. It is still useful, however, for printed communications and remains in use for a variety of purposes, both internally and between close business associates externally. Some uses include:

Confidential communications

Long documents

Policy documents

Informal reports

Cover pages for internal documents and reports

Transmittal of paper documents or other materials

67a Basic Memo Parts

Memo forms typically have the company name and logo at the top. Forms may be created from word processing templates or on plain paper with the word *Memorandum* or *Memo* in large letters at the top and the **guide words** *Date, To, From,* and *Subject* (see Figure 8.3).

The notation for copies may or may not be included among the guide words at the top. It can be inserted as needed or indicated with the notations at the bottom of the message (see 67c). Other guide words that may be added at the top include the following:

cc:
Department:
Floor number:
Email:
Extension:

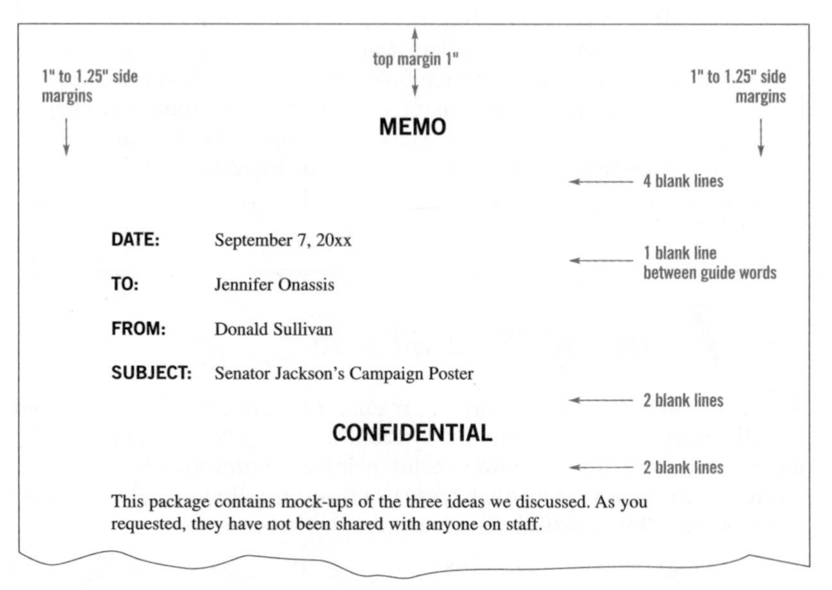

FIGURE 8.3 Memo guide words and notation

67b Filling in the Memo Form or Template

Use the default tab or set a tab that aligns the entries at least two spaces from the longest guide word. See the sample memo in Figure 8.4.

THE TO LINE

- Include the first and last name of the primary recipient(s).
- Type the names of the recipients across on one line if they fit; if not, list them.
- Including job titles or department names is optional.

To: Ellen Johansen, Bill Harris, Bonita Rodriquez

To: Ellen Johansen, Human Resources, Eastern Region
Bill Harris, Human Resources, Midwest Region
Bonita Rodriguez, Human Resources, Southern Region

- If the list is too long to fit at the top, type **Distribution** in the To space and list the names at the bottom of the memo with the notation "Distribution" (see Figure 8.4).

THE FROM LINE

Fill in your full name or that of the sender if you are preparing the memo for someone. It is optional for the sender to initial the typed name before the memo is sent.

THE DATE LINE

Enter the date the memo is being sent, not the date it was originally drafted. Write the full date as follows:

Date: July 27, 2008 NOT 7/27/08

THE SUBJECT LINE

Like email, memos should be confined to one topic. Be as specific and use as few words as possible. Capitalize the main words in the subject line.

Subject: Promotion Recommendations

THE MESSAGE

Begin the message two or three lines below the Subject line. Type the message single-spaced with a double-space between paragraphs.

67c Special Notations on Memos

Notations are words or lines below the Subject line or at the bottom of the memo. These may include:

- **CONFIDENTIAL** or some other special notation about the contents of the memo. A notation at the top should be typed in bold, capital letters two lines below the Subject line (see Figure 8.3).
- **Preparer's initials.** If someone other than the writer prepares a memo, that person types his or her initials in lowercase letters below the last line of the message.
- **Enclosure or attachments.** If other documents or materials are being sent, use one of these notations:

  Enclosure or Enc.

  Attachment or Att.

  To indicate the number of enclosures or attachments:

  2 Enclosures

  Attachments (2)

To specify what is enclosed or attached:

Enclosure: Summer Furniture Catalog

- **Copy notation.** As a courtesy to the main recipient, list the names of those receiving a copy of the memo. Use the abbreviation *c* for *copy* or *cc* for *courtesy copy*.

c: Savannah Bourne

cc: Ellington Persley

United Computer
Corporation

MEMO

Guide Words: Tab two to three spaces from longest word to align

TO: Mario Adolpho
FROM: Anne McKenna
DATE: August 1, 20xx
SUBJECT: Fall Collection

← 2 blank lines

Left margin flush with guide words or a minimum 1" margin

Enclosed is the report you requested on possible jewelry selections for the upcoming Fall Collection.

← 1 blank line between paragraphs

I have included the suppliers' names and their mailing and Web site addresses. I have also included the first and last dates on which these items will be available.

Each of these pieces is stunning and will enhance our fall line.

Here's to a successful season!

← 1 blank line

bfg

← 1 blank line

Enc.

← 1 blank line

Distribution:

← 1 blank line

L. Donnelly
R. Walden
F. Osborne
G. Jorgensen

1" bottom margin

FIGURE 8.4 Format for a preprinted interoffice memo

- **Blind copy notation.** Type at the bottom of the file copy and the recipient's copy only:

  bc: Heaven Hodges

- **Distribution.** When sending a memo to a large number of recipients, list the names at the bottom of the memo instead of on the To line.

67d Continuing Pages of Memos

Type the second and subsequent pages of a memo on plain paper. Use the header function to insert the recipient's name, page number, and date at the top of each additional page. The header can be typed in either of the two styles shown following.

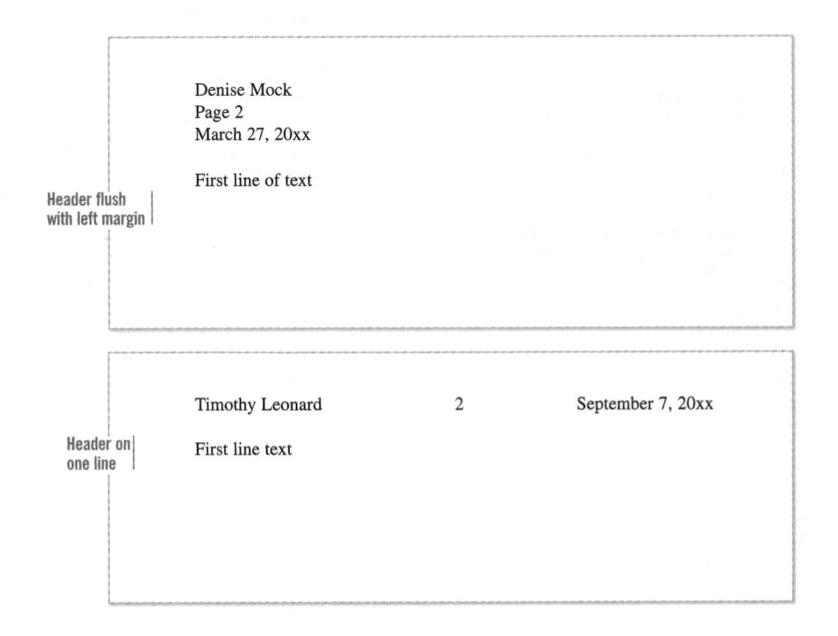

68 BUSINESS LETTER STYLES

Business letters are formatted in one of three styles: **block** (Figure 8.5), **modified block** (Figure 8.6), and **simplified** (Figure 8.7).

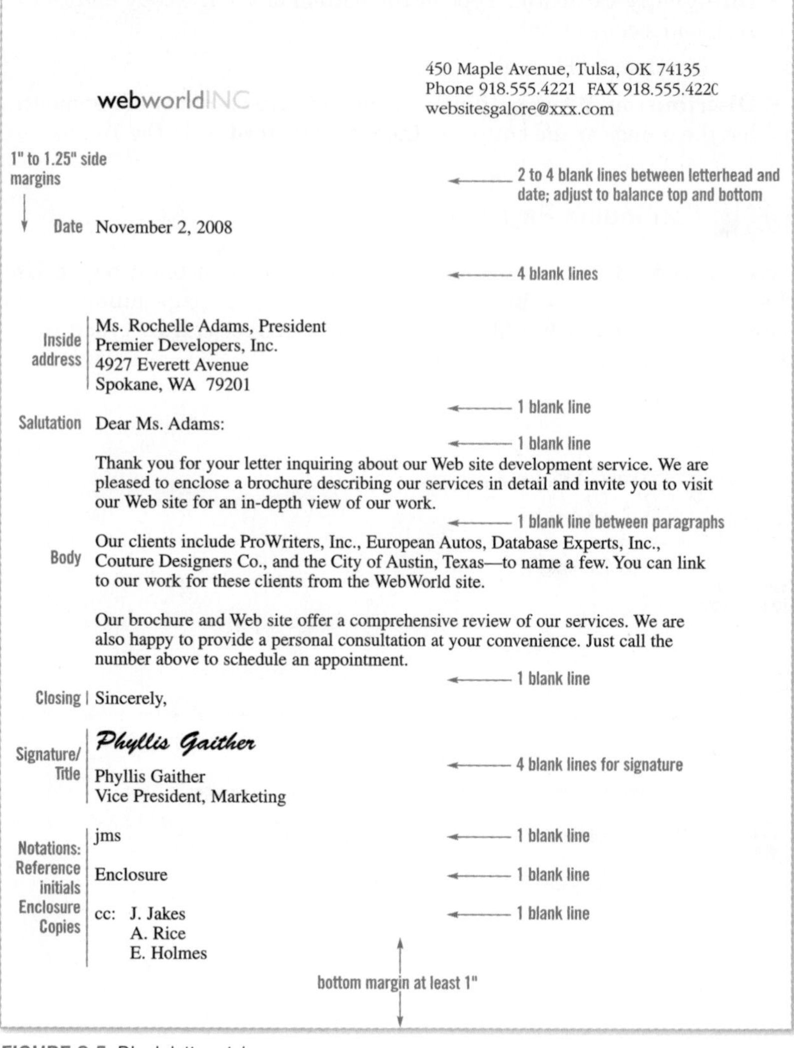

webworldINC

450 Maple Avenue, Tulsa, OK 74135
Phone 918.555.4221 FAX 918.555.4220
websitesgalore@xxx.com

November 2, 2008

Ms. Rochelle Adams, President
Premier Developers, Inc.
4927 Everett Avenue
Spokane, WA 79201

Dear Ms. Adams:

Thank you for your letter inquiring about our Web site development service. We are pleased to enclose a brochure describing our services in detail and invite you to visit our Web site for an in-depth view of our work.

Our clients include ProWriters, Inc., European Autos, Database Experts, Inc., Couture Designers Co., and the City of Austin, Texas—to name a few. You can link to our work for these clients from the WebWorld site.

Our brochure and Web site offer a comprehensive review of our services. We are also happy to provide a personal consultation at your convenience. Just call the number above to schedule an appointment.

Sincerely,

Phyllis Gaither

Phyllis Gaither
Vice President, Marketing

jms

Enclosure

cc: J. Jakes
A. Rice
E. Holmes

FIGURE 8.5 Block letter style

68a Block Style

All elements of the letter (except the designed letterhead) are typed flush with the left margin. The block style is recommended for its streamlined appearance. It is the most efficient letter style since tabs are eliminated.

68b Modified-Block Style

In the standard modified-block letter, the date and signature begin at the center of the page. The modified-block style may also be typed with indented paragraphs; this is rarely used today.

United Computer Corporation

SALES · SERVICE · LEASING
7005 Technics Drive, Box 227, Dayton, OH 45409
Telephone 937-555-1000 Fax 937-555-1200
uccorp@xxx.com

← 2 to 4 blank lines between letterhead and date; adjust to balance top and bottom

1" to 1.25" side margins

December 21, 20xx ← begin date at center

← 2 to 4 blank lines

Inside address | Mr. Peter J. Pososki
7800 Bridgeway
Dayton, OH 45409

← 1 blank line

Salutation | Dear Mr. Pososki:

← 1 blank line

Body |

Thank you for your letter of inquiry regarding the position of sales manager in our Marketing Department here at UNICOM. We are not currently recruiting to fill that position, however, since the vacancy has not been confirmed by our executive staff or the person currently in that position.

← 1 blank line between paragraphs

Your credentials are certainly impressive, and we will keep your information in our active file, although we do not anticipate an opening before April of next year. Your file will remain active for the next six months.

Thank you again for your interest in being a part of the UNICOM team. I am also enclosing our recruitment packet to acquaint you further with our organization.

In the meantime, if you have any computer needs, please think of us. We think you will be pleased with both our sales and our service.

← 1 blank line

Closing and signature centered |

Sincerely,

← 4 blank lines

Martin J. Eckerd
Martin J. Eckerd
Manager, Human Resources

← 1 blank line

Notations: Preparer's initials and enclosure |
llp
Enc.: Recruitment Packet

bottom margin at least 1"

FIGURE 8.6 Modified-block letter style

68c Simplified Style

This style was developed by the Administrative Management Society many years ago. It simplifies the standard format by omitting the salutation and complimentary closing. It includes a Subject line typed in all caps. It is useful when writing letters to a large number of people or when writing to groups or to people whose names you do not know.

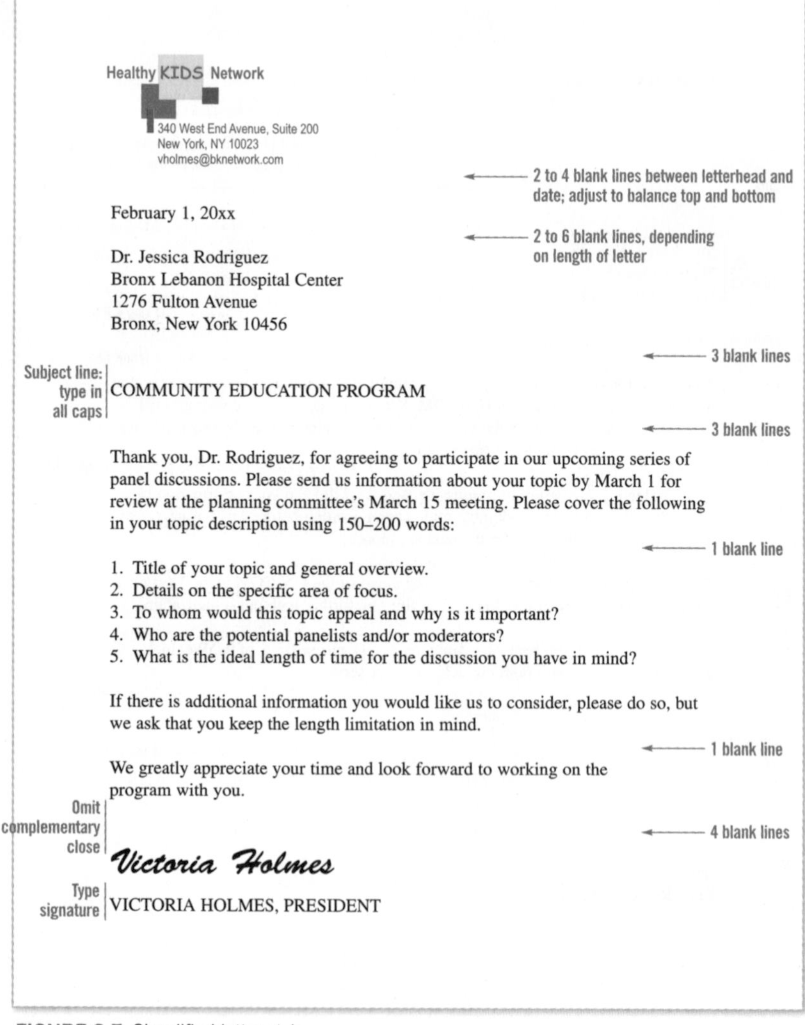

Healthy KIDS Network
340 West End Avenue, Suite 200
New York, NY 10023
vholmes@bknetwork.com

← 2 to 4 blank lines between letterhead and date; adjust to balance top and bottom

February 1, 20xx

← 2 to 6 blank lines, depending on length of letter

Dr. Jessica Rodriguez
Bronx Lebanon Hospital Center
1276 Fulton Avenue
Bronx, New York 10456

← 3 blank lines

Subject line: type in all caps | COMMUNITY EDUCATION PROGRAM

← 3 blank lines

Thank you, Dr. Rodriguez, for agreeing to participate in our upcoming series of panel discussions. Please send us information about your topic by March 1 for review at the planning committee's March 15 meeting. Please cover the following in your topic description using 150–200 words:

← 1 blank line

1. Title of your topic and general overview.
2. Details on the specific area of focus.
3. To whom would this topic appeal and why is it important?
4. Who are the potential panelists and/or moderators?
5. What is the ideal length of time for the discussion you have in mind?

If there is additional information you would like us to consider, please do so, but we ask that you keep the length limitation in mind.

← 1 blank line

We greatly appreciate your time and look forward to working on the program with you.

Omit complementary close

← 4 blank lines

Victoria Holmes

Type signature | VICTORIA HOLMES, PRESIDENT

FIGURE 8.7 Simplified letter style

68d Letter Formatting

Figures 8.4, 8.5, and 8.6 show standard formats for block, modified block, and simplified letter formats. The finished document should appear similar to a picture in a frame with margins of at least 1″ all around, single-spacing within paragraphs, and double-spacing between them. Use the Print Preview feature of your software to make sure the letter layout is balanced.

QUICK REFERENCE 68.1

Standard letter formatting

Margins

Top and bottom

- The top margins are already established on preprinted letterhead or an electronic letterhead template.
- On created letterhead, aim for at least a ½″ to 1″ top margin; the bottom margin should be at least 1″.
- Top and bottom margins should appear to be approximately equal on a letter that fills the page. If a letter is shorter, it is acceptable to have a larger bottom margin. Spacing above the date can also be increased for balance.

Sides

- Side margins should be equal; 1″ is standard.
- Your word processing default settings may be different (the Microsoft Word default is 1.25″).
- Adjust margins to accommodate the length and visual appeal of the copy.
- **Justification** (even margins on both sides) is not appropriate in business letters.

Line Spacing

Top of letter

- Leave two to five lines between the last line of the letterhead and the date; adjust for balance.
- Double-space between the date and the salutation.
- Double-space between the salutation and the body.

Body paragraphs

- Single-space paragraphs.
- Double-space between paragraphs.

CONTINUED→

QUICK REFERENCE 68.1 → CONTINUED

Bottom of letter

- Double-space between the last line of the body and the closing.
- Leave four spaces between the closing and the signature.
- Double-space between notations following the closing.

Type Font

- Times New Roman or Century Schoolbook are the two most commonly used type fonts for business documents.
- 12-point type is the standard size; adjust size to 11 point or 10 point if a letter is running over to a second page by only one or two lines; do not enlarge it.

QUICK REFERENCE 68.2

Standards for letterhead

Company letterhead (preprinted stationery) sizes

A letterhead should not take up more than 2″ at the top of the sheet.

- **Standard.** 8½″ × 11″—used for general business correspondence
- **Executive** (also called Monarch). 7½″ × 10″—used by some executives
- **Half sheet** (also called Baronial). 5½″ × 8½″—used for notes

Standard information on company letterhead

- Business/organization name
- Logo (optional)
- Street address
- Suite number or floor (optional)
- Telephone and fax numbers
- Email address

Optional information on company letterhead

- Web site address
- Names (executives, board members)

CONTINUED →

QUICK REFERENCE 68.2 → CONTINUED

- Addresses of branch offices
- Company tag line

Standard information on personal letterhead

- Name
- Address
- Telephone number
- Fax number
- Email address
- Web site address

69 GUIDELINES FOR PARTS OF BUSINESS LETTERS

69a Date

Type the dateline about 1.5″ from the top of the page or a double-space below the letterhead. Military and international organizations use the inverted date style: 27 January 2008.

Standard style: May 11, 20xx

Military and international style: 11 May 20xx (no comma needed)

69b Special Notations

Reference and *confidential* notations are the most frequently used at the top of a letter, but these guidelines apply to any notation in that space. Type the notation two lines below the date (double-spaced) and space down two more lines to begin the inside address. See Figures 8.8 and 8.9.

Reference: Re: Order #35706-2 (vase with copper trim)

Confidential: CONFIDENTIAL or PERSONAL

(**Note:** To address a letter to the attention of a specific person in an organization, use the name in the first line of the inside address. An Attention line is not necessary.)

Letterhead

July 10, 20xx

Marshall S. Kinzer
Director of Finance
Suite 201
Global Corporation
235 Park Avenue South
New York, NY 10021

Dear Mr. Kinzer:

← 1 blank line

Reference line | RE: Consulting Agreement for Investment Strategy

← 1 blank line

We are pleased to send you the contract for the work you will be doing on our strategies . . .

FIGURE 8.8 Placement of reference line

Letterhead

March 30, 20xx

← 1 blank line

Special Notation | CONFIDENTIAL

← 1 blank line

Ms. Mae Al-Jamal
Manager
Glorious Bed and Breakfast
146 Old Bay Road
Kennebunkport, ME 04046

← 1 blank line

Dear Mae:

← 1 blank line

We are pleased that you have chosen our company to handle background checks on your new employees. We know how important it is for your business to hire trustworthy and . . .

FIGURE 8.9 Placement of confidential notation

69c Inside Address (Recipient's Name and Address)

The inside address should include the following:

Recipient's name and courtesy title	Ms. Jeannette Dibble
Recipient's job title/ Department	Director, Engineering Department
Company name	Zonars Corporation
Suite/Room number	Suite 900
Address	132 N. Jefferson Blvd.
City/State/ZIP code	Newark, NJ 07076

Use either the two-letter state abbreviation in the inside address or spell it out. However, use only the two-letter postal code on the envelope.

NAME AND COURTESY TITLE

Use a courtesy title (Mr., Mrs., Ms.) in the inside address and on the envelope. It is permissible to omit the courtesy title in the following instances:

- When you do not know the person's gender and cannot be sure from the name; for example, Leslie, Lee, Pat
- In bulk mailings for which the addresses are generated from a database
- When you do not know the name of the person who should receive your letter (see 69d)

Director of Sales
ABC Software Corporation
3876 South Shore Drive
Long Island City, NY 11101

JOB TITLE, DEPARTMENT, AND ORGANIZATION

- Type the job title immediately after the name, separated by a comma, or on the next line. Decide based on a balanced appearance of the address block.
- Type the organization name in full; always check spelling.

Mr. Jerome Neal, Director
Engineering Division
Eastern Aeronautics Inc.
1465 Oriental Way
Los Angeles, CA 95201

Margaret Elliot
Director, Human Resources
General Accounting Services Group
Walker Smith & Associates
156 Main Street
Austin, TX 08876-1111

ADDRESS

- When a letter is addressed to two people, type the inside addresses one under the other or side by side. Use the format that best suits the length of the letter.
- If an address has both a street address and a postal box number, type the box number on the line above the city and state.
- With the two-letter state abbreviation, leave two spaces between the abbreviation and the ZIP Code.
- If there is a room or suite number, type it on the same line or on the line below the street address. If it is too long to fit on the same line, type it on a separate line just above the street address.

Mr. Sarkis Hagopian
6688 Walnut Lane
Bloomfield Hills, MI 48323

Mr. Max Albertson, Treasurer
Tulsa Oil Corporation
Box 340
Tulsa, OK 74114

OR

Ms. Miriam Yong
Director of Marketing
Chester Building
Suite 806
Framingham, MA 01702

Mr. Max Albertson, Treasurer
XYZ Oil Corporation
2400 South Berry Avenue
Box 340
Tulsa, OK 74114

69d Salutation

- Address the recipient by first name or courtesy title (Mr., Ms., and Dr.) and last name, as appropriate to your relationship with the individual. In business it is no longer customary to use the titles *Miss* or *Mrs.* to denote marital status.
- Begin the salutation at the left margin, two lines below the last line of the inside address.
- Place a colon at the end of the salutation; do not use a comma.

Dear Mr. Norris:

Dear James:

- Spell out professional titles: Lieutenant Ricardo, Professor Edgerton

- When you are not writing to a specific person, use a general salutation:

  Ladies and Gentlemen:

  Dear Sir or Madam:

  Dear Madam:

  Dear Sir:

  Dear Customer Service Department:

[Read more about courtesy titles and abbreviations in Topic 46.]

69e The Body of the Letter

- Begin typing two lines below the salutation.
- Always single-space paragraphs and double-space between paragraphs.
- Continue onto a second page if copy runs over by at least three to six lines.
- Never go to a second page for only the complimentary closing; instead, edit the letter and adjust spacing to fit one page.

See Quick Reference 70.1 for guidelines on adjusting letters to fit one page.

69f Complimentary Closing and Signature

- Type the closing two lines below the body of the last line of text.
- Begin at the left margin for block style letters and at the center for modified block style.
- Capitalize only the first word of the closing.
- Place a comma after the closing.

Standard closings	**More formal closings**	**Informal closings**
Sincerely yours,	Respectfully yours,	Best,
Sincerely,	Respectfully,	My best,
Cordially,	Very truly yours,	Best wishes,
Best regards,		
Regards,		

- Leave four lines between the closing and the name. Type the writer's job title and department on the line below the name, *unless the letterhead contains this information*.

Cordially,

Jennifer Olmstead
Manager, Marketing Services

- When it is important to emphasize that the message represents the views of the company as a whole and not just the views of the writer, type the company name in all capital letters one line below the complimentary closing:

  Sincerely,

  JOHNSON CLEANING SERVICES, INC.

69g Typist's Reference Initials

Use reference initials to indicate that you have typed a letter for someone else. Include only the initials of the person who types the letter; do not include the writer's initials, as was done in the past.

- Type the initials at the left margin.
- Begin two lines below the last typed line in the closing block.
- Use lowercase letters: lfb

69h Copy Notations

- Use the designation *cc* for *courtesy copy* or *c* for *copy*.
- Begin two lines below the last typed line in the closing block or reference initials, if any.
- Type the list of names single-spaced. You can spell out the full name or use the first initial and last name.

cc:	A. Burns	c:	Audrey Burns
	D. Everett		Denis Everett
	F. Gregory		Frank Gregory

- List the names in alphabetical order or in order of rank in the business organization.
- If a blind copy or copies are sent, type the notation *bc* and the name on the recipient's copy and the file copy only.

69i Enclosures

- Align the word *Enclosure* or the abbreviation *Enc.* two lines below the signature or the copy notation, if any. Use one of the following formats:

  Enclosure or Attachment

  Enc. or Att.

- If a single item is enclosed, it is not necessary to list it, but list the items if there are two or more enclosures or if one enclosure is of value, such as a check.

  Enclosures: Letter of Agreement
  Project Specifications

70 CONTINUING PAGES IN LETTERS

Before beginning a second page, make sure the letter needs to be longer than a page. Consider cutting copy instead of adding pages, particularly if the letter is running long by only a few lines.

70a Formatting the Second and Subsequent Pages

- Use plain paper, never letterhead, for continuing pages.
- Use a continuation page heading at the top of each additional page. The heading has three parts:

  (1) the recipient's name

  (2) the page number (using the word *page* before the number is not necessary)

  (3) the date of the letter

- Never start a new page unless you have at least three lines of copy to carry over in addition to the complimentary closing, signature, and any notations. If not, shorten the letter to make it fit on one page.

See Quick Reference 70.1 on adjusting length of letters.

- Always begin the first line of a continuation page with a full line of text.

Aaron Burch
Page 2
December 19, 20xx

Please return your response in the enclosed envelope no later than January 15, 20xx. If you are unable to mail your response by that date, I will not be able to schedule a hearing during the first week of February.

Your attorney, Ms. Adams, is away from the office on business for the next two weeks. If you have any questions or need her assistance during that time, please let me know and I will arrange for her to call you.

Sincerely,

Donald L. Boatwright
Paralegal

FIGURE 8.10 Header for continuation pages aligned at left margin

- **Type the heading in the header section of the page in one of the styles shown in Figures 8.10 and 8.11.**
- **Begin typing the continued copy on the first line of the second page.**
- **Set the top margin to a 1″ margin or your word processor's default.**

Aaron Burch   Page 2   December 19, 20xx

Please return your response in the enclosed envelope no later than January 15, 20xx. If you are unable to mail your response by that date, I will not be able to schedule a hearing during the first week of February.

FIGURE 8.11 Header for continuation page on one line

QUICK REFERENCE 70.1

Adjusting format for short or long letters

To achieve a balanced appearance for exceptionally long or short letters, the following margin and spacing adjustments are acceptable:

- Place the date higher or lower on the page.
- Add or delete spaces between the date and the inside address.
- Adjust side margins from a minimum .75″ to 1.5″ maximum.
- Adjust the spacing from four blank lines to three between the complimentary close and the typed signature line, leaving enough space for the written signature.
- Decrease size of type (12-point is standard; minimum is 10-point, depending on the font).
- Allow the text to go to a second page if the copy is at least three lines, but never for only the closing and signature.
- Use a header on every page after the first (see Figures 8.10 and 8.11).

71 COMPOSING DIFFERENT TYPES OF BUSINESS MESSAGES

The primary purpose for writing business documents varies, but all business communications have a common secondary purpose—*to establish and maintain rapport*. Whereas it is easy to build rapport when messages are positive, circumstances often require writing messages that will not be positively received by the reader. It is possible, however, to maintain goodwill while saying no, pointing out a problem, criticizing an employee's work, or refusing a request.

The guidelines in the following sections will help you formulate messages for both routine and sensitive situations. The examples are categorized according to the main purposes for most business writing:

- To inform
- To direct or instruct
- To request
- To respond
- To persuade

72 WRITING TO INFORM

Communications written to inform are usually passing along routine business information. To look at the various ways of constructing information messages, it is helpful to categorize them in three ways: as positive, negative, and neutral.

72a The Direct and Indirect Approach

When writing positive or neutral information messages, there is no reason to build up to the essential point. Use the **direct approach**, which means immediately stating your purpose for writing, as shown in Figure 8.12.

The **indirect approach**—explain first and then inform—is recommended when imparting information that may be troublesome or outright bad news. Be concise in the explanation. Base the level of detail and the amount of information on what you know about the recipient. Don't assume what is known or what is important to the recipient;

QUICK REFERENCE 72.1

Writing information messages

The direct approach

- Be straightforward; provide the necessary information immediately.
- Write short sentences rather than complex explanations.
- Say it once; don't be repetitive.
- Use words that are concrete.
- Use the active voice.

The indirect approach

- Begin with the reasons for the communication, and then state the point as positively possible.
- Choose tactful words that will avoid upsetting or offending the recipient.
- Use the passive voice where it will help soften impact.
- Close courteously and, whenever possible, leave the door open for a more positive outcome in the future.

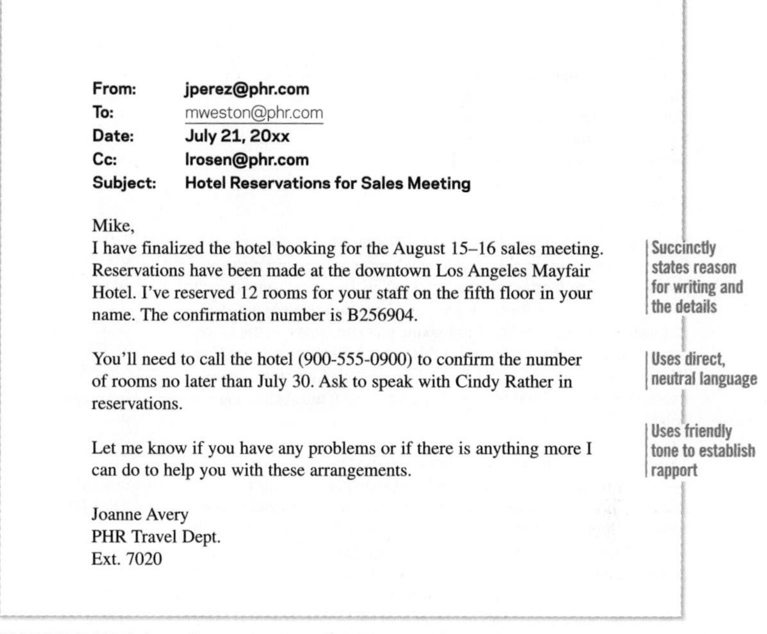
From: jperez@phr.com
To: mweston@phr.com
Date: July 21, 20xx
Cc: lrosen@phr.com
Subject: Hotel Reservations for Sales Meeting

Mike,
I have finalized the hotel booking for the August 15–16 sales meeting. Reservations have been made at the downtown Los Angeles Mayfair Hotel. I've reserved 12 rooms for your staff on the fifth floor in your name. The confirmation number is B256904.

You'll need to call the hotel (900-555-0900) to confirm the number of rooms no later than July 30. Ask to speak with Cindy Rather in reservations.

Let me know if you have any problems or if there is anything more I can do to help you with these arrangements.

Joanne Avery
PHR Travel Dept.
Ext. 7020

FIGURE 8.12 Information message—direct approach

err on the side of including more rather than less. The goal is to be honest and prepare the reader for what is coming. See the example in Figure 8.13.

72b Confirming an Oral Agreement

Written confirmations of business arrangements help avoid misunderstandings and disagreements over matters both trivial and important. Confirmations can be as simple as writing an email to establish the time, date, and place for a lunch appointment, or as complex as writing a letter to a contractor to confirm the outlines of a project and agreement before drawing up an official contract.

Confirmations are often written to follow up on oral agreements. When confirming an agreement, include all of the details and be specific, rather than relying on any assumptions about what the recipient already knows or understands. Seeing the points in writing is the surest way to clarify any discrepancies in understanding. Figure 8.14 is an example of a confirmation to solidify meeting arrangements.

From: lrosen@phr.com
To: rdoherty@phr.com
Date: October 18, 20xx
Cc: jperez@phr.com
Subject: Attendance at NEPC

Rick,

I know you have registered to attend the National Event Planners Convention in Houston next month, and I appreciate the effort you've put into planning for the time out of the office. However, I am concerned about your absence in the week preceding the relocation of your staff; it is just too risky. Therefore, I am asking that you remain in the office August 20-23 and forego attending this year's NEPC convention. There is a good possibility that without you there to "mind the store" some important business could be lost during this crucial time before the holiday selling period.

Begins positively and sets up the bad news with a compliment.

States the message tactfully and provides a strong reason.

Anticipates objections, but makes it clear that the decision has been made.

I know you will be disappointed, but I hope you will understand that it is a matter of necessity. Since you have already paid the registration fee and made hotel arrangements, I see no reason why you shouldn't select someone from your staff to attend in your place. I think Nina would be an excellent choice, since she's fairly new and hasn't had the chance to go before; but I will leave that decision up to you.

Suggests an alternative plan.

I really appreciate your cooperation on this, Rick. You are one of my most trusted managers, and your staff needs your problem-solving skills to keep abreast of business while dealing with this complex relocation. I will personally see to it that nothing stands in the way of your attending the convention next year.

Closes with a positive paragraph that includes personal and professional reassurances.

Linda

FIGURE 8.13 Information message—indirect approach

72c Confirming Receipt

Acknowledging receipt can be a necessity or just a courtesy. Either way, be specific when confirming receipt of documents, information, or materials in case your reader made a mistake or does not recall what was sent. Figure 8.15 confirms receipt of a check.

QUICK REFERENCE 72.3

Writing confirmation messages

- Include all of the details that are important to a mutual understanding.

CONTINUED →

QUICK REFERENCE 72.3 ➤ CONTINUED

- Use a level of formality appropriate to your relationship with the recipient and the situation.
- Express whatever positive thoughts are appropriate to building goodwill and rapport.
- Attach supporting documents, if necessary.

Dear Ms. Johnson:

This will confirm our telephone conversation about the June 11–12 staff retreat of Patterson & Associates Consulting at the Downtown Hyacinth Hotel. We need the following reservations and meal arrangements:

Opening states the purpose and refers to specific details.

1. Four single rooms at the special rate of $250 each for the night of June 12 for the following individuals: Judy Patterson, Leo Frailey, Peter Haritan, and Randall Estevan.

Confirms pertinent points of agreement in an itemized list.

2. A private meeting room on June 12 from 8 a.m. to 5 p.m. We would like to have a table in the center of the room that will seat ten, plus side tables for materials. (There will be no charge for this room.)

3. Your gourmet service for a morning coffee break at 10:30 a.m. and afternoon beverage break at 2:30 p.m.

4. A luncheon for ten people at 12:30 p.m. will be set up in the Roof Garden restaurant private dining room to be ordered from the restaurant menu.

I would appreciate it if you would confirm these arrangements in writing today, so that I can get Ms. Patterson's approval to execute a formal agreement.

Tells the reader what is needed and the next steps.

Thank you for your assistance. I really appreciate your many helpful suggestions and the offer of the free meeting room. We look forward to gathering at your facility.

Builds rapport with a closing statements.

Sincerely yours,

Randall Estevan
Vice President, Marketing
Patterson & Associates, Consulting

FIGURE 8.14 Confirmation of an oral agreement

Dear Mr. Paxton:

Thank you for your check for $1,200 as the first payment on Exhibit Space K for the Association of Rare Book Dealers Convention, to be held on December 13-16.

Describes in detail what was received.

As stated in the convention packet, should your plans for exhibiting at the convention change, the deposit is refundable in full if we are notified of your cancellation by November 1, and 50 percent refundable upon notification by November 15; after that date, the deposit is not refundable.

Reminds the reader of an important company policy to prevent future problems.

Please don't hesitate to let us know if we can be of assistance to you as the convention date draws near.

Closes cordially to build rapport.

Sincerely,

FIGURE 8.15 Confirming receipt of information or materials

72d Transmittal Messages

Transmittal messages are usually short, cordial, informal communications that don't require much information. The two purposes of a transmittal

To: **Amanda Beaulieu, Marketing Manager**
From: **Rolf Moriarty, Design Supervisor**
Date: **May 7, 20xx**
Subject: **Photos for Annual Report Cover**

Enclosed is a CD with five photos for you to consider for the Annual Report cover. This includes only the shots of major architectural projects completed in the past year, as you requested.

Describes the enclosure.

I hope you like the shots I selected. I have my preferences from the standpoint of aesthetics, and would be happy to meet with you to discuss them.

Builds rapport with offer to provide assistance.

If you can select the cover shot by tomorrow, we can complete the layout and be ready to go to the printer next week.

Lets the reader know what is needed and what is at stake.

FIGURE 8.16 Transmittal message

document are to inform the recipient of what is being sent and to make a record of the transaction. Figure 8.16 is an example of a transmittal message.

QUICK REFERENCE 72.4

Writing transmittal messages

- Give a brief description of the item(s) being transmitted; include details, for example, the number and amount of a check.
- Explain why the item is being sent, if necessary.
- State any actions you want the recipient to take.
- Include information the recipient needs in order to respond, such as deadlines or instructions for completing a transaction.

73 WRITING TO INSTRUCT

Clarity—important in anything you write—is essential when composing instructions or directions. It is critical to avoid making assumptions about what the reader already knows; include more rather than less.

The following two examples show how instructions can be improved. The message in Figure 8.17A uses vague phrases and lacks details; while an efficient assistant can get the job done, it will be more difficult and time consuming. Compare the highlighted wording in 8.17B where pertinent details are provided. Key phrases are in blue type.

QUICK REFERENCE 73.1

Writing instructions

- Keep in mind that instructions need to be both understood and applied. Therefore, using precise simple language is the best approach.
- Write instructions or directions in a logical sequence.
- Number the items for clarity.
- Try to anticipate questions that might arise and answer them.

To: **Jonathan Elwood**
From: **Kendra Ali**
Date: **December 2, 20xx**
Subject: **Items needing attention in my absence**

Please take care of the following items while I'm on vacation next week

1. Send Ira King a copy of my presentation and ask him to review it by the time I get back. **[Which presentation? Where is it?]**
2. Find out what additional support data he can supply. **[What is needed?]**
3. If Courtney Adams calls about the committee meeting, **[What committee?]** find out if George Shapiro has scheduled it yet. **[Find out from Courtney or George?]**
4. Please attend the weekly staff meeting in my place and take notes on anything important so we can talk about it on Monday. **[What is important?]**

Thanks for your help. Call me at the hotel if you need anything. **[Which hotel?]**

Have a great week!

FIGURE 8.17A Giving instructions—draft

To: **Jonathan Elwood**
From: **Kendra Ali**
Date: **December 2, 20xx**
Subject: **Items needing attention in my absence**

Please take care of the following items while I'm on vacation next week

1. Send Ira King a copy of my End-of-Year Review presentation and ask him to review it by the time I get back. It is in the file called Presentations and my final draft has today's date (12/2).
2. Find out if he can supply additional support data on sales increases by territory and where pricing changes influenced sales.
3. If Courtney Adams calls about the Governance Committee meeting, ask her to call George Shapiro to find out if he has scheduled it yet. I've asked her to attend in my absence if the meeting is held next week.
4. Please attend the weekly staff meeting in my place and take notes on the agenda items so we can talk about it on Monday.

Thanks for your help. Call me at El San Juan Hotel if you need anything. A copy of my itinerary is underneath the paperweight on my desk.

Have a great week!

FIGURE 8.17B Giving instructions—revised draft

74 WRITING TO MAKE A REQUEST

74a Requesting Information, Assistance, or a Favor

Requests for routine information need comparatively little explanation or persuasion to get action. The goal is to elicit a positive response and avoid any misunderstanding about what is being requested. See Figures 8.18 and 8.19 and Quick Reference 74.1.

When requesting that someone perform a service or provide help that could be characterized as a favor, it is especially important to show courtesy and gratitude. See Figure 8.20.

74b Requesting Resolution of a Problem or Complaint

Writing to request help with a problem or to make a complaint requires especially careful wording. Aim for a neutral tone with words that come across as rational, even-tempered, and clear. If a problem has caused you to become emotionally upset, wait until you cool down before writing. If

Alicin,

I would like permission to attend the National Association of Accountants conference in San Diego, October 13–16. The seminar will focus on technology-related matters and I am particularly interested in the workshops on network security. One of my six-month goals is to identify areas where the security of our system can be improved.

Asks directly; provides sound reasoning.

This will require me to be out of the office for four days that week, but I think it will be well worth the time and cost. I'm attaching a copy of the brochure and registration form to give you an overview of the meeting. In order to take advantage of the early registration fee of $495, I need to send in the form by the end of next week.

Includes information to support a positive response.

I hope you'll agree that this would be a worthwhile travel expense and approve my request for this trip. Thanks.

Builds rapport with the closing.

Doug

FIGURE 8.18 Request for permission

Dear Mr. Ricci:

Thank you for sending me the confirmation of accommodations for our conference on August 18-20. I appreciate your efforts in making sure the meeting is successful.

Builds rapport with a courteous opening.

I am planning to be in Phoenix July 9-12, and would like to have the opportunity to meet with you to finalize the arrangements and take a look at the Golden Valley Lodge and Conference Center facilities.

States the request immediately.

I will be arriving the afternoon of the 9th, so if you could you block out a couple of hours for me on July 10 or 11, that would be great. Please let me know which day and what time would be convenient for you and I will arrange my itinerary accordingly.

Provides necessary details and shows respect by offering to meet at the recipient's convenience.

Cordially,

FIGURE 8.19 Request for an appointment

Dear Mr. Lipscomb:

Our company is planning an expansion and modernization of its library, and I have been asked to assist in putting together a proposal for the project.

Explains the nature of the request.

The library was organized many years ago when we were a very small company, and we find that it no longer meets the needs of our staff—especially engineers, chemists, and scientists. We are looking for guidance in expanding our present space and equipment as well as making more information accessible online.

Provides background information and reason for the request.

It occurred to me that perhaps the SLA has model layouts and suggestions for equipment and materials. If so, I would be grateful if you would share this information with us, and would be happy to pay any fee. If you do not have such information, perhaps you could recommend another source.

Offers compensation as an incentive for a positive response.

Thank you very much, Mr. Lipscomb. If we succeed in our plans, I will make it a point to share the results with you, complete with diagrams and photographs.

Builds rapport with warmth and a sincere offer to reciprocate.

Cordially,

FIGURE 8.20 Request for a favor

QUICK REFERENCE 74.1

Guidelines for writing a request

Basic elements

- Use direct language and be explicit about what you want.
- Use concrete words that show courtesy and gratitude.
- Write with a "you attitude," and, when possible, indicate how your reader will benefit from honoring your request.

Requests to resolve problems

- Give a straightforward explanation of the problem.
- Avoid language that might be interpreted as sarcastic, accusatory, or a personal attack.
- Provide precise information or reasoning that supports your position and aids the reader's understanding of it.
- Provide a proposed action or resolution based on what you consider acceptable.
- Be courteous and tactful, but firm in indicating any further action you might take.

you are writing just to vent, think twice about writing at all. Figure 8.21 focuses on the purpose for writing and avoids using angry words, yet the writer's dissatisfaction is clear.

Dear Jim:

We placed an order with you on April 14 for 20 navy blue binders embossed with our company name and logo in gold. When the order arrived this morning, we were disappointed to find aqua blue instead of navy binders. I am returning the order by overnight mail with a copy of the original order form specifying the correct color.

Provides precise information and explains the problem without a long buildup.

We need this mistake corrected as quickly as possible. Please let me know immediately how soon you will be able to supply the binders as ordered.

Proposes an action to resolve the problem.

Thank you for your attention to this matter. We have always received good service from you and would like to continue to give you our business.

Closes courteously, but firmly indicates that future business is at stake.

Sincerely yours,

FIGURE 8.21 Request to correct a mistake

75 WRITING TO RESPOND

Written responses in business include form responses with **boilerplate** (standard) wording, adaptations of boilerplate to fit individual situations, and totally individualized communications. The following sections provide guidelines for responding positively and negatively. In both cases, using the direct approach is recommended.

75a Responding Positively to an Inquiry

A positive response to an inquiry is similar to a straightforward information message (see Figure 8.22). Use the direct approach as discussed in 72a.

Dear Mr. Moberly:

Your request for information about our "executive on-the-go" briefcase was forwarded to me. I am very pleased to tell you that it can be ordered in burgundy. The blue and black shown in our catalog are the standard colors we keep in stock. There is a charge of $5 per item for the special order color. Thus, the price would be $59.95 per briefcase, and your company logo could be imprinted for an additional charge of $2 each.

Refers to reader's original request and provides a complete answer to the inquiry.

You will be pleased to hear that we can offer you a 10 percent discount if the size of your order will be at least 50, as you estimated. The total cost would be computed as follows:

Offers incentive to offset bad news of higher price.

50 gift briefcases @ $59.95:	$2,997.50
Add logo imprint at $2:	100.00
Total:	$3,097.50
Less 10% discount:	309.75
Net price:	$2,787.75

Provides details to help the customer make a decision quickly.

We would be delighted to have your business. We guarantee delivery within 15 business days after the receipt of the order.

Asks for the order and provides a time frame to help the customer plan.

I will be happy to answer any additional questions you may have, so please don't hesitate to contact me. I look forward to hearing from you.

Builds goodwill by offering further assistance.

Sincerely yours,

FIGURE 8.22 Positive response to a query

QUICK REFERENCE 75.1

Writing a positive response to an inquiry

- Refer to the original inquiry and express appreciation, such as, "Thank you for your inquiry about our photography services."
- Include specific details about the original request, unless you are responding to an email that includes the recipient's original message.
- Provide details about the actions being taken to fulfill the request.
- Use the opportunity to build goodwill and cultivate future business.

75b Responding Negatively with an Alternative

When it is not possible to fulfill a request, try to find a way to turn the negative into a positive. A standard tactic is to explain the reason in terms of company policy. This can build goodwill by communicating that all such requests are treated the same. Whenever possible, offer an alternative solution. See the example in Figure 8.23.

75c Responding Negatively Outright

When it is necessary to flatly turn down a request or proposal, let the recipient down as gently as possible. The best rejection letters provide a straightforward explanation, but do not go overboard in trying to make

QUICK REFERENCE 75.2

Writing a negative response to an inquiry or request

- Express appreciation for the inquiry or request and refer to it in specific terms where possible (it might not be possible in a form response).
- Communicate that the request has been taken seriously.
- Provide the reason(s) for the negative response.
- When possible, build goodwill by asking the recipient to consider an alternative or an offer of future assistance.
- When applicable, ask for a continuing relationship and/or remind the recipient of past favorable relations.
- Close warmly.

Dear Mr. Vetter:

Thank you for your inquiry about pricing of our AutoPulse phone dialer software—our superior time saver for telemarketing sales calls. TeleSolutions offers commercial software products designed for a variety of business purposes. For a company of your size, with fewer than ten employees, we are unable to offer the price and free installation for the system as advertised on our Web site. The AutoPulse is designed for large operations.

Expresses appreciation and tactfully states negative response.

Please take a look at the enclosed catalog to learn more about our many cutting-edge products designed to meet the needs of smaller telemarketing and customer service businesses. You will find that most of these products do not require installation service, as they are easily and quickly installed by the purchaser.

Offers an alternative.

If you see a product that would fulfill your needs, simply complete and mail the attached order form. You can also place an order online, which guarantees receipt within ten business days.

If you need assistance, please don't hesitate to contact me by phone or email to discuss how we might be able to help you find the best system for your business.

Builds goodwill with a friendly tone, offer of quick service, and personal attention.

Sincerely yours,

FIGURE 8.23 Negative response with an alternative

excuses or give complicated reasons. One honest reason, worded with consideration, is usually enough to maintain goodwill.

If a form letter is appropriate, consider whether the response can be individualized in some way, if company policy allows. Whenever feasible, offer a suggestion that might lead to a positive response in the future.

In Figure 8.24, the writer must flatly turn down a request.

76 WRITING TO PERSUADE

A request is written to ask for a specific action, but in most cases, the recipient is in some way obligated to perform or to at least acknowledge the request and explain why its compliance is not possible. Writing to persuade is different because there may be no legal, ethical, or professional obligation on the part of the recipient. When the purpose is to sell

Dear Mr. Pruitt:

Thank you for offering us the opportunity to sponsor a merit award at the Elmwood Community College graduation ceremony. Your proposal for establishment of a "Wallingford's Prize" for each year's outstanding retail merchandising graduate is highly commendable, and we are complimented by the invitation.

Builds rapport by expressing appreciation and commenting favorably on the proposal.

Because Wallingford's receives many similar proposals each year, we have had to establish the policy of declining these opportunities. I'm sure you will understand that lending our support to your institution would mean that other fine colleges in our locale would have every right to expect the same. Unfortunately, the cost of such an endeavor would become prohibitive.

Gives a general reason for rejecting the proposal based on an easily accepted principle.

We will, of course, continue to offer internships and work closely with your job placement office on the recruitment and hiring of many of the fine graduates of Elmwood.

Thank you again for your offer and we wish you all the best in finding a suitable sponsor for your merit award program.

Maintains goodwill with a reminder of past favorable actions and a warm closing.

Sincerely yours,

FIGURE 8.24 Rejection of a request

an idea, a product, or a service under these circumstances, persuasiveness is an art and a skill.

Quick Reference 76.1 lists key elements to consider including in communications written to persuade. Figures 8.25 and 8.26 provide examples involving sales of a product and a service.

QUICK REFERENCE 76.1

Key elements of a persuasive message

- **A hook to attract attention.** Appeal to the reader's interests, needs, and wants—this is the "you attitude."
- **A focus that builds interest.** Focus immediately on what will interest the reader in learning more.
- **A description that creates desire.** Use concrete, specific, and incisive terms to describe your idea, service, or product. The

CONTINUED→

QUICK REFERENCE 76.1 → CONTINUED

description should help the reader visualize how your offer will satisfy a need.

- **An incentive to act upon the message.** Make the reader want to take the action you desire and provide clear information about how to do so.
- **A message that is credible.** Choose words that will convince the reader that you are honest and reliable. Avoid exaggeration—it destroys credibility and is not persuasive. Also avoid flattery if there is any chance that it will strike a false note.

Dear Ms. Sullivan:

You are invited to join a small group of discriminating individuals who truly appreciate fine art—people who are keenly aware of a work's aesthetic as well as economic worth.

Attracts attention with appeal to feeling exclusivity.

Please take a look at the enclosed catalog. In a colorful and exciting way, it shows how you may acquire individually signed and numbered, authenticated, and framed original lithographs and etchings, from limited editions, by renowned modern artists. All are priced from only $1,000 to $10,000.

Builds interest on the basis of quality and price.

Our board of advisors seeks out only those living artists whose works have been praised by respected critics and displayed in galleries and museums all over the country. Each edition has been chosen both for its artistic beauty and its investment potential. The beauty will speak for itself; the investment potential will be proved later, when your works of art have increased dramatically in value!

Provides specifics to prove that the product is worth considering.

You risk nothing by joining the Art Collector's Guild. You will never be required to make a single purchase. Your $50 membership fee will be billed only after you have requested, received, and approved the free (framed) original etching or lithograph we send you.

Motivates with offer of a "free" item with no future obligation.

I hope you will want to take advantage of this unique opportunity. All you have to do right now is fill in and return the enclosed card. It needs no postage.

Provides a simple and easy way to accept the offer.

Sincerely,

FIGURE 8.25 Persuasive letter—selling a membership

Dear Mr. Lasser:

As I looked over my file on Arthur Lasser and the United Air-Conditioning Institute this morning, I wondered, What can I say to Mr. Lasser that will convince him that Golden State Coastal Inn is the ideal spot for his annual convention? If I were he, why would I choose this particular hotel? And I thought about the following:

Builds rapport with personalized opening that focuses on the individual instead of the company.

The staff. Golden State employees know the meaning of hospitality. Although they're efficient (they know why people have meetings), they are also friendly (they want serious convention goers to have a good time). Everyone aims to act as a personal host to every guest.

Lists benefits that will interest and motivate the reader to learn more.

The facilities. No other hotel has our oceanfront views, our two Olympic-size swimming pools, our magnificent auditorium, our luxurious guest rooms, our culinary skills, or our elegant baroque atmosphere in a twenty-first-century setting. And we're not just beautiful—we're conveniently located and reasonably priced.

Uses concrete descriptions to create a mental picture.

The climate. Spring comes to the Oceanside region in early March. The flowers are blooming, the winds are soft and gentle, the sun is assertive, and the water is inviting.

So, there are many other reasons for you to choose Golden State Coastal Inn—but, you really need to see it for yourself.

Boosts credibility by admitting that "seeing is believing".

This is why I am inviting you and a companion for a complimentary weekend (two nights) on a date of your choosing. All I ask is that you make your reservation within the next 30 days. Simply return the enclosed card or reserve online.

Persuades the reader with the offer of a free weekend and motivates him with a deadline of "within 30 days."

I look forward to greeting you personally on your arrival!

Sincerely,

FIGURE 8.26 Persuasive letter—selling a convention site

77 WRITING PERSONAL MESSAGES

Relationships with coworkers, clients, or customers often require communications that convey a personal message. There is no formula for writing such messages—other than the goal of making sure that they are thoughtful and appropriate to the situation and the relationship. Some key considerations that apply to a variety of situations are listed in Quick Reference 77.1.

QUICK REFERENCE 77.1

Considerations for writing personal messages

- **The message.** A personal message need not be lengthy, but it must be sincere. Use direct, but sensitive language that avoids flowery or overly sentimental phrases.
- **Typing versus handwriting.** Nothing builds rapport better than a handwritten personal note. Although typed messages—printed and mailed or emailed—are better than none, handwriting is the most sincere (and classy) way to write personal messages. This is especially the case with thank-you notes for important occasions and letters or cards expressing condolence. An email thanking a colleague for a favor or to congratulate someone on a promotion or a project well done is perfectly appropriate.
- **Promptness.** Personal messages conveying appreciation, congratulations, or condolences need to be sent promptly. Otherwise, the recipient might interpret the message as an afterthought or an obligation rather than a sincere expression of concern or appreciation.
- **Sincerity.** The purpose is to make a personal connection, which is done best in language that shows sincerity and genuine interest. A thank-you note should mention the specific act or gift; a condolence should acknowledge the person or relative, rather than referring to a generic "loss." Take advantage of the opportunity to express a bit of the real you when writing a personal message to a business associate.
- **Appropriate level of formality.** Aim for a level of formality that reflects your true relationship with the reader. Don't become formal because you are offering condolences or too familiar because you are offering congratulations.

77a Thank-you Notes

Never neglect an opportunity to send a written "thank-you," even when you are sure the recipient does not expect one. It is a way of building rapport and showing appreciation that outranks all others.

A thank-you note should get right to the point—don't weaken it by starting with the pointless phrase "I want to . . ." Express your thanks simply—by stating what was given to you or done for you—and why it was meaningful, enjoyable, or important. At the end, avoid the trite and redundant phrase "Thanks again."

Dear Mrs. Aguirre:

Thank you for attending our conference and for your informative and enjoyable keynote talk, "How to Motivate Your Students." It set exactly the right mood for the National Secondary School Counselors' conference. You will be pleased to know that counselors who attended the conference are feeling better about themselves and their work because of your supportive, enthusiastic message. Several wrote to tell me how much they enjoyed your talk. I have enclosed copies of their letters.

Says "thank-you" simply and directly.

Makes courteous and genuine complimentary statements and supports them with concrete evidence.

As you know, a keynote address can make or break a conference. Evaluations of this one indicate that it was one of the best we have had, and we truly appreciate your contribution to that success.

Reinforces the positive message in the close.

Sincerely yours,

FIGURE 8.27 Thank-you letter—guest speaker

Figure 8.27 is an example of a note anyone would be happy to receive—the writer actually provides proof that the audience was pleased with the speaker. Think how pleased the reader will be to see that others at the conference shared this writer's feelings. Figure 8.28 gets to the point promptly, but instead of starting with a description of what the reader did, it starts with an attention-getting lead about the outcome for the writer.

Dear Dr. Downing:

As you know, the goal of any graduate of Weston Business School is a position with a prestigious firm like R. L. Justen, Inc. Because of your help, Professor Downing, I will be joining the firm when I graduate in June.

Begins by describing the favorable outcome of the reader's actions.

Thank you for the convincing letter of reference you wrote to Jerome Hastings on my behalf. I shall always be grateful for your help.

Expresses appreciation and describes the specific act.

When you are looking for sponsors for your student internship program next year, please remember me. I would consider it an honor and a pleasure to help one of your future students.

Closes with a sincere offer to return the favor.

Sincerely yours,

FIGURE 8.28 Thank-you letter—job reference

77b Condolences

Letters of condolence are not easy to write, and for that reason many people put off writing them. Like all personal messages, a letter of condolence should be written promptly—preferably the same day you receive the news.

Aim for a serious tone, but avoid sounding gloomy or morose. Refer to the event that has occurred in language that you feel comfortable using, and then follow with an expression of sympathy. Some people prefer such phrases as *passed away* or *loss of;* while others feel comfortable using more direct language, including the word *death*. Do what feels best for you, but avoid clichéd euphemisms like *tragic event.* The same is true with words like *condolences* and *sympathy*. Although you might choose to express your feelings in a more individual way, there is nothing wrong with using these traditional words.

In some instances, you might be able to suggest something you could do to help. If so, be specific. Most people will not respond to "call me if you need me." Figure 8.29 was written to a business colleague who experienced a fire. In this case, the writer was in a position to offer concrete assistance. Whether or not the recipient accepts, she will remember his generosity in making the offer.

Figure 8.30 expresses sympathy for the death of a company official. The message is sincere and succinct. If you knew the deceased person, as in this case, it is always nice to say something complimen-

Dear Margaret:

We were all shocked and sorry to hear of the fire in your office building last night. We were relieved to learn that no one was in the building at the time, but heard that it must be temporarily vacated.

Expresses sympathy without dwelling on the cause.

Dave Atkinson has asked me to extend an invitation to use the recently vacated suite on the second floor of our Central Street building. He hopes that you will use it as a base of operations until you can return to your own office. Let me know if this arrangement might work for you; we can iron out the details whenever you're ready. If not, let me know if we can assist you in any other way.

Goes a step further by offering concrete help.

Leaves the reader an opening to turn down the offer.

Mark O'Reilly

FIGURE 8.29 Condolence letter—tragic event

Dear Paul,

All of us here at the Benson Foundation are grieved by the news of the death of your president, Jean Rollenstein. Please accept our sincere condolences. Those of us who knew Jean revered her as a true leader and an example to everyone in the community. Her leadership in organizing our volunteers for the annual fundraising event will be long remembered.

Sincerely yours,

Uses concrete words instead of euphemisms.

Expresses condolences.

Pays compliments to the deceased.

FIGURE 8.30 Condolence letter—death of a colleague

tary or to refer to your relationship and what it meant to you. If not, an expression of solidarity is an appropriate closing, as shown in Figure 8.31.

Dear Jennifer,

I was very sorry to hear about the loss of your mother. I recall from our lunch conversations that the two of you were very close, and I want you to know that my thoughts and prayers are with you. When you return to the city, please know that you have me to lean on as a friend.

Let's get together as soon as you have the time.

My sincerest condolences to you and all your family members.

Sincerely yours,

Opens with expression of sympathy.

Makes a personal reference that shows thoughtfulness.

Offers both abstract and concrete support.

Respectfully acknowledges others who are affected by the loss.

FIGURE 8.31 Condolence letter—death of colleague's family member

77c Expressions of Congratulations

It is appropriate to send a letter, note, or email of congratulations to business associates when they receive promotions, awards, or other kinds of recognition. Avoid flattery in such messages, even if you are truly enthusiastic about someone's performance or achievements. Praise comes across

Dear Chris,

Congratulations on your promotion to vice president of advertising at Kerry & Company. I read about it in the newspaper yesterday. Two years ago when you hired and trained me, I thought you were a terrific teacher and manager. I know your promotion is well deserved and that you will do a great job.

Best of luck!

FIGURE 8.32 Congratulations message

as more sincere when it is offered in a reasonable-sized dose. You may wish to show your enthusiasm with an occasional exclamation point, but use them sparingly and one at a time.

Figure 8.32 is a short email of congratulations that helped the writer stay in touch with a former, well-liked boss. Figure 8.33 is also a networking letter congratulating a colleague on an achievement that received publicity. Both are short notes that impart enthusiasm that sounds sincere. This is a good way to establish or maintain a relationship with an acquaintance that might be of assistance in the future.

Dear Mr. Carr:

Congratulations on the success of your conference on "Human Relations and Customer Service." The excellent write-up in this month's *HR Today* must have pleased you after all the hard work you put into planning it. I attended the morning session and particularly liked the seminar conducted by Frances Winger on dealing with dissatisfied customers. I was sorry that a prior commitment made it impossible for me to stay for the afternoon sessions. Are you planning to provide transcripts of the speeches? I know at least two other people who are also interested.

I am looking forward to next year's conference.

Sincerely,

FIGURE 8.33 Congratulations letter

REPORTS, PROPOSALS, AND REFERENCES

section nine

78 BUSINESS REPORTS

Business reports are informative documents written for a specific purpose and for a designated audience. Reports present findings and data, summarize activities, analyze and discuss a specific issue, and fulfill a variety of other purposes. Most reports include recommendations or solutions for consideration. A report should cover only one topic, although a long report might have many sections covering relevant subtopics.

A good business report presents information in a style and format that helps the reader digest information and extract the essentials quickly and efficiently. Therefore, both format and content are critical to developing a successful report. Much thought should be given to the best way to present the information clearly and meet the expectations of the reader.

78a Defining Purpose and Audience

The following questions will help you focus on your purpose and audience when writing reports:

- What is the purpose for writing the report?
- Who are the primary readers?
- What do you want your readers to do with the information?
- Is there a secondary audience for the report; for example, the local or national media?

78b Gathering Information

- What specific information are your readers looking for?
- What decisions do you expect to be made as a result of the report?
- How much background information will readers need in order to make the best-informed decisions?
- Does the content need the support of tables, charts, graphs, or other graphics?
- What source materials are needed to substantiate information in the report? Will these sources need documentation?
- Are there materials that need to be included as attachments or appendixes?

79 INFORMAL REPORTS

Informal reports are short and are usually written for routine business purposes—for example, a travel report after a field trip or conference, a status report on a project, or an analysis of the viability of a new project or process. These types of reports are usually written for internal audiences.

79a Informal Report Formats

A typical format for an informal report is a printed memo of one or two pages, or several unbound pages of typed copy on plain paper. (See Figures 9.1 and 9.2.) This assumes that the intent is to have the report printed and read. Since a short report does not need a binding, it can be distributed via email as an attachment, and, depending on the audience, it might be appropriate to send an informal report as an email.

Some informal reports follow a prescribed format used routinely by an organization or department for reporting that recurs frequently. Otherwise, an informal report is best structured according to the writer's judgment of how to most clearly and coherently present the content.

79b Parts of Informal Reports

Three standard parts that will work for almost any type of informal report are described below.

INTRODUCTION

Begin with a brief statement that tells the reader the purpose of the report and provides whatever amount of background is needed to set the information in context. A heading is not always necessary; for example, in routine reports a subject line and/or a one- or two-sentence opening paragraph might be sufficient. When a heading is desired, the words *Introduction, Overview,* or *Summary* are appropriate.

BODY

Depending on the amount of information and its complexity, consider breaking up the body with subtopic headings. This helps the reader see the scope of the report immediately and makes it easy to find information at a glance.

CONCLUSION

The conclusion summarizes the main points from the writer's point of view in a succinct paragraph or two. It might be labeled *Conclusion, Summary,*

Recommendations, or *Proposed Solutions,* depending on the type of report. Figure 9.1 shows a report typed on plain paper. Note the following characteristics:

- The introduction indicates the purpose of the report and provides background that leads into the body.

Report on Employee Suggestions for Revamping *Tabs*
Submitted to the Employee Communications Task Force

Wanda Roundtree, Employee Representative
September 25, 20xx

INTRODUCTION

An informal survey of employees was conducted to determine the future of the company's newsletter, *Tabs*, which was renamed and revamped five years ago.

A two-page questionnaire was emailed to the entire staff. They were offered the option of responding by email or printing out the survey form and sending it back inter-office if they wished to remain anonymous. Approximately 35 percent of the employees responded, the majority by email. I also talked informally to about 20 employees at random and sought out 10 staff members to interview in-depth, based on their responses to the questionnaire.

The questionnaire and interviews sought to answer the following general questions:

1. Is the newsletter still meeting the needs of the employees?
2. What do employees see as its strengths and weaknesses?
3. Which features of the newsletter are outdated, irrelevant, or uninteresting?
4. What new story ideas and features would employees like to see in a revamped newsletter? What information do they find most/least useful?
5. Do employees like the title of the newsletter or would a new title be more appealing?
6. Should the newsletter be redesigned?

FINDINGS AND RECOMMENDATIONS

Is the newsletter still meeting the needs of the employees?

Employees are generally very satisfied with *Tabs*. They see its value as a vehicle for keeping them informed about company news, and appreciate the timeliness and

FIGURE 9.1 Informal report

Report on Employee Suggestions for Revamping *Tabs* **2**

the tone. Employees feel that the newsletter succeeds in keeping them involved in the organization by letting them know what is going on at the management level. Their main concern, however, is an overemphasis on management activities. They recognize these as important, but see them as out of balance with the amount of coverage given to the workforce itself.

What do employees see as its strengths and weaknesses?

Strengths:

1. Generally, they like the format of the newsletter and find it easy to read online or print out to read on the way home.

2. Employees recognize the publication by the name *Tabs*; the majority like the title and find it entirely appropriate.

Weaknesses:

1. Employees feel that *Tabs* has too many stories on activities of management and too few about the typical worker. They want a newsletter that is principally a publication for and about employees—not a management PR publication.

CONCLUSION

While employees appreciate *Tabs* in its current form, a revamped version that focuses more on employees at all levels of the organization will be even more highly valued. The recommended changes are designed to create an employee-oriented focus with more balanced coverage. This new focus will provide employees with a true sense of ownership of this important communications tool.

Thank you for the opportunity to handle this aspect of the project. I will be happy to explore or clarify further any of these findings and recommendations for the entire Task Force or for individual members.

FIGURE 9.1 (Continued)

- The body is structured with three main headings: Introduction, Findings and Recommendations, and Conclusion. The headings reflect the questions listed in the introduction.
- The concluding paragraph summarizes the report without being repetitious.

- The tone of the writing is friendly and informal, reflecting the working relationship the writer has with the recipients and the people-oriented nature of the project.

Figure 9.2 shows the same report written as a memo; the title becomes the subject line. The header for page 2 would be the same as that shown on page 2 in Figure 9.1. [Read more about headers and footers in documents in Section Ten: Document Design, Graphics, and Multimedia.]

MEMO

To: Employee Communications Task Force (see Distribution)

From: Wanda Roundtree

Date: September 25, 20xx

Re: Report on Employee Suggestions for Revamping *Tabs*

An informal survey of employees was conducted to determine the future of the company's newsletter *Tabs*. The newsletter was renamed and revamped five years ago. ECTF wanted answers to the following questions:

Distribution:
Thomas Allen, Human Resources
Jeffrey D'Artagnan, Corporate Communications
Deanna Huff, Corporate Communications
Janie Kwan, Chief of Staff
Dorsey Miller, Human Resources
Theresa O'Loughlin, Creative Services

FIGURE 9.2 Memo report

80 FORMAL REPORTS

Reports have been called "the workhorses of business." **Formal reports** are typically lengthy enough to require a well-planned organizational structure. They contain standard parts that readers expect to see in a report of a particular kind, such as a research report, an annual report, a problem analysis, and so on. This Topic provides guidelines for a standard business report that analyzes a problem and presents recommended solutions. It covers the standard parts included in such reports. It also has guidelines that can be applied to any type of report. In general, it is critical that reports communicate clearly through their organizational structure, writing style, and overall visual presentation. Business reports must also be designed so the reader can extract information quickly and accurately.

80a Parts of Formal Reports

Formal reports have three main elements:

1. **Front matter:** preliminary material at the beginning of the report
2. **Body:** text of the report
3. **Back matter:** attachments, appendixes, and reference material, including bibliography

Quick Reference 80.1 lists the standard parts that make up these three elements in the order in which they should appear. The parts labeled "required" are those included in almost all formal reports; the others are optional and should be included as needed.

Formal reports also frequently include graphics (illustrations, charts, graphs, and photos), tables, and source documentation. Section Ten in this book covers graphics, tables, and page layout; documentation of sources is covered in Topics 82-84 of this section.

QUICK REFERENCE 80.1

Standard parts and their order in formal reports

Front matter

- Letter or memo of transmittal (optional)
- Cover (required)
- Title page (optional)
- Copyright notice, credits (optional)

CONTINUED→

QUICK REFERENCE 80.1 → CONTINUED

- Table of contents (required)
- List of tables and/or figures (optional)
- Preface or foreword (optional)
- Acknowledgments (optional)

Body

- Executive summary (optional, but used in most reports)
- Introduction (required)
- Findings (optional)
- Recommendations (optional)
- Conclusion (required)

Back matter (all parts are optional)

- Reference list or bibliography of sources cited in the report and/or used to develop the report
- Appendixes containing supporting materials
- Attachments; copies of source materials

80b Cover and Title Page

Place the following information on the cover page:

- Title of the report
- Name and professional title of the author(s) of the report
- Name and professional title of the person for whom the report was prepared (or the group or organization)
- Date the report is distributed
- Company logo, if desired

Figure 9.3 shows how to format these elements for readability and visual appeal. Select font size and use spacing according to the amount of text on the page.

TITLE PAGE

A title page is optional. Some writers prefer to have a title page between the cover and Contents page in a professionally bound report. A title page repeats the text printed on the cover. The back of the title page may be used for a copyright notice, credits and/or acknowledgments, or other publication notes.

A Study of Nurse Retention at People's Hospital

Prepared by
Evelyn T. Jones
Human Resources Director

Submitted to

People's Hospital
Executive Staff & Board of Directors

October 15, 20xx

FIGURE 9.3 Report cover page

Begin the contents on the first right-hand page after the cover or title page. If the contents does not continue onto a second page, leave the back of it blank (if no other front matter is included—see Quick Reference 80.1) and begin the body of the report on the next right-hand page. Figure 9.4 shows the layout of the cover and table of contents for a report with double-sided pages and no title page. (See Quick Reference

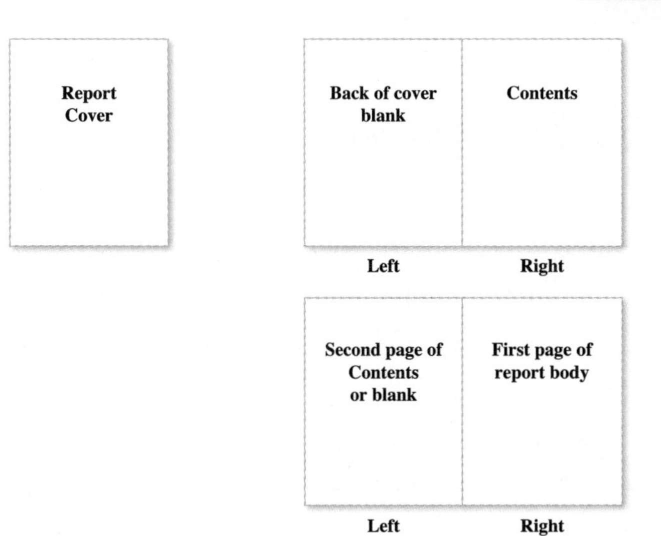

FIGURE 9.4 Layout of opening pages printed on both sides. See Figure 9.10 for layout of remaining front matter pages

80.3 for guidelines on numbering front matter pages and Figure 9.10 for layout of front matter and numbering of front matter pages.)

80c Letter or Memo of Transmittal

The transmittal document introduces the report to the reader. It should appear first—either attached to the front of the report or bound into the document as the first page. When the report is being transmitted outside the organization, it should include a **letter of transmittal.** When the report is being distributed inside the organization, it should be accompanied by a printed **memo of transmittal** (see Figure 9.5). This may be sent as an email attachment if the report is being transmitted electronically, or you may wish to embed the transmittal information in the email.

The transmittal document should include the following:

- A brief description giving the title and purpose of the report
- If appropriate, a brief statement as to why the report is being sent to the recipient(s)
- What action, if any, is expected of the recipient(s)

When you send a report by email, it is a good idea to reformat it as a PDF file rather than send it as a word processing document. **PDF** is the file format for representing documents in a manner that is independent of the original application software, hardware, and operating

MEMO

Date: November 28, 20xx

To: Executive Staff and Board Members

From: Evelyn T. Jones, Human Resources Director

Re: A Study of Nurse Retention at People's Hospital

I am transmitting for your review a report that was prepared to determine the reasons for a chronic shortage of nurses at People's Hospital. The study focuses on turnover rates of nursing staff and provides a comparison of practices at People's and three other hospitals in our region. We looked at a variety of factors, including salaries and benefits, recruitment efforts, work conditions, and advertising and public relations.

The report provides a number of specific recommendations that involve working with a cross-section of People's staff and the board. Implementing these changes will substantially improve our ability to retain nursing staff and increase our patient population.

Please be prepared to discuss your response to this report at the next board meeting scheduled for December 15. If you have any questions in the interim, feel free to contact me by phone (000-000-000) or email: ejones@xxx.org.

FIGURE 9.5 Transmittal memo

system used to create it. A PDF will ensure that none of the information is distorted, which can happen in transmission, especially if the material contains graphics and tables. It also ensures that recipients cannot alter the document.

[Read more about writing transmittal documents in Section Eight: Email, Memos, and Letters.]

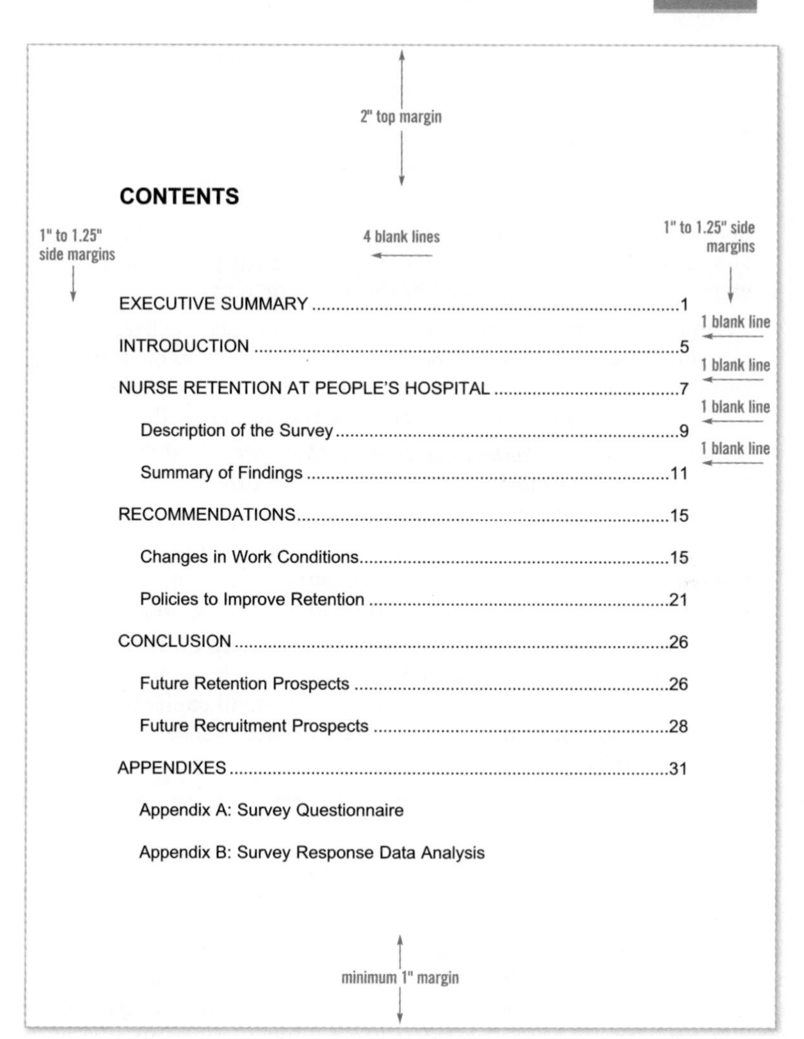

CONTENTS

EXECUTIVE SUMMARY 1

INTRODUCTION 5

NURSE RETENTION AT PEOPLE'S HOSPITAL 7

Description of the Survey 9

Summary of Findings 11

RECOMMENDATIONS 15

Changes in Work Conditions 15

Policies to Improve Retention 21

CONCLUSION 26

Future Retention Prospects 26

Future Recruitment Prospects 28

APPENDIXES 31

Appendix A: Survey Questionnaire

Appendix B: Survey Response Data Analysis

FIGURE 9.6 Report table of contents

80d Table of Contents

A table of contents follows the cover or title page and lists the main sections of the report. Include front matter items, body text main headings (and subheadings, if appropriate), and all back matter, when applicable. Format the contents for readability; see Quick Reference 80.2 for formatting guidelines and Figure 9.6 for a readable and visually attractive format.

QUICK REFERENCE 80.2

Formatting a report table of contents

- **Margins:** See Figure 9.6 for standard margins; make adjustments as needed to accommodate length.
- **Line spacing:** Double-space between entries. Leave more space between the title and the first entry if the contents page is very short, but do not space out the entries to fill the page. For a short contents list, start further down on the page.
- **Page numbering:** Use roman numerals to number the front matter. The contents is page i of the front matter, but if you have only a cover and table of contents, you need not put a number on the contents page; instead begin numbering the report body with page 1.
- **Title:** Use the title *Contents* or *Table of Contents*, typed flush at the left margin. Centering the title and using *Table of Contents* is considered traditional; flush left and *Contents* is the modern style.
- **Second and subsequent pages:** Do not repeat the words *Contents* or *Table of Contents* on top of subsequent pages. Continue the listing with the next heading appropriately aligned.
- **Headings:** Type headings to reflect the structure of the body of the report; they do not necessarily have to match the font size and style of the text, however. Font size, color, all capitals, and cap/lowercase can be used to create an attractive look and a clear hierarchy of parts of the report.

80e Foreword and Preface

A **preface** is written by the author of a report; a **foreword** is written by someone other than the author such as an executive in the company or an outside expert. A report might include one or both or neither. Purposes for including a preface and/or foreword are to discuss some or all of the following: (1) why the report was written; (2) what it is intended to accomplish; (3) how the research or background information was gathered; (4) how the conclusions were reached; (5) acknowledgment of individuals and/or groups who assisted in preparing the report. Because these points can also be covered in an introduction, most reports do not need a preface written by the author, particularly if the report has a foreword.

A foreword includes the name and title of the writer because he or she is someone other than the author of the report. Type this information at the end of the text, centered or flush with the right margin. Including the writer's signature above the printed name is optional.

Figure 9.7 shows the format for a foreword. Use the same format for a preface, but without the name and title.

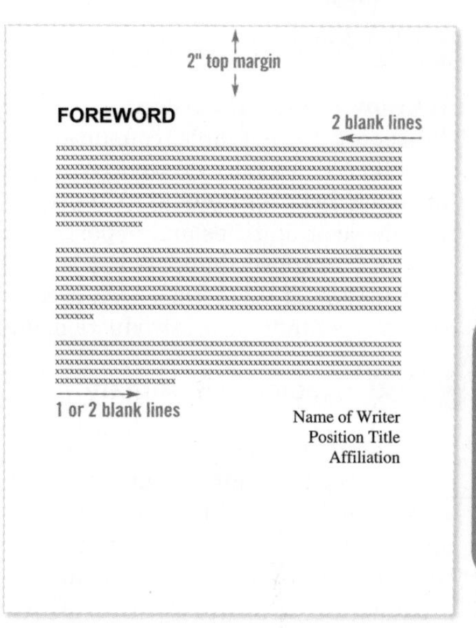

FIGURE 9.7 Format for a foreword

80f List of Figures and Tables

In a report that has a large number of figures and/or tables, a list in the front matter provides a convenient reference tool. Place the list after the contents, formatted to match. List each figure or table number and its title and provide the page number. See the example in Figure 9.8. If there are numerous figures, consider clustering them under main topic titles corresponding to the text.

[For more information on formatting titles and captions for figures and tables see Section Ten: Document Design, Graphics, and Multimedia.]

LIST OF FIGURES

Figure 1	Five-Year Hiring/Retention Rates	7
Figure 2	Average Annual Salary by Level of Employee	16
Figure 3	Percentage of Budget Allocated to Salaries	17
Figure 4	Average Salary: Industry Comparison	17
Figure 5	Percent of Budget Allocated to Benefits	18

FIGURE 9.8 List of figures

80g Acknowledgments

Acknowledgments list people or groups who made contributions to the report; for example, consultants, interviewees, and providers of resources. Names may be written in paragraph form or in list format following a brief statement of appreciation. In addition to the names, include position titles and department or organizational affiliations.

If the acknowledgments list is long, make it a separate section of the front matter. If the list is short, it can be placed at the end of the preface, executive summary, or introduction, under the heading *Acknowledgments*.

80h Executive Summary

An **executive summary** (also called **summary)** is a brief but thorough synopsis of the contents of a report. Its purpose is to provide readers with an overview of the report's major points including the conclusions and recommendations. An executive summary is useful in any report that has several main sections, and is essential in a long report.

Keep in mind that conciseness is important; the executive summary is not meant to entirely replace a thorough reading. Figure 9.9 illustrates an executive summary written for a report to a hospital board of directors to study the problem of a nurse shortage.

80i Introduction

The **introduction,** which follows the executive summary, is a brief discussion of the report contents. It is the writer's opportunity to set the stage for the reader's interpretation and response to the information.

An introduction may cover any or all of the following:

- An overview of the report's main focus
- A summary of the scope of information covered
- Background information to help the reader put the report in context
- Methods used for gathering the information
- Explanation of how the information is presented
- Highlights of key findings or conclusions
- Acknowledgments (optional) (see 80g)

80j Body of the Report

The **body** contains the main content of the report. Logical order is a key element to ensure a clear, comprehensive treatment of the topic. Break the body into subtopics and structure them with headings. Use parallel wording and font size/style for headings of the same level of importance.

EXECUTIVE SUMMARY

This report was prepared to determine the reasons for a chronic shortage of nurses at People's Hospital. The findings are based on a formal study of turnover rates of nursing staff and a comparison of practices at People's with the three other hospitals in our region, all of which have grown in demand for services and which have a lower patient-nurse ratio. We compared a variety of factors, including salaries and benefits, recruitment efforts, work conditions, and advertising and public relations.

States the problem

During the past five years, our area population base has doubled from 175,000 to 350,000. Our facility population has declined 12 percent in that time period. The other three hospitals in our service area (Sunrise, Westview, and Grayson) have grown at an average rate of 3 percent each year.

Summarizes background information

Summary of Findings

1. Our hospital's nursing staff has decreased 5 percent in each of the past five years. The patient-nurse ratio is 12 to 1, the second highest in our region. By comparison, Sunrise Hospital enjoys a patient-nurse ratio of 5 to 1.
2. Our nurses work an average of 50 hours per week; the regional average is 44 hours per week.
3. Forty-three percent of People's former nurses are employed elsewhere in the region; our average turnover of nursing staff is one year to 18 months.
4. People's salaries are not competitive with the regional standards.

Summarizes findings and recommendations

Recommendations

1. Develop new policies that support recruitment and retention of nursing staff and address the causes of dissatisfaction that contribute to turnover, including salaries, work hours, level of staffing per shift, benefits, and other issues.
2. Initiate a policy with Human Resources to conduct exit interviews, which has never been done.
3. Establish a task force consisting of a cross-section of People's staff—nurses, doctors, and administrators—to implement a series of administrative changes that will contribute substantially to retention of nursing staff.
4. Once changes are implemented, identify advertising/PR firms that would be invited to bid on creation of an advertising campaign dedicated to recruitment of nursing staff, with the added benefit of attracting patients to our services.

Summarizes recommendations

FIGURE 9.9 Executive summary

See Figure 9.11 for an example of the body of a report and Quick Reference 80.3 for guidelines on formatting body text. Quick Reference 80.4 shows how to style headings.

[Read more on organizing and planning documents in Section Six: Writing Process and Style and structuring and formatting headings in Section Ten: Document Design.]

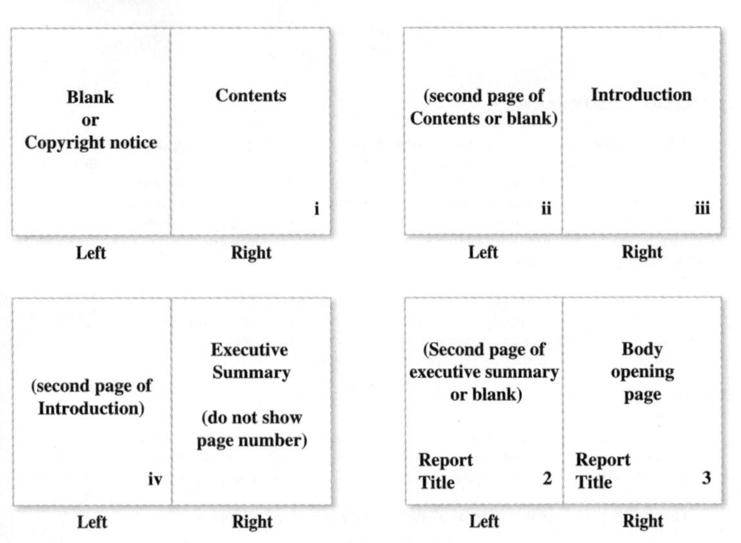

FIGURE 9.10 Layout and numbering of front matter pages

QUICK REFERENCE 80.3

Formatting a report

Font

- Use a standard font, preferably, 12-pt. Times Roman,

Margins

- Top and bottom margins: 1 inch
- Side margins: 1 inch for unbound reports; 1.5 inches for bound reports
- Line spacing: Single-space long reports; in shorter reports 1.5-inch line spacing is acceptable to enhance readability.

Header/footer options

- Report title and page number
- Report title, section title, and page number

[For examples of formatting header/footer, see Topic 85.]

Numbering pages

Front matter

- Use lowercase roman numerals; *do not place a number on the cover or title page.*
- If you have a title page, the contents will be page iii; otherwise it will be page i (see Figure 9.10).

CONTINUED →

QUICK REFERENCE 80.3 → CONTINUED

Body

- Number the first page 1 (arabic).
- Begin each main section on a right-hand page, regardless of how the text falls.
- If title pages are created for each main section of the report, do not show the number on these pages. Use your word processor's automated numbering system to suppress the number, but always count these pages in the overall numbering.

Back matter

- Continue numbering consecutively from the body of the report.
- If any materials, such as appendixes and attachments, are already numbered, these numbers can stand. In that case, make a title page for the appendix and number it as part of the text. Use this number reference in the contents, and then list the titles of the appendixes or attachments without numbers.

(**Note:** Microsoft Word has downloadable templates for business reports.)

80k Recommendations

Recommendations are suggestions for consideration; for example, a list of possible actions to solve a problem, suggestions for organizational changes, or a plan for implementation of an idea. The need to include recommendations depends on the purpose of the report.

Recommendations may be listed at the end of each major section or at the end of the report. If listed at the end, organizing them under headings that match the corresponding section of the report is useful. A matrix or chart keyed to main sections is also an option. Numbering recommendations is also a good way to provide a reference for discussion of specific points. Choose a format and place that makes the recommendations easy to digest and reference by skimming.

If applicable, this section can include a follow-up or implementation plan, such as a chart detailing delegation of responsibility, resources needed, or a suggested time frame for implementation of the recommendations.

QUICK REFERENCE 80.4

Formatting headings in a report

Following is a standard way of structuring headings in body text.

Level 1 Heading

- Cap/lowercase, centered or flush with the left margin.
- Start each new section on a right-hand page.
- Type the section title 1 inch from the top of the page.
- Use a display font, such as Arial (14 pt. or 16 pt.).
- For color printing, a second color, such as navy blue or burgundy looks elegant and enhances readability by emphasizing the headings.
- Begin text two spaces below.

LEVEL 2 HEADING

- All caps, boldface, flush with the left margin.
- Match either the Level 1 heading font or the text font.
- Do not use a third font.
- If color is used for the Level 1 headings, this heading may also be typed in the same color.
- Begin text two spaces below.

Level 3 Heading

- Cap/lowercase, boldface. This heading should be in black type and match the text type, whether or not color is used for the Level 1 and 2 headings.
- Begin text two spaces below.

Level 4 heading.

- Cap/lowercase, boldface, in the same font as text in black type.
- Run this heading into the first line of the paragraph.

80I Conclusion

The **conclusion** of a report lists or summarizes the writer's interpretation of the contents. This is a standard element that needs to be included in most any report. In most instances, one concluding section is sufficient. However, it is not out of the ordinary to end major sections with a conclusion or summary as well.

The conclusion may be written in paragraph form, as a numbered or bulleted list, or as a combination of both these forms. The goals of the re-

Nurse Retention at People's Hospital

The nursing staff is the "heart" of any medical facility. Nurses quite literally can make or break a hospital's reputation. People's Hospital values its nursing staff highly. Yet, in the latest annual review of the hospital it was noted that the number of nurses People's employs had dropped from the previous year. Further study revealed that such a drop was not unusual. The data showed that the number of nurses on staff has dropped an average of 5 percent for the past five years. In the past five years, our population base has doubled from 175,500 to 350,000. Our facility population has declined 12 percent in that same time period. The other three hospitals in our service area (Sunrise, Westview, and Grayson) have grown at an average rate of 3 percent each year. The Board of Trustees expressed a genuine concern about this situation, and funded a survey to be conducted by an external research firm.

DESCRIPTION OF THE SURVEY

The entire nursing staff at People's Hospital was asked to complete a written questionnaire designed to determine their levels of satisfaction and areas of dissatisfaction.

The survey instrument was reviewed by all of the supervisory nursing staff and a representative sample of doctors and administrators. Based on feedback from these groups, the survey focused on key areas identified as primarily accountable for the low retention rate: (1) compensation compared to nearby facilities; (2) interactions with supervisors and administrative staff members; (3) staffing levels that equitably share the workload; (4) hours required per week; and (5) level of difficulty of the work.

The survey was completed voluntarily, with nurses signing in to complete the questionnaire under the supervision of a proctor to ensure that each nurse completed only one questionnaire, yet was able to do so anonymously. There was extensive cooperation on the part of the staff; out of a total of 250 nurses employed by the hospital, 222 responses were filed.

Key Findings

Appendix 1 contains a copy of the survey instrument, and Appendix 2 contains a table summarizing its data. Following is a summary of key findings addressed in the rest of this report.

FIGURE 9.11 Report body

port, the type of content, and its readability will determine the best format to use.

80m Appendix

An **appendix** to a report contains supplemental information. For example, the body of a report might discuss a topic or present data that is

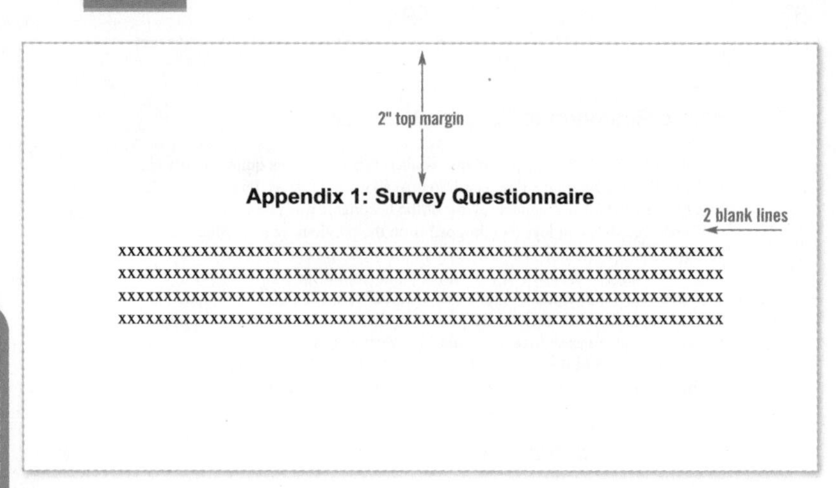

FIGURE 9.12 Opening page of appendix

part of a separate analytical or source document; for the reader's reference, you may opt to include the complete document as an appendix. Examples of typical appendix materials include detailed data analysis; survey instruments, such as questionnaires or interview questions; and complete copies of source documents that are referenced or shown in part in the body.

If you have more than one appendix (*appendixes* is the preferred plural spelling; *appendices* is also correct), number or letter them consecutively as Appendix 1, Appendix 2, or Appendix A, Appendix B, and so on. Type the title at the top of the page, centered or flush left, according to the style used in the body of the document. Double-space between the title and the body, as shown in Figure 9.12.

If an appendix has an exceptionally long title, break it as needed, as shown in Figure 9.13.

If the appendixes are separate documents that have their own titles and page numbering systems, create a section-opening contents page and list the specific titles underneath, as shown in Figure 9.14.

80n References

Another element required in the back matter of some reports is a list of references cited and sources used. (For guidelines on documenting sources and compiling a reference list or bibliography, see Topic 83.)

Appendix A

Executive Summary
Health Care Policy and the Nursing Profession:
Report of the National Association of Nursing Professionals, 20xx

FIGURE 9.13 Appendix title

APPENDIXES

A. Executive Summary–Health Care Policy and the Nursing Profession: Report of the National Association of Nursing Professionals, 20xx

B. Salary Survey of Nursing Professionals in the United States 20xx-20xx

FIGURE 9.14 Appendix contents page

80o Glossary

A **glossary** of terms may be necessary in reports that contain specialized language. A glossary always lists words alphabetically; definitions should be concise and clear. The standard style is to use boldface for the defined term. Capitalizing terms is optional, but be consistent; typically capitalize only the first word of the entry. See Figure 9.15 for a typical glossary opening page and standard style for entries.

For assistance with putting items in order—such as acronyms, abbreviations, or names with numbers—see Topic 55.

Glossary

Ablation The erosion of a solid body by a high-temperature gas stream moving at high velocity, e.g., a reentry vehicle's heat shield that melts or chars under the effects of air friction.

ABMA Army Ballistic Missile Agency (US).

Abort To cancel or cut short a mission.

Absolute zero The temperature at which all heat action ceases, 2273.16°C (2459.69°F).

Acceleration A change in velocity, including changes of direction and decreases as well as increases in speed.

FIGURE 9.15 Glossary opening page

81 BUSINESS PROPOSALS

A **proposal** is a document written to make a request, for example, funding a project, purchasing a service, or approving a reorganization of staff. Its essential purpose is to persuade. Like reports, proposals may be short and simple—in memo or two- to three-page document format—or complex, lengthy documents.

While all proposals have in common the desired outcome of getting someone to do something, the needs of each proposal and, thus, the content and structure may be approached with more flexibility than the standards followed for business reports. Therefore, this Topic presents some very broad guidelines that can be adapted for formulating the basic parts of a proposal. Many excellent books and Web sites are devoted to the topic of writing proposals and business plans.

81a Types of Proposals

When writing a proposal, the first thing to consider is whether the audience is internal or external. **Internal proposals** are written for use inside an organization, for example, a supervisor's proposal to a manager to add a new position to the department. **External proposals** are written for parties outside an organization, for example, to request funding for a project or to convince a potential client to purchase services.

Either of these two types of proposals may be solicited or unsolicited. **Solicited proposals** are prepared at the receiver's request. Many firms that solicit proposals provide guidelines for how they want them written. Some organizations distribute a **Request for Proposal,** commonly referred to as an **RFP,** a document that describes in detail what is needed and outlines the specifics for submission. **Unsolicited proposals** are prepared without official guidelines.

81b Parts of Proposals

The following elements (parts) are described broadly as guidance that can be applied to most proposals. Do not be constrained by the names of the parts used here; label your proposal with words that best explain what each part of the proposal covers. (Remember to request guidelines whenever you respond to a solicited proposal or when you have the opportunity to ask a potential recipient for suggestions on what to include.)

OPENING

The goal of this part is to paint a picture of the context for the proposal —to help the reader understand the *who, what, where,* and *why* of it. Describe the purpose of the proposal and why it is needed, in vivid language that will grab the reader's attention. Depending on the type of proposal, the style can vary widely. The opening—which can be given a heading that is appropriate to the tone you want to set—might include the following:

- **An anecdote:** relate a dramatic incident that will elicit an emotional reaction
- **A historical perspective:** explain what has led up to the need and/or why past solutions have failed
- **Statistics:** cite studies and facts that dramatize the situation
- **A description of the current situation:** describe what is creating an urgent need for what you are proposing

DESCRIPTION

This part provides a detailed discussion of the product, service, or project that is being proposed. It should have as much information as is necessary to give the reader a clear idea of the *what* and *how.* It most likely would include:

- **Facts and figures:** data that supports the rationale for the proposed product or service

- **Research:** primary (conducted by you) or secondary (conducted by others) studies that will add to the recipient's understanding of the situation in a concrete and quantifiable way
- **Methods:** information that reassures the reader that you will be able to implement what you are proposing; as much detail as necessary to show that you have thought through the steps and have the capability to carry them out

The goal is to make sure the reader feels fully informed about what you are proposing. Care needs to be taken to make this section complete and balanced—you are not selling; you are building a case.

BUDGET OR FINANCIAL IMPACT

This part summarizes the financial dimensions of the proposal. It covers funding needs, allocation of the budget, and potential revenue associated with the proposal. These elements might be described in the following formats:

- **Charts and graphs:** visual depictions of proposed income and/or costs and allocation
- **Milestones and time lines:** stages of development tied to funding of the project; outlining this in advance is part of answering the *how* and *when*
- **Staffing requirements:** changes (usually additions) to staff that will be required for implementation; for example, a list of persons and/or position descriptions to show that qualified people will be brought on board to implement the project

The goal is to give the people who review and approve the proposal a clear understanding of the cost/benefit tradeoff associated with it. Failure to provide this in a clear, well-thought-out form often leads to the rejection of a proposal.

CONCLUSION

A brief summary of the "why" of the proposal. If appropriate, this section can include a sales pitch for the proposer, focusing on the track record of the person or organization and why it is well qualified to provide the service or product being proposed.

81c Example of a Short Proposal

Figure 9.16 is an example of a short proposal requesting funding. The main sections and headings used are based on the author's assessment of what the reader will be looking for and the key elements of the project.

[For the formatting of short proposals, cover page, and table of contents, follow the guidelines for reports shown in Figures 9.1, 9.3, and 9.6.]

Proposal for Funding
Helping Children Cope Project (HCCP)
Emergency Preparedness Publications

Submitted by Darlene Gray, Director, HCCP
January 3, 20xx

SITUATION ANALYSIS

Each year, extreme weather events force families to evacuate their homes. One of the most severe examples in recent times was Hurricane Katrina, a catastrophe that struck the Gulf Coast in 2005. In the months following Katrina, the National Center for Missing and Exploited Children (NCMEC) received reports of 4,710 children missing or displaced in Louisiana, 339 in Mississippi, and 39 in Alabama. Hurricane Rita hit the same region shortly after, resulting in a total of 5,192 missing children.

The intense media coverage of Katrina brought national attention to the gaps in emergency preparedness. Impoverished areas of Louisiana, Alabama, and Mississippi lacked a multitude of resources, and the impact fell more heavily on families already struggling with a burden of poverty. Unfortunately, the majority of these families did not have emergency or evacuation plans. They thought they would return to their homes in a couple of days as they had done in the past. Many of them did not even have identification, and taking important documents was not even a thought.

Children were especially vulnerable in this situation. During the evacuation from New Orleans, the nation witnessed the tragedy of children being separated from their parents by rescue teams. With no means of identifying them or finding family members, children were taken to shelters that lacked any special preparation for them. Many were deemed "lost" in the ensuing weeks. All of the families and children were traumatized, and continue to suffer from the effects of this trauma.

GOAL OF HELPING CHILDREN COPE PROJECT

The goal of the project we are proposing is to help parents, caregivers, and others in under-resourced communities effectively prepare for natural disasters.

FIGURE 9.16 Short proposal

DESCRIPTION OF THE PROJECT

To accomplish the goal, we will develop two easy-to-use publications designed to help families and responders be more effective in handling the needs of children in the wake of a national or local emergency or natural disaster.

Publication I: ***A Parent's Guide to Emergency Preparedness***
Target audience: parents and caregivers residing in low-income or underserved communities who have children 12 years old and younger.

Objectives
- To educate parents about the feelings and fears that children experience during an emergency or natural disaster.
- To give parents tips and information about how to communicate with children in the process of being prepared for, and in the aftermath of emergencies/natural disasters—including dealing with children's exposure to media coverage of disastrous events elsewhere.
- To provide information on emergency preparedness at home and in the event of evacuation.

Publication II: ***Helping Children and Families Cope with Emergencies and Natural Disasters***
Target audience: shelter volunteers and staff; elementary and middle school administrators and teachers; school social workers, psychologists and guidance counselors; physicians and nurses, clergy, and volunteers at centers of worship.

Objectives
- To educate the target audience about the special needs of children.
- To provide a resource that can help them meet the needs of children and their families before, during, and after an emergency or natural disaster.

Timeline
- Both publications will be completed six months from the start of the project.

2

FIGURE 9.16 (Continued)

PROJECT DEVELOPMENT PLAN

The tools we are proposing will be developed by HCCP staff in collaboration with mental health professionals, parents, educators, volunteer workers, and first responders that will guide the work of the project.

Project Staff Positions and Consultants

The following staff will be required to implement this project:

- **Project Manager** – Will manage the staff, monitor budgets and schedules, coordinate work with consultants, and oversee project development.
- **Research Assistant** – Will work with the Project Manager to identify information and materials for the content and assist with day-to-day duties.
- **Writer/Editorial Consultant** – Will work with the project monitor on planning content, write and edit drafts, and manage production.
- **Graphic Design Consultant** – Will design layouts and oversee printing.
- **Professional Consultants/Reviewers** – Will represent the target audience for each publication.

Project Budget

The total cost of the project will be $80,000. The table gives a budget outline.

Item	Description	Cost	
Project Manager	On staff	Portion of Salary & Benefits	$9,500
Research Assistant	On staff	Portion of Salary & Benefits	$5,500
Consultants/Reviewers	Paid on per-diem basis	Consulting Fee	$25,000
Writer/Editorial Consultant	Paid on flat-fee basis	Fee and Expenses	$25,000
Graphic Design & Layout	Paid on flat-fee basis	Fees	$15,000

continued

FIGURE 9.16 (Continued)

CONCLUSION

Hurricane Katrina was a devastating event that cost many lives. Families experienced severe trauma that might have been mitigated through greater preparedness. As our country continues to experience the effects of severe weather due to climate change, the threat of domestic and international terrorism, and disasters such as hurricanes, tornadoes, and wildfires, families and communities will need to continue to work toward a greater level of preparedness and establish the capability for coping with the aftermath of these events. The HCCP project will provide an essential resource for families and communities, especially those in under-resourced areas.

ATTACHMENTS

1. Preliminary outlines for Publications I & II
2. List of Consultants/reviewers

4

FIGURE 9.16 (Continued)

82 DOCUMENTING SOURCES

When you paraphrase, summarize, or quote from sources, you need to let readers know what portions of your work are not original. The need to provide documentation of sources stems from both an ethical obligation to be honest in what you present as your own work and a legal obligation not to violate the copyright laws of the United States. Documentation is necessary not only for information from printed and published sources (in print or electronically), but also for such sources as information obtained from an oral presentation or broadcast.

82a Definition of Copyright-Protected Material

WHAT IS PROTECTED BY COPYRIGHT?

The US copyright laws protect ownership of original works of authorship. Violation of these rights is known as **copyright infringement.** Use of copyrighted material without permission is restricted and subject to legal sanctions if such use is determined to be infringement. This protection applies to both published and unpublished works, and it includes material published on the World Wide Web (which did not exist when the law was originally written). Copyrightable works include the following categories:

- Literary works
- Musical works, including any accompanying words
- Dramatic works, including any accompanying music
- Pantomimes and choreographic works
- Pictorial, graphic, and sculptural works
- Motion pictures and other audiovisual works
- Sound recordings
- Architectural works

These categories are viewed broadly and encompass media that did not exist at the time the law was enacted. For example, computer programs and most compilations of works from a variety of sources may be registered with the US Copyright Office in the category of literary works; maps and architectural plans may be registered as pictorial, graphic, or sculptural works.

WHAT IS NOT PROTECTED BY COPYRIGHT?

Several categories of material are generally *not* eligible for copyright protection. These include (among others):

- Works that have *not* been fixed in a tangible form of expression; for example, choreographic works that have not been notated or recorded, or improvised speeches or performances that have not been put in writing or recorded

- Titles of works, names, short phrases, and slogans; commonly used symbols or designs; mere variations of typographic ornamentation, lettering, or coloring; mere listings of ingredients or contents
- Ideas, procedures, methods, systems, processes, concepts, principles, discoveries, or devices—as distinguished from a description, explanation, or illustration
- Works consisting *entirely* of information that is common property and containing no original authorship; for example, standard calendars, height and weight charts, tape measures and rulers, and lists or tables taken from public documents or other common sources

LENGTH OF COPYRIGHT PROTECTION

Works that were created (fixed in tangible form for the first time) on or after January 1, 1978, are automatically protected from the moment of creation. Protection lasts for the author's life plus an additional 50 years after death. In the case of joint works, the period applies to the last surviving author's death.

82b Form of Written Copyright Notice

The copyright symbol © is used to signify copyright protection on materials where it can be made visually perceptible; there is no obligation to post a copyright notice on works that do not physically permit it. In fact, *the use of a copyright notice is no longer required under US law.* Therefore, you may not use material that is in print or from the World Wide Web or in other forms simply because it does not bear a copyright notice.

Although not required by law, it is beneficial to use a copyright notice on work you create for wide distribution since some people may not be aware of this provision. Note that, because prior law did contain such a requirement, the use of such notice is still relevant to the copyright status of older works.

The notice for copyrighted material should contain all three of the following elements:

1. The symbol © (the letter *c* in a circle) or the word *Copyright*
2. The year of first publication of the work
3. The name of the copyright owner

Following are typical ways of writing a copyright notice.

© 2002 John Doe

Copyright © 2002 John Doe

Copyright © by John Doe, 2002

Additional information may be included in the copyright notice to explain the copyright holder's policy regarding use of the material. Here is typical wording for such a policy:

© 2002 John Doe. All rights reserved. No part of this book may be reproduced in any form or by any means without the written permission of the author.

82c Use of Copyrighted Material

It is illegal to violate an owner's copyright; however, you can seek permission for use of copyrighted material. In addition, some limited use of copyrighted material is allowed under the statute without permission. This is known as fair use, as described below.

PERMISSION FOR USE

A copyright owner can grant permission for use of copyrighted material, and, thereby, provide exemption from copyright liability. This might take the form of a letter or standardized form of permission, which grants rights for specific use with a credit to the original source that includes the copyright notice. A fee for use may or may not be required. In other instances, the limitation takes the form of a license under which certain limited uses of copyrighted works are permitted upon payment of specified fees or royalties and compliance with statutory conditions. Both of these exemptions require a specific request to the copyright owner.

When permission is granted, the usual practice is to place the credit as a footnote at the bottom of the page where the material is used. Here is an example:

*Source: Christopher F. Monte, *Merlin: The Sorcerer's Guide to Success in College.* Belmont, CA: Wadsworth, 1994. Reprinted with permission.

THE DOCTRINE OF FAIR USE

One major limitation of copyright that does not require a specific request or the granting of permission or license is the **doctrine of fair use,** which is a part of the 1976 Copyright Act. However, the distinction between fair use and copyright infringement is not always easily defined. There is no specific number of words, lines, or musical notes that may safely be taken without permission. Acknowledging the source of the copyrighted material does not substitute for obtaining permission. Always proceed with caution when you use copyrighted material, even in a very limited way.

The law provides guidance with a list of the various purposes for which the reproduction of a particular work *may* be considered fair. Examples of what is generally regarded as fair use include:

- Quotation of excerpts or short passages for purposes of illustration, comment, or clarification of the author's observations, or for review in a publication
- Use of portions of content in a parody
- Summary of an address or article with brief quotations in a news report
- Reproduction by a teacher or student of a small part of a work to illustrate a lesson
- Reproduction of a work in legislative or judicial proceedings or reports
- Incidental and fortuitous reproduction in a newsreel or broadcast of a work located on the scene of an event being reported

Keep in mind that copyright protects the particular style in which an author has expressed himself or herself; it does not extend to ideas, systems, or factual information conveyed in the work.

The safest course is always to get permission from the copyright owner before reproducing copyrighted material. When this is impracticable, the use of copyrighted material should be avoided unless you are certain the doctrine of fair use clearly applies to the situation.

(**Note:** For further information about the limitations of copyrights, consult the U.S. Copyright Office.)

THE CONCEPT OF PUBLIC DOMAIN

Works in the **public domain** are not copyrighted. They may be referenced freely without concern about infringement. For example, many classic literary works are in the public domain because they were published before copyright laws were written. Other works are public domain because their owners have surrendered copyright protection or because a copyright has expired. Such works should still be sourced; however, you don't have to seek permission to use them.

Many works created by agencies of the US government are automatically in the public domain. You don't need permission to use them, but they should still be given credit. Also, be aware that many works published by the government are produced by outside contractors, and these are subject to copyright protection.

Before 1978, copyright was generally secured by the act of publication with notice of copyright, assuming compliance with all other relevant statutory conditions. US works in the public domain on January 1, 1978 (for example, works published without satisfying all conditions for securing copyright under the Copyright Act of 1909) remain in the public domain under the 1976 Copyright Act.

82d Plagiarism

QUICK REFERENCE 82.1

Avoiding plagiarism

Plagiarism is the presentation of another's intellectual property as your own. It is both a legal and an ethical violation. Although you might not be technically violating copyright laws by using another person's words (because of the fair use doctrine), it is still unethical to do so. Writers often claim that their plagiary is unintentional—in the process of researching, they lose track of what is theirs and what came from another source. That claim, however, will not be accepted, and it can lead to serious legal or ethical sanctions. The following guidelines will help you avoid plagiarizing:

- Do not assume that paraphrasing another's work or combining a number of sources and revising heavily will eliminate the need to document those sources. Cite the sources you use, even though you feel you have synthesized the work and made it your own.
- When you directly quote the work of another, always enclose the exact words in quotation marks. (Never use quotation marks when you paraphrase.)
- Keep track of sources as you write. One system is to put the citation in boldface type as you go along and move it later to the appropriate place as a reference note. Relying on memory or written notes kept separate from the document can lead to incomplete citations (as well as extra time and work reconstructing the information).
- Do not assume that lack of a copyright notice on source material means a work is not protected. This is not the case under the law (see 82b).

83 SOURCE CITATION

This section explains the various types of source citations used in business documents. Documentation consists of two elements: (1) An indicator within the text that clearly signals that particular words or paragraphs are taken from an outside source. In most cases, this will be a **superscript number** (a number raised above the line) or a number enclosed in parentheses. (2) Information about the source that must contain certain specific elements and appear in a specified order, depending on the type of documentation style you are using. See 83d for specific guidelines and examples of bibliographic reference list formats.

83a Text Notes

Text notes (also called **in-text citations**) are complete citations placed within parentheses at the point of reference in the text. Text notes are efficient if you have very few references. However, because they are commonly used in academia, they can tend to make a business document look too "academic." They should also be avoided in documents that have many citations because they disrupt the flow of text and interfere with readability. In the following example, the text note is shown in colored type.

> The impending retirement of 76 million baby boomers will have a significant impact on the composition of the nation's workforce. (Richard W. Judy and Carol D'Amico, *Workforce 2020*, Hudson Institute, Washington, DC, 1999, p. 87.) Our study of the regional workforce indicates that we can expect a 30% decrease in the number of qualified entry-level employees over the next decade, unless we begin to enact plans to counter this impact within the next three to five years.

83b Footnotes

Footnotes are citations indicated with a superscript (above the line) number keyed to source citations and/or explanatory comments at the bottom of the page. Place the superscript number at the end of the sentence (or word or phrase within a sentence) that corresponds to the source citation. Number footnotes consecutively, beginning with the number 1, all the way through a document.

Footnotes are efficient because the reader can simply glance at the bottom of the page to scan the citation, if desired, or ignore the number and continue reading without disruption. If your reader will be influenced by the sources cited in terms of authenticity, currency, or other factors, footnotes at the bottom of the page are a good choice.

Footnotes are also easy to format because word processing software can automatically insert and number footnotes in the text. It places the numbered note at the bottom of the page and automatically renumbers if you add or delete a note.

EXAMPLE OF A FOOTNOTE

> The impending retirement of 76 million baby boomers will have a significant impact on the future composition of the nation's workforce.[1] Our study of the regional workforce indicates that we can expect a 30 percent decrease in the number of qualified entry-level employees over the next decade, unless we begin to enact plans to counter this impact within the next three to five years.
>
> ---
>
> [1]Richard W. Judy and Carol D'Amico, *Workforce 2020,* Hudson Institute, Washington, DC, 1999, p. 87.

Footnotes can become a distraction when they are numerous or long, in which case they might flow onto a second page. They also tend to make a document look more academic. To avoid this in business documents, use endnotes or a bibliography instead.

83c Endnotes

Endnotes are references with superscript (raised above the line) numbers in the text that are keyed to a numbered list of citations and/or comments placed at the end of sections or at the end of the document. If your reader will have only a mild interest in the sources, endnotes are a better option.

Number and list endnote entries in the order they appear in the text. If you have numbered them consecutively in each section and have a combined list at the end, use section headings that match the text headings exactly to make the sequence clear; sections headings are not needed if you number consecutively throughout.

A list of endnotes at the end of the document should be the first item in the back matter, directly following the last page of text. Start the list on a right-hand page; leave the left-hand page blank if necessary. Continue numbering from the body-text page numbers.

EXAMPLE OF AN ENDNOTE

> Adult learners are an increasing segment of the college population. While this is a trend nationwide, this campus has not seen a significant increase in students over the past five years. According to a recent study by the American Council on Education (ACE), "Institutions have developed several types of special academic programs that are particularly convenient or relevant for adult students."[1] The task force is recommending that we review our offerings and prepare to modify programs in ways that will make us more attractive to adult learners. According to the ACE, popular program

modifications include accelerated degree programs, night and weekend programs, distance education, and contract programs for local employers, unions, or other organizations. Overall, 76 percent of institutions offer at least one of these special programs.[2]

Endnotes

1. Bryan Cook and Jacqueline E. King, *Improving Lives Through Higher Education: Campus Programs and Policies for Low-Income Adults,* American Council on Education, Center for Policy Analysis, Washington, DC, 2005, p. 15.
2. Ibid.

83d Bibliography

A **bibliography** (also called a **reference list**) is an alphabetic listing of sources, always placed at the end of a document. It may include sources cited in text notes or footnotes, as well as those consulted but not specifically mentioned in the main text of the document. When you want to provide your reader with sources consulted as well as sources quoted or summarized, a bibliography will be the best form to use. Quick Reference 83.1 provides guidelines for formatting a bibliography using business style.

QUICK REFERENCE 83.1

Formatting bibliographic entries

- Start the bibliography on a right-hand page, and type **Bibliography** in the same style as the document's main section headings.
- Set the margins the same as those of the body of the report.
- Begin each entry at the left margin and indent turnovers with 0.5-inch tabs (called a **hanging indent**.
- Type the entries single-spaced and end each with a period.
- Double-space between entries.
- The entries may be numbered, but this is not necessary because they are listed alphabetically.
- If more than one work by the same author is listed, do not repeat the author's name each time; instead use a long dash after the first listing.
- When there are multiple authors, invert the name of the first author only.

EXAMPLE OF A BIBLIOGRAPHY

BIBLIOGRAPHY

Christensen, Clayton M., Erik A. Roth, and Scott D. Anthony, *Seeing What's Next: Using Theories of Innovation to Predict Industry Change,* Harvard Business School Press, Cambridge, MA, 2004.

De Kluyver, Cornelis A., and John A. Pearce, II, *Strategy: A View From the Top,* 3rd ed., Prentice Hall, Upper Saddle River, NJ, 2006.

Drucker, Peter F., *Innovation and Entrepreneurship,* Collins, New York, 2006.

_____, *The Essential Drucker: The Best of Sixty Years of Peter Drucker's Essential Writings on Management,* Collins, New York, 2003.

Farris Paul W., et al., *Marketing Metrics: 50+ Metrics Every Executive Should Master,* Wharton School of Publishing: Pearson, Upper Saddle River, NJ, 2006.

Hamel, Gary, *The Future of Management,* Harvard Business School Press, Boston, 2007.

FIGURE 9.17 Bibliography

84 REFERENCE STYLES—BUSINESS, MLA, AND APA

A reference list at the end of a document needs to include a number of basic elements. The information and the order of it vary, depending on the preferred documentation style and the type of source listed. Basic elements include:

1. Name of author(s) or editor(s)
2. Complete title of the source, including edition number (if applicable)
3. Name of the publication, if the source is from a larger publication
4. Name of publisher
5. Location of publisher
6. Date of publication
7. Page reference (if applicable)
8. Volume number (if applicable)
9. Web site URL (if applicable)

The examples in the preceding sections follow a common business citation style. Many organizations use this style or the format recommended in the *Chicago Manual of Style,* which is slightly different. Others prefer one of two widely used academic styles—the Modern Language Association (MLA) style or the American Psychiatric Association (APA) style. Quick Reference 84.1 lists guidelines that apply to all the styles; Quick Reference 84.2 lists variations.

84a Books

The main style variations among business, MLA, and APA style are in the order of information, style of titles, and punctuation

BOOK WITH ONE AUTHOR

Business style

Blumenthal, Karen, *Grande Expectations: A Year in the Life of Starbucks' Stock,* Crown, New York, 2008.

MLA style

Blumenthal, Karen. Grande Expectations: A Year in the Life of Starbucks' Stock. New York: Crown, 2008.

APA style

Blumenthal, K. (2008). *Grande expectations: A year in the life of Starbucks' stock.* New York: Crown.

BOOK WITH TWO OR THREE AUTHORS

Business style

Neck, Chris, and Charles Manz, *Mastering Self-Leadership: Empowering Yourself for Personal Excellence, 4th edition,* Prentice Hall, Upper Saddle River, NJ, 2007.

MLA style

Neck, Chris, and Charles Manz. Mastering Self-Leadership: Empowering Yourself for Personal Excellence. 4th ed. Upper Saddle River, NJ: Prentice Hall, 2007.

APA style

Neck, C., & Manz, C. (2007). *Mastering self-leadership: Empowering yourself for personal excellence* (4th ed.). Upper Saddle River, NJ: Prentice Hall.

QUICK REFERENCE 84.1

General bibliographic entry style guidelines

These guidelines can be applied to all three citation styles: business, MLA, and APA. See Quick Reference 84.2 for details about the variations in these styles.

Author's name

- In a bibliography, list sources alphabetically by the primary author's last name.
- If no author's name is given, alphabetize by the first significant word in the title.

Title

- If a title begins with an article (*a, an, the*), disregard it when alphabetizing entries.
- Do not capitalize articles (*a, an, the*) unless they are the first word of the title; also do not capitalize prepositions with four and fewer letters and conjunctions in titles.
- Include the edition number of the publication, if other than the first edition.

Publisher's name and location

- Use a shortened form of the names of well-known publishers. For example, Random House, Inc./Random House; The McGraw-Hill Companies/McGraw-Hill; Vantage Press/Vantage.
- Many large publishers have several imprints under their corporate umbrella; in this case, you need list only the name of the imprint that published your source:

  Sources for checking publishers' names and common usage are amazon.com, barnesandnoble.com, publishers' Web sites, and directories available in libraries.
- List only the city where the publisher is located if it is a major city such as Chicago, New York, or Boston; otherwise list the city and two-letter state abbreviation.

Date

- List the date of publication; for books list the year only; for articles in periodicals, list the month and year or month, day, and year, as applicable.
- If there is a volume or issue number, list it in front of the date.
- If you are citing a book that has more than one edition, list the publication date of the edition you are using.

QUICK REFERENCE 84.2

Style variations in business, MLA, and APA entries

Business style
Each element separated with a comma and a period at the end of the entry.

- Author's full name, inverted
- Do not invert coauthors' names
- Title in italics
- Titles of parts (chapters, articles) in quotation marks
- Main words of titles and subtitles capitalized
- Name of publishing company
- Location of publisher
- Year of publication

Smith, Leila R., *English for Careers: Business, Professional, and Technical, 10th edition,* Pearson Prentice-Hall, Upper Saddle River, NJ, 2006.

MLA style
Each element separated with a period and a period at the end of the entry.

- Author's full name, inverted
- Do not invert coauthors' names
- Main title underlined
- Titles of parts (chapters, articles) in quotation marks
- Main words of titles and subtitles capitalized
- Location of publisher
- Name of publisher
- Year of publication

Smith, Leila R. <u>English for Careers: Business, Professional, and Technical</u>. 10th ed. Upper Saddle River, NJ: Pearson Prentice Hall, 2006.

APA style
Each element separated with a period and a period at the end of the entry.

- Author's name, inverted—last name, initials only
- Invert coauthors' names—last name, initials only
- Date of publication in parentheses
- Title in italics
- Titles of parts (chapters, articles) not in quotation marks
- First word only of titles and subtitles capitalized
- Location of publisher
- Name of publisher

Smith, L. R. (2006). *English for careers: Business, professional, and technical* (10th ed). Upper Saddle River, NJ: Pearson Prentice Hall.

BOOK WITH MORE THAN THREE AUTHORS

If an entry has more than three authors, list the first author's name followed by *et al.* (Latin for *and others*) without italics. Place a period after *al.*

Business style

Tripp, Valerie, et al., *Samantha's Short Story Collection,* American Girl Publishing, Middleton, WI, 2006.

MLA style

Tripp, Valerie, et al. Samantha's Short Story Collection. Middleton, WI: American Girl Publishing, 2006.

APA style

Tripp, V., et al. (2006). *Samantha's short story collection*. Middleton, WI: American Girl Publishing.

BOOK EDITOR INSTEAD OF AUTHOR

When an editor's name is listed in place of an author's name, follow it with *ed.* in parentheses for business style and APA. Use *eds.* when more than one editor is involved.

Business style

Kinnerman, Suzanne (ed.), *Secrets of Success: Profiles of Top Executive Women,* Salamander Books, Albany, NY, 2009.

MLA style

Kinnerman, Suzanne, ed. Secrets of Success: Profiles of Top Executive Women. Albany, NY: Salamander Books, 2009.

APA style

Kinnerman, S. (Ed.). (2009). *Secrets of success: Profiles of top executive women*. Albany, NY: Salamander Books.

MULTIPLE WORKS BY THE SAME AUTHOR(S)

For business and MLA style, list the author's name in the first entry only; use three hyphens or a long dash followed by a comma for subsequent titles. For business style, list the works in order of most recent publication date; for MLA style list the works alphabetically (ignoring articles, *a, an, the*). For APA style, repeat the author's name in each entry and arrange the entries chronologically by date of publication.

Business style

Covey, Stephen R., *The Eighth Habit Workbook: Strategies to Take You from Effectiveness to Greatness,* Free Press, New York, 2006

———, *The Seven Habits of Highly Effective People: Powerful Lessons in Personal Change,* Free Press, New York, 2004.

MLA style

Covey, Stephen R. The Eighth Habit Workbook: Strategies to Take You from Effectiveness to Greatness. New York: Free Press, 2006.

—. The Seven Habits of Highly Effective People: Powerful Lessons in Personal Change. New York: Free Press, 2004.

APA style

Covey, S. R. (2004). *The seven habits of highly effective people: Powerful lessons in personal change.* New York: Free Press.

Covey, S. R. (2006). *The eighth habit workbook: Strategies to take you from effectiveness to greatness.* New York: Free Press.

BOOK WITH NO AUTHOR LISTED

Business style

Harvard Business Review on Managing Yourself, Harvard Business School Press, Cambridge, MA, 2005.

MLA style

Harvard Business Review on Managing Yourself. Cambridge, MA: Harvard Business School Press, 2005.

APA style

Harvard business review on managing yourself. (2005). Cambridge, MA: Harvard Business School Press.

84b Periodicals and Anthologies

Newspaper and magazine article entries include the name of the author (if known), the title of the article, the name of the publication, the volume number (if given), the date, and the page number. Articles may be signed or unsigned. The following examples illustrate formatting for a signed and an unsigned article, and an article with a volume number.

MAGAZINE (MONTHLY, WEEKLY, OR BIWEEKLY)

Business style

Smith, John, "The Competition is Gaining on You," *Time,* November 3, 2009, pp. 10-11.

"The Teflon Tech Companies," *PC World,* November 10, 2009, pp. 14-18.

MLA style

Smith, John. "The Competition Is Gaining on You." Time 3 Nov. 2009: 10-11.

"The Teflon Tech Companies." PC World 10 Nov. 2006: 14-18.

APA style

Smith, J. (2009, November). The competition is gaining on you. *Time*, 10-11.

The Teflon Tech Companies. (2006, November 10). *PC World*, 14-18.

PROFESSIONAL JOURNAL

Business style

Davis, Michael, "Eighteen Rules for Writing a Code of Ethics," *Science and Engineering Ethics,* Vol. 13, No. 2, June 2007, pp. 171-189.

MLA style

Davis, Michael. "Eighteen Rules for Writing a Code of Ethics." Science and Engineering Ethics 13.2 (2007): 171-89.

APA style

Davis, M. (2007). Eighteen rules for writing a code of ethics. *Science and Engineering Ethics, 13*(2), 171-189.

NEWSPAPER

Most newspapers use capital letters for section numbers. These should be indicated as part of the page number.

Business style

Jones, Joseph, "Entertainment Dollars and Sense," *Los Angeles Times,* April 15, 2005, p. C24.

MLA style

Thomas, Joseph. "Entertainment Dollars and Sense." Los Angeles Times 15 Apr. 2005: C24.

APA style

Jones, J. (2005, April 15). Entertainment dollars and sense. *Los Angeles Times,* p. C24.

ANTHOLOGY

Business style

Espinosa, Linda M., "Social, Cultural, and Linguistic Features of School Readiness in Young Latino Children," in Barbara Bowman and Evelyn K. Moore (eds.), *School Readiness and Social-Emotional Development: Exploring Diverse Cultural Perspectives,* Washington, D.C., National Black Child Development Institute, 2007, pp. 33-47.

MLA style

Espinosa, Linda M. "Social, Cultural, and Linguistic Features of School Readiness in Young Latino Children." <u>School Readiness and Social-Emotional Development: Exploring Diverse Cultural Perspectives</u>. Ed. Barbara Bowman and Evelyn K. Moore. Washington, DC: National Black Child Development Institute, 2007. 33-47.

APA style

Espinosa, L. M. (2007). Social, cultural, and linguistic features of school readiness in young Latino children. In B. Bowman and E. K. Moore (Eds.), *School readiness and social-emotional development: Exploring diverse cultural perspectives* (pp. 33-47). Washington, DC: National Black Child Development Institute.

84c Online Sources

Works published online follow the same general styles as printed works, with an added notation indicating the date the article was retrieved and the URL (Web address) of the Web site.

The following examples show documentation for online articles, Web page documents, and reports. When an Internet document is more than one Web page, provide a URL that links to the home page or entry page for the document. Also, if there is no date available for the document use *n.d.* for *no date*.

ARTICLE FROM AN ONLINE PUBLICATION

Business style

Holahan, Catherine, "Tis the Season for E-vites," *BusinessWeek*, December 17, 2007. Retrieved May 25, 2008 from www.businessweek.com/technology/content/dec2007

MLA style

Holahan, Catherine. "Tis the Season for E-vites." BusinessWeek. 17 Dec. 2007. 25 May 2008. <http://www.businessweek.com/technology/content/dec2007>

APA style

Holahan, C. (2007, December 17). 'Tis the season for E-vites. *BusinessWeek.* Retrieved May 25, 2008 from www.businessweek.com/technology/content/dec2007

ARTICLE FROM A DATABASE

Business style

Rumbaut, Ruben G., "Acculturation, Discrimination, and Ethnic Identity Among Children of Immigrants, 2001." Retrieved March 1, 2003 from http://www.ksg.harvard.edu/inequality/seminar/papers/Rumbautl.pdf

MLA style

Rumbaut, Ruben G. "Acculturation, Discrimination, And Ethnic Identity Among Children Of Immigrants, 2001." Retrieved March 1, 2003 from http://www.ksg.harvard.edu/inequality/seminar/papers/Rumbautl.pdf

APA style

Rumbaut, R. (2001). Acculturation, discrimination, and ethnic identity among children of immigrants. Retrieved March 1, 2003 from http://www.ksg.harvard.edu/inequality/seminar/papers/Rumbautl.pdf

WEB DOCUMENT, WEB PAGE, OR REPORT

Business style

National Center for Education Statistics (NCES). "Readiness for Kindergarten: Parent and Teacher Beliefs," U.S. Department of Education, Washington, DC, 2001. Retrieved March 23, 2005, from http://nces.ed.gov/pubs93/web/93257.asp

MLA style

National Center for Education Statistics (NCES). Readiness for Kindergarten: Parent and Teacher Beliefs. U.S. Department of Education, Washington, DC, 2001. Retrieved, March 23, 2005, from http://nces.ed.gov/pubs93/web/93257.asp

APA style

National Center for Education Statistics. (2001). Readiness for kindergarten: Parent and teacher beliefs, U.S. Department of Education, Washington, DC. Retrieved March 23, 2005, from http://nces.ed.gov/pubs93/web/93257.asp

84d Other Sources

The following examples are shown in business style only; follow the examples in the preceding sections to adapt these business style entries to APA or MLA style.

GROUP OR CORPORATE PUBLICATIONS

List the full name of the corporate author or name of the organization first. If the corporate author is also the publisher, list the organization's name only once.

Business Education 1900-2000, *Delta Pi Epsilon Conference Summary,* New York, 2005.

A Guide to the Project Management Body of Knowledge, Project Management Institute, Philadelphia, 2004.

If you list the organization as the author, you may indicate "Author" as publisher.

Project Management Institute, *A Guide to the Project Management Body of Knowledge,* Author, Philadelphia, 2004.

UNPUBLISHED WORKS

Indicate that the work is unpublished and the type of work.

Alexander, Houvras E. Jr., *DNAs: The Critical Element in Family Trees,* unpublished doctoral dissertation, Northwestern University, Chicago, 1995.

GOVERNMENT PUBLICATIONS

If a government publication does not include an author, list the agency or division name as the author. Then list the governmental agency responsible for the report. Most U.S. governmental publications are published by the Government Printing Office (GPO).

Michigan Department of Social Services, *Medical Coverage for Medicare-eligible Members,* Michigan Department of Budget and Management (DMB), Lansing, MI, January, 2006.

SPEECH

List the speaker's name, the title of the speech, and the place and date that it was given.

Venduzi, C., Keynote Address, Twenty-fifth Annual Meeting of Midwest Bar Association, Chicago, December 19, 2009.

DOCUMENT DESIGN, GRAPHICS, AND MULTIMEDIA

section ten

85 DESIGNING DOCUMENTS FOR READABILITY

Business documents have the greatest degree of readability when information is presented in segments. Choice of type and page layout—headings, paragraphs, a fair amount of open space on the page, and elements set off for emphasis—are the tools available for formatting text for optimum readability and visual appeal.

- **Type:** What standard fonts and font combinations will most enhance readability? Should only black be used or should color be added?
- **Page layout:** What arrangement of text on the page will best guide the reader through the organizational structure of the document?

85a Sizes and Styles of Type

The following definitions are essential for understanding the basics of type styles and sizes and for communication with professional graphic artists, designers, and printers.

- **Type:** a shortened form of *typeface*.
- **Typeface** (or **font**)**:** the design of a complete set of letters, numbers, and symbols; for example Arial, Times (New) Roman, Verdana, Garamond, Book Antiqua. (Note the variation in size, even though all are shown here in 12 point). Today, the word *font* is commonly used to refer to a typeface.
- **Type font:** the complete assortment of point sizes (8 pt., 9 pt., 10 pt., 12 pt., 14 pt., etc.) and style variations (regular or roman, *italic,* **boldface,** ***boldface italic***) for one typeface, although, as stated previously, the word *font* is used widely to refer to the typeface as well. The "normal" style for a font is technically called "roman," but today most people refer to it as "regular."

  Many type faces also have additional fonts, such as condensed, light, and medium.
- **Point size:** the measurement from the highest part of the tallest letter (*h* or *l*) to the lowest part of the longest letter that extends below the baseline (*p* or *y*). All type that is the same point size is the same height, but the width of characters and height of lowercase letters varies, giving a different **yield**—the number of characters per line—and **leading**—the spacing between lines of type. (This term stems from the use of lead—pieces of metal—that were formerly used in the typesetting process.)

Courier New 12 point

In everyday usage, the distinction between *typeface* and type *font* has receded, and many people refer to the whole gamut as *fonts*.

Times (New) Roman 12 point

In everyday usage, the distinction between *typeface* and type *font* has receded, and many people refer to the whole gamut as *fonts*.

- **Serif:** a typeface that has little strokes at the top and bottom of most letters. Examples are Times Roman, Century, and Courier New. Serif fonts are recommended for body text copy because the serifs increase readability.
- **Sans serif:** a typeface without the little strokes (*sans* is French for *without*), such as Arial, Tahoma, and Verdana. Sans serif fonts are recommended for titles and headings.

85b Selecting Type for Business Documents

The purpose for varying the type within a document is to guide the reader by signaling structural changes.

- **Display headings,** in large bold type and possibly in color signal a major change of topic. Use display headings to open major sections (equivalent to chapter or level 1 topics in an outline) in large documents.
- **Main heading,** in a larger type size and different font (e.g., 14 point, boldface), signals major points within a main topic.
- **Subheadings,** smaller than main headings, signal points within those topics, and so on.

Too much type variation in a document is distracting. One font will usually suffice for most business documents, and it is rarely necessary or desirable to use more than two or three in one document. See Quick Reference 85.1 for guidelines on selecting type for text and headings.

QUICK REFERENCE 85.1

Selecting type fonts for business documents

Standard font sizes

- 12 point for text copy
- 11 or 12 point for page numbers
- 14 to 16 point for display headings (may be centered or flush left)

CONTINUED →

QUICK REFERENCE 85.1 → CONTINUED

- 12 to 14 point for regular headings
- 9 or 10 point for footnotes

Body text

- **Use serif fonts.** Serif fonts are easiest on the eyes. Times (New) Roman, 12 point, is recommended for business documents. The size and style are ideal for readability and are recognized as the business standard.
- **Use standard type sizes.** Use standard 12-point type for routine documents—letters, memos, and reports. At times, for example when a letter is running only a couple of lines over one page, it makes sense to use a smaller point size to avoid going to a second page (if it is not possible to cut text to fit one page). Avoid going smaller than 10 point.

Headings

- **Use sans serif fonts and vary font size for display headings.** Sans serif type is easier to read from a distance and it looks clear and crisp in **display headings**—section titles or Level 1 heads in long documents. [Read more about levels of headings in 85d.]
- **Vary font style for regular headings.** Use **boldface,** *italics,* ***italics/bold,*** ALL CAPS, and Cap/Lowercase underlined to distinguish levels of headings (see 85d). In some cases, you might also increase size from 12 point to 14 point for differentiation.

(**Note:** To access half-point sizes, e.g., 8.5 or 11.5, highlight the copy and type the number in the Font Size window, then hit Enter on the keyboard.)

85c Page Layout

An attractive and appropriate visual appearance of each document page and the document as a whole will be achieved through attention to page layout. **Page layout** is the placement of all the elements that make up a document page. The process of page layout is also called **composition.** Thinking of page layout as composition brings awareness that visual and text components must work in harmony for the benefit of the reader.

Display and main headings help the reader skim through a document to get an overview and to locate specific sections and topics. It is very likely that a document of a few pages or more has a use beyond the first reading—certainly the writer would like to think so. Page layout techniques facilitate use of a document as an information resource. A good page layout achieves the following:

- Is appealing to the eye on first glance
- Helps readers quickly grasp the overall organization of the document
- Helps readers see how each part of the document relates to the whole
- Makes the information easy to read and understand
- Helps readers find information quickly

Document format should be part of the initial consideration at the outline stage of a project. The more complex and varied the information, the more important it is to consider layout from the start.

85d Heading Structure

Headings provide a roadmap that guides the reader through the organizational structure of a document. Key considerations are wording, format, and style.

Headings should clearly reflect the hierarchy of a document's content. Figure 10.1 illustrates a title page with a large part title display heading. Title pages give a professional look to longer, complex documents that have several main parts. They also provide the opportunity to add graphic elements that illustrate something important about the topic. Another advantage of part title pages is that they can be tabbed—providing a useful tool for using the document as a resource.

Figure 10.2 shows a page that could follow a part title or stand on its own. It reflects the standard structure of a main section title, centered in large type, and three levels of heads. Note that the third and fourth subheadings are the same size, but the fourth level heading is run-in with the text.

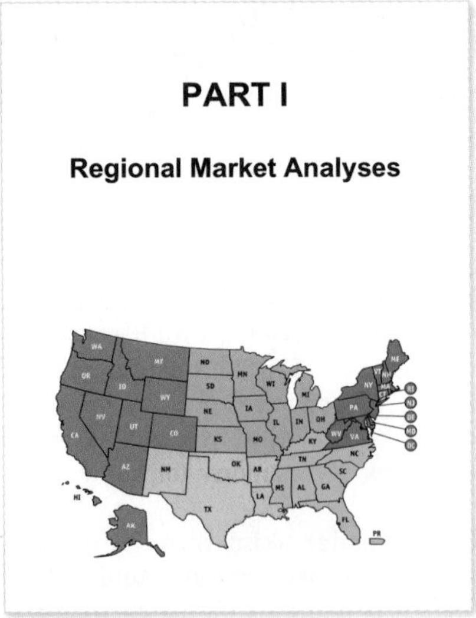

PART I

Regional Market Analyses

FIGURE 10.1 Part title heading

85e Parallel Construction of Headings

Each level of heading in a document should be worded consistently. In a typical document, such as a report, short descriptive headings of one to three words are the best way to identify main and subtopics. Other styles are shown in Quick Reference 85.2.

In long documents the word patterns and styling of headings at different levels may vary. For example, main headings can be descriptive noun phrases and subheadings can begin with *-ing* words. Select the style that best suits the tone and content of your document. A report that summarizes a study might read well with headings in question format. A document that presents a solution to a problem or one that provides a set of instructions might read better with headings worded as statements.

[Read more about heading structure in Quick Reference 80.4.]

Always double-check for heading consistency during the proofreading stage of the writing process. Changes made in a draft during revisions often affect the headings, and it is easy for this to go unnoticed unless you do a careful check.

CONSISTENT FORMAT AND STYLE

Format all headings of the same level exactly the same throughout each document. Vary font size, style, and placement to indicate levels. This can be done in various ways: center heads or left-justify them (flush left); vary the type font by using boldface or italics, or underlining; or use capitalization. See Figure 10.2 for an example that works for most documents. Figure 10.3 is another example, using numbered headings.

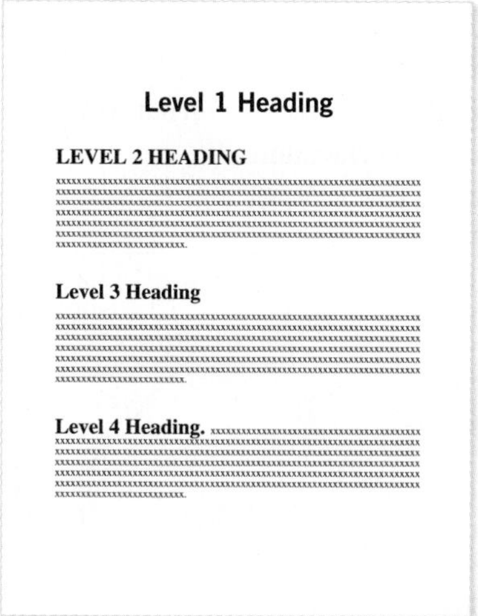

Level 1 Heading

LEVEL 2 HEADING

Level 3 Heading

Level 4 Heading.

FIGURE 10.2 Page layout with standard headings

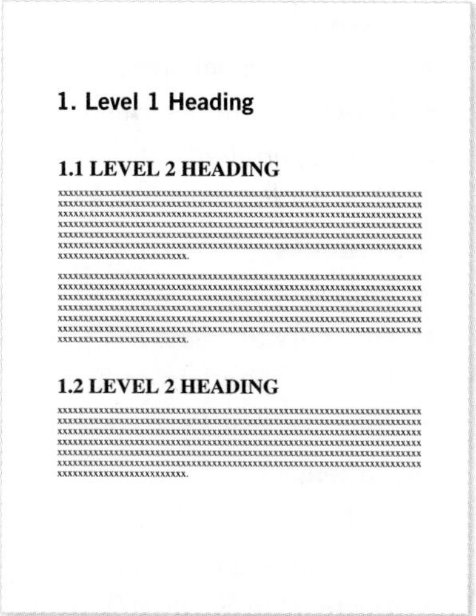

1. Level 1 Heading

1.1 LEVEL 2 HEADING

1.2 LEVEL 2 HEADING

FIGURE 10.3 Page layout with numbered headings

QUICK REFERENCE 85.2

Parallel construction of part titles and headings

For each level of heading in a document, use consistent word patterns, capitalization, and punctuation. Here are some commonly used constructions for headings:

Short descriptive noun phrases

- School Size
- Student Body Makeup
- Student/Teacher Ratios
- Test Performance Scores

Longer descriptive phrases

- Relationship of School Size and Student Performance
- Composition of Student Body and Student Performance
- Student-to-Teacher Ratios and Test Scores
- Standardized Tests and Student Performance

Statements

- School size and student performance are related.
- Composition of student body affects performance.
- Ratio of students to teachers affects test scores.
- Standardized tests fail to measure student performance.

Questions

- How are school size and performance related?
- How does composition of the student body affect performance?
- How do student/teacher ratios impact performance?
- How does performance correlate with test scores?

Statements

- Reduce School Size
- Diversify Student Body Makeup
- Decrease Student-to-Teacher Ratios
- Improve Test Performance Scores

***-ing* phrases**

- Reducing School Size
- Diversifying Student Body Makeup
- Decreasing Student/Teacher Ratios
- Improving Test Performance Scores

85f Balance of Text and White Space

A good balance between the amount of text and white space on the page is needed to provide an open, inviting appearance and enhance readability. Striking this balance involves making decisions about text margin width and alignment (justification) and placement of elements that break up blocks of text to introduce white space. The following guidelines will help you in balancing these four elements on the page. They are illustrated in Figures 10.4 through 10.7, which show different ways to balance text and white space.

WHITE SPACE

Dense blocks of type and long line lengths are hard on the eyes and a turnoff to readers. Look at white space in juxtaposition to blocks of text and the line spacing between them; size of the top, bottom, left, and right margins; and other elements on the page that might be indented, placed in boxes, set up in lists, and so on.

BULLETED AND NUMBERED LISTS

Whenever you have a series of items, consider arranging them in list format. This not only helps break up the text to make it more visually appealing, it helps the reader find information and conveys order, logic, and relative importance of items. Using parallel construction—consistent wording patterns and type style—is essential in listed items, just as it is in headings.

[See 85e and Quick Reference 85.1.]

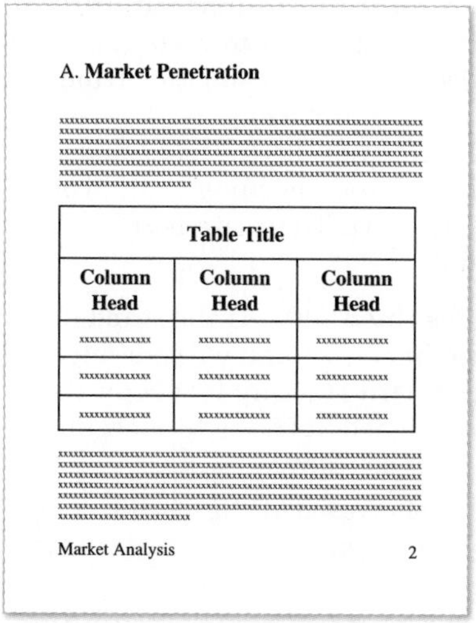

A. **Market Penetration**

Table Title		
Column Head	**Column Head**	**Column Head**
xxxxxxxxxxxxxx	xxxxxxxxxxxxxx	xxxxxxxxxxxxxx
xxxxxxxxxxxxxx	xxxxxxxxxxxxxx	xxxxxxxxxxxxxx
xxxxxxxxxxxxxx	xxxxxxxxxxxxxx	xxxxxxxxxxxxxx

Market Analysis 2

FIGURE 10.4 Table set off from text

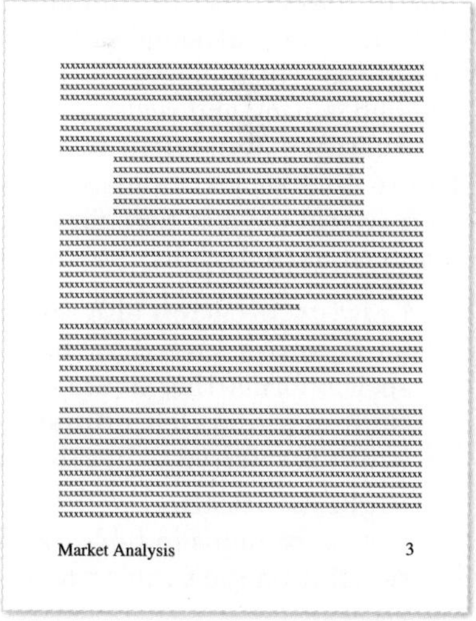

Market Analysis 3

FIGURE 10.5 Extract set off from text

FIGURE 10.6 Numbered list set off from text

FIGURE 10.7 Bulleted list set off from text

85g Margins and Justification

Margins provide white space on the page and should be within the comfort zone of the reader's visual path from left to right. Readers are thrown off when they see nonstandard margins. Therefore, it is advisable to consistently use standard 1-inch margins for unbound and 1.5-inch margins for bound documents. Resist the urge to make margins smaller to control length. Rare is the document that cannot be trimmed through editing and revising when length is a problem.

Justification refers to how text is aligned at the side margins. Figure 10.8 shows standard justification of text, headings, and footers on a typical page of text, for example, a report. There are four kinds of justification: left, right, centered, and full.

- **Left justification** also referred to as **flush left**—is the standard for **running text,** copy that is typed in one column without any special formatting treatment. In standard running text copy, the right margin is left **unjustified,** unaligned at the right margin—which is referred to in printing as "ragged right."
- **Right justification**, or **flush right,** is often used to align headers and footers, columns in tables, and in other instances where material is set off from the running text copy.

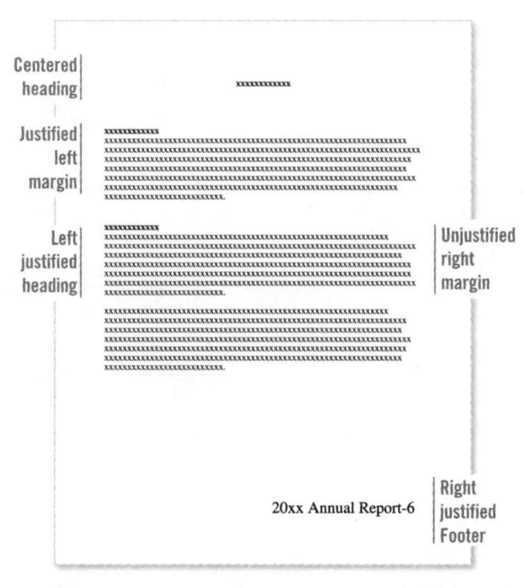

FIGURE 10.8 Standard justification of text, headings, and header/footer

- **Fully justified** text is aligned at both right and left. This is commonly done with two-column text and with text that is set off with borders, a format that is known as a **sidebar.**

85h Color and Shading

Use color sparingly in business documents, and never use it for text copy or headers and footers. Elements where color can be used include headings, shaded blocks of text, borders, and graphics. For color choice, gray, dark blue, or burgundy provide attractive but still conservative accents.

Shading is the use of color as a background for text or graphics. Color can be used for shading in documents where a second color (one color in addition to black) is used. Otherwise, a light gray can be used. A common use of shading is to set off columns or rows in a table by alternating color with white background. See Figures 10.9, where colored headings and shading are used along with a border (see 85i) to set off introductory text. In Figure 10.10 colored shading is used for clarity in alternating columns of a table.

I. Market Analysis

REGION 1-SUMMARY

Competition Analysis

Market Analysis 1

Table 1

Title							
Hd	Hd	Hd	Hd	Hd	Hd	Hd	Hd

Market Analysis 2

FIGURE 10.9 Use of color for emphasis

FIGURE 10.10 Use of color for emphasis and clarity

For standard documents printed in black, bold type and light gray shading or solid black shading with white type can be used sparingly as a design element. Figures 10.11 and 10.12 show the same effect achieved in black and white text.

I. Market Analysis

REGION 1-SUMMARY

Competition Analysis

Market Analysis 1

Table 1

Title		
Column Head	Column Head	Column Head
xxxxxxxxxx	xxxxxxxxxx	xxxxxxxxxx
xxxxxxxxxx	xxxxxxxxxx	xxxxxxxxxx
xxxxxxxxxx	xxxxxxxxxx	xxxxxxxxxx

Market Analysis 2

FIGURE 10.11 Gray shading used to set off section-opening text

FIGURE 10.12 Black shading used to set off column headings

85i Rules and Borders

Setting off elements of a document with rules and borders is another technique for highlighting segments, creating white space, and structuring content.

RULES

Rules are vertical or horizontal lines used to separate or highlight text and graphics. A rule can be created by using underline on the keyboard or by accessing the application in a word processing software program. When you use the automated software application, the thickness of rules is measured in points.

¼ point

¾ point

1 point

3 points

Use horizontal rules to separate parts of text for emphasis. For example, a lightweight horizontal rule can be used to separate the last line of text type from a header, as shown. (The Automated Footnote feature automatically places a rule above footnotes.) Figure 10.13 has this style of rule above the footer and a heavier rule under the centered main heading.

FIGURE 10.13 Rules used to set off main heading and footer

BORDERS

Borders (also called **boxes** or **boxed rules**) frame an element that you want to set off—a segment of text, a visual, a list, or a combination. These set-off segments are known as **sidebars** when they contain material that is related to the surrounding copy but could also stand alone. Figure 10.14 shows a figure set off with a border, and Figure 10.15 shows a numbered list set off with a border.

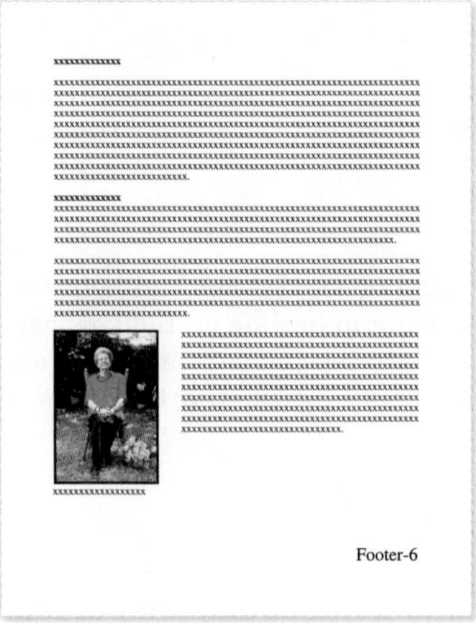

Footer-6

FIGURE 10.14 Figure with border

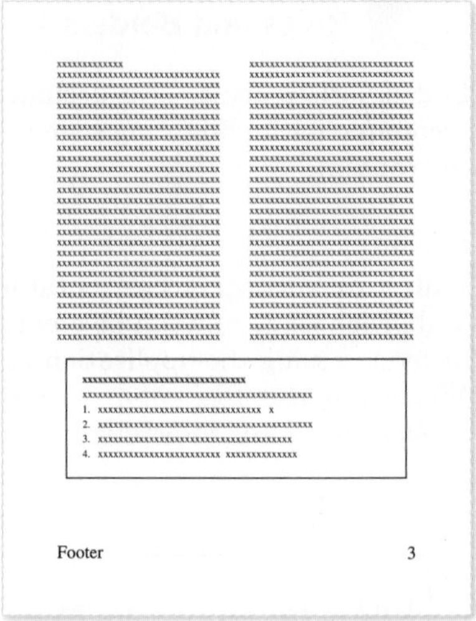

1.
2.
3.
4.

Footer 3

FIGURE 10.15 Text set off with border

85j Headers and Footers

When inserting a header or footer, consider the following:

- **Font:** Match the type to the body or use a common sans serif font, such as Arial.
- **Size:** For best readability, use a font that is one or two points smaller than the body type.
- **Placement:** Page numbers alone are more easily seen when centered or right justified (aligned with the right margin). For balance, position headers/footers and page numbers at the left and right margins respectively.
- **Titles:** Titles on headers and footers should be short; use abbreviated forms if section headings are longer than two or three words. Limit the header or footer to one line that includes the title and page number. To include additional information, for example, part and section title, consider using both a header and footer, but only if the information is essential to the reader.
- **Page numbers:** Whether or not a header or a footer is included, always number the pages of a document. The word *page* is unnecessary; the number alone is sufficient. The page number should be centered or right justified. Automated page numbering allows the

QUICK REFERENCE 85.3

Pagination in documents with front and back matter

When numbering long documents that have a cover page and/or front matter, follow these guidelines.

Front matter

- Use roman numerals to number frontmatter.
- Begin numbering on the first page following the cover (or title page). For single-sided copy, this is usually the table of contents, which would be page i.

Body and back matter

- Begin the first page of the body with arabic numeral 1.
- Begin each main section on a right-hand page.
- If title pages are used as dividers of main sections, do not show the number on these pages, but do count them. Use the automated numbering system to suppress the number.
- Numbering of back matter continues from the body of the document.
- If materials such as appendixes and attachments are already numbered, an option is to create one or more "title pages" listing these documents under the heading Appendixes and/or Attachments. This page can then be listed in the table of contents for numbering continuity, then list the titles of the individual documents without numbers.

[Read more about formatting back matter in Topic 80.]

insertion of the total number of pages after the page number (2 of 35, for example). This is useful at times, but as a rule it isn't necessary. Readers are accustomed to seeing the page number standing alone.

- **Date:** When the date is included in a header or footer using the automated insertion feature, be aware that it will be automatically updated each time the document is opened. To avoid this, the options are to type it instead of using the automated feature or to convert the document to PDF format before distributing it.

(**Note:** Use only a header on printed memos and letters that run more than one page. For specifics on the wording of second and subsequent pages of memos and letters, see 67d and 70a.)

85k Number Long Documents (Frontmatter, Text, and Backmatter)

In long documents such as reports and book manuscripts, frontmatter is numbered separately from the body, but backmatter is not. Use lowercase roman numerals to number frontmatter and do not show numbers on the title page or back of the title page. Usually, the first page with a number showing (usually iii) is the table of contents. Quick Reference 85.3 provides guidelines for numbering long documents.

[See 80i in Part Nine: Reports, Proposals, and References for illustrations of frontmatter pages and numbering.]

86 INTEGRATING TEXT AND VISUALS

Representing information in graphic and tabular format is vitally important to communication. Visuals add clarity and interest to the content of a document so long as they are relevant to the topic and effectively used to summarize data and communicate essential information. Visuals may be used purely as decorative items on covers and title pages, but otherwise, they should be labeled and placed in context with a brief discussion or reference in the text.

86a Tables

Tables are used primarily for summarizing numerical data, but they can also be useful for text matter that can be more easily understood (and used for reference) in columnar format. Some tables are clearer with gridlines showing and some without; it depends on the type of data, the number of columns, and the length. Table formatting without gridlines works well for organizing information without labeling it as a table. This is a good way to break up blocks of paragraphs to create visual interest without using tabs for spacing, which often loses formatting when documents are closed and reopened or transmitted by email.

The following example shows tabular information that can be set up without gridlines.

Following are the annual salaries of our current department managers:

Robert Griffin General Manager	$65,000
Julia Muhammad Telemarketing Supervisor	$45,300

Vicki Brown Communications Manager	$41,900
Debra Souder Director of Sales	$39,000
Sally Jamison Office Manager	$29,000

Here is how the same table can be set up with gridlines and shading: In a document with a large amount of tabular information, tables will most likely need to be numbered and labeled so they can be referenced in the text.

Robert Griffin General Manager	$65,000
Julia Muhammad Telemarketing Supervisor	$45,300
Vicki Brown Communications Manager	$41,900
Debra Souder Director of Sales	$39,000
Sally Jamison Office Manager	$29,000

86b Formatting Tables

TABLE GRID

Table title and number identify the table and its subject matter.

Table columns present information vertically (top to bottom).

Table rows present information horizontally (left to right).

Cells contain column headings, row headings, and data.

Footnotes contain reference or explanatory information.

Figures 10.16 through 10.18 show several table formatting options.

SPACING

- Leave at least two lines of space above and below a table; adjust for overall page balance.
- Single-space copy within cells for most tables; always use consistent spacing for column heads and consistent spacing in cells.
- Use consistent spacing above and below entries within cells; adjust to increase or decrease the size of the table as a whole.

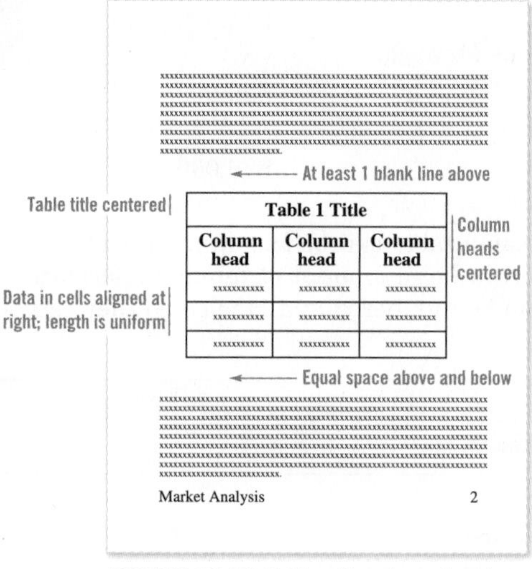

FIGURE 10.16 Table with column heads

TITLE AND NUMBER

- Type the table number and title in boldface on one or more lines; if on one line, separate the number and title with punctuation. Use all capital letters or cap/lowercase.

Table 6
Monthly Overtime Hours for Union Employees
December 1–January 31, 20xx

Table 9—Maintenance Fee Schedule

- The word *Table* and the number can be placed outside the grid line, flush left or centered.

Table 1

Dropout Rates* for First-year Students 1990–2010				
2010	**2005**	**2000**	**1995**	**1990**
45.2	44.1	43.9	39.5	38.7

*Percentage of first-year students who did not return for a second year

Table title flush left

Table 1 Title			
	2000	**2005**	**2010**
Row Head	xxxxxxxxx	xxxxxxxxx	xxxxxxxxx
Row Head	xxxxxxxxx	xxxxxxxxx	xxxxxxxxx
Row Head	xxxxxxxxx	xxxxxxxxx	xxxxxxxxx

Column heads

Row heads flush left

Data entered in cells

Footer 2

FIGURE 10.17 Table with column heads and row heads

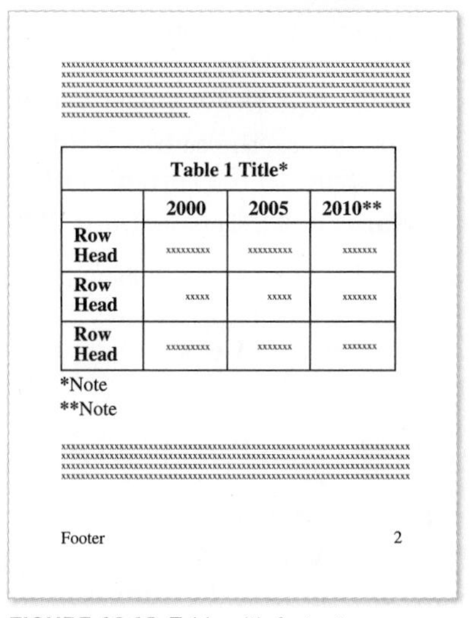

Table 1 Title*			
	2000	**2005**	**2010****
Row Head	xxxxxxxxx	xxxxxxxxx	xxxxxxx
Row Head	xxxxx	xxxxx	xxxxxxx
Row Head	xxxxxxxxx	xxxxxxx	xxxxxxx

*Note
**Note

Footer 2

FIGURE 10.18 Table with footnotes

HEADINGS

- Center column headings and use a boldface font.
- Begin row headings at the left margin (left justified) and use a boldface font.
- Use a consistent style for capitalization of column and row heads: initial cap, title style, or all caps.

ENTRIES IN CELLS

- If cells have an uneven number of lines, match the width of the cells with the one that has the longest line length and align copy at the top of the cell.
- Unless all cell entries are complete sentences, omit periods or other end punctuation.
- Align cell data at the left margin or center it (whichever is the most visually appealing alignment).
- Align large numbers at the right margin and align at decimals and/or commas. [See 86e.]

86c Table Footnotes and Source Notes

- Place footnotes or source notes outside of the table grid, at the bottom.
- Use footnotes or source notes to explain information in a table—for example, unfamiliar terms, abbreviations, missing data, and guidelines or caveats about interpreting the data.

- For only a few footnotes, number them or use symbols for identification. For one to three notes, use asterisks or a series of symbols, such as (*), (§), (¶). For longer lists of notes, use consecutive numbers.
- To indicate the source of information in a table, place a note directly underneath the bottom border:

  Source: US Census Data, 2000

For a table that does not show gridlines, insert a rule above the source note:

Source: US Census Data, 2000

86d Formatting Figures in Table Cells

UNITS OF MEASURE

- Identify units of measure either in column headings or with abbreviations after the number in each cell; do not use periods after abbreviations.
- Be consistent in units of measure listed and expression of the numerical data.

  120.3 lb
  240.5 lb
  122.0 lb

LARGE FIGURES

- Truncate (shorten) large round figures by omitting zeroes and indicate in the column heading whether the numbers are expressed in thousands, millions, or billions.
- If the amount represented applies to the entire table, put the spelled out amount in parentheses below the title. If it pertains to a column of figures, insert it in parentheses below the column head.

Table 10 Variable-rate Bonds (in millions)

Year Ending December 31	Principal	Interest	Net swap payments	Total
2006	$ 1.4	$ 59.5	$ (5.1)	$ 55.9
2007	1.5	59.5	(3.4)	57.5
2008	1.5	59.4	(3.4)	57.5
2009	1.6	59.3	(3.4)	57.6
2010	1.7	59.3	(3.4)	57.6

- When listing figures in columns that represent different types of numbers, use words and/or symbols in the column heading to label the figures.

Complete figure	Millions ($)	(%)	(Days)
25,849,000	25.8	14.2	34
97,047,000	97.0	2.0	12
240,739,000	240.7	7.6	188

DOLLAR FIGURES

- Columns of money require only a dollar sign before the first figure and a dollar sign before the total. The two dollar signs in each column should align one beneath the other.

2nd Quarter Sales (millions)			
	June	July	August
Spring Line	$ 2,950.2	$ 590.5	$ 27.2
Summer Line	1,200.0	1,303.5	840.0
Fall Line	489.5	913.0	1,910.4
Total	$ 3,699.7	$ 2,837.0	$ 2,777.6

86e Integrating Tables with Text

REFERENCING TABLES

Refer to numbered tables as Table 1, Table 2, and so on; for unnumbered tables refer to the title:

> See “Employee Ratings by Year” on page 22.

Integrate references to tables in running text or show them in parentheses:

> New products did not do well this year. Table 3 lists monthly sales for the top 10 new products introduced since January 20xx.
>
> Sales were sluggish throughout the year as shown by the lackluster performance of the top 10 new products introduced since January 20xx (see Table 3).

When referring to a table that is not on the same page as the reference, provide the page number.

> Table 3 (p. 15) provides sales figures for the top 10 new products introduced this year.
>
> Sales figures for our top 10 new products have been sluggish all year (see Table 3, page 15).

PLACEMENT OF TABLES

Place a table as close as possible to the point in the text where it is first mentioned and where it will not disrupt the flow of the content. Ideally, this would be directly following the paragraph in which it is referenced.

When fitting a table within the margins of the text copy is challenging, try adjusting the size of type overall. Eliminating words in column and/or row headings might also help reduce the width. See Quick Reference 86.1 for tips on how to stay within the parameters of standard layout as you manipulate table features.

QUICK REFERENCE 86.1

Placement of tables in text documents

- Tables look best centered on the page within the text margins or even with the text margins, whenever possible.
- If a table is too wide to fit vertically on the page, place it horizontally on a page by itself, with the top of the page facing the left margin. Center it and allow at least 1-inch top, bottom, and side margins.
- Place a table as close as possible to the point in the text where it is first mentioned and where it will not disrupt the flow of the content, but never break up a table or chart to make it fit on the same page as the reference. Place it on the following page.
- Do not divide a table at the bottom of a page. If a table takes up two-thirds of a page or more, place it on a separate page and adjust surrounding text as needed.
- If a table is longer than one page, begin it at the top of a page (not at the bottom) and continue it onto the next page; repeat the title and column headings on the second page, even if the two pages face each other. See Figures 10.19a and 10.19b.

Table 4 Title		
Column Head	**Column Head**	**Column Head**
xxxxxxxxxx	xxxxxxxxxx	xxxxxxxxxx
xxxxxxxxxx	xxxxxxxxxx	xxxxxxxxxx
xxxxxxxxxx	xxxxxxxxxx	xxxxxxxxxx
xxxxxxxxxx	xxxxxxxxxx	xxxxxxxxxx
xxxxxxxxxx	xxxxxxxxxx	xxxxxxxxxx
xxxxxxxxxx	xxxxxxxxxx	xxxxxxxxxx
xxxxxxxxxx	xxxxxxxxxx	xxxxxxxxxx
xxxxxxxxxx	xxxxxxxxxx	xxxxxxxxxx

Footer 2

FIGURE 10.19a First page of two-page table

Table 4 Title (continued)		
Column Head	**Column Head**	**Column Head**
xxxxxxxxxx	xxxxxxxxxx	xxxxxxxxxx
xxxxxxxxxx	xxxxxxxxxx	xxxxxxxxxx
xxxxxxxxxx	xxxxxxxxxx	xxxxxxxxxx
xxxxxxxxxx	xxxxxxxxxx	xxxxxxxxxx

Footer 2

FIGURE 10.19b Second page of two-page table with "continued" notation

86f Integrating Graphics and Text

The term **graphics** includes charts, graphs, photographs, diagrams, and illustrations (drawings). They all fall under the category of **figures** and should be labeled, numbered, and referenced in text.

To integrate graphics with text, place each graphic as close as possible to the paragraph where it is first discussed. Include a reference to the figure number; for example:

> Figure 9.1 shows the relationship of sales to promotion dollars spent over the last six months.

Use the sizing and formatting options in your word processor to fit the graphic within the text area as seamlessly as possible. Figures 10.20, 10.21, and 10.22 show examples of various formats for integrating text and graphics.

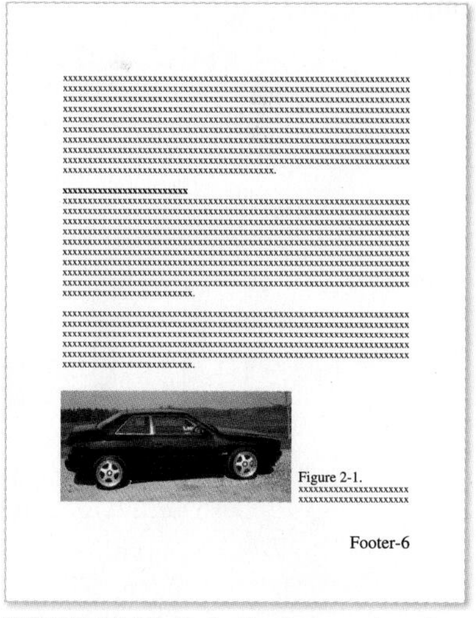

FIGURE 10.20 Text with photograph and caption

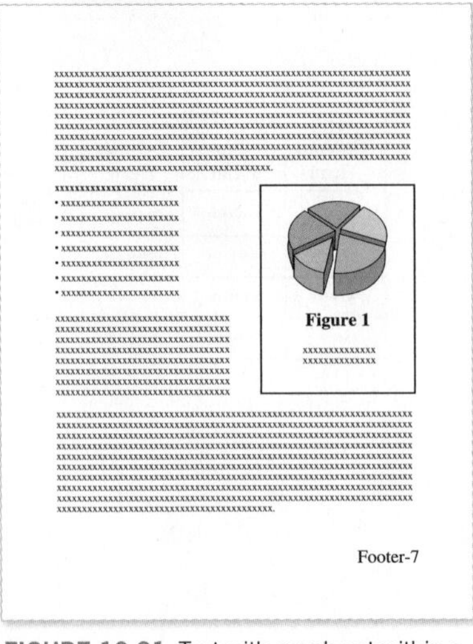

FIGURE 10.21 Text with graph set within a border

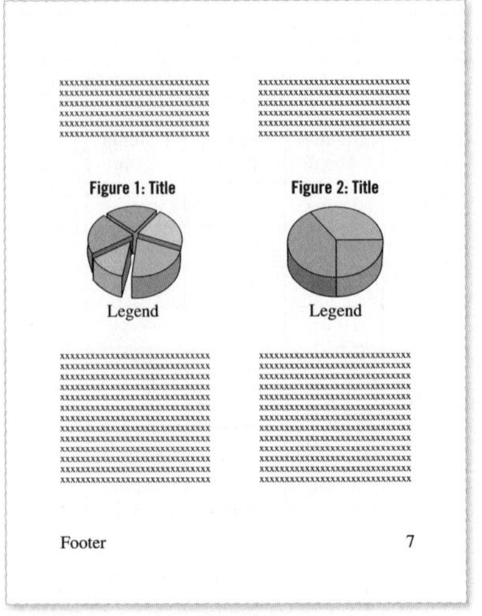

FIGURE 10.22 Double-column text with graphs aligned

86g Selecting Appropriate Graphics

Different types of graphics serve various purposes, depending on the type of data and the information the writer wishes to illustrate. The following illustrations represent standard types of graphics and their purposes:

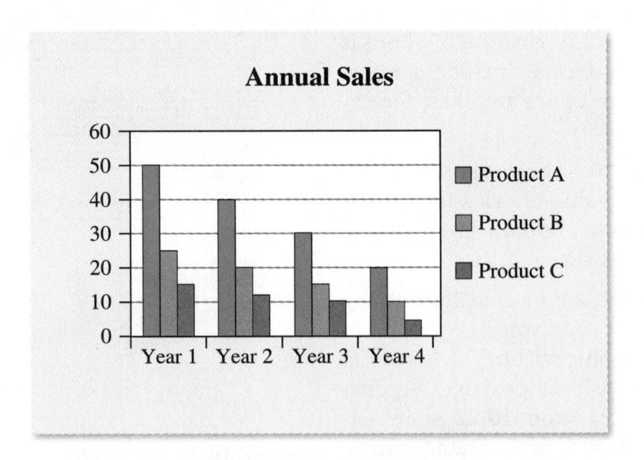

FIGURE 10.23 Bar graph shows the relationship between two or more sets of data.

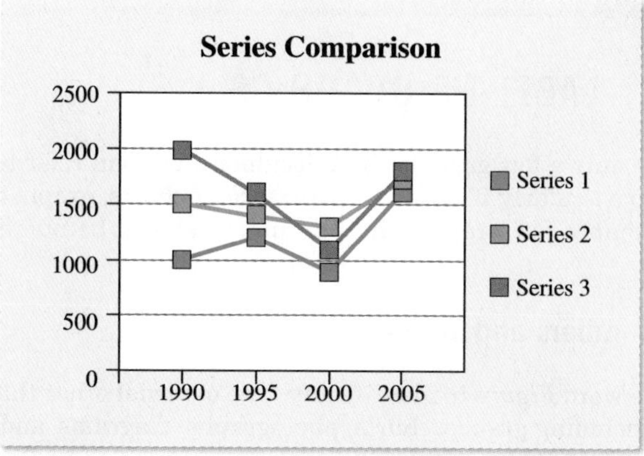

FIGURE 10.24 Line graph: Shows the relationship of information or data to a time line.

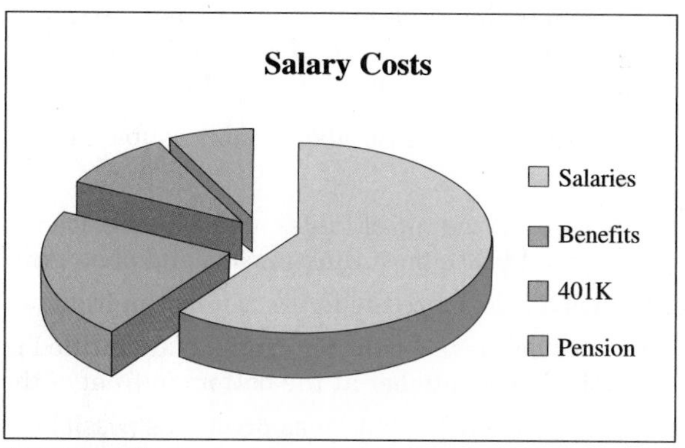

FIGURE 10.25 Pie graph: presents simple data for comparison, such as percentages of a whole.

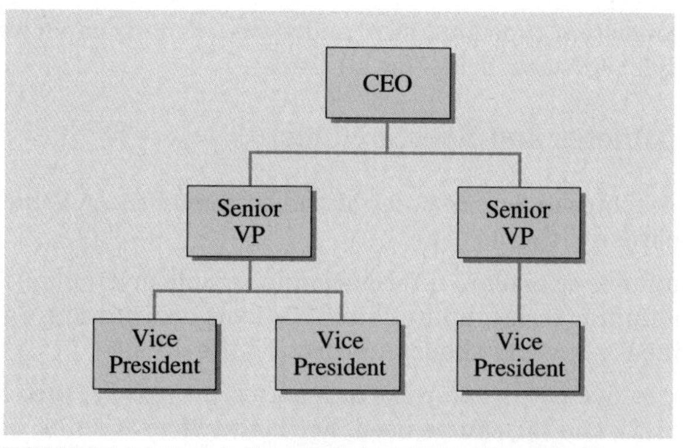

FIGURE 10.26 Organization chart: depicts the hierarchy of items—usually positions in an organization.

87 LABELING GRAPHICS

If you have only a few graphics in a document, you can refer to them by title only, particularly if they are a mixture of charts, graphs, and photos. More than a few graphics in a document should be numbered consecutively.

87a Numbers and Titles

- Use the word *Figure* to identify any type of visual other than a table, including graphs, charts, photographs, diagrams, and illustrations.
- Figures can be numbered consecutively throughout a document or double numbered within each section when main sections of a report or other publication are numbered. (Figure 1, Figure 2, Figure 3, and so on or Figure 1.1, Figure 1.2, Figure 1.3, and so on).

(**Note:** When figures are double-numbered, also double number tables if a document has both.)

- Always place titles at the top of tables and graphics. Charts, graphs, and diagrams need titles; most illustrations and photographs do not.
- If a graphic has a title, place the figure number in front of the title.
- If a graphic does not have a title, for example an untitled photograph, place the figure number at the bottom in front of the caption.
- Use short, descriptive titles, but be as precise as possible.
- When multiple graphics have similar content—for example, figures for various periods of time, include specifics in the title.
- Use a consistent type font, size, and style—usually cap/lowercase (title style), all caps, bold—for all titles.

87b Footnotes and Source Notes

- Place footnotes or source notes at the bottom of the graphic outside of the border, if there is one.
- Use footnotes to explain information in a table or graphic; for example, unfamiliar terms, unfamiliar abbreviations, missing data, and guidelines or caveats about interpreting the data.
- For one to five notes, asterisks or a series of symbols, such as (*), (**), (†), (‡), and (§), can be used. For longer lists of notes, use consecutive numbers.

- A **source note** should include relevant information about the source, such as author, title, and date. If a graphic is used with permission from the copyright owner, this should be noted.
- For a table that does not show gridlines or a graphic without a border, insert a short rule above the footnote or source note:

---

*Data does not include the years 1999–2001.

87c Captions, Legends, and Callouts

Figure 10.27 shows the elements listed here.

- A caption is a short explanation (one or two sentences) or description of a graphic. Position it directly beneath the graphic, or alongside it, depending on layout. Captions are often set in a smaller type font than running text; a sans serif font, such as Arial, 10 point, is a good choice.

If a graphic does not have a title, indicate the figure number below the graphic with the caption. When a photographer, illustrator, or source is to be credited, place this information below the caption.

- A **legend** is a key to the scheme of colors or patterns in graphs and charts. Place the legend at the bottom of the graphic. Keep legends short and use consistent wording and capitalization.
- **Callouts** are labels used to identify or provide brief explanations of parts of graphics, such as drawings and diagrams.

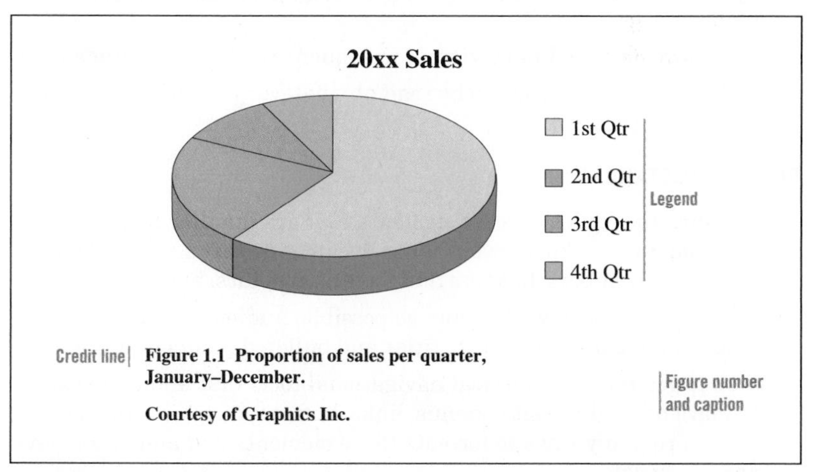

FIGURE 10.27 Figure with caption, legend, and callouts

(**Note:** When using material from outside sources, make sure that you are not infringing on anyone's copyright ownership. For information about copyright and fair use, see Topic 82.)

88 WRITING FOR MULTIMEDIA

Preparing materials for publication through media other than printed documents requires a shift in the perception of your audience's needs. This topic provides guidelines for developing material for slides and Web pages.

88a Page Versus Screen

Writing for media other than print requires a shift in thinking about how your audience will perceive and use the information. Here are some important differences to consider *from the readers' point of view.*

VISUAL PERCEPTION

- The reader of a printed page reads from left to right and top to bottom.
- The reader of a slide focuses on the center of the screen first.
- The reader of a Web page focuses on whatever is designed to be the central focal point.

SEQUENCE

- Printed documents are designed to be read in sequence at the reader's pace.
- Slides are designed to be viewed in sequence at the presenter's pace.
- Web pages are designed to be read at whatever pace and sequence the reader chooses.

DESIGN EXPECTATIONS

- Documents require specific elements that are familiar to the reader and common to almost every other document—text sections, headings, page numbers, headers and footers, graphics, and so on.
- Slides require as few elements as possible. Audiences expect them to follow a typical format—e.g., titles and bulleted points or graphics.
- Web pages require technical navigational tools that allow the user to move around the site: menus, links, buttons, graphics, and so on. There are many ways to formats these elements and audiences have varied expectations.

89 PREPARING SLIDE PRESENTATIONS

Although Microsoft PowerPoint is probably the most widely known and used application for slide presentations, the information in this section is general enough to apply to any slide presentation software.

89a Purpose

The traditional use of a slide show is to augment a live spoken presentation. However, today, slide shows are often designed to stand on their own as presentations to be read or with audio included. Standalone uses include sales presentations, proposals, corporate information published on Web sites, work portfolios, photography shows, and audiovisual presentations on the Web.

89b Audience

In the case of a slide presentation delivered in person, the audience expects the slides to be shown in a logical sequence that augments the speaker's words. The audience does not expect to have any control over the medium, placing the burden on the speaker to integrate slides and oral content in a way that engages the listener/viewer.

Audiences expect standalone presentations to provide short bites of information, but in a thorough enough fashion that they are not left hanging. Nevertheless, audiences will not be content with text-heavy slides, any more than they would in a presentation delivered in person. Nor can the number of slides be overwhelming. The point of using slides is to present a focused and interesting package that will hold the viewer's attention for a short period. Impact is key; thus, standalone presentations should hit only the high points of the subject and be supplemented with print information if necessary.

89c Drafting

Begin writing by outlining the presentation on a blank black-and-white slide. This will prevent you from getting distracted by design considerations, while forcing you to attend to the most important element of the design—not overloading the slides.

In PowerPoint, the Outline view lets you review your draft outline and print it out for editing. Another option is to storyboard the presentation. A **storyboard** is a method of writing in two columns, one for graphics and one for the points about each image. This works well for presentations that include a lot of graphics, and is an excellent way to avoid having the slide show become a "script" of your spoken message. The worst presentations are those in which the speaker simply stands and reads what is on the slides. Slides should augment your message—they should not be the message itself. An interesting presenter has things to say that are not on the slides.

Either method of developing the draft allows you to manipulate the order of the slides and edit the text of each before beginning the actual design process.

89d Revising and Editing

Keep the time allotted to the presentation in mind and revise with the goal of limiting the number of slides. A rule of thumb for words per slide is:

- One key point for each line of text
- Not more than six to eight words per line
- No more than six to eight lines per slide

Use headlines and key phrases on the slides that will keep the audience's attention focused on what you are saying. Package key points together when they relate as a whole, and use **builds**—having content appear on the screen line by line—when you need to spend time on points individually. This technique helps to hold the audience's attention. You don't want them focused on reading point number three while you're still discussing point number one. Select a consistent, simple manner for the build, for example, from left to right, and use this feature only when necessary. Overusing it becomes a distraction.

89e Design and Layout

Various colors and background displays are provided on the software templates. If these are not suitable, use a blank slide or software templates available from commercial sources. Settle on one consistent set of style elements—font styles, colors, and sizes and background—for all slides. Design a consistent arrangement of text and graphic elements as well. For longer presentations, vary the slide design to some extent to avoid monotony. Text and image, text alone, bulleted or numbered lists, and graphics can be matched to the content to create an interesting presentation.

Figures 10.28, 10.29, and 10.30 provide examples and guidelines for how to make text and visuals work together.

BACKGROUND DESIGN AND COLOR

Select a template that is appropriate to your purpose and audience. Use contrasting colors for text and background: light text on a dark background (Figure 10.28) or dark text on a light background (Figure 10.29)

Limit the number of colors on a single screen to three for text screens and four for charts.

89f Special Effects

Be sure that any special effects, such as animation and sound, are used only when appropriate to the audience and subject matter. For a serious business presentation, select one unobtrusive **transition mode (animation)**—the movement from one slide to the next—and use it throughout the presentation. Use nondramatic modes such as left to right or top to bottom. For situations where other modes might be appropriate, be careful about overusing the more dramatic ones—they tend to become annoying upon repetition.

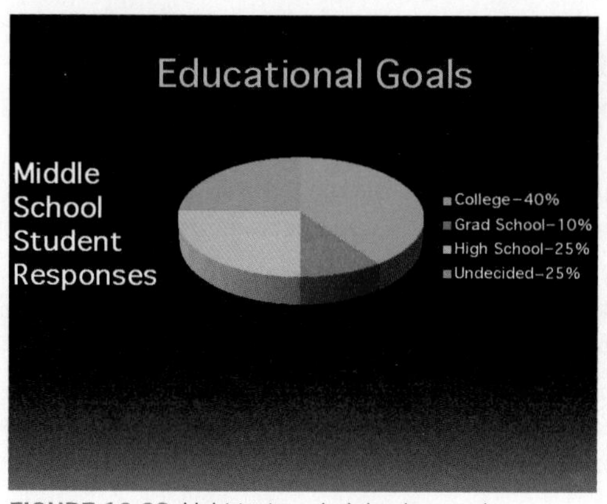

FIGURE 10.28 Light text on dark background

Layout

When applicable, place titles of the main presentation sections at the top to aid clarity. Use all caps or lowercase.

Use a smaller font size, and caps/lowercase or sentence case for text.

Leave empty space around the text and graphics. Use more slides if necessary to ensure empty space on each slide.

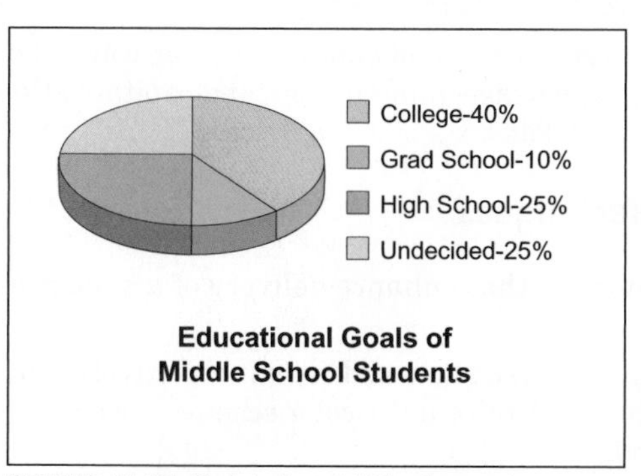

FIGURE 10.29 Dark text on light background

Font

Use a single sans serif font.

Vary the size to achieve levels of emphasis.

Use sizes ranging from 24- to 48-point.

Do not use all caps except for titles.

Avoid italics or fancy fonts that are hard to read.

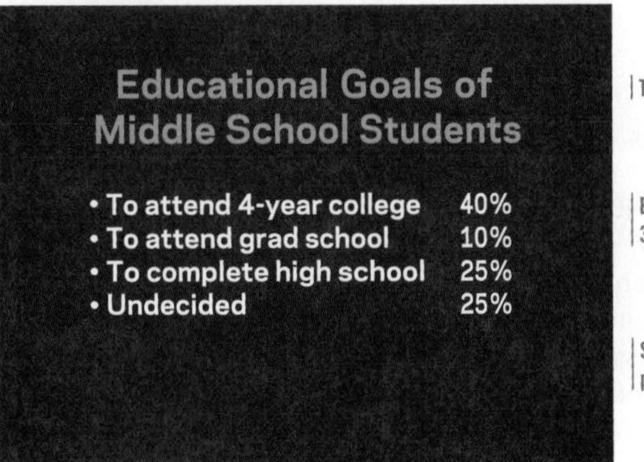

FIGURE 10.30 Text only—light type on dark background

TEXT DESIGN AND STYLE

- Follow the rule of parallel structure for items listed in a series. [See 85e.]
- Punctuation can make slides look cluttered. Avoid it by using phrases instead of sentences to eliminate periods and most commas, but be consistent.
- Avoid using all capital letters; they are more difficult to read. Instead, use a larger or different style font.
- Avoid fancy fonts; the sans serif fonts that work well in print are most readable on slides as well; however, they require at least 18 point and larger for readability at a distance. [See 85b for guidelines on type and font selection.]
- Limit lines of text on each slide to no more than six to eight.
- Print the slides and proofread them.
- Go through the text several times and edit for spelling, consistency of wording, style, language usage, punctuation, and capitalization. [See proofreading guidelines in Part Six: The Writing Process.]

89g Presentation Techniques

Following are some techniques that enhance delivery of a slide presentation.

- Run the presentation as a slide show and view it objectively (critically), as the audience will. Notice if the color scheme is working and adjust it if needed.
- Run through the presentation on the same type of screen that will be used in the actual presentation, when possible, to confirm readability.

- Learn how to manipulate the presentation efficiently; for example, navigating by jumping ahead or back without having to page through every slide.
- Provide a copy of the presentation in handout form *after the presentation* to avoid having audience members reading instead of watching and listening. Let the audience know beforehand so they won't be distracted by taking notes.
- Remember to face the audience and not the screen while speaking.
- Do not read the presentation from the slides; the slide text should be used as a cue to the more substantive message of your spoken presentation.
- Put nothing on a slide that will be hard for the audience to decipher or read. Eliminate anything you would need to apologize for or ask the audience to "excuse."
- When you want to speak without the support or distraction of a slide, press the B key on the keyboard and the screen will go to black; press B again to return to the slide show.
- Practice the presentation and avoid reading from the slides; get an honest critique of a first-time presentation and slide show.

90 WEB PAGES

If you need to create a Web page or Web site, consult the many online sources, books, and professionals who specialize in this work. If you need to create text or otherwise contribute material for use on Web pages for a particular audience, this topic provides some guidelines for understanding audiences for this medium and developing content accordingly.

90a Purpose

The purposes for business Web sites are no different from those of printed documents and publications. Web pages exist to inform, to persuade and sell, to instruct and direct, and to respond to questions and requests. A Web site as a whole might have one or more of these purposes, and any page on the site might have several objectives. When developing material for a Web site, consider the multiple purposes the site might serve.

90b Audience

The audience for Web pages is not so much a *reader* as a *user* or *consumer* of information. The user expects to be able to **navigate**—move around the site at will—and anticipates that certain tools will be available to aid this navigation. These **navigational tools** include menus, buttons, and graphics, and underlined words that provide **links**—connections between Web pages. Users expect these tools to be available, and they expect them to work efficiently—that is move them with one or two clicks of the mouse to the information they want.

Generally, there are two types of users of business Web sites: internal users and external users. External users are the customers and clients who come to the Internet site, the site that is accessed by the public; internal users are the employees who have access to their organization's **intranet,** the site reserved for company use, which is protected from access by those outside it.

90c External Web Sites—the Internet

Some key categories of information found on external business Web sites are the following:

- **Company information:** such topics as company history, biographical data on principals, and information on the organization's mission, achievements, divisions, branches, and so on.
- **Product/service information:** describes what the company or organization does or provides, divided into as many segments and/or links as necessary to satisfy the user's needs.
- **Communications and public relations information:** pro-vides the media and the public with current and historical information on the company's activities. Includes annual reports, press releases, newsletters, brochures, interviews, feature stories, and other publications that define and promote the company's mission.
- **Investor information:** documents and reports on the company's financial picture; includes information on performance, holdings, subsidiaries, and current business strategies.
- **Events and calendars:** advertises past and upcoming activities and events related to the company and possibly outside of the company.
- **Careers and job opportunities:** promotes the company as an employer and lists job openings; might include profiles of employees and information on community-related activities.
- **Frequently asked questions (FAQs):** answers questions asked most often by visitors to the Web site.
- **Downloadable information:** brochures, reports, publications, and other materials made available in PDF format for printing.

90d Internal Web Sites—the Intranet

An **intranet** is a private computer network designed to be accessed only by company employees. Organizations use intranet sites to provide a broad range of information to employees that used to be provided exclusively through printed material. Some of the most common categories of information available on intranets are the following:

- **Policies and procedures:** human resources policies related to aspects of employment and the policies and procedures of individual departments.
- **Benefits:** details of benefit plans or links to providers' plans, along with necessary forms, applications, and so on.
- **Employment opportunities:** job postings and applications.
- **Communications:** newsletters, executive messages, and internal reports.
- **Calendars:** schedules of holidays, annual events, and special events.
- **Bulletin boards:** a place where employees can exchange information with one another.

90e Writing for the Web

Writing for internal or external Web sites requires the same level of attention to style, accuracy, consistency, and correctness that applies to writing print materials. In fact, in today's businesses, a large number of materials are created for use in both print and electronic format. When writing only for the Web, keeping in mind the differences in how it will be consumed. Following are some of the key differences (see also 89a):

- **Timeliness:** It is understood by readers that print publications might contain information that is not up to date. Users of Web sites, however, expect to find timely information. If you are responsible for information posted on a Web site, make sure it is updated regularly—monthly, weekly, or even daily—to keep visitors coming back.
- **Integration of text and graphics:** Rare is the Web page that has only text. Most will have at least a banner across the top and a menu down the left side. Graphics are often integrated with text, so it is important to know exactly how much text will appear on a screen and how it will be viewed by the user. Images and other design elements must work in harmony with text, so that neither one overwhelms the other. Consult a design professional if you need to build a Web site from scratch.
- **Amount of text:** Just as with print, text and white space need to be balanced for readability. An additional consideration for a Web page is what will be most comfortable visually and most convenient for the user. Short blocks of text broken up with formatting (i.e., headlines, headings, bullets) and color used as a visual cue make a page easy for the reader to navigate. Judge how many lines of text will appear on a screen before the reader needs to scroll or click a link to

continue reading. A menu of topics at the top of a page leaves the home page free of dense copy while making it easy for users to link to those topics elsewhere on the site.

- **Navigational tools:** Web users expect to find information by clicking a button on a menu or a link elsewhere on the page indicated by an underline. Understand the structure of the Web site for which you are writing and where your copy fits. Use underlining only to denote links. Using it for other purposes will be confusing.
- **Proofread:** Proof copy carefully, using the same rules applied to print. [See Topic 8 for proofreading guidelines.]

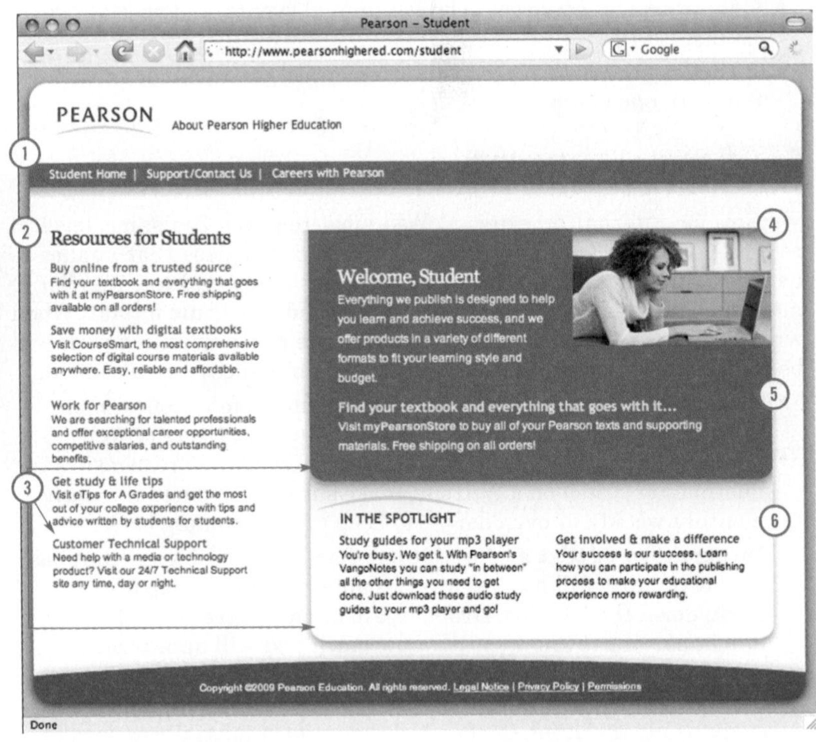

1. Menu items positioned at the top.
2. Structure of the site is summarized in five succinct paragraphs with links.
3. Only three sections of text make the page easy to scan or read quickly.
4. White space on the page leaves it uncluttered and easy to read.
5. The eye is drawn to one focal point that provides information about the site.
6. The user doesn't need to scroll down; copy fits on one screen.

FIGURE 10.31 Effective Web page design

BUSINESS AND EMPLOYMENT COMMUNICATIONS

section eleven

91 MEETING AGENDAS AND MINUTES

Meetings range from small, routine group sessions to large, highly structured business conferences, seminars, and workshop events. For any kind of meeting, it is essential to have an **agenda,** a document that lists items for discussion, activities, and the order of business.

Agendas for meetings to discuss routine business matters are usually informal. Items for discussion can be listed in an email announcing the meeting or in a document attached to the email so that participants may prepare in advance. When an agenda is distributed in advance of a meeting, copies should also be available for distribution at the start of the meeting.

91a Informal Meeting Agenda

Quick Reference 91.1 lists the standard items to include in a meeting agenda and Figure 11.1 provides a format for a routine business meeting agenda.

Department of Administrative Management
Chippewa Hall, Room 325
April 18, 20xx
3 – 5 p.m.

AGENDA

Executive Committee Meeting

Dr. Amelia Jackson, Department Chair, Presiding

Purpose: Closeout of preparations for summer and fall semesters

1. Staff awards luncheon agenda and awardees – Dr. Harrison
2. Summer Seminar responsibilities and schedules – Dr. Draper
3. Curriculum Committee recommendations for course changes/additions – Dr. Mushen
4. Goals and timetables for summer/fall committee work – Committee Chairs
5. Annual Report – Dr. Jackson

List of Attendees:

J. Baer	F. Jenkins
H. Draper	P. Mushen
L. Harrison	I. O'Hara
A. Jackson	

FIGURE 11.1 Meeting agenda

QUICK REFERENCE 91.1

Items for an informal meeting agenda

- Name of the group or individual convening the meeting
- A title indicating the meeting's purpose
- The date, time (start or start/finish), and location
- List of attendees
- Topics to be covered in order of discussion
- Presenter or discussion leader for each topic (optional)
- Time allotment for each topic (optional)

91b Agenda for Meetings Using Parliamentary Procedure

Formal meetings of government and civic agencies, corporate boards, nonprofit organizations such as churches, unions, and professional associations traditionally follow the procedures set forth in *Robert's Rules of Order, Newly Revised.* This is the guide to **parliamentary procedure,** a method of conducting meetings to ensure that each participant has a voice and a vote in the decision-making process.

See Quick Reference 91.2 for guidelines on the order of business to list in an agenda for a meeting that follows parliamentary procedure.

QUICK REFERENCE 91.2

Items to include in a parliamentary procedure agenda

- Call to order
- Opening ceremonies (optional)
- Roll call (if customary)
- Reading and approval of last meeting's minutes
- Reports of officers, boards, and standing committees
- Reports of special committees (announced only if such committees are prepared or instructed to report)
- Special orders (announced only if there are special orders)
- Unfinished business and general orders
- New business
- Announcements
- Program (if a program or a speaker is planned for the meeting)
- Adjournment

(Source: The National Association of Parliamentarians Web site: http://parliamentarians.org/basics-presiding.php)

91c Conference and Seminar Agendas

Formal conferences and seminars usually have a professionally produced program; however, businesspeople frequently hold less formal one- or two-day conferences, seminars, and training sessions that require an agenda. Such an agenda is essentially an outline of scheduled activities, presenters, locations, and times. These can be created with word processing software templates or by designing a format of your own. Figure 11.2 is an agenda for a two-day training seminar prepared with a Microsoft Word template.

AGENDA

Entrepreneurial Endeavors
Training Seminar
Century Plaza Hotel & Spa, Los Angeles
April 2 – 3, 20xx

Tuesday, April 2

8 – 9 a.m.	Continental Breakfast & Welcome	Grand Salon II
9 – 10:30 a.m.	Business Plan Workshop—Part I	Palisades Room
10:30 – 11 a.m.	Beverage Break	Main Lobby and Patio
11 a.m. – Noon	Business Plan Workshop—Part II	Palisades Room
Noon – 1 p.m.	Luncheon	Grand Salon I & II
1 – 3 p.m.	Marketing Plan Breakout Sessions	
	Level I	Encino Room
	Level 2	Palisades Room
	Level 3	Santa Monica Room

Free time—network and enjoy the pool and spa!

7 p.m.	Cocktails	Poolside

Wednesday, February 6

8 – 9 a.m.	Continental Breakfast	Grand Salon II
9 – 10:30 a.m.	Panel—Financing Options Moderator—Douglas Frasier US Small Business Administration	Grand Salon II
10:30 – 11 a.m.	Q & A Session	Grand Salon II

Networking and Business Card Exchange

Departure – Checkout by Noon

FIGURE 11.2 Seminar agenda

91d Informal Meeting Minutes and Summaries

Minutes provide a written record of the discussion, actions, and decisions on meeting agenda items. For informal meetings, it is common practice to record the proceedings in the form of a brief summary that focuses on decisions and assignments for follow-up on agenda items. See Figure 11.3 for an example and QuickReference 91.3 for items to include.

Department of Administrative Management
Summer Seminar Committee
Minutes, November 12, 20xx

Members present: R. Witowsky, S. Lorenzo, B. Weston, A. Levine, G. Baker, L. Merriweather, J. Donaldson, F. Lopez

The meeting was convened at 8 a.m. in Room 816.

Ron and Al presented costs and details for the proposed 20xx summer seminar in Scotland. The tentative agenda was distributed and discussed. Members made a few minor changes, but were in favor of the subcommittee moving forward.

A motion was made and seconded to proceed with making plans for the Scotland seminar.

The budget was discussed, and the committee concluded that a minimum number of participants would be 20 and the maximum to aim for is 30. A preliminary mailing to potential participants will be sent out as soon as the agenda is firmed up. The target date for the mailing was established as December 1 to give participants at least six months advance notice. A draft of the mailing will be distributed to committee members for input by no later than next Friday.

Gordon suggested a policy change to offer the summer seminar every other year. The committee decided to bring this up for discussion at the next full staff meeting.

The minutes of the November 1, 20xx meeting were approved as circulated.

The meeting adjourned at 9 a.m.

Linda Carlson
Department Secretary

FIGURE 11.3 Informal meeting minutes

91e Formal Meeting Minutes

Minutes for formal meetings follow a more rigid format that correlates to the parliamentary procedure order of business as summarized in Quick Reference 91.3. An example is shown in Figure 11.4.

REAL TIME INFORMATION SERVICES

Meeting of the Executive Committee

June 4, 20xx

ATTENDANCE

The monthly executive committee meeting was held in the office of J. H. Hudson, Vice President and General Manager, at 2 p.m. on June 4, 20xx. Jay Hudson presided. Those present were Leslie Amato, Albert Button, George Johnson, Fay Peterson, and Judith Smith. Randolph Miller was absent.

AGENDA ITEMS COVERED

1. Leslie Amato presented the marketing plans for the new product, ART INFO ON-LINE. It was decided to move the launch date from June 1 to September 1, due to delays in getting the program up and running. The rest of the plan was approved.
2. George Johnson presented the production status report. ART INFO is the only major project not on schedule. It was agreed to reschedule it as stated in item #1 above.
3. Al Button reviewed second-quarter expenditures. All departments were within or under budget for the quarter to date.
4. Fay Peterson reviewed the creative services budget for third quarter. It was estimated that an additional $30,000 would be needed to cover promotional plans for the launch of ART INFO. It was decided that Fay would meet separately with Leslie and George to develop a strategy for implementing the original plan without going over budget. Jay Hudson asked Fay to present a report and recommendation by June 15.

DISCUSSION

Judith Smith presented a proposal for a new product that would supply information to businesses on convention sites in the United States and internationally. Members of the committee were asked to review the proposal and prepare a response for next month's meeting.

ADJOURNMENT

The meeting was adjourned at 3:30 p.m.

FIGURE 11.4 Formal meeting minutes

QUICK REFERENCE 91.3

Guidelines for meeting minutes

Items for all meeting minutes

- Name of the group
- Time, date, and location
- Title or purpose of the meeting
- Name and title of the person presiding over the meeting
- Names of attendees and standing members who were absent, if applicable
- Summary of resolution of each agenda item—for example, decisions, follow-up activities, outstanding issues
- Plans for next meeting, if applicable

Items for formal minutes

- If the meeting follows parliamentary procedure, the headings in the minutes should match those in the agenda (see Quick Reference 91.2).
- Record the exact wording of motions or proposals for action, the name of the persons who introduced and seconded each motion, and how the group voted on each item or why it did not go to a vote.
- Record the specifics of decisions made, matters set aside for further discussion, notices or correspondence read to the group, outside speakers who addressed the group, reports presented, and any other actions that took place.

92 ITINERARIES

92a Travel Itinerary

An **itinerary** is a detailed schedule of activities routinely used for travel plans. The following items may be included in a **travel itinerary** (see Figure 11.5):

- Name of the individual or group that will use the itinerary
- A line describing the destination and purpose of the trip
- Transportation details: provider, departure/arrival times for all segments of the trip; details specific to the mode of transportation (flight numbers, rental car pickup location, train station, etc.)

Travel Itinerary for Kelly Thomas

Trip to Seattle, WA
October 7–9, 20xx

Wednesday, October 7

9:34 a.m.	***Leave Detroit, Northwest Airlines, Flight #750 (no meal)*** Electronic Ticket (confirmation attached)
11:24 a.m.	Arrive Seattle-Tacoma International Airport Taxi to W Seattle Hotel, 1112 4th Avenue Seattle, 206-264-6000
1:00 p.m.	Meet Anderson Roswell in hotel lobby for drive to Microsoft corporate campus in Redmond, Washington Mr. Roswell's cell number: 206-555-7800
2 – 5 p.m.	Meeting with Noel Din, Microsoft Marketing VP and staff Mr. Roswell will drive you back to the hotel
7:00 p.m.	Dinner with Jeffrey Ortega and his wife in downtown Seattle. Phone Jeffrey if any changes: 206-555-6500

Thursday, October 8

8:00 a.m.	Breakfast with Horace Wilcox at the W hotel and return to Microsoft campus
10:00 – noon	Meeting with Microsoft Product Launch Team
Noon – 2 p.m.	Lunch at Microsoft
	Return to Seattle for free afternoon and evening

Friday, October 9

9:20 a.m.	***Leave Seattle, Flight #141 (no meal)*** Electronic Ticket (confirmation attached)
11:32 a.m.	Arrive Detroit

FIGURE 11.5 Travel itinerary

- Hotel arrival/departure dates; type of room booked; reservation guarantees; check-in/checkout times
- Telephone numbers of hotel and transportation services
- Contact information related to business being conducted
- Locations and phone numbers of local restaurants or meal reservations made

92b Event Itinerary

Group outings and other events that involve multiple locations and time schedules often require an informal itinerary. Following are items to include; an example is shown in Figure 11.6.

- Name and date of the event
- Names of participants

Interior Design Students Tour of Modern Home Design, Inc.

May 2, 20xx

ITINERARY

8:30 - 9 a.m.	Board Bus - Bishop Hall, Arbor Street Entrance
9:15 a.m.	Departure (Prompt)
9:30 - 11 a.m.	Guided Tour of Show Rooms and Facilities Judy Biagas, MHD Design Manager
11 a.m. - noon	Presentation and Round Table MHD Design Consultants
noon - 1 p.m.	Lunch - Executive Conference Room
1 - 2:30 p.m.	Demonstration - Design in Progress
2:30 - 3 p.m.	Q & A with Designers
3:15 p.m.	Departure for Return to Campus

Wear comfortable walking shoes.
Please leave large bags on campus.

Enjoy the day!

FIGURE 11.6 Event itinerary

- Contact information for leader/trip planner
- Activities, locations, and scheduled times
- Transportation information
- Special notations concerning meals, clothing requirements (e.g., for outdoor activities), accommodations for people with disabilities, and the like

93 PRESS RELEASES

93a Purpose and Audience for a Press Release

A **press release** (also called a **news release**) is a document distributed by an organization to media outlets with the goal of getting information out to the public. News releases announce new products and services, staff changes, organizational restructuring, special events and openings, appearances by company representatives, and myriad other items businesses might wish to publicize.

The audience for a news release is the media professional who will decide whether or not your news is of interest to the ultimate intended audience. News release copy needs to be attention-grabbing, with a clearly worded and catchy headline and a concise summary at the top that captures the essence of the news. If you email the news release, use the subject line to capture the recipient's attention.

The release should be written with the assumption that the media outlet can pick it up verbatim. Media outlets are free, however, to summarize news releases or print them with changes and cuts. Generally, a length of two pages at most is considered optimum for a news release. Many organizations post news releases online and also send them out as email attachments. Online posting provides the option of linking the reader to additional information.

93b What to Include in a Press Release

THE TOP OF THE RELEASE

Include the following information at the top of the news release (see Figure 11.7) whether it is published in print or online.

- Name of the organization
- Mailing address
- Name of contact person(s)
- Telephone and fax numbers

News Release

PRESS OFFICE

Release Date: December 24, 2008
Release Number: 08-127

Contact: Christine Mangi (202) 205-6948
Internet Address: http://www.sba.gov/news

Baruah Welcomes Nomination of Karen Mills To Be SBA Administrator

WASHINGTON – U.S. Small Business Administration Acting Administrator Sandy K. Baruah issued the following statement on President-Elect Barack Obama's nomination of Karen Mills to be the next SBA Administrator:

"I applaud, and welcome, President-Elect Obama's selection of Karen Gordon Mills to serve as the next Administrator of the SBA.

"Karen Mills has been a friend and professional partner over the years in both my roles as the assistant secretary of Commerce and the head of the SBA. She is ideally suited to lead the agency. Mills' background is a combination of management, venture capital, and public policy, three elements key to leading the agency successfully. In addition, Mills has a record of bi-partisanship which is important to SBA and the small business community the agency serves.

"I am proud of the agency's record of reform, which has opened opportunity to small business owners throughout America, achieved record loan volume to small businesses, and ensured that communities affected by disaster have the resources to rebuild. Mills will head an agency that has vastly improved its delivery of services and has a dedicated team of civil servants to help carry out the agency's mission.

"Along with the entire SBA team, I am committed to ensuring a smooth and collaborative transfer of power to the new Administration. Mills will have my full support in her new role during the transition and beyond."

FIGURE 11.7 Press release posted online

- Email address
- Web site URL
- A headline that clearly states the essence of the announcement of primary interest to the reader.
- A blurb may follow the headline, where appropriate.

THE BODY OF THE RELEASE

- Single-space paragraphs block style.
- Double-space between paragraphs, with no indent.
- Lead with the most important information in the first paragraph.
- Write the copy as you would like the information to appear.
- Concisely summarize the *who, what, when where, how,* and *why* of the announcement.
- Write in a style that will "hook" the media professional and is suitable for the intended end user of the information—which is the media outlets' audience.
- If possible, confine the length to two pages, preferably one.
- Make sure all information is accurate.
- Include a brief description of your organization, if the target audience might need this information.

94 RESUMES

Employment communications are sales tools; they need to be persuasive and must sell you and your qualifications for a job. A **resume** is a summary of your employment background and experience, highlighting personal facts that relate to the position you are seeking. Many excellent books and Web sites are available to guide you in preparing a quality resume. Review resume samples from many sources and combine ideas to arrive at a format that fits your situation.

Before preparing a resume, find out all you can about the job for which you are applying. Armed with this information, you can focus on those aspects of your background, education, experience, personality, and interests that will make you the person best suited for the position. The checklist in Quick Reference 94.1 contains questions that will help you create employment documents to achieve the results you want.

QUICK REFERENCE 94.1

Employment documents checklist

- Did I show I understand the major requirements of the position?
- Did I show that my education, training, and experience meet these requirements?
- Did I use a positive but not a boastful tone?
- Did I present the key personal qualifications and characteristics that attest to my experience/training in accordance with the employer's needs?
- Did I offer references that will vouch for my experience, education, and character?
- Did I request an interview?

94a Contact Information

List the following at the top of the page: your name, address, telephone number (home and mobile, if desired), email address. If you have a Web site that is related to the job application, list it below the email address.

Use an email address that lists your name in a professional manner; a "cute" email name sends a signal that you are unfamiliar with business protocol. Following are two sample formats; no heading is required.

BARBARA R. EUBANKS
17 Cayuga Lane
Redwood City, California 94064
415-000-000
breubanks@xxx.com

BARBARA R. EUBANKS

17 Cayuga Lane	**415-000-000**
Redwood City, California 94064	**breubanks@xxx.comc**

94b Summary or Professional Profile

A statement or short paragraph can be used to summarize key skills and areas of work experience. It is an attention-getting device designed to motivate the reader to look farther. Use as few words as possible to convey the most relevant aspect of your background that relates to the position you are seeking.

SUMMARY

Nonprofit project manager with 10 years experience in fund-raising, conference planning, and special events management with top-tier charitable organizations.

Use a heading and place this section at the top of the resume directly following the contact information. In addition to or in place of the summary, consider including a keyword summary of your skills. **Keywords** are phrases, terms, and industry jargon used to describe skills and jobs. This style is useful to companies that use database searches of resumes to look for qualified candidates, as well as providing readers an at-a-glance summary of your key qualifications.

Professional Profile

CONSUMER SALES AND MARKETING MANAGER
with more than 10 years of experience in

- Retail Merchandising
- Pricing and Packaging
- Trade Show Promotions
- Advertising and Sales

94c Objective

This is a short statement specifying the type of job you want. Stating an objective is optional, but it can be useful on an application that focuses on a particular position. A more broadly worded career or job objective is less effective because most resume screeners have seen such statements so many times that they are not likely to pay much attention. Here is an example of how to word a specifically targeted objective statement.

OBJECTIVE: A position as production assistant with a television news broadcast that offers training and potential career growth.

94d Employment History and Work Experience

This section lists detailed information on current and previous employers, including company name and address, dates of employment, and positions held. This information can be combined with a list of items describing job functions and achievements, or it can be listed separately. The two most widely used ways of organizing work experience are chronological and functional. A third method combines the two. See examples in 94i, 94j, and 94k.

94e Keywords and Action Verbs

Use keywords to describe work experience and concrete "action" words that are up to date in your field. If language in your field has changed, to the extent possible describe earlier jobs in terms that are current. Use the present tense for current employment and the past tense form for previous jobs. See Quick Reference 94.2 for a list of action words and examples of wording in Figures 11.8, 11.9, and 11.10.

94f Education

This section includes all education-related information starting with the highest level of education for which you obtained a degree or diploma. If you have a higher education degree (associate's or above), it isn't necessary to list your high school diploma, unless you feel it would be of interest to the employer (for example, attendance at a specialized, job-related high school).

The following may be listed where applicable. Examples are shown in Figures 11.8, 11.9, and 11.10.

- Schools attended, date of graduation, majors, diplomas and degrees
- Certificates and licenses earned and the dates
- Number of hours acquired toward a higher education degree with school, dates attended, and relevant courses
- For high school graduates, courses relevant to the job being sought
- Adult education or non-degree/certificate courses that are job related
- Training programs and seminars related to the position

If you have little work experience, you might opt to list your educational background before work experience and include courses of study as shown in Figure 11.10.

94g Special Skills and Achievements

Include in this section special training, technical skills, memberships in and contributions to professional or civic organizations, awards or other types of recognition, publications, or any other achievements—professional or personal—relevant to your career goal. You might elect to break this list into several headings, for example: Publications, Presen-

QUICK REFERENCE 94.2

Resume action words

accomplished	delegated	identified	performed
achieved	demonstrated	implemented	planned
allocated	designed	improved	prepared
analyzed	developed	increased	presented
arranged	devised	influenced	processed
assigned	directed	initiated	produced
assisted	diversified	innovated	promoted
attained	educated	instituted	publicized
authored	eliminated	introduced	restructured
chaired	established	investigated	reviewed
coached	evaluated	launched	revitalized
collected	executed	led	saved
compiled	expanded	maintained	scheduled
conceptualized	expedited	managed	screened
conducted	facilitated	marketed	solved
consolidated	fashioned	mediated	streamlined
contracted	focused	monitored	strengthened
contributed	forecast	motivated	supervised
controlled	formulated	negotiated	systematized
coordinated	founded	operated	trained
created	generated	organized	traveled
cut	guided	originated	upgraded
decreased	headed up	oversaw	wrote

tations, Awards, Professional Activities, Technology Skills, or other specialized training.

94h References

Use this heading if references and contact information are being listed on the resume. If references will be supplied "upon request," indicate this in a cover or application letter, not on the resume.

94i Chronological Resume

A **chronological resume** lists employers and work experience together in reverse chronological order—from most recent to earliest. Employers perceive this resume style as fact-based, and it can be easily skimmed.

For job seekers with solid experience and a logical job history, the chronological resume is the most effective. It is a good way to emphasize the progression of your career. If you have a long work history, consider omitting early positions that are no longer relevant.

Career changers and those who lack formal on-the-job experience (such as new graduates) find this resume the most difficult to write. A functional or combination resume might be more suitable in these cases.

Jill Jones
103 Ortega Street, San Francisco, CA 92116
415-000-0000
jjones@xxx.com

OBJECTIVE
Fund-raising for nonprofit organization with opportunity for managing campaigns.

EXPERIENCE
2007–present
Supervisor/Director, Telemarketing Concepts, Berkeley, CA

Directed four telephone fund-raising campaigns—for a political party, an environmental organization, a local candidate, and a ballot initiative campaign

- Raised in excess of $10 million
- Developed fund-raising strategies
- Wrote email campaign communications
- Supervised phone bank workers
- Coordinated interactions with campaign liaisons

2004-2007
Tour Coordinator, Poetry Players, El Cerrito, CA

Booked performances for a nonprofit theater company with schools, libraries, senior citizen and community centers throughout Northern California and Oregon.

- Marketed the shows
- Coordinated performance dates
- Arranged travel logistics for the company (motels, transportation, food, etc.)
- Executed actor and performance contracts

2002-2004
Canvasser and Canvass Coordinator, Concerned Neighbors in Action, Oakland, CA

Supervised canvass crews raising money for healthcare reform.

- Trained new crew members
- Organized and coordinated activities with other campaigns in the same territory
- Averaged $85/night as a canvasser

EDUCATION
Antioch College, BA, 2003
Major: Political Science. Minor: Anthropology
Editor, *Critics Choice*, campus literary magazine
Laney College Berkeley Extension, course in municipal government, 2002

FIGURE 11.8 Chronological resume

94j Functional Resume

A **functional resume** (Figure 11.9) arranges employment history into sections that highlight areas of skill and accomplishment with employer information listed separately. This organization highlights work experience, specialized skills, and professional achievements that match the requirements of the position being sought. It emphasizes relevant qualifications in cases where employment history by itself might not. It works well for people who have changed jobs often, worked in different fields, or who have not been steadily employed.

To make it easier for employers to match skills with actual job titles, level of responsibility, and dates of employment, you can include the company name in parentheses at the end of the "bullet" describing each accomplishment. After the listing of skills and accomplishments, the employer information—organization names, addresses, and years with each employer—are listed in reverse chronological order.

Using headings to summarize the functional part of the resume also helps emphasize important qualifications and skills.

94k Combination Resume

A **combination resume** merges the chronological and functional styles. It lists important skills, educational background, and achievements first (functional), and then specific employment data and brief descriptions of responsibilities and achievements with each employer (chronological). Figure 11.10 is a combination resume for an applicant who is a recent college grad. The resume emphasizes the education that is relevant to the job being sought, and then lists current previous employment in chronological order.

94l Resume Formatting

Formatting on resumes needs to be minimal unless you are absolutely certain the document will not be transmitted electronically (for example, when it is submitted as part of a printed proposal). In the days when resumes were always printed and sent by mail, high-quality paper and design elements used for highlighting—boldface, underlining, bullets, indents, and so on—were the norm. Today's employers want simply formatted resumes that can withstand electronic transmission through online application systems and scanning into electronic databases. Some employers request a specific document format, for example they prefer a word processing document as opposed to PDF format.

Quick Reference 94.3 provides guidelines for producing an attractive resume that is suitable for use by an employer in both print and electronic format. It also provides additional tips for producing a scannable resume.

REX T. ROBINSON
4001 Tremont Street • Casper, WY 12345 • (123) 555-1234

OBJECTIVE: A Senior Management position in a credit union with responsibilities in branch administration and lending

HIGHLIGHTS OF QUALIFICATIONS

- 15 years experience in financial environments, including mortgage and consumer lending.
- Successfully turned around two credit union operations and three bank branches.
- Continuously achieved designated profitability and market share growth goals.

PROFESSIONAL ACHIEVEMENTS

MANAGEMENT

- Managed Maplewood Savings' new branch in Casper, turning a deficit of $93,000 to a profit of $450,000 and increasing loan base by $8.3M and deposits by $4.6M.
- Administered all aspects of daily operations at Union Credit.
- Projected Maplewood's budgets for staffing, loan demands, and deposit growth.
- Developed a reporting system to keep Union's senior management abreast of achievements.
- Motivated staff at each institution to extend their best effort in meeting customers' expectations.

LENDING

- Managed loan portfolios of up to $55M at First Interstate.
- Hired, trained, and supervised staff of up to 25 in credit analysis, presentations, lending regulations, and product development and marketing at Maplewood Savings.
- Utilized lending expertise in real estate (secondary market sales/servicing), consumer lending, and VISA credit and debit cards to achieve Union's profitability and market share growth.

WORK HISTORY

1999-Present	Senior Branch Manager	Maritime Credit Union, Casper, WY
1994-99	Vice President/Manager	Maplewood Savings, Casper, WY
1990-94	Senior Development Lender	Union Credit, Casper, WY
1989-90	Business Development Lender	First Interstate Bank, Orinda, CA
1987-89	Commercial Loan Officer	Bank of America, Oakland, CA
1985-87	Commercial Loan Officer	Wells Fargo Bank, Lafayette, CA

SPECIALIZED TRAINING AND EDUCATION

Maplewood Savings:	Consumer Lending	Management Training Program
AIB Training:	Tax Return Analysis	Advanced Financial Statement Analysis
Seminars:	Negotiating Skills	Bank Management

B.A./A.B, University of California, Los Angeles, CA, 1985

Source: CareerOneStop a US Department of Labor-sponsored Web site that offers career resources and workforce information.

FIGURE 11.9 Functional resume

STEPHEN R. LUDLUM
518 Burnett Road
Randallstown, Maryland 21123
301-555-1234

JOB TARGET
Management Trainee in Marketing Research

EDUCATION
BA University of Baltimore, June, 2009.
Major: Marketing Minor: General Business
G.P.A. 3.50; Dean's List 2008 and 2009

MARKETING COURSES
Marketing Principles
Marketing Research
Advertising Media
Marketing Management
Motivation Research
Principles of Distribution

OTHER BUSINESS COURSES
Business Statistics
Business Communication
Accounting 1 and 2
Business Law
Business Finance
Information Technology

EXPERIENCE
2008-Present
WAREHOUSE CLERK – TRACY'S DISCOUNT STORE, RANDALL, MD
Fill customer orders, maintain inventory, supervise two part-time workers.

2007
SALESPERSON – HIGGANBOTHAM'S PHARMACY, RANDALL, MD
Made special deliveries, assisted customers, assisted with stock.

2006
SALES REPRESENTATIVE – CAVELL HOME PRODUCTS, BALTIMORE, MD
Sold house wares.

FIGURE 11.10 Combination resume

QUICK REFERENCE 94.3

Resume format

Electronic transmission of resumes requires simple formatting. You can create an attractive print resume that can be scanned or transmitted online without becoming unreadable.

Length, margins, and spacing

- The conventional wisdom is that people simply do not read long resumes. While it is impossible to generalize, stick to one or two pages unless you are in a field, such as academia, where long resumes are customary.
- Place your name at the top of each subsequent page, but do not repeat contact information on the second page.
- Always print single-sided pages.
- Single-space parts within sections and double-space in between.
- Try to leave 1-inch margins on all sides; make small adjustments if slightly smaller ones will help limit the length.
- Leave ample white space for ease of reading.

Font

- Use an easy-to-read font, such as Times Roman or Arial. Arial, a sans serif font, has a crisp look that is attractive and works well for controlling length.
- The acceptable font size range is 10- to 12-point for text and 12- to 14-point for headings.
- Use only black type; no color.

Text

- Use all caps for major headings; avoid italics and underlining altogether; be aware that boldface type might be lost in an online application system.

Producing a scannable resume

- Use a one-column format and avoid horizontal or vertical lines, boxes, or shading to set off sections.
- Use only capital letters or boldface to emphasize important information. Do not use italics, underlining, or graphics.
- Use bullets and double-space between items in each section; be aware that bullets might be lost in an online application system.
- Avoid asterisks, dashes, parentheses, and brackets as they may also be lost in transmission.

CONTINUED

QUICK REFERENCE 94.3 → CONTINUED

Sending the resume

- When sending a resume by regular mail, print it on a laser printer on high-quality white bond paper. Do not fold or staple pages.
- When faxing, use fine resolution and follow with a mailed original.
- When using email, find out what format (word processing document, PDF file, text only) the prospective employer prefers. First, email a copy of your resume to yourself to make sure it looks the way you meant it to look.
- Consider creating two versions of your resume: one to send for the computer to read (scannable format and detailed descriptors) and one for people to read during an interview (a creative layout, enhanced typography, and summarized information).

95 COVER LETTERS

95a Writing the Cover Letter

A cover letter introduces you and your resume; it explains why you are interested in the company and/or a specific position, and when you will contact the recipient. Figures 11.11 and 11.12 are examples of cover letters for an experienced worker and a recent graduate.

Always address a cover letter to a specific person. The following are key features of a quality cover letter:

- Explains why you are writing and gives the source of information about an open position (e.g., advertisement, recommendation of colleague, interest in the company).
- Highlights key qualifications/achievements related to the position.
- Emphasizes strengths, but avoids overkill and exaggeration. Refers to your attached resume.
- Expresses interest in the company and the position desired and gives professional reasons for making the contact (e.g., interest in the company's mission, what you can offer in the position).
- Is short (no more than a page), written in a professional and courteous tone, carefully formatted, and error-free.

Dear Ms. Mayheu:

Mr. Ralph Meadows, the executive director of The Gold Leaf Education Fund, suggested that I contact you about the position of Director of Fund Development with your organization, which you spoke to him about earlier this week. The job sounds very interesting and challenging, and I would like to be considered for it.

As you will see in the enclosed résumé, I have been special projects director with the Stay in School Program, a pilot project funded by the Chicago Public Schools system. My work with this project has given me the opportunity to develop relationships with businesses and agencies throughout the city to gain their support and sponsorship. I would be able to bring these contacts and relationships to bear on fund-raising activities for Gold Leaf. I have a strong interest in and commitment to your organization's mission of providing mentoring and scholarship programs to ensure that all students have access to higher education. I can also offer strong written and oral communication skills, a key element of my successful work on the Stay in School project.

I would like to meet with you to discuss the position and my qualifications in-depth. I will call you in a week or so to arrange a meeting at your convenience.

Sincerely yours,

FIGURE 11.11 Cover letter—experienced worker

- Closes courteously and requests an interview and/or indicates how you intend to follow up.
- Printed out and signed if sent by regular mail; if sent by email, as many employers request, use a complimentary close and type your name.

95b Formatting the Cover Letter

Use standard business letter formatting. See Section Eight: Email, Memos, and Letters for guidelines on formatting parts of business letters.

- Type on personal letterhead (preprinted with your name and contact information—address, phone, fax, email).
- Use standard business letter block style (see Figure 8.5).
- Use standard Times Roman, 12-point, black font.

Dear Mr. Goddard:

The position you advertised in the May 14 *Sun* for a management trainee in marketing research is exactly the opportunity I had hoped to find. As I read the ad, I felt that you were talking to me.

As you will see in the enclosed résumé, I will graduate from the University of Baltimore in early June with a major in marketing. I have acquired an excellent marketing education (18 semester hours), supported by a broad program in general business. Of special interest to me was learning about global markets. We not only studied international trends and modern data-gathering techniques, but were also required to read and report on significant books focusing on corporate growth strategies and the global marketplace. Two that I found especially interesting were *The World Is Flat* (Thomas Friedman) and *Blue Ocean Strategy* (W. Chan Kim), on which I wrote papers that received special honors.

I would like very much to meet you and tell you in person why I believe I could be useful to your organization. I have an intense interest in and deep commitment to marketing, and I am most eager to apply what I have learned in your company, which covers the many facets of this exciting field.

I can be reached each weekday at 410-555-0819. I will follow up with your office in about a week to request an appointment.

Sincerely yours,

FIGURE 11.12 Cover letter—college graduate

96 REFERENCES

96a Requesting a Reference

It is a cardinal rule never to use a person's name as a reference without first asking for permission. Figure 11.13 is a request for a reference from a family connection.

96b Thank-you Letter for a Reference

An important aspect of networking is expressing appreciation for assistance. Figure 11.14 is a letter thanking a former professor for a reference.

Dear Judge Toffler:

Graduation is only a few weeks away, and if everything goes right, I will receive my bachelor's degree in business administration from the University of Baltimore on June 2. I don't know who will be happier—me or Dad! It was he who suggested that I contact you to request the use of your name as a reference as I start my job hunt.

I have just begun to look for a position. My interest is in marketing research, and I hope to find a management trainee position in a large company in the area or not too far away. May I include your name as a reference on my application? If you are willing to vouch for me and my work ethic (as you remember it from all those summer jobs), it would mean a great deal to me.

Best wishes to you and Mrs. Toffler. I will be in Randallstown around June 8, and I hope to see both of you then.

Sincerely yours,

FIGURE 11.13 Request for a reference

Dear Professor Hale:

I think you will be pleased to hear that I have been hired by Cantrell Corporation, in Silver Spring, for a position in the Marketing Research Department. The company develops computer systems, and I have been told that my first assignment will be to research computer applications in the agricultural industry.

Please be assured that I appreciate your allowing me to use your name as a reference. I am certain your recommendation was influential in Cantrell's decision to hire me, and I will do my best to prove that I deserve your confidence.

I hope to see you from time to time to let you know what (and how) I am doing. When you are next in Silver Spring, I hope you'll visit my office. As soon as I get my business cards I will send you one! Meanwhile, my contact information is listed below.

Sincerely,

FIGURE 11.14 Thank-you letter for a reference

97 JOB SEARCH FOLLOW-UP

97a Thank-you Letter for a Job Interview

A thank-you letter or email message following a job interview is a required courtesy. Send the message no later than a day after the interview. It should be very brief—a simple expression of appreciation written in a warm, sincere manner. Use the opportunity to reinforce your interest in the job, if this is the case. Note how the letter in Figure 11.15 indicates the writer's interest by offering to provide more information quickly.

Dear Mr. Revere:

Thank you for allowing me to meet with you this week and discuss the position of sales correspondent at Rector Industries. The job is most attractive to me and would offer the kind of opportunity that I have been looking for.

I feel certain that I would find the work challenging and interesting and I hope you have concluded that my skills are right for the job. If you need any additional information or work samples, please let me know, and I will send them to you immediately.

Sincerely yours,

FIGURE 11.15 Thank-you letter for job interview

97b Letter Withdrawing Application

If you have lost interest in a job after an interview, it is courteous to let the potential employer know so you can be taken out of consideration. Simply express appreciation for the interviewer's time and interest.

Dear Mr. Goddard:

This is to let you know that I have accepted a marketing research position with another company and am no longer a candidate for position of sales correspondent.

I appreciate the time you spent with me during the interview and the consideration you gave my application.

Sincerely,

FIGURE 11.16 Withdrawal of application

part four

USER REFERENCE TOOLS

GLOSSARY AND INDEXES

section twelve

98 GLOSSARY

This glossary lists important terms of grammar, language, writing, and document design. The references in parentheses indicate the handbook sections where the term is highlighted and defined in context.

absolute phrase A group of words that contains a noun or pronoun and a participle and modifies the whole sentence. (3c)

acknowledgments A listing of contributors, such as consultants, interviewees, and providers of source material, placed in the front matter of a report or publication. (80g)

acronym An abbreviation formed from the first letters of a name or group of words and pronounced as a word. (*NATO—North Atlantic Treaty Organization; WYSIWIG—what you see is what you get.*) (45d)

action verb A verb that tells what the subject of the sentence is doing. (5a)

active voice A way of constructing the subject and verb in a sentence that directly emphasizes that the subject is the *performer* of the action. This construction is the opposite of the *passive voice,* which places the emphasis on the subject as the *receiver* of the action. (5f, 64b)

adjective A word that describes, identifies, or quantifies a noun. Adjectives are one of three types: *descriptive, limiting,* and *pointing.* The articles *a, an*, and *the* are also adjectives. (1a, 7a, 7b)

adverb A word that describes, identifies, or quantifies a verb, an adjective, or another adverb. Many adverbs end in *ly.* (1b, 7c)

agenda A list of topics and order of business to be discussed at a meeting. (91)

agreement Consistency in number and gender of subjects and verbs and pronouns and antecedents in sentences. (2a, 6c)

antecedent A noun or pronoun that is referred to by another pronoun in a sentence. (2f)

appendix A part in the back matter of a report or publication that is supplemental to the main part (the *body*). (80m)

article The words *a, an,* and *the;* used in front of nouns, adjectives, and adverbs to tell *which one*. (7b)

aside Information that is useful but not essential to meaning. (15c)

back matter Parts that appear at the end of a report or other publication, e.g., reference lists, glossaries, and indexes. (80a)

bibliography An alphabetic listing of sources used as references in a report or other publication. May include sources cited in text notes or footnotes, as well as those consulted but not specifically mentioned in the main text of the document. (83d)

blind copy A copy of a communication sent without the other recipients' knowledge. (66a, 69h)

block style A letter format in which all elements (except the letterhead) are typed flush with the left margin. (68)

body The main part of a document or publication. (80j)

boilerplate Standard wording for a communication such as a form letter or contract. (75)

borders A rule that frames a segment of text or graphic element to set it off from other elements on a page; also called **boxes** or **boxed rules.** (85h)

builds The feature in slide presentation software that makes content appear on a slide line by line or section by section. (89d)

caption A short explanation (one or two sentences) or description of a graphic element in a document or other publication. (87c)

callout A label used to identify or provide brief explanations of parts of graphics, such as drawings and diagrams. (87c)

chemical formula A group of chemical symbols that represent a chemical compound, such as H_2O (water). (52b)

chemical symbol An abbreviation that represents the name of a chemical element, such as Au for gold. (52b)

chronological resume A resume organization that lists employers and work experience together in reverse chronological order—from most recent to earliest. (94i)

clause A group of related words containing a subject and a verb. (4)

coherence The quality of writing that shows relationships between main ideas and their supporting details, and between main ideas from one paragraph to the next; achieved by providing introductory statements, transitions, and summary statements. (63b)

collective noun A word that refers to groups; may be either a common or a proper noun. (1b, 2d)

combination resume A resume organization that merges the chronological and functional styles, listing important skills, educational background, and/or achievements first (functional), and then specific employment data and brief descriptions of responsibilities and achievements with each employer (chronological). (94k)

comma splice A sentence with a comma between two or more independent clauses without a conjunction to connect the two. (4c)

common noun A word that names classes or groups of people, places, and things and begins with a lowercase letter. (1b, 23a)

comparative form (second degree) adjective The adjective form used to compare two things; usually ends in *er* or is preceded by *more* or *less*. (7h, 7j)

comparative form (second degree) adverb The adverb form used to compare two things; usually ends in *er* or adds *more* or *less* to the positive form. (7h, 7j)

complement A word or group of words that follows a helping verb and completes the meaning of the verb. (5e)

complex sentence A sentence composed of one independent clause and one or more dependent clauses. (4a)

complimentary closing The words at the end of a piece of correspondence that indicate the end; placed above the writer's name. (66b)

compound-complex sentence A sentence composed of at least two independent clauses and one or more dependent clauses. (4a)

compound modifier An adjective-adjective or adverb-adjective combination functioning together. A compound adjective may or may not require hyphenation; there is no need to hyphenate adverb-adjective combinations because the grammatical construction makes the meaning clear. (53d)

compound noun Two nouns that form a unit and may be written as one word, two words, or as a hyphenated construction. (53c)

compound sentence A sentence composed of at least two independent clauses. (4a)

compound verb Two or more words functioning together as a single verb. Common compound verbs are often written as single words: *brainstorm, download.* (53e)

compound word Two or more words that function together to form a single unit. Compound words may or may not be hyphenated. (53c)

conclusion A paragraph or section of text that lists or summarizes the writer's key points or interpretation of the main contents. (80l)

conjunction A part of speech that connects two or more words, phrases, or clauses. See *coordinate conjunctions, dependent (subordinate) conjunction,* and *correlative conjunction.* (1b, 4b)

consonant All the letters of the alphabet except the vowels: *a, e, i, o, u*. (54)

contraction A shortened form of two words written as one with an apostrophe in place of the missing letters. (19a)

coordinate conjunctions The words *and, but, or, nor, for, yet, so;* used to join words and parts of sentences. (4b)

copyright infringement A violation of the US copyright law that protects ownership and usage of original works of authorship. (82a)

correlative conjunction Connecting words that occur in pairs, e.g., *either . . . or, not only . . . but also, even though.* (4d)

courtesy copy (or copy) Copy of a document sent to persons other than the addressee. This term replaces the former term: *carbon copy*. (67c)

dash A mark of punctuation used to replace other punctuation marks—most often commas, parentheses, colons, and semicolons—to emphasize, de-emphasize, or set apart parts of sentences. The two types of dashes, based on their length, are *em dash* (—) and *en dash* (–). (15a)

declarative sentence A sentence that makes a statement; ends with a period. (9a)

demonstrative pronoun A pronoun that refers to a specific person, place, or thing (*this, that, those, these . . .*). (6l)

dependent clause A clause that has a subject and a verb but cannot stand alone; it depends on the rest of the sentence for its meaning. A dependent clause capitalized and punctuated as a sentence is a *sentence fragment*. (4, 11a)

dependent conjunction (subordinate conjunction) A word such as *although, while, because* that precedes a dependent clause—a word group that cannot stand by itself as a sentence. (4d)

descriptive adjective A modifying word that tells "what kind." (7b)

direct approach A method of imparting information by immediately stating your purpose for writing. (72a)

direct question A sentence that directly asks a question and ends with a question mark. (9c)

direct quotation A quotation of the exact spoken or written words of someone other than the writer; always enclosed in quotation marks. (17a)

display heading A main heading of text styled in large bold type and possibly in color to signal a major change of topic. (85b)

editing A review of a draft that involves detailed analysis—sentence placement within a paragraph, sentence structure, tone, and word choices. (60)

ellipsis A mark of punctuation that indicates an omission; made by typing three periods with no spaces in between (. . .). (14)

elliptical expression A sentence that omits one or more words to avoid repeating words in the first part of the sentence. (11e)

elliptical question A shortened form of a question that should end with a question mark. (9d)

email correspondence Formal emails that are sent in place of traditional printed memos and letters for business communication within and outside of an organization. (66)

empathy A feature of writing that shows, through style and tone, that the writer has a sense of how the receiver will feel. (65g)

endnote A text reference indicated with a superscript (raised above the line) number keyed to a numbered list of source citations and/or explanatory comments placed at the end of a section or at the end of a document. (83c)

essential phrase (also called **restrictive**) A phrase that is essential to the meaning of a sentence. Essential phrases are not set off by commas. (3a, 6j)

euphemism A word or expression that states unpleasant or politically incorrect words in more acceptable or pleasant terms. (65e)

exclamatory sentence A sentence that expresses strong emotion or emphasis; ends with an exclamation point. (9b)

executive summary (also called **summary**) A relatively brief but thorough synopsis of the contents of a report. Its purpose is to provide readers with an overview of the report's major points, including the conclusions and recommendations. (80h)

external proposal A proposal written for parties outside an organization, for example, to request funding for a project or to convince a potential client to purchase services. (81a)

fair use The legal use of a limited amount of copyrighted material without permission. (82c)

flush left/right (also called **left/right justification**) Text that is evenly aligned at the left or right margin of a page or column. (85g)

footnote A text citation indicated with a superscript (raised above the line) number keyed to a source citation and/or explanatory comment placed at the bottom of the page. (83b)

foreword A short writing at the front of a document or publication written by someone other than the author. (80e)

formal report A multi-page, informative document written for a specific purpose for a designated audience; contains front matter and back matter formatted according to business standards. (80a)

format The physical layout of type on a page; may also be used to refer to type and graphics or a pattern used throughout a document or publication. (59c)

fragment A group of words sounding like a sentence but lacking some essential element. (4e)

front matter The section of a business report or other publication that contains introductory material: title page, table of contents, preface, foreword, introduction, and so on. (80a)

functional resume A resume organization that places employment history into sections that highlight areas of skill and accomplishment with employers and dates of employment listed separately. (94j)

future perfect tense A verb form that refers to action that will have been completed before a specific time in the future. (5b)

future tense A verb form that refers to action that will occur at some time in the future. (5b)

gerund A verb ending in *ing* that acts as a noun. (Also see *verbals.*) (3b)

gerund phrase The *ing* form of a verb used with other words functioning as a noun. (3b)

glossary An alphabetical listing of words and definitions in a report or other publication. (80o)

graphics Refers to illustrations such as charts, graphs, photographs, drawings, and diagrams; may also refer to the type in a designed document. (86g)

guide words The words *Date, To, From,* and *Subject* at the top of a memorandum. (67a)

helping verb (also called **auxiliary verb**) A verb form used with other verbs to show time, possibility, or emphasis. (5a)

imperative mood The mood of verbs that gives a command or makes a request. (5g)

imperative sentence (also called **a command**) A sentence that issues a command or makes a polite request; ends with a period even though it might be worded as a question. (*Will you please let me know as soon as you decide.*) (1c, 9a)

indefinite pronoun A pronoun that refers to nonspecific people, things, and activities (e.g., *each, everyone, somebody*). (2f, 6h, 6m)

independent clause A clause that has a subject and a verb and can stand alone as a sentence because it expresses a complete thought. (4, 11a)

indicative mood The mood of verbs that makes a statement or asks a question; it conveys a concrete message or asks a question that is specific in the present, past, or future. (5g)

indirect approach A method of imparting information by explaining first and then delivering troublesome or outright bad news. (72b)

indirect question A sentence that restates a question and ends with a period. (*He asked if we plan to attend the seminar.*) (9c)

indirect quotation A sentence in which the words or the order of the words of a quotation are changed. (17b)

infinitive Verb form that includes the word *to*—*to come, to go.* (5h)

infinitive phrase A group of words that looks like a verb because it begins with the word *to* but is acting as a noun in a sentence. (3b)

informal report A short report usually written for routine business purposes; may be written in memo format or as a document on plain paper. (79a)

initialism An abbreviation formed from the first letters of a name or group of words and pronounced letter by letter (IBM, DMV, YMCA). (45d)

interjection One of the eight parts of speech; a word or short phrase that expresses strong emotion and usually ends with an exclamation point. (*Wow! Super! You're kidding!*) (1b, 9b)

internal proposal A proposal written to persuade a person or group within an organization. (81a)

international date style (also **military date style**) The style used by the US military and many countries; reverses the day and month and does not require punctuation: 12 November 2016. (69a)

international time (also called **military time** and **24-hour clock**) Time designated in 24-hour periods as opposed to 12-hour periods; begins at 0:00 (midnight) and ends at 23:00. When used to indicate international time, it is usually written with a colon; military usage does not include a colon. (36f)

interoffice memo (short for **memorandum**) A traditional format used for writing internal business communications on printed forms. (67)

interrogative pronoun A pronoun that introduces a question: *who, whom, what, which, whose.* (6k)

intranet A private computer network designed to be accessed only by company employees and protected from access by those outside it. (90d)

intransitive verb A verb that does not need an object to complete its meaning. (5a)

introduction An overview of a report or other published document written by the author. (80i)

irregular verb A verb that forms the past and past participle by changing spelling in different ways. (5c)

itinerary A detailed schedule of activities, commonly used for travel and group activities. Itineraries are routinely used for travel plans and events of short duration. (92a)

jargon Words and acronyms used and understood within a given industry or profession. (64b)

justification Alignment of text with the side margins; may be left justified, right justified, or centered. See also definition of **flush left/right.** *Unjustified text* is usually aligned at the left margin and unaligned at the right, also known as "ragged right." *Fully justified* text is aligned at both right and left. (68d, 85g)

keyword A phrase, term, industry jargon, or title used to describe work on a resume. (94b)

leading The spacing between lines of type. (85a)

legalese Words and expressions appropriate in the legal field that have found their way into everyday language. (64b)

legend A key to the scheme of colors or patterns in graphs and charts. (87c)

letterhead A heading at the top of stationery listing the name and address of the organization or person sending the letter. (68d)

limiting adjective A describing word that "limits" a noun in the sense of quantity; it tells "how many." (7b)

linking verbs (also called **state-of-being verbs**) Forms of the verb *to be* and verbs of the senses, as well as others that "link" the subject of the sentence to a word or words that tell something about the subject. (5a, 7f)

links Elements such as underlined words that provide connections between Web pages. (90b)

main heading A section or part opening headline that designates a main topic in a document. (85b)

margins The white space at the top, bottom, and sides of a page. (85g)

memorandum (memo) A form of business correspondence that has a standard heading (*To, From, Date,* and *Subject*) and is typically used for interoffice communication. (67)

minutes A written record of what occurred at a business meeting. (91d)

mixed number A number made up of a whole number and a fraction. (42)

modified-block letter The style of formatting a letter with the date, closing, and signature beginning at the center of the page; may also be typed with indented paragraphs. (68)

modifier A word or group of words that functions as an adjective or adverb. (11b)

mood of verbs The form of a verb that conveys the manner in which you want the action in a sentence to be interpreted by the reader. (5g)

navigate The act of using the mouse on a computer to move from place to place on a Web site. (90b)

navigational tools Menus, buttons, graphics, and other elements that the user can operate with a mouse click to activate movement within a Web site. (90b)

netiquette Coined from the word *etiquette,* a set of statements that describe good manners when using email and the Web. (66e)

nominative case The pronoun form that is used as the subject of a sentence. (6b)

nonessential phrase (also called **nonrestrictive**) A phrase that describes or adds information about the element it modifies, but is not essential to the meaning of the sentence; usually set off by commas. (3a, 6j)

noun A word that names people, animals, places, and things; abstract concepts and qualities; activities; time and measurements. *Common nouns* are nonspecific and are not capitalized unless part of a proper name, a title, or the first word in a sentence; *proper nouns* are specific and should always be capitalized; *collective nouns* refer to groups and may be either common or proper. (1a)

noun phrase A group of words functioning as a noun; may be the subject or object of a sentence. (3b)

object A word in a sentence that answers the question *whom?* or *what?* after the verb; it receives the action directly or indirectly. (1d)

objective case The pronoun form that is used as the object in a sentence. (6b)

ordinal number A number indicating a ranking or place within a series; formed by adding *st, nd, rd,* or *th* to an arabic number. (35)

page layout The placement of elements that make up a printed page; the process of page layout is also called *composition*. (85c)

parallel construction Consistent construction of word forms, verb tenses, and phrasing to connect related ideas in a sentence, list, or headings. (64d)

paraphrase A summary of a speaker's words using your own words. (17b)

parliamentary procedure A method of conducting meetings that follows Robert's Rules of Order to ensure that each participant has a voice and a vote in the decision-making process. (91b)

participial phrase A group of words that contains a present or past participle. (3c)

parts of speech The eight forms of words used in sentences—as *nouns, pronouns, verbs, adjectives, adverbs, prepositions, conjunctions,* and *interjections*. (1a)

passive voice A way of constructing the subject and verb in a sentence that places the emphasis on the subject as the *receiver* of the action directly. This construction is the opposite of the *active voice,* which emphasizes that the subject is the *performer* of the action. (5f, 64b)

past participle A verb form that refers to action that has been completed. (5b)

past perfect tense A verb form that refers to action that was completed before another past action. (5b)

past tense A verb form that refers to action that occurred at an earlier time. (5b)

PDF (portable document format) A format for text files that is universally compatible with any computer system. PDF files will not change format in the transmission process and the text cannot be manipulated by the recipient. (66c)

personal pronouns Pronouns that substitute for nouns in the first person (e.g., *I, me, we*); second person (*you*); or third person (e.g., *he, she, it*). (6d)

personal titles *Mr., Mrs., Ms.,* and *Dr.* (*Miss,* the title that designates a single woman, is rarely used anymore; *Ms.* is generally preferred.) Always use a period and a space after these abbreviations. (46b)

phrase A group of related words in a sentence that does not contain both a subject and a predicate. (3, 11b)

plagiarism The presentation of another's intellectual property as your own; it is both a legal and an ethical violation. (82d)

point size A measurement of type that encompasses the highest part of the tallest letter (*h* or *l*) to the lowest part of the longest letter that extends below the baseline (*p* or *y*). (85a)

pointing adjectives The words *this, that, these,* and *those;* they tell "which one." (7b)

positive form (first degree) adjective The simple form of an adjective that describes the quality of the noun it modifies without making a comparison. (7h)

positive form (first degree) adverb The simple form of an adverb that describes the quality of the noun it modifies without making a comparison. (7h)

possessive case The form of a pronoun that shows possession. (6b)

possessive pronoun A pronoun showing ownership (*my, your, our, his, hers, their*). (6o)

predicate The verb and words that modify the verb in a sentence; the *simple predicate* is the verb itself. (1c)

preface A short piece in the front matter of a report or other publication, usually focusing on its purpose; written by the author. (80e)

prefix Letters added to the beginning of a root to form a new word. (53f)

preposition A word that connects a noun or pronoun to another word in a sentence, e.g., *in, off, with, to, above.* (1b, 8a)

prepositional phrase A group of words that begins with a preposition and ends with a noun or pronoun, which is called the *object of the preposition*. (1b, 3c, 8a)

present participle A verb form that refers to action that is in the process of taking place (ending in *ing—walking, eating, running*). (5b)

present perfect tense A verb form that refers to action that began in the past, has been completed in the present, or is continuing into the present time. (5b)

present tense A verb form that refers to an action or state of being in the present. (5b)

press release (also called a **news release**) A written announcement distributed in print or online by an organization to media outlets with the goal of getting information out to the public; written in a form that can be picked up verbatim by news outlets. (93a)

pronoun A word that substitutes for nouns, e.g., *he, she, it, them, who, everybody*. (1b, 6a)

pronoun case The form of a pronoun that is used as a subject (*nominative case*), as an object (*objective case*), or to show possession (*possessive case*). (6b)

pronoun reference The word or group of words to which a pronoun refers (the *antecedent*); they must agree in number (singular or plural) and in gender (male, female, or neutral). (6c)

proper adjective A word derived from a proper noun; should be capitalized. (7a, 23a)

proper noun A noun that refers to specific people, places, or things; always begins with a capital letter. (1b, 23a)

proportion A number that expresses an amount compared to a whole. (43b)

proposal A bid to perform services; a *solicited proposal* is requested from the recipient; an *unsolicited proposal* is initiated by the writer. (81)

public domain The status of a work that is not copyrighted and may be referenced freely without concern about copyright infringement. (82c)

ratio A numerical expression of two numbers that shows a comparison in quantity, amount, or size; a colon separates the numbers. (43b)

recommendations A section of a report that presents suggestions for consideration. (80k)

redundancy The use of unnecessary repetition. (64a)

reflexive pronoun A pronoun that refers back to the subject or a clause in a sentence: *myself, themselves, yourself* and other words with the suffixes *self* or *selves;* also *each other, one another.* (6n)

regular verb A verb that forms the past tense and past participle in the "regular" way, by adding *ed* or *d: walk/walked, look/looked, die/died, propose/proposed.* (5c)

relative pronoun A pronoun that refers to a noun preceding it in the sentence: *who, whom, that, what,* and *which.* (6j)

report (business report) An informative document written for a specific purpose and for a designated audience; reports may present findings or data, summarize activities, or analyze issues. A *formal business* report typically has three major parts: *front matter, body,* and *back matter*; an *informal report* may take the form of a memo, letter, or short document. (78)

Request for Proposal (RFP) A document soliciting proposals that describes in detail what is needed and outlines the specifics for submission. (81a)

resume A summary of personal history, highlighting work-related experience and skills that relate to the position being sought. (94)

revising A review of a draft from the "big picture" perspective—scope of content, clarity of expression, logical flow of ideas, and the structure of the document as a whole. (60)

routine email message A message that does not require certain elements such as a salutation and closing that are needed in more formal emails. (66)

rule A vertical or horizontal line used to separate or highlight text and graphics. (85i)

running text The body of written material—text copy excluding headings, tables, and graphics. (85g)

run-on sentence Independent clauses that are run together without punctuation. (4c)

sans serif A typeface that does not have little strokes (*sans* is French for *without*), such as Arial, Tahoma, and Verdana. Sans serif fonts are recommended for titles and headings. (85a)

sentence A group of words that expresses a complete thought; it must include a *subject* and a *verb,* which in grammar terms is called the *predicate*. (1c)

sentence fragment A group of words intended as a sentence but lacking one of the essential components—a subject or a verb. (4e)

serif A typeface that has little strokes at the top and bottom of most letters, such as Times Roman, Century, and Courier New. Serif fonts are recommended for body text copy because the serifs increase readability. (85a)

sidebar A segment of text that is set off with a border or rule. (85g)

signature block In email, includes the sender's full name and contact information listed at the end of the message. In a letter, includes the sender's name and title when full contact information is included at the top of the letterhead stationery. (66b)

simple sentence A sentence consisting of one independent clause. (4a)

simplified style letter A letter format that omits the salutation and complimentary closing; it includes a subject line typed in all caps. (68c)

solicited proposal A proposal prepared at the receiver's request. (81a)

source note A note at the bottom of a table or graphic that provides information about the source, such as a reference. (87b)

storyboard A method of preparing a visual and audio script by writing in two columns, one for graphics and one for the points about each image. (89c)

subheading A heading used in reports to introduce subdivisions of the main heading. (80j, 85b)

subject The noun or pronoun in a sentence that tells *who* or *what* is doing the action or being. The *simple subject* may be one word or a group of words; *the complete subject* may be a phrase that includes modifiers. (1c)

subject line (window) A heading appearing at the top of a memo or email that specifies the topic of a message. (66a, 67b)

subject-verb agreement Consistency in number—if the subject is singular, the verb must be singular; if the subject is plural, the verb must be plural. (2a)

subjunctive mood The mood of a verb that expresses doubt, a wish, or a condition contrary to fact. (5g)

suffix Letters added to the end of a root to form a new word. (53g)

summary sentence A sentence, usually the final sentence in the paragraph, that ties together the details and points the reader forward. Not every paragraph needs a summary. (63a)

superlative form (third degree) adjective The comparative form of an adjective used when comparing three or more people, places, or things. The superlative form of regular adjectives ends in *est* or is preceded by *most* or *least*. (7h, 7j)

superlative form (third degree) adverb The comparative form of an adverb used to compare three or more people, places, or things. The superlative adverb is formed by adding *est* or *most* or *least* to the positive form. (7h, 7j)

superscript number A number raised above the line used to indicate a footnote or text note. (83)

template A preset format for letters, memos, forms, and other documents. (67b)

tense Forms of verbs that indicate the *time* that an action takes place. (5a)

text notes (also called **in-text citations**) Source citations placed within parentheses at the point of reference in the text. (83a)

tone The quality of writing that reflects the writer's attitude and relationship to the reader. (62b)

topic sentence A sentence in a paragraph that tells the reader in a general way what the paragraph is about; it is usually the first sentence, but doesn't have to be. (63a)

transitional word or expression A word or phrase that links elements of a sentence. Frequently used transitional expressions are *therefore, furthermore, also, too, however, in fact, for example*. (4b, 11c, 63c)

transitive verb A verb that requires an object to complete the meaning of the sentence. (5a)

transmittal letter/memo A message that accompanies a document or other material to inform the recipient of what is being sent and to make a record of the transaction. (72e, 80c)

travel itinerary A detailed schedule of flight information and activities for a traveler. (92a)

type A shortened form of *typeface*. (85a)

typeface (or font) The design of a complete set of letters, numbers, and symbols; for example, Arial, Times (New) Roman, Verdana, Garamond, Book Antiqua. Today, the word *font* is commonly used to refer to a typeface. (85a)

type font The complete assortment of point sizes (8 point, 9 point, 10 point, 12 point 14 point, etc.) and style variations (regular or roman, *italic,* **boldface, *boldface italic***) for one typeface, although, the word *font* is used widely to refer to the typeface as well. The "normal" style for a font is technically called *roman,* or *regular.* (85a)

unity The quality of writing that focuses the sentences of a paragraph on the main idea to show a logical relationship. In document design, unity is achieved through logic and balance of visuals and text. (63b)

unsolicited proposals A proposal initiated by the writer. (81a)

verb A word (or words) that express action or state of being in a sentence. (1b, 5a)

verbals Words made from verbs, but that do not act as verbs; they serve as *subjects, complements,* or *modifiers*. The three types of verbals are *gerunds, participles,* and *infinitives.* (3b)

voice of verbs The way the subject and verb are constructed in a sentence to emphasize whether the subject is the *performer* of the action (the ***active voice***) or the *receiver* of the action directly (the ***passive voice***). (5f)

vowels The letters *a, e, i, o,* and *u.* (54)

writer's block The inability to begin the process of writing; usually caused by stress and a lack of planning. (59b)

yield The number of characters per line of type. Although all type that is the same point size is the same height, the width of characters and height of lowercase letters varies, giving a different yield with different fonts. (85a)

99 QUICK REFERENCE BOXES AND WRITING SAMPLES INDEX

100 TOPIC INDEX

101 GENERAL INDEX

GLOSSARY AND INDEXES